Ferdinand de Lesseps

The Suez Canal

Letters and Documents Descriptive of its Rise and Progress in 1854-1856

Ferdinand de Lesseps

The Suez Canal
Letters and Documents Descriptive of its Rise and Progress in 1854-1856

ISBN/EAN: 9783744763608

Printed in Europe, USA, Canada, Australia, Japan

Cover: Foto ©Andreas Hilbeck / pixelio.de

More available books at **www.hansebooks.com**

THE SUEZ CANAL.

LETTERS AND DOCUMENTS DESCRIPTIVE OF ITS RISE AND PROGRESS IN 1854–1856.

BY

FERDINAND DE LESSEPS.

TRANSLATED BY

N. D'ANVERS,

AUTHOR OF "THE ELEMENTARY HISTORY OF ART,"
ETC.

HENRY S. KING AND CO., LONDON.
1876.

TO THE MEMBERS

OF THE

ACADEMY OF SCIENCES, PARIS.

I owe the distinguished honour of my seat in the Academy of Sciences to the execution of the Suez Canal.

My colleagues have expressed a wish to know the history of the labours they have so frequently aided by their assistance and influence, and which, spread over a period of twenty years, have resulted in a successful completion of the work, supported as it has been by the verdict of Science and the progress of Civilisation.

It is not for me to compile a complete history of an enterprise in which much opposition and contest, years before the formation of a financial company, necessarily compelled me to make myself conspicuous.

But, in order to prepare an outline of the history and to comply with the wish of the Academy, I have collected my private and official correspondence, together with such of my notes as have been written according to the requirements of events as they occurred.

This collection contains an account of the principal circumstances which occurred during and after the opening of the Egyptian Bosphorus to navigation, an occasion honoured by the presence of a numerous deputation of members of the Institute of France.

FERD. DE LESSEPS.

PARIS, *May* 1875.

CONTENTS.

1852.
			PAGE
July 8*th*.	LETTER TO M. S. W. RUYSSENAERS, CONSUL-GENERAL FOR HOLLAND IN EGYPT		1
November 15*th*.	LETTER TO THE SAME...		2

1854.
September 15*th*.	LETTER TO THE SAME		2
Nov. 7*th to* 26*th*.	LETTER TO MADAME DELAMALLE		3
,, 27*th*.	LETTER TO MR. BRUCE, HER BRITANNIC MAJESTY'S AGENT AND CONSUL-GENERAL IN EGYPT... ...		32
,, 27 & 28*th*.	LETTER TO MADAME DELAMALLE		33
,, 29*th*.	LETTER TO M. SABATIER, AGENT AND CONSUL-GENERAL FOR FRANCE IN EGYPT...		35
,, 30*th and* December 2*nd*.	LETTER TO M. RUYSSENAERS		36
,, 3*rd*.	LETTER TO MR. RICHARD COBDEN, M.P....		36
,, 6*th*.	LETTER TO M. ARLES DUFOUR, SECRETARY-GENERAL FOR THE INTERNATIONAL EXHIBITION, PARIS		38
,, 10*th*.	LETTER TO MADAME DELAMALLE		38
,, 14*th*.	LETTER TO M. ARLES DUFOUR		39
,, 16*th. to* *Jan.* 15, 1855.	LETTER TO MADAME DELAMALLE		40

1855.
January 15*th*.	INSTRUCTIONS TO LINANT BEY AND MOUGEL BEY ...		67
,, 16*th*.	LETTER TO M. ARLES DUFOUR...		69
,, 18–22*nd*.	LETTER TO MADAME DELAMALLE		74
,, 26*th*.	LETTER TO M. S. W. RUYSSENAERS		77
,, 27*th*.	LETTER TO M. ARLES DUFOUR		78
February 2*nd*.	LETTER TO THE SAME		79
,, 15*th*.	NOTE FOR THE VICEROY OF EGYPT AND COMTE THEODORE DE LESSEPS, MINISTER OF FOREIGN AFFAIRS		80
,, 19*th*.	LETTER TO HIS HIGHNESS RESCHID PACHA, GRAND VIZIER		83
,, 19*th*.	NOTE FOR THE COUNCIL OF HIS IMPERIAL MAJESTY THE SULTAN		83
,, 24*th*.	LETTER TO HIS HIGHNESS RESCHID PACHA		84
,, 24*th*.	LETTER TO HIS EXCELLENCY BARON KOLLER, INTERNUNCIO FOR AUSTRIA AT CONSTANTINOPLE		85

1855.

			PAGE
February 26*th*.	ANSWER FROM BARON KOLLER	... ...	86
,, 26*th*.	LETTER TO HIS EXCELLENCY LORD STRATFORD DE REDCLIFFE, ENGLISH AMBASSADOR AT CONSTANTINOPLE		86
,, 27*th*.	ANSWER FROM LORD STRATFORD		87
,, 26*th*.	LETTER TO COMTE DE LESSEPS		88
,, 28*th*.	LETTER TO VISCOUNT STRATFORD DE REDCLIFFE		90
March 1*st*.	LETTER TO BARON KOLLER		94
,, 1*st*.	LETTER OF THE GRAND VIZIER TO HIS HIGHNESS MOHAMMED SAID PACHA, VICEROY OF EGYPT		95
,, 3*rd*.	LETTER TO COMTE DE LESSEPS		95
,, 3*rd*.	LETTER TO M. SCHEFER, FIRST DRAGOMAN TO THE FRENCH EMBASSY AT CONSTANTINOPLE		98
,, 10*th*.	LETTER TO COMTE DE LESSEPS		101
,, 16*th*.	LETTER TO M. BENEDETTI, CHARGÉ D'AFFAIRES FOR FRANCE AT CONSTANTINOPLE		101
,, 18*th*.	LETTER TO COMTE DE LESSEPS		104
,, 22*nd*.	LETTER TO M. HIPPOLYTE LAFOSSE		105
,, 23*rd*.	LETTER TO HIS ROYAL HIGHNESS THE DUKE OF BRABANT		108
,, 26*th*.	LETTER TO HIS HIGHNESS MOHAMMED SAID (Private Letter)		110
April 5*th*.	LETTER TO COMTE DE LESSEPS		111
,, 8*th*.	LETTER TO THE SAME		115
,, 8*th*.	LETTER TO THE SAME		119
,, 14*th*.	LETTER TO M. BENEDETTI		120
,, 14*th*.	LETTER TO THE SAME		121
,, 21*st*.	LETTER TO MADAME DELAMALLE		122
,, 18*th*.	MEMORANDUM TO HIS HIGHNESS MOHAMMED SAID (Confidential)		124
,, 30*th*.	REPORT TO HIS HIGHNESS MOHAMMED SAID		126
May 6*th*.	LETTER TO COMTE DE LESSEPS		128
,, 12*th*.	LETTER TO THE SAME		130
,, 19*th*.	LETTER TO THE SAME		132
June 5*th*.	MEMORANDUM FOR THE EMPEROR		132
,, 7*th*.	MEMORANDUM FOR COUNT WALEWSKI		133
,, 9*th*.	MEMORANDUM FOR THE EMPEROR		134
,, 14*th*.	LETTER TO M. S. W. RUYSSENAERS		137
,, 18*th*.	CIRCULAR TO THE ORIGINAL SHAREHOLDERS IN EGYPT		139
,, 18*th*.	LETTER TO M. ARLES DUFOUR		140
,, 19*th*.	ROUGH DRAFT OF A REPLY TO AN ENGLISH MEMORANDUM		141
,, 25*th*.	LETTER TO COMTE DE LESSEPS		148
,, 28*th*.	LETTER TO BARON VON BRÜCK, MINISTER OF FINANCE, VIENNA		153
,, 30*th*.	LETTER TO COMTE DE LESSEPS		155
July 4*th*.	LETTER TO HIS MAJESTY THE EMPEROR		158
,,	THE SUEZ CANAL QUESTION SUBMITTED TO ENGLISH PUBLIC OPINION		159

CONTENTS.

1855.

			PAGE
July 9th.	Letter to M. S. W. Ruyssenaers		162
„ 29th.	Letter to Baron von Brück		164
August 3rd.	Letter to Mr. Rendel		165
„ 8th.	Circular Addressed to Members of Parliament, Merchants, &c.		166
„ 9th.	Letter to his Highness Mohammed Said	...	166
„ 17th.	Letter to her Majesty the Empress		167
„ 17th.	Letter Delivered by the Empress to the Emperor		168
„ 31st.	Letter to Mr. James Wilson		170
September 13th.	Letter to Comte de Lesseps		173
„ 24th.	Letter to M. S. W. Ruyssenaers		174
October 28th.	Letter to Baron von Brück ... ·		179
„ 11th.	Circular to the Members of the International Scientific Commission		181
„ 30th.	Letter to the Editor of the "Times"		182
November 13th. and 19th.	Letter to Madame Delamalle		194
„ 22nd.	Letter to M. Thouvenel, French Ambassador at Constantinople		195
Nov. 27th. to December 6th.	Letter to Madame Delamalle		198
„ 16th.	Message to the Members of the International Commission		220

1856.

January 2nd.	Condensed Report of the International Commission		220
„ 4th.	Memorandum sent to Friends and Supporters		222
„ 4th.	Circular to the Members who did not go to Egypt		224
„ 5th.	Letter to Chevalier Revoltella		224
„ 6th.	Letter to Madame Delamalle		225
„ 10th.	Letter to M. de Chancel		226
„ 14th.	Letter to M. Barthélemy Saint-Hilaire	...	228
„ 19th.	Letter to N. de Negrelli		230
„ 20th.	Public Notice in the European and American Journals		231
„ 20th.	Letter to Madame Delamalle		232
„ 25th.	Letter to M. Barthélemy Saint Hilaire	...	232
„ 26th.	Letter to M. Kœnig Bey, Private Secretary to the Viceroy		233
„ 28th.	Letter to M. Mougel Bey		234
February 3rd.	Letter to Chevalier de Negrelli		234
„ 4th.	Letter to Madame Delamalle		236
„ 10th.	Letter to Comte de Lesseps		238
„ 7th.	Letter to Madame Delamalle		239
„ 28th.	Letter to M. Barthélemy Saint-Hilaire...	...	240

CONTENTS.

1856.

		PAGE
March 21st.	Letter to M. de Negrelli	241
,, 25th.	Report to the Viceroy of Egypt	243
,, 29th.	Memorandum for the Emperor of the French	245
April 4th.	Letter to M. de Thouvenel	246
,, 8th.	Memorandum for the Viceroy of Egypt	247
,,	Memorandum for Count Walewski, Minister of Foreign Affairs	250
,, 17th.	Letter to M. de Negrelli ... ... , ...	254
,, 17th.	Letter to M. Barthélemy Saint-Hilaire... ...	256
,, 21st.	Letter to M. S. W. Ruyssenaers	257
,, 22nd.	Letter to M. Thouvenel...	259
May 6th.	Letter to M. S. W. Ruyssenaers	261
,, 20th.	Letter to the Viceroy of Egypt	264
June 13th.	Letter to M. Elie de Beaumont	265
,, 23rd.	Account given at the Opening of the General Meeting of the Engineers to the International Scientific Commission	266
,, 25th.	Summary of Resolutions passed by the International Scientific Commission	270
July 8th.	Letter to Comte de Lesseps	272
,, 16th.	Letter to Madame Delamalle	273
,, 20th.	Letter to M. Thouvenel...	273
,, 20th.	Report to the Viceroy on the Fellah Workmen to be Employed	274
	Extract of a Report to the King of Holland	278
August 10th.	Remarks on the Official Inquiry relating to Piercing the Isthmus	279
,, 25th.	Remarks on Egypt Published in the "Isthmus of Suez" Newspaper	280
,, 28th. and Sept. 3rd.	} Letters to M. Thouvenel	288
October 12th.	Memorandum for the Emperor	290
November 5th.	Letter to M. S. W. Ruyssenaers	292
,, 9th.	Opinion of General Albert della Marmora with Regard to the Geology of the Isthmus	305
,, 22nd.	Letter to Madame Delamalle	306
,, 22nd.	Letter to Mr. Richard Cobden, M.P.	307
,, 24 & 25.	Memorandum for the Viceroy of Egypt	310

THE SUEZ CANAL.

I.

To M. S. W. Ruyssenaers, Consul-General for Holland in Egypt.

Paris, *July* 8, 1852.

Three years ago, after my mission to Rome as Envoy Extraordinary, I asked for and obtained leave from my office as Minister Plenipotentiary.

Since 1849 I have studied incessantly, under all its aspects, a question which was already in my mind when we first became friends in Egypt twenty years ago.

I confess that my scheme is still a mere dream, and I do not shut my eyes to the fact that so long as I alone believe it to be possible, it is virtually impossible.

To make the public take it up it requires a support still wanting to it, and I ask for your assistance with a view to obtaining that support.

The scheme in question is the cutting of a canal through the Isthmus of Suez. This has been thought of from the earliest historical times, and for that very reason is looked upon as impracticable. Geographical dictionaries inform us indeed that the project would have been executed long ago but for insurmountable obstacles.

I enclose a minute, the result of my former and more recent studies, which I have had translated into Arabic by my friend Duchenoud, the best interpreter to the Government. It is strictly confidential, and you must judge whether the present Viceroy, Abbas Pacha, is likely to recognise its importance for Egypt and to aid in its execution.

II.

To the Same.

Paris, *November* 15, 1852.

When you wrote to me that there was no chance of getting Abbas Pacha to entertain the idea of the Suez Canal, I communicated my project to my friend M. Benoit Fould, the financier, who was about to take part in the formation of a Crédit Mobilier at Constantinople. He was struck with the grandeur of the scheme and with the advantage of including the privilege of making the Suez Canal amongst the concessions to be demanded of Turkey.

The agent sent to Constantinople met with such difficulties as led to the abandonment of the project. One argument brought to bear against it was the impossibility of taking the initiative in a work to be executed in Egypt, where the Viceroy alone has a right to undertake it.

Under these circumstances I shall lay aside my minute on the Canal until a more convenient season, and occupy myself meanwhile with agriculture and in building a model farm on a property recently acquired by my mother-in-law, Madame Delamalle.

III.

To the Same.

La Chenaie, *September* 15, 1854.

I was busy amongst bricklayers and carpenters, superintending the addition of a storey to Agnes Sorel's old manor house, when the postman, bringing the Paris mail, appeared in the courtyard. My letters and papers were handed up to me by the workmen, and my surprise was great on reading of the death of Abbas Pacha and the accession to power of the friend of our youth, the intelligent and warm-hearted Mohammed Said. I hurried down from the scaffolding, and at once wrote to congratulate the new

Viceroy. I told him that I had retired from politics, and should avail myself of my leisure to pay my respects to him as soon as he would let me know the date of his return from Constantinople after his investiture.

He lost no time in replying, and fixed the beginning of November for our meeting at Alexandria. I wish you to be one of the first to know that I shall be punctual at the place of meeting. How delightful it will be for us to be together again in dear old Egypt! Not a word to any one, before I arrive, on the Canal project.

IV.

To Madame Delamalle, Paris.

(*Journal.*)

Alexandria, *November* 7, 1854.

I LANDED at Alexandria at eight o'clock a.m., from the Messageries packet *Le Lycurgue*. I was met, on behalf of the Viceroy, by my friend Ruyssenaers, Consul-General for Holland, and Hafouz Pacha, Minister of Marine. I got into a state carriage, which was to take me to one of his Highness's villas, a league from Alexandria, on the Mahmoudieh Canal; and thinking it as well not to pass through Alexandria without calling at the French Consulate, I delivered some despatches to M. Sabatier, of which I had taken charge in Paris, where nothing had been said of my Canal project, as I had mentioned it to no one, not even to my brother, secretary to the Minister of Foreign Affairs. I was very well received by M. Sabatier, who begged me, should I remain a night in Alexandria, to take up my quarters in the French palace, which had been commenced under my own superintendence in 1835, when I was at the head of the French Consulate-General.

I then proceeded on my way to Villa Cérisy, with my escort of Kawas and Sais, and on my arrival I found an entire staff of servants drawn up on the staircase, who saluted me three times by stretching their right hand to the ground and then raising it to their forehead. They were Turks and Arabs, under the control of a Greek *valet de chambre* and a Marseillaise cook named Ferdinand.

Here is a description of my residence, of which I myself witnessed the construction by M. de Cérisy, the celebrated French naval engineer, founder of the Arsenal of Alexandria, from which he has turned out twelve vessels of the line and twelve frigates in a short space of time. Under Mehemet Ali, M. de Cérisy contributed much to the enfranchisement of Egypt. The chief pavilion rises from the centre of a beautiful garden between two avenues, one leading to the plain of Alexandria, on the side of the Rosetta Gate, the other to the Mahmoudieh Canal. This pavilion was occupied a few days back by the princess who has recently presented Said Pacha with a son, named Toussoum. The reception-rooms and dining-room are on the ground floor; and on the first storey we have the drawing-room, a very cheerful apartment, with luxurious divans all round and four large windows overlooking the two avenues; the bedroom, with a soft canopied couch and fine yellow lampas curtains, fringed and embroidered with gold, and supplemented by double inner curtains of worked net; a first dressing-room, well stocked with perfumes and with rosewood and marble furniture; and beyond that again a second dressing-room, not less elegant, provided with a large basin, a silver ewer, and long soft towels, embroidered with gold, hanging from pegs.

I had just inspected my quarters when some friends of the Viceroy came in. I made them talk of the habits of Said Pacha since his accession; of his tastes, his mental tendencies, the persons about him, who was in favour and who in disfavour: all matters which it is well to be informed of beforehand when the guest of a prince. These gentlemen told me that since his return from Constantinople the Viceroy has often spoken of my visit, and has talked to those about him of his old friendship for me. I was informed that he had waited for me to accompany him on a journey he is about to make to Cairo, by way of the Desert of Libya, at the head of an army of 10,000 men. This trip will certainly be interesting, and will take eight or ten days. The start is fixed for next Sunday.

Presently additional servants arrived, including a Kaouadji bachi (chief coffee-maker), accompanied by several assistants; and a Chiboukchi bachi (superintendent of pipes), escorted by four acolytes with their insignia, consisting of a dozen long pipes with large amber bowls set with diamonds. The office of these men is no sinecure, for in well-ordered homes, belonging to great Turkish seigneurs, fresh pipes and little cups of coffee (findjanes) are served to every visitor.

Now came one of the Viceroy's officers to inform me that his Highness would receive me at noon in his palace of Gabbari.

I reflected that, having known the prince when he was in a totally different position, it would be desirable to treat him with the respectful deference always so acceptable to the human heart. I therefore wore my dress coat, with my medals, decorations, and orders.

The Viceroy received me very cordially, and talked about his childhood: of the way in which I had sometimes protected him from his father's severities; of the persecution and misery he had endured in the reign of Abbas Pacha; and, lastly, of his desire to do good and restore prosperity to Egypt. I congratulated him on his intentions, adding that it must be for some good end that Providence had entrusted the most despotic Government in the world to a prince who had received a good education when young, and had subsequently been sorely tried by adversity. I also expressed my conviction that he would be worthy of his mission.

The approaching march through the desert, amongst the Bedouin tribes, was discussed, and it was agreed that I should join the expedition without having to make any preparations myself.

I returned by way of Alexandria, and paid a second visit to M. Sabatier, meeting at his house all the officers of the Consulate-General and some old French friends, who, one and all, welcomed me enthusiastically.

Later I went to the French Post-office, still presided over by M. Gérardin, whom I had myself appointed eighteen years ago, at the time of the inauguration of the packet-boat service by M. Philibert Conte, son of the celebrated Postmaster-General.

Then came a grand dinner at the hospitable mansion of the Pastrés, who had invited the "ban" and "arrière-ban" of my old friends in Egypt to meet me.

On returning to my pavilion at eleven at night I found my entire staff of servants drawn up as before, and the head cook called my attention to a well-spread table decked with flowers. He told me he had orders to serve a similar meal morning and evening, and I replied that I should only require breakfast, and was now going to my room. Two footmen offered to assist me to ascend the brilliantly-illuminated staircase, and I accepted their services with the gravity and indifference proper to the guest of a Sovereign accustomed to similar attentions.

November 8th.

I was up at five this morning, and opened the two windows of my room, shaded by the branches of trees the names of which I am unable to give. The air was laden with the scent of their blossoms and of the jasmines lining the avenue leading to the canal, beyond which, though the sun had not yet risen, I could see Lake Mareotis swept by a deliciously soft fresh breeze.

I went to make a morning visit to the Viceroy, and he left his apartments as soon as he heard of my arrival. We seated ourselves on a comfortable sofa in a gallery opening on to the garden. After we had had a pipe and some coffee my host led me to the balcony of the gallery to show me a regiment of his guard, which was to accompany him on his journey. We then went into the garden to try some revolving pistols I had brought him from France.

Our walk ended I told Mohammed Said I must leave him to receive some people at his house, whom I had invited in his name. He thanked me for doing the honours of *my* house so well.

Later I called on the Viceroy's brother, Halim Pacha, whose house is near my own. The young prince speaks French fluently, and said that, from what he had heard of me, he was sure we should soon be good friends, as we were both fond of riding and hunting. He is to be of our party in the desert, and will take his falcons and greyhounds with him. He placed his servants and weapons at my disposal.

November 9th.

I went this morning to see the Viceroy at his father's palace at Raz-el-Tyn, on the further side of the port, and he invited me to assist at the first audience of the new Consul-General for Sardinia, who was about to present his credentials.

After the ceremony we retired to the private apartments, where we had a long and very interesting conversation on the best principles of government; but not a word was said about the Suez Canal, a subject I shall not broach until I am quite sure of my ground and the scheme is sufficiently matured for the prince to adopt it as his own rather than mine.

I must act with the greater prudence that Ruyssenaers remembers having heard Said Pacha remark, before his accession to power, that if ever he became Viceroy of Egypt he should follow the example of his father, Mehemet Ali, who had declined to have anything to do with cutting a canal across the Isthmus because of the difficulties it might lead to with England.

This is not an encouraging precedent; but I am confident of success.

November 11th.

This morning I received a fine horse from the Viceroy, for which he sent to Syria, and I was informed that there would be a review of troops this morning on a plain between Alexandria and Lake Mareotis. I mounted and joined my host. Soliman Pacha superintended the manœuvres, which included field exercise. As we were galloping along, a diamond ornament fell from the prince's cartridge-box; but he would not have it picked up, and we rode on.

November 12th.

The Viceroy sent me word that his troops are to begin their march to Cairo, under his leadership, to-day, and he has given orders to his aide-de-camp to bring me to his first halting-place to-morrow.

November 13th.

I left the Viceroy's pavilion at six o'clock this morning on the horse he gave me, escorted by two mounted Kawas and two Sais on foot, and followed by a second led horse and two camels laden with my baggage. We were to meet Zulfikar Pacha at the Gabarri Palace, and then, going round Lake Mareotis, to join the head-quarters of the Viceroy. To avoid delays our camels and baggage were placed under the care of a Kawas. After leaving the ancient baths of Cleopatra and the Arab tower on our right, we came to a well by which the Viceroy had encamped the previous night. He had started again at four a.m., to cross the lake where it was almost dry. Following the deep furrows made in the sand by the wheels of his carriage, and noticing how our own horses sunk here and there, we were able to judge of the difficulties the troops had had to contend with in their passage. Throughout the entire ride I discussed my project with Zulfikar Pacha, who was an old acquaintance of mine. He fully recognised the importance of my scheme for Egypt, and promised to turn his intimacy with the Viceroy to account by trying to prepare him to give my proposals a favourable hearing.

After having crossed the lake we entered that part of the Desert of Libya which was formerly an inhabited and civilized country, but has been abandoned to a few Bedouin tribes since the Arab conquest. Here and there, by ancient wells, we saw black camel-skin tents, such as those alluded to in the Scriptures, and which are alike in Palestine, Syria, Arabia, and along the whole coast of Africa from Egypt to Morocco.

The sky now became slightly overcast and a gentle breeze made it cooler than on the other side of the lake. I was here witness of a true scene of the desert, for a dog was tearing a dead animal to pieces, whilst some birds of prey stalked solemnly about, waiting their turn, quite undisturbed by our approach.

At eleven o'clock Zulfikar and I, without drawing rein, eat some biscuits and chocolate, with which we had filled our holsters; pistols being unnecessary.

We now caught sight of the Viceroy's camp from a

neighbouring eminence, and a Bedouin told us we should be there in half-an-hour; but here, as everywhere else, peasants always shorten distances; so I judged that we had still two hours at least to ride. Dreading neither heat nor fatigue I pressed on, without once dismounting, arriving at the camp, at half-past two, to find the Viceroy enjoying his siesta, and a tent pitched next to his for Zulfikar Pacha and myself, containing an iron bedstead with a good mattress and a quilted silk coverlid, a mat, some folding chairs, and a mahogany table.

Pipes and coffee were brought at once, succeeded by basins and silver ewers; we were then sprinkled with rose-water, a ceremony which always immediately precedes a meal.

A collation was served on a tray set on a stool, by which we took our places. Seven or eight courses succeeded each other. I was about to use my fingers, like my companion, when a spoon, fork, knife, and a Sèvres porcelain plate were put before me. We obeyed the injunction of the Prophet and took no wine, contenting ourselves with pure water cooled by pieces of ice floating on the top.

Presently military music announced that the Viceroy was awake, and he and I left our tents at the same moment. He wished me to join him, and we went into his pavilion. He then told me how he had got his artillery across the lake, galloping from one battery to another encouraging and urging on the men, adding that everybody had prophesied that the passage could not be made, so he had made it a point of honour to accomplish it. He was in very good spirits, and we remained alone together for more than two hours, talking on many interesting subjects, all bearing more or less on my host's wish to signalise the commencement of his reign by some great and useful enterprise. All I said was listened to with attention, and the prince seemed to place entire confidence in me. The time passed rapidly until the ceremony of ablution warned us that dinner was ready.

After that meal a courier arrived from Alexandria, bringing the Viceroy's correspondence from Constantinople, which had come by one of his steamers. His Highness had the letters read aloud by Zulfikar Pacha, and translated part of their contents for my benefit.

They consisted of despatches from his Agent at Constantinople and from Reschid Pacha, the Grand Vizier. Amongst them he showed me one from the Sultan's female favourite, thanking him for a present of 150,000 piastres. The letter also complimented him on the part of his Imperial Majesty on the excellent condition of some Egyptian troops recently sent to Turkey.

News from Sebastopol to the 2nd, when the town was not yet taken. The Admirals had given the Generals notice that the sea would no longer be tenable a month hence; which fact will probably lead to a decisive attack, costing the Allied Armies the lives of some ten to fifteen thousand men. I left the Viceroy at ten p.m.

We are to remain here three days, to wait for two regiments of infantry, which will arrive to-morrow, and two of cavalry, expected the day after that.

November 14th.

I was on foot at five o'clock this morning; the soldiers were beginning to leave their tents; and the vast moonlit plains, though bare and desolate, were not entirely without beauty.

Hearing the Viceroy's voice I went to wish him good morning. We smoked a pipe together, drank some coffee, and mounted our horses ready to receive the expected troops, who soon came up, fresh and in good condition, having left Alexandria yesterday morning with only three biscuits for each man. The Arabs are very temperate, and seem to thrive on their abstinence. The review over, we all returned to our tents.

I was interrupted by a visit from Halim Pacha, the Viceroy's brother, who has pitched his tent a league from our camp. He tells me that his Bedouin scouts report having sighted herds of gazelles two or three hours' march off, and that he proposes arranging a hunt for the day on which we resume our journey.

At ten o'clock we were summoned to breakfast by the Viceroy, and went to his tent with Halim Pacha.

Directly after our meal, Prince Halim's horses were brought round, and he returned to his camp. We retired at the same time, and, saddling my horse, I galloped about over the level plains and occasional hills near the camp. On one side the desert stretched away as far as the eye could reach, whilst on the other it was bounded by Lake Mareotis, with the sea beyond. Presently a large jackal started up almost from beneath my horse's feet, and I followed it at close quarters for some ten minutes, nearly touching it with the end of my whip, but finally losing sight of it in the brushwood. It had probably taken up its position at a good starting-point for nocturnal visits to our camp in search of food.

On my return I found the Viceroy outside his tent, and, dismounting, I went with him to an howitzer, planted 450 mètres from a target, on which two companies of light infantry were trying their skill. Several shells had been thrown, but, though often near the mark, none had actually hit it.

And now night closed in upon the camp, and the watch-fires were lit. The Viceroy's military band struck up airs and marches of every nationality, including the "Marseillaise" and the "Hymn of Riégo." The Egyptians, the most lively nation on earth, grouped themselves before their tents and sang their national airs, beating time with their hands. The Viceroy, who had lost his appetite, probably because of the failure of his gunners, retired to his own tent, and sent his dinner to me in mine!

November 15th.

I was not dressed at five o'clock this morning. Any one who had happened to see me outside my tent in my red dressing-gown, like the robe of a Scherif of Mecca, washing my arms up to the elbows, would have taken me for a true believer, and in the time of the Inquisition I should have been burnt alive; for you know that washing the arms to the elbow was one of the high misdemeanours punishable with tortures and *autos da fé*.

The camp soon began to show signs of life, and the freshness of the air gave notice of the approaching sunrise.

I put on something warmer than my dressing-gown, and returned to my observatory. The horizon was already illuminated by the first rays of the dawn, and the east, on the right, was clear and bright, whilst the west was still dark and cloudy.

Suddenly to the left of my tent I beheld a rainbow of the most brilliant colours, the ends dipping, one into the east, the other into the west. I confess that my heart beat violently, and I was obliged to check myself from jumping to the conclusion that this sign of the covenant alluded to in the Scriptures was a proof of the moment having arrived for the true union of the West and East, and that this day was marked out for the success of my scheme.

The Viceroy's approach roused me from my dream, and we wished each other good morning with a hearty shake of the hand, in thoroughly French style. He told me he thought of adopting my suggestion of yesterday, and riding to some of the neighbouring heights to examine the dispositions of his camp. We mounted, preceded by two lancers and followed by an aide-de-camp. Arrived on a prominent hill, strewn with relics of ancient stone constructions, the Viceroy decided that it would be a good place from which to arrange the start of to-morrow; so he sent an aide-de-camp to order his tent and carriage to be brought to him. The latter is a kind of omnibus, with sleeping accommodation inside, and is drawn by six mules. The mules brought the carriage to the top of the hill at a gallop, and we sat down beneath its shade.

The Viceroy had a circular parapet of stones, picked up on the spot, erected opposite to us by some of his light infantry. An embrasure was then made, through which a cannon was pointed, and a salute fired for the benefit of the rest of the troops arriving from Alexandria. The heads of the columns could be seen beyond the camp.

At half-past ten, the Viceroy having breakfasted before he started, I went to get something to eat with Zulfikar Pacha. I wanted to show my host that his horse, the sturdy qualities of which I had proved on the first day of the journey, was a first-rate jumper; so, as I saluted him, I made my steed clear the stone parapet with one bound, and gallop down the slope to my tent. As you will see, this piece of imprudence probably had something to do with my winning the necessary approbation of the Viceroy's suite for my scheme. The Generals, with whom I breakfasted, complimented me, and I noticed that I had gained greatly in their esteem by my boldness.

I thought the Viceroy was now sufficiently prepared by my previous conversations to recognise the advantage to every Government of having great works of public utility executed by financial companies, and, encouraged by the happy omen of the rainbow, I hoped that the day would not pass over without a decision on the subject of the Suez Canal.

At five p.m. I remounted and returned to the Viceroy's tent, again clearing the parapet. His Highness was in a very good humour, and taking my hand, which he held for a moment in his own, he made me sit down beside him on his divan. We were alone, and through the door of the tent we could see the beautiful setting of that sun the rising of which had affected me so deeply in the morning. I felt strong in my composure and self-control at a moment when I was about to broach a question on which hung my whole future. My studies and reflections on the Canal between the two seas rose clearly before my mind, and the execution seemed to me so practicable that I did not doubt I should be able to make the prince share my conviction. I propounded my scheme without entering into details, laying stress on the chief facts and arguments set forth in my minute, which I could have repeated from end to end. Mohammed Said listened with interest to my explanations. I begged him if he had any doubts to be good enough to communicate them to me. He brought forward several objections with considerable intelligence, to which I replied in a satisfactory manner, for he said at last: *"I am convinced; I accept your plan. We will talk about the means of its execution during the rest of the journey. Consider the matter settled. You may rely upon me."*

Thereupon he sent for his Generals, made them sit down

on chairs opposite to us, and repeated the conversation he had just had with me, inviting them to give their opinion on the proposals of *his friend*. These impromptu counsellors, better able to pronounce on an equestrian evolution than on a vast enterprise of which they could not in the least appreciate the significance, opened their great eyes, and, turning towards me, seemed to be thinking that their master's friend, whom they had just seen clear a wall on horseback with so much ease, could not but give good advice. Whilst the Viceroy was speaking to them they raised their hands to their foreheads every now and then in sign of assent.

The dinner-tray now appeared, and with one accord we plunged our spoons into the same bowl, which contained some first-rate soup. This is a faithful account of the most important negotiation I ever made or am ever likely to make.

Towards eight o'clock I took leave of the Viceroy, who told me we should start again to-morrow morning, and I returned to my tent. Zulfikar Pacha guessed my success as soon as he saw me, and rejoiced with me. The Viceroy's playmate in his childhood and the most intimate friend of his mature years, he has done much to contribute to the favourable result just obtained.

I was not inclined for sleep, so I set about working up my notes on the journey, and putting the finishing touches to an *impromptu* minute asked for by the Sultan, which had already been drawn up for two years.

This is the minute, dated Mareia Camp, November 15, 1854, and addressed to his Highness Mohammed Said, Viceroy of Egypt and its dependencies :—

> The scheme of uniting the Mediterranean and the Red Sea, by means of a navigable canal, suggested itself to all the great men who have ruled over or passed through Egypt, including—Sesostris, Alexander, Cæsar, the Arab conqueror Amrou, Napoleon I., and Mohammed Ali.
>
> A canal effecting a junction between the two seas, viâ the Nile, existed for a period of unknown duration under the ancient Egyptian dynasties ; during a second period of 445 years, from the first successors of Alexander and the Roman conquest to about the fourth century before the Mohammedan era ; and, lastly, during a third period of 130 years, after the Arab conquest.

On his arrival in Egypt Napoleon appointed a commission of engineers to ascertain whether it would be possible to restore and improve the old route. The question was answered in the affirmative; and when M. Lepère presented him with the report of the commission, the Emperor observed: "It is a grand work; and though I cannot execute it now, the day may come when the Turkish Government will glory in accomplishing it."

The moment for the fulfilment of Napoleon's prophecy has arrived. The making of the Suez Canal is beyond doubt destined to contribute more than anything else to the stability of the Ottoman Empire, and to give the lie to those who proclaim its decline and approaching ruin by proving that it is possessed of prolific vitality and capable of adding a brilliant page to the history of civilization.

Why, I ask, did the Western nations and their rulers combine as one man to secure the possession of Constantinople to the Sultan? Why did the Power which menaced that possession meet with the armed opposition of Europe? Because the importance of the passage from the Black Sea to the Mediterranean is such, that the European Power commanding it would dominate over every other, and would upset the balance of power, which it is to the interest of each one to maintain.

But suppose a similar though yet more important position be established on some other point of the Ottoman Empire; suppose Egypt to be converted into the highway of commerce by the opening of the Suez Canal; would not a doubly impregnable situation be created in the East? for, afraid of seeing any one of themselves in possession of the new passage at some future date, would not the European Powers look upon the maintenance of its neutrality as a vital necessity?

Fifty years ago M. Lepère said he should require ten thousand men for four years and thirty or forty million francs for the restoration of the old indirect canal. He thought, moreover, that it would be possible to cut across the isthmus from Suez to Pelusium in a direct line.

M. Paulin Talabot, who was associated, as surveying engineer for a maritime canal society, with the equally celebrated Stephenson and Negrelli, advocated the indirect route from Alexandria to Suez, and proposed using the *barrage* already existing for the passage of the Nile. He estimated the total cost at 130 million francs for the canal and twenty million for the port and roadstead of Suez.

Linant Bey, the able director for some thirty years of the canal works of Egypt, who has made the Suez Canal question the study of his life in the country itself, and whose opinion is therefore worthy of serious respect, proposed cutting through the isthmus, at its narrowest part, in an almost direct line, establishing a large internal port in the basin of Lake Timsah, and rendering the harbours of Suez and Pelusium accessible to the largest vessels.

Gallice Bey, general of engineers and founder and director of the fortifications of Alexandria, presented Mohammed Ali with a canal scheme coinciding entirely with that proposed by Linant Bey.

Mougel Bey, director of works at the *barrage* of the Nile and chief engineer *des ponts et chaussées*, also had some conversation with Mohammed Ali on the possibility and desirability of making a maritime canal; and in 1840, at the request of Count Walewski, then on a mission in Egypt, he was commissioned to take some preliminary measures in Europe, which were, however, prevented by political events from leading to any definite results.

A careful survey would decide which would be the best route; and the scheme having once been recognised as possible, nothing remains to be done but to choose the readiest means for carrying it out.

None of the necessary operations, difficult though they may be, are really formidable to modern science. There can be no fear nowadays of their failure. The whole affair is, in fact, reduced to a mere question of pounds, shillings, and pence—a question which will, without doubt, be readily solved by the modern spirit of enterprise and association, that is to say, if the advantages to result from its solution are at all proportionate to the cost.

Now it is quite easy to prove that the cost of the Suez Canal, even on the largest estimate, will not be out of proportion with its value, shortening, as it must do, by more than half the distance between India and the principal countries of Europe and America.

To illustrate this fact I add the following table, drawn up by M. Cordier, Professor of Geology :—

Names of the Chief Ports of Europe and America.	Leagues.		Difference.
	Viâ the Suez Canal.	Viâ the Atlantic.	
Constantinople	1800	6100	4300
Malta	2062	5800	3778
Trieste	2340	5980	3620
Marseilles	2374	5650	3276
Cadiz	2224	5200	2976
Lisbon	2500	2350	2830
Bordeaux	2800	6650	2850
Havre	2824	5800	2976
London	3100	5950	2850
Liverpool	3050	5900	2850
Amsterdam	3100	5950	2850
St. Petersburg	3700	6550	2850
New York	3761	6200	2439
New Orleans	3724	6450	2726

(Distance from Bombay.)

With such figures before us comment is useless, for they demonstrate that Europe and the United States are alike interested in the opening of the Suez Canal and in the maintenance of its strict and inviolable neutrality.

Mohammed Said is already convinced that no scheme can compare either in grandeur or in practical utility with that in question. What lustre it would reflect upon his reign! What an inexhaustible source of wealth it would be to Egypt! Whilst the names of the sovereigns who built up the pyramids, those monuments of human vanity, are unknown or forgotten, that of the prince who should inaugurate the great maritime canal would go down from age to age, and be blessed by the most remote generations!

The pilgrimage to Mecca henceforth rendered not only possible but easy to all Mussulmans, an immense impulse given to steam navigation and travelling generally, the countries on the Red Sea, Persian Gulf, the east coast of Africa, Spain, Cochin China, Japan, the empire of China, the Philippine Islands, Australia, and the vast archipelago now attracting emigration from the Old World brought 3000 leagues nearer alike to the Mediterranean, the north of Europe, and to America, such would be the immediate results of the opening of the Suez Canal.

It has been estimated that six million tons of European and American shipping annually pass round the Cape of Good Hope and Cape Horn; and if only one-half went through the Canal, there would be an annual saving to commerce of 150 million francs.

There can be no doubt that the Suez Canal will lead to a considerable increase of tonnage; but counting upon three million tons only, an annual produce of thirty million francs will be obtained by levying a toll of ten francs per ton, which might be reduced in proportion to the increase of traffic.

Before closing this note, I must remind your Highness that preparations are actually being made in America for making new routes between the Atlantic and Pacific, and at the same time call your attention to the inevitable results to commerce generally, and that of Turkey in particular, should the isthmus separating the Red Sea from the Mediterranean remain closed for any length of time after the opening of the proposed American lines.

The chief difference between the Isthmus of Panama and that of Suez would appear to be that the mountainous nature of the former presents insuperable difficulties to the construction of a continuous ship canal, whereas on the latter such a canal would be the best solution of the difficulty. For America a kind of compromise has been made, the route consisting partly of a canal and partly of a railway. Now if, with a view to effecting only a partial success, the nations chiefly interested have come forward at once in a case where the advantages to be obtained are fewer and the expenses far greater than they would be in the Suez Canal scheme, and if the conventions for insuring the neutrality of the American route were accepted without difficulty, are we not forced to conclude that the moment has come for considering the question of the Isthmus of Suez? that the scheme for a canal which is of far more importance to the whole world than the Panama line, is perfectly secure from any real opposition, and that, in our efforts to carry it out, we shall be supported by universal sympathy and by the active and energetic co-operation of enlightened men of every nationality?

(Signed)   FERDINAND DE LESSEPS.

The site of our encampment on the Mareia, called Gheil in Arabic, retains some vestiges of antiquity. I have noticed, for instance, several shafts of columns and an immense half-ruined reservoir with some dozen horse-shoe arches. The neighbouring hills, too, are strewn with hewn stones. Water is plentiful and excellent. My servant, Ibrahim, a certain officious personage who merits special mention, had hastened to draw some at the reservoir. This Ibrahim seems to me a very good specimen of the crafty, self-interested Arab when familiarised with Europeans. He met Clot Bey in the square of Alexandria, claimed to have been previously under his protection, and declared that he was attached to his service. So he came to the camp with the master on whom he had forced himself. On my arrival, however, he saw that I was treated with more distinction than any one else in the Viceroy's suite and his attentions were transferred to me. He told me that I was "the apple of his eye," that he was very fond of me, and had decided to remain with me as long as I was in Egypt. This sudden conversion, of which I took care to tell my comrades, did not give me a favourable opinion of Ibrahim's morality; but he took such good care to anticipate our wants from morning till night, and was so intelligent in his service, that we let him keep the work he already arrogated to himself of looking after all the details of our encampment, lading the camels, taking down the tent and setting it up before our arrival at the next halting-place, where he would be ready to give us fresh water and a cup of coffee as soon as we dismounted.

November 16*th.*

I was up this morning with the dawn, and Ibrahim, who was already on the alert, brought me a jug, basin, soap, &c. There were as yet no signs of life about the camp, and the Viceroy's tent, always the first to be taken down, was still standing. I began the day by writing to tell you of my good news, and Zulfikar Pacha will send my letter to Alexandria by a courier on a dromedary. Next I packed my portmanteau (which I never let any one do for me) and had my bedding folded up. Meanwhile my horses were saddled and waiting, held by my Saïs. Then I went to inquire after the Viceroy, and he kept me to breakfast. Whilst coffee was being served a cannon-shot announced the order to raise the camp. In an instant thousands of tents were rolled up and packed on camels. The baggage caravan was the first to pass before us, and, turning its back on Lake Mareotis, it made for the desert, soon looking like a long ribbon unrolling itself in the distance. The infantry regiments formed in three columns, flanked by skirmishers and followed by the artillery and cavalry. The Viceroy now mounted, with me on his right and Selim Pacha, his cavalry general, on his left. This Selim was educated at the school of Ghizeh, and I was present at his *début*, under the French Colonel Varin, in 1833. We galloped off to take up our position on an eminence opposite our tent and watch the army defile beneath us, the soldiers cheering and presenting arms as they passed the Viceroy. The weapons glittered in the sunbeams, and I noted particularly the fine bearing of a squadron of cuirassiers wearing the old Saracen helmet. The brown faces of the Arabs were well set off by these helmets. The march past over, we rode to the head of the army, preceded by a dozen mounted Bedouins, who served as scouts and guides, and greeted by fresh acclamations and military music. This part of the world has not witnessed an army on the march since Napoleon's expedition. Our brave soldiers of the Republic went through many fatigues and hardships where we, half a century later, are performing a military march with every possible comfort.

We took an easterly direction, and, after two hours' march, the Viceroy ordered a halt by the tomb of the late Sheik Abou-Hadidja, a Marabout. We rested there for half-an-hour.

The Viceroy had his "carriage bed" brought forward, and as the rate of progress of the troops would not admit of their reaching the next stopping-place before night, Zulfikar and I rode on in advance, arriving at sunset at the little village of Gavazi, inhabited by a mixed population of Bedouins and Fellahs.

3 *

The Viceroy and the troops did not arrive until two hours later. His Highness sent his compliments to me, and gave orders that dinner should be served for us, but he himself retired to rest. Our meal was prepared by a squad of some twenty-five or thirty cooks and scullions, by the light of a dozen *machallas*, or torches. I went to have a look at the open-air kitchen, and saw three rows of coppers ranged above holes in the earth filled with burning fagots —a kind of stove by no means economical in its consumption of fuel, but one that can be very readily constructed.

I returned to my tent to find dinner awaiting me. Zulfikar Pacha and the chief officers shared it with me. Our meal over, the table was removed and the tent became for a time the head-quarters of the staff, messengers coming to make inquiries, ... Zulfikar Pacha writing letters, receiving and sending out couriers, giving orders in the name of his master, and so forth.

November 17th.

The Viceroy was on foot outside his tent, next to ours, at seven o'clock this morning. I joined him, and he told me he had been disturbed too early by the trumpets of the cavalry, and that he must have his tent moved some three hundred yards farther off, to some spot where he could be out of hearing of the annoyance, and also have a clear space in front for setting up targets, at which his artillery and infantry could practise. I left the Viceroy to his preparations, and after a ride returned to find him watching his men practise on a target at a distance of 500 mètres. None of them had as yet done any execution, and taking a rifle from one of them I showed them how to hold it in taking aim, resting the butt-end firmly on the shoulder and avoiding loosening the trigger, as they did, by a sudden rebound. Their officer begged me to add example to precept, and I hit the target exactly in the centre. The Viceroy then sent for his own gun, of German manufacture, which I tried, hitting the mark the first shot. I made no further attempts, as I was afraid of compromising my newly-acquired reputation as a good marksman.

I returned to my tent, where breakfast was waiting. A

certain Sheik Masri, who had given proofs of devotion to
the Viceroy when he was persecuted by Abbas Pacha, and
was now attached to his household, told us all about a war
which took place six months ago between his own tribe of
Oulad Aly and a numerous one from Upper Egypt. The
former occupies the deserts between Lake Mareotis, on
the coast, and the frontiers of Tripoli, and cultivates the
districts bounded by the canals separating the desert from
Lower Egypt. They number 50,000 souls, and can arm
10,000 men. Expecting an attack from their enemies,
instigated by Abbas Pacha, the Oulad Alys, to the number
of more than 6000, including some women, who were to
cheer on the combatants with cries and shouts, entrenched
themselves behind earthworks and fascines near Hoche,
a village we shall reach to-morrow. In the battle which
ensued the attacking party lost 300 men, whilst the
besieged escaped with four women and three men killed.
In such a contest the women are mounted on camels, and
are more exposed than the men. The Bedouins from
Upper Egypt took to flight, and have never reappeared.

November 18th.

We started this morning two hours before daybreak.
The Viceroy was already *en route*, and we caught him up
at ten o'clock at Hoche, where he was waiting for us in
the tent of the provincial governor. There are more than
a hundred Bedouin chiefs of the tribe of Oulad Aly in this
village, all tall, fine, intelligent-looking men. Presently the
troops arrived, and the tents were set up. It was terribly
hot, and all were eager to get under shelter.

We had a visit from the chief who commanded in the
fight described above. He was accompanied by his son,
a strapping fellow, six feet high, like himself.

We started again with the Viceroy at three o'clock, the
troops remaining at Hoche. We were preceded by some
Bedouins, whilst others escorted us on the right hand and
the left. Every now and then they set spurs to their
horses, wheeled round and fired off their guns, a performance they called a *fantasia*.

We arrived at Zaoui-el-Khamour at sunset. The

Viceroy, who takes his meals very irregularly, begged me not to wait for him, and told Zulfikar Pacha to have dinner served in my tent, to which we retired, finding everything prepared for us by Ibrahim. Towards nine o'clock, just as I was going to bed, I heard women singing to the accompaniment of tambourines and castanets. Then came Paolini Bey with a message from the Viceroy inviting me to join him, as he had given some *Almehs* from the neighbouring town permission to perform in his presence. His Highness made room for me on his own divan. The Almehs were squatting in a circle on a carpet, and one of them was very richly dressed. "That hussy," observed the Viceroy, "has ten thousand francs' worth of embroidery and jewellery about her." The singing, consisting of verses in honour of the Viceroy, now began, and at occasional intervals the Kaouadji bachi (chief coffee-maker) went in front of the performers and, patting their cheeks as if they were children, gave them sweets and syrup. When the singing was over, two Almehs got up and, standing opposite each other, like Spanish ballet-dancers, began to dance. Two others succeeded them, after which the whole troupe passed before the Viceroy, kissed his feet respectfully, and retired.

November 19*th.*

We began marching at seven o'clock and halted at nine. The Viceroy dismounted and got into his carriage. We went on in advance with Halim Pacha, and arrived about noon at Yahoudieh, a regular Egyptian village. We had to ride over a cultivated and partially inundated plain, which gave our horses rather heavy work, and crossing a dyke we came to a little islet, a charming place for a rest, shaded by tamarind, sycamore, willow, and mulberry trees, surrounded by a piece of water, and forming a little circular wood. A delightful oasis, contrasting strongly with the sand hillocks just traversed, which are likely to make the passage of the troops very arduous.

At two o'clock the Viceroy appeared on horseback on the other side of the dyke, followed by a company of light infantry. The baggage had been sent on before, and the tents were already set up amongst the sand dunes. I went to look for mine and found Zulfikar resting in it. The Viceroy was fatigued, and had retired to his own tent. I went to see him at once, and spent an hour with him. He told me he had given orders for ten steamers to assemble on the Nile, near Neguileh, which we shall reach to-morrow, and added that he should expect me to read my minute on the Canal quietly over to him on board his steamer, together with my draught of the Firman of Concession.

The Viceroy was anxious to go to bed in good time, that he might be up early the next morning; so I left him and returned to my tent, where I found Halim Pacha and some Generals, who remained to dinner.

November 20th.

The Viceroy did not get up as early as he intended, for he did not get a very quiet evening after all. A message was brought to him to say that the artillery could not cross the sand dunes, and that a dozen horses had already succumbed to fatigue. A reinforcement was at once sent, and with the help of men and mules the difficult passage was finally effected.

At eight o'clock orders were given to prepare to start, and as our tent was being rolled up an eagle came and hovered above us. Zulfikar Pacha at once sent for his gun. I fired, and the bird fell at my feet. I cite this fact, of little importance in itself, because it may influence public opinion in Egypt in favour of the success of my scheme.

We mounted at the same time as the Viceroy, and after half an hour's march across a dyke we dismounted just outside a village, beneath the shade of two immense sycamore trees, with vast green fields of corn in the blade stretching away from us on every side. The Viceroy had a bad cold, so I urged him to rest in his carriage, and he took my advice. I then went to join Halim Pacha, who had taken a shorter route to the Nile than that followed by the troops. Half an hour's gallop enabled me not only to join him, but to ride with him to the anchorage of the steamers. I was delighted to see the beautiful river again, which is said irresistibly to attract strangers who have once drank of its waters. A boat took us to the Viceroy's steam yacht, which his predecessor, Abbas Pacha, had had built in England at a cost of £200,000. It would be impossible to convey an idea of the luxury of the arrangements, paintings, and furniture of this vessel: doors of oak and citron wood, locks and hinges of solid silver, medallions, paintings of rivers and animals by celebrated artists, staircases with silver balusters and railings, divans covered with cloth of gold, a saloon forty feet long, a dining-room, boudoir, retiring-rooms, bedrooms, all furnished in the style of the grandest palace. It was positively dazzling.

The arrival of the Viceroy was announced, and we hurried to the ladder to receive him. I went over his floating palace again with him, and he observed: "You will guess that I should not have been guilty of this folly; but I profit by it." He placed his old steamboat, *El Ferusi* (the Turquoise), at my disposal for the two or three days we are to remain on the Nile, whilst waiting for the troops and seeing them off for Cairo. A second steamboat was assigned to Halim Pacha. The Viceroy lent me his own boat to go and take possession of my apartments on board the *Turquoise*. My saloon is twelve feet long, and is surrounded by a spacious divan covered with fine Lyons fabrics brocaded with gold. At the end is a sleeping apartment; on the right as you go in is a dressing-room, and on the left a second retiring-room, with a large slab of white marble forming the floor. Clot Bey, Hassan Pacha, and two generals occupy other rooms. We met in the saloon, where a good dinner was served in the Turkish style.

ON THE NILE, NEAR NEGUILEH.
November 21st.

I went to see the Viceroy this morning, my minute in my pocket. I read it to him, and he pointed out several passages for alteration; I also read him my draught of the Firman of Concession, of which he entirely approved.

I then paid a visit to Prince Halim Pacha. The conversation turned on his family. He will help me to bring about a reconciliation between the Viceroy and his heir, Achmet Pacha. We breakfasted with Mohammed Said. It was settled that we should have a hunt on an island near Neguileh, which is said to be tenanted by boars. The Viceroy, who decided to join us, had steam got up on his own yacht. We landed on the island and rode about for some time, but saw nothing of the expected game, though there were plenty of fresh traces. The animals probably only come out at night.

We re-embarked and returned to our former anchorage. Mustapha Pacha, younger brother of Achmet Pacha and nephew of the Viceroy, arrived on a steamer from Cairo with passengers from Alexandria. His Highness invited him to make the rest of the voyage with us. He told him about my scheme, and asked him to look at my minute. We retired to the *Turquoise*.

November 22nd.

I had a talk with Mustapha Pacha about the maritime canal. I found the prince very intelligent and well informed. He speaks French like a Parisian. We breakfasted on board the Viceroy's vessel.

His Highness informed me that troops would be embarked on the *Turquoise* in the evening, ready to start for Cairo during the night with all the other steamers except his own, which will not leave till to-morrow. I transferred my effects to the Viceroy's vessel.

November 23rd.

I was on deck early, and Mustapha Pacha made me read him my report. He seemed very pleased with it, warmly advocated my scheme, and engaged to find the necessary capital.

Just then the Viceroy came on deck and invited us into his saloon. He himself introduced the subject of the Canal, and asked me what engineer had better make the preliminary surveys. I recommended Linant Bey, and suggested the association with him of Mougel Bey, adding that their report would have to be examined by English, German, and French engineers, whose statements would, in their turn, be submitted to a commission, over which I should preside, and which would decide on the best plan. The steamer started whilst we were at breakfast.

This evening we stopped for an hour to cross the dam by torchlight, and arrived at Boulac at eleven o'clock. I passed the rest of the night on board.

CAIRO, *November 24th.*

I was up at six this morning. The Viceroy had already started incognito for the Citadel. He had told Zulfikar Pacha to beg me to wait for a carriage, which would convey me to the Palace of Muçafirs (foreigners), near the mosque of Setti Zeneb (St. Zenobia), where apartments were assigned to me. At seven o'clock a large "Berlin" and four arrived on the quay with two Chiaous (officers of the Viceroy's household), whose insignia consisted of a cane with a silver chain. I ordered a halt near the Place d l'Esbekie, the house of Linant Bey, who was enthusiastically delighted when I told him that the Suez Canal, of which he had dreamt so long, was to become a reality, by decision of the Viceroy. I went up to call on Madame Linant, for whom I performed the marriage service when I was French Consul at Cairo, but had not since seen.

Lubbert Bey, Secretary General to the Ministry for Foreign Affairs, who lives close by, heard of my arrival, and came to call on me at Linant Bey's. When I first came to Alexandria as attaché in 1832, Lubbert was the friend and guest of my beloved chief, M. Mimaut, one of the most distinguished diplomatic agents of France. I shall never forget how M. Mimaut, with the grand work of the French expedition into Egypt on hand, initiated me into the mysteries of the maritime canal, a subject of which, I confess, I was till then totally ignorant.

But it was time to take possession of my new residence. Conducted there by my brilliant equipage, I made a solemn entrance through a line of Mamelukes and servants. The Nazir (steward), a worthy effendi resembling the portraits of Francis I., rushed to the carriage door as I was about to alight, made me take his arm, and led me, thus supported, into my apartments, where we were quickly joined by the Chiaous and people of the house. The Foreigners' Palace was the home of the Institute of France during the French expedition, and the commission of savans sent to report on the maritime canal met in it. A singular coincidence that, fifty years later, the same place should witness the inauguration of the work they studied under the inspiration of the great man of the century. I was informed that there were ten carriages and ten saddle horses at my disposal in the stable, a large gilt chariot for state occasions, the "Berlin," an open carriage, and a brougham.

Breakfast was laid for twelve persons.

The Viceroy had advised me to lose no time in calling on Mr. Bruce, the Agent and Consul-General for England, to inform him that his Highness intended to make a canal across the Isthmus of Suez, and to show him my documents relating to it. I therefore ordered the brougham, and went to Mr. Bruce's residence.

I had a conference with him of two hours' duration. He assured me that, although he could not speak yet in the name of his Government, whom he would inform of my visit, he did not hesitate to express his private opinion, that, so long as there was no question of the intervention or influence of any one Power, but merely of the free combination of capital in an enterprise authorised by the head of the country, he could not foresee any opposition on the part of England. I told him that I had thought as much, and that the cutting of the Isthmus of Suez, formerly an affair of such grave import, but now freed from the political difficulties by which it was complicated, had become a mere question of practicability and capital. As to its practicability, scientific men had already spoken and would again speak, whilst capital would surely not be wanting for a work which must not only enrich the commercial world, but, according to the most modest calculations, would be a profitable speculation to the shareholders.

It was arranged with Mr. Bruce that I should write to him, enclosing a copy of my report and the scheme for the Firman of Concession. I let the Viceroy know of all the details of this conference, with which he was satisfied.

Kœnig Bey, formerly the Viceroy's tutor and now his private secretary, is to translate into Turkish the documents relating to the Canal.

CAIRO, *November 25th.*

The Viceroy had requested me, without assigning any reason, to present myself at the Citadel at nine o'clock this morning. I entered the large divan, where I found my host seated on the very spot where his old father, Mehemet Ali, had often received me, and where one day he described to me his tragedy of the massacre of the Mamelukes. All the public functionaries were to pay their respects to the Viceroy to-day, on the occasion of his arrival at the capital. I came in at the same time as the Consuls-General of the various Powers. M. Sabatier had not yet returned from Alexandria, where he went to be married.

Scarcely had the Consuls, in uniform, taken their places on the divan and made their salutations when, to my great surprise, the Viceroy publicly announced that he had determined to throw open the Isthmus of Suez by means of a maritime canal, and had commissioned me to form a company of capitalists, of all nations, to whom he would concede the right of working this enterprise. He added, addressing me: "Are we not going to do so?" I then addressed the meeting, and briefly commented on the announcement of the prince, leaving him the credit of originating and deciding on the scheme, and taking great care not to offend foreign susceptibilities.

The Consul-General for England appeared slightly embarrassed.

The Consul-General for the United States of America, however, to whom the Viceroy had said, "Well, Monsieur de Léon, we are going to compete with the Isthmus of Panama, and shall have finished before you," had fully made up his mind, and answered so as to convey the idea of a favourable opinion.

The Consuls retired, whilst I remained with the Viceroy. He was struck with the coincidence of my being in the home of the old Institute of Egypt, where the question of the maritime canal was first studied. He sent for some of his most intimate friends, to tell them about it, and they congratulated him on the announcement to the Consuls. I told him that I should not have dared to recommend such a course, but that I thought he had taken the best means of anticipating many objections and difficulties by suddenly challenging public opinion on a project the general utility of which is incontestable. He replied: "Upon my word, I hadn't thought much about it; it was an act of impulse. You know that I am not much given to following the usual rules, and that I don't like doing things like everybody else."

We went with the Viceroy to his private apartments, and the arrival of Soliman Pacha, who wished to see his Highness, was announced. He was admitted, and I returned to my state carriage with its four white horses. The negro coachman was very skilful in driving at a brisk trot or gallop along the narrow streets of Cairo and across the bazaars. It was like driving a carriage through the Passage des Panoramas.[1] It is true that, in spite of my orders to the contrary, the Chiaous and Sais administered blows right and left to make the people leaning against the walls and shops get out of the way. The poor creatures did not complain, they even uttered admiring exclamations, such as: "Oh, here's a great lord passing, Machallah!" (Glory be to God!). Such is the East, such has it been from time immemorial and as it is described in the Bible, where we read, after the acccount of Joshua's massacre of the inhabitants of Jericho, including the women, children, and asses: "So the Lord was with Joshua, and his fame was noised throughout all the country."

In the course of the day I went to see the three sons of Ibrahim Pacha. The eldest, Achmet Pacha, is a well-educated man, who has successfully followed the course of study at our Ecole Polytechnique. Like his father he is very successful in the management of his immense property, and he converses in French with perfect ease on any subject. He had been to call on the Viceroy on the very

[1] The Passage des Panoramas is an arcade of Paris, out of the Boulevard Montmartre.

morning of his arrival, and had been well received. He knew that I had aided in the reconciliation, and thanked me, and hoped we should be friends.

I have already spoken of Ibrahim Pacha's third son, Mustapha Pacha; as for the second, Ismail Pacha, he is full of sympathy for me, and I was delighted with his reception. He has a fine, intelligent, and distinguished countenance, and he is really of the race of Mehemet Ali. When he ceases to be quite so much addicted to pleasure, I fancy he will distinguish himself usefully. Although only twenty-five years old, he is already father of a dozen children. He inherited the finest palace of Cairo, on the banks of the Nile, and has spent more than a million francs on furniture imported from France. He showed me over the vast and magnificent apartments on the ground floor, and part of those on the first storey, the rest were reserved to the harem. In crossing a grand room, longer than the Salle des pas Perdus in the Palais de Justice, Paris, I saw some tapestry hangings moving, before which eunuchs were on guard.

The staircase railing is of carved rosewood inlaid with silver, with crystal balusters by Baccarat.

I went thence to see Prince Halim Pacha, who lives in one of Mehemet Ali's residences, approached by an avenue, a league in length, shaded by huge sycamore trees, which were very beautiful when I last saw them and now form a thick green canopy. This fine avenue was planted by the French in 1800. I was most graciously received by Halim Pacha, who is delighted with his brother's announcement to the Consuls on the subject of the Suez Canal. He has the bearing and vivacity of a Frenchman from the south, with a very pure Parisian accent.

Later I visited Herr von Hüber, Agent and Consul-General for Austria. He spoke to me of the interest taken by his Government in the opening of the Suez Canal. He has instructions to support the scheme heartily when the proper time arrives.

Herr von Hüber had just dined at home with Mr. Bruce, Baron Pentz, Consul-General for Prussia, Count Escayrac, a French traveller, Linant Bey, &c.

Clot Bey has become my guest. The Viceroy invited him to stay with me through Zulfikar Pacha. He introduced his children's tutor to me, a young poet of two-and-twenty, from Marseilles, M. Reynier by name, with a charming face and frank pleasing manners. His father is public librarian at Marseilles. He very obligingly offered to assist me with my writing, and I found him a first-rate secretary. After having made a few copies of my report and firman, he no longer required the originals to make others, for he knew them by heart.

November 26th.

To-day I received a visit from Talat Bey, First Secretary of Turkish Affairs to the Viceroy; Kœnig Bey, who holds the same office for European Affairs, accompanied him, and acted as interpreter.

I went up to the Citadel at ten o'clock, and the Viceroy invited me to breakfast with him. The conversation turned on what he calls *my affair*. It was arranged that Mougel Bey should be associated with us in the survey we are to make with Linant. His Highness made some objections on the ground of the difficulty of getting these two engineers to agree, but ended in consenting to my proposal, which I had very much at heart.

I then returned to Setti Zeneb, and received a visit from Achmet Pacha, whom I like more than ever.

Other visits followed, including one from our fellow-countryman, Arnaud Bey, the traveller who ascended the White Nile for 1200 leagues, no one before him having advanced further than 900 leagues. He gave us some very interesting details of his strange excursion. The expedition was sent out by Mehemet Ali, who placed 800 men under Arnaud's orders. He could not go further on account of the opposition of some of the officers. All the expenses were covered by the elephants' tusks with which the boats were loaded on their return. Arnaud spoke highly of the reception given to them by the negro populations through which they passed, who had never before seen a sailing vessel. Not one of the soldiers was killed by the natives. As he ascended towards the equator, which he neared within two degrees, the people of the country told him that the river was navigable for four degrees beyond the equator, but that it would take a month to traverse them, on account of the winding of the river, representing some 150 leagues. In the lofty regions on either side of the Nile are vast forests, inhabited by elephants, lions, and all sorts of animals. Arnaud's party sometimes fired upon the herds of hundreds of elephants, which hurried rapidly along without ever looking behind them. But they took no more notice of the bullets than if they had been pelted with sugar-plums, not even quickening their pace after the discharge. On one occasion an elephant was surrounded, and dashing up to a man he lifted him with his trunk and tossed him in the air. The animal, however, finally succumbed to a volley fired at close quarters.

V.

To Mr. Bruce, her Britannic Majesty's Agent and Consul-General in Egypt.

November 27th.

I HAVE already had the honour of conversing with you on the Viceroy of Egypt's project of cutting a canal through the Isthmus of Suez. His Highness, who intends to authorise me to form a *compagnie universelle*, to which will be accorded the right to execute the works and carry on the business of the new route, has requested me to forward you a copy of the report, drawn up at his desire, on this question, in which he is anxious to consult the interests of England, as well as those of other nations.

Everything which leads to the extension of the commerce, industry, and navigation of the world has a special interest for England, a Power which outweighs others by the importance of its navy, its manufactures, and its commercial relations.

A deplorable prejudice, founded on the political antagonism which unfortunately so long existed between France and England, has alone countenanced the opinion that the opening of the Suez Canal, a work of civilisation and progress, would not be conducive to the interests of Great Britain. The frank and complete alliance of the two nations placed at the head of civilisation, an alliance which has already proved the possibility of the solving of many questions hitherto considered insoluble by common tradition, will allow, amongst many other advantages, of the impartial consideration of the great Suez Canal question, of the taking of an exact estimate of its influence on the prosperity of all nations, and must make it appear a heresy to suppose that an enterprise which is to shorten by half the distance between the East and West could be detrimental to England, mistress as she is of Gibraltar, Malta, the Ionian Islands, Aden, important colonies on the Eastern coast of Africa, India, Singapore, and Australia.

England, as much as and even more than France, ought therefore to promote the cutting through of this neck of land of forty leagues, which no one interested in civilisation and progress can see upon the map without an earnest desire to remove the sole obstacle remaining on the grand route of the commerce of the world.

The copy of my report, which I have the honour to enclose, and of the powers the Viceroy proposes conferring upon me, render it unnecessary for me to enter into the further details of an enterprise, in which you will observe there is no question of privileges for any State in particular, but merely of the formation of a free company, open on equal conditions to shareholders of every nationality.

VI.

To Madame Delamalle, Paris.

(Continuation of Journal.)

CAIRO, *November 27th.*

I AM about to call on Zulfikar Pacha, Kœnig Bey, and Talat Bey, who live in the Citadel. I have other visits to pay in the town. Everywhere I meet with compliments and congratulations on the grand scheme of the Suez Canal. The French Consul-General, M. Sabatier, has not yet arrived, and I am waiting to show him my letter to Mr. Bruce before sending it. Not knowing whether I should succeed, I could not say a word to him when at Alexandria about what I was going to attempt; but his reception of me was so hearty and cordial that I should be sorry for him to learn from any one but myself of an affair of so much importance, and of which he is as yet completely ignorant, though it is already the chief topic of conversation in Cairo. I have, therefore, begged to be informed immediately of his landing.

November 28th.

M. Sabatier arrived yesterday evening, and I at once told him all the details of my journey across the desert. He seemed to understand my reserve with him when I passed through Alexandria, and rejoiced for France at the realisation of a scheme which his instructions authorised him to propose to the Viceroy two years ago. In accordance with his usual character, having once made up his mind, he will frankly and vigorously carry out his views, and he is disposed to support me to the fullest extent of his power. He read and approved of the report, firman, and letter to Mr. Bruce, which last he undertook to deliver.

I paid a visit to the Viceroy at nine o'clock, and entered the divan of the Citadel at the same time as M. Sabatier. The French Consul-General hastened to congratulate the Viceroy on the Canal affair, telling him of the instructions authorising him to support a project, the execution of which had always been desired by the French Government, in a word, saying everything necessary to strengthen the Viceroy in his resolve.

After M. Sabatier had taken leave, the Viceroy made me go into his apartments with Prince Mustapha. The conversation turned on the preliminary measures for the execution of the scheme, such as drawing up the list of the first founders, &c. "It will be for you," said my host, "to name the sum I am to put down."

VII.

To M. Sabatier, Agent and Consul-General for France in Egypt.

Cairo, November 29th.

On your arrival at Cairo, I informed you of the circumstances which, during my journey with the Viceroy, had called the attention of his Highness to the great enterprise of cutting a canal across the Isthmus of Suez, and I discussed with you the Viceroy's proposal for conceding the execution of the work to a company of capitalists belonging to all nations.

I now beg you to be good enough to inform the Imperial Government of the decision of Mohammed Said, and to entrust to me the task of forming and directing the Maritime Canal Company. I shall hasten, on my approaching return to Paris, to solicit the personal honour of submitting to his Imperial Majesty the measures to be adopted and the result of a survey I am about to make of the isthmus in conjunction with M. Linant Bey, Director of Public Works in Egypt, and M. Mougel Bey, Chief Engineer des Ponts et Chaussées, whom the Viceroy has permitted to join us.

Meanwhile I think it my duty to forward to you:

1. The report on the proposed canal across the Isthmus of Suez, drawn up by me at the request of the Viceroy.

2. A translation of the powers to be conferred on me by the Viceroy.

3. A copy of the letter I wrote to Mr. Bruce, and which you were good enough to undertake to remit after having read and approved of it.

The Viceroy, whose present friendly relations with the Porte are known to you, tells me that he has no doubt of the Sultan's acquiescence in his scheme for the maritime canal, and that he will discuss the matter personally with his suzerain as well as with Reschid Pacha.

VIII.

To M. Ruyssenaers, Consul-General for Holland in Egypt.

Cairo, November 30th.

I GAVE you a verbal account of the circumstances which enabled me, during the journey I recently took with the Viceroy from Alexandria to Cairo, to persuade his Highness to concede the right of making the Suez Canal to a company of capitalists of all nations.

You, who have concurred with me for the last two years in endeavouring to realise this scheme, of such special importance to the interests of Holland, will rejoice with me in the resolution come to by our mutual friend, Mohammed Said.

I have the honour of forwarding to you the report drawn up at the request of his Highness, and the translation of the powers signed this very day by him for constituting and directing the Universal Maritime Suez Canal Company.

December 2, 1854.

Documents sent to all the Consuls-General, and a letter, in which I inform them that the Viceroy will himself discuss the matter with the Porte.

IX.

To Richard Cobden, Esq., M.P., London.

Cairo, December 3, 1854.

As the friend of peace and of the Anglo-French alliance I am going to tell you some news which will aid in realising the words, *Aperire terram gentibus.*

I arrived in Egypt a short time back, as the invited guest of the Viceroy, with whom, since his boyhood, I have been on terms of friendship, and I have had an opportunity of calling his attention to the advantages which would result to the commerce of the world and the prosperity of Egypt from the opening of a maritime canal between the Mediterranean and the Red Sea. Mohammed Said has understood the importance of this great enterprise, and wishing to see it carried into execution, he has authorised me to form a company of capitalists of all nations. I forward you a translation of the Firman of Concession. The Viceroy has requested me to communicate it to her Britannic Majesty's Agent and Consul-General as well as to the other Consuls-General in Egypt.

Some people maintain that the Viceroy's project will meet with opposition in England. I cannot believe it. Under existing circumstances your statesmen must be too enlightened for me to admit such an hypothesis. What! England monopolises half the general commerce with India and China; she possesses an immense empire in Asia; she can reduce by one-third the charges on her commerce and the distance from her metropolis by one half, and she will not have it done! And why? In order to prevent the countries on the Mediterranean from profiting by their geographical situation to carry on a little more commerce in the Oriental seas than they do at present, she will deprive herself of the advantages, material and political, of this new communication, merely because others are more favourably situated than herself, as if geographical position were everything, as if, having regard to all the circumstances, England had not more to gain by this work than all the other Powers put together. Lastly, England deprecates, it is said, the diminution in the number of vessels trading with India which will result from the reduction by more than one-third of the length of the voyage. Has not our experience with railways proved, in a manner surpassing the expectations of the most sanguine, that the abbreviation of distances and of the duration of journeys lead to an immense increase in the number of passengers and the amount of traffic?

It is difficult to understand why those who admit this last objection do not advise the English Government to compel vessels for India to take the Cape Horn route, for it would employ more ships and turn out better sailors than that of the Cape of Good Hope.

If, though it seems impossible, the difficulties with which we are threatened have actually arisen, I hope that public spirit, so powerful in England, will soon have done justice to interested opposition and superannuated objections.

Allow me, in case of need, to count upon your legitimate influence. I have already written to our friend M. Arles Dufour, Secretary-General to the Imperial Commission at the Universal Exhibition of Paris, asking him to communicate with you.

X.

To M. Arles Dufour, Secretary-General of the International Exhibition, Paris.

CAIRO, *December* 6, 1854.

My letter of the 30th of November will have informed you of the Viceroy's intention to open the maritime canal, and to grant a concession for its construction to a company of capitalists, of all nations, which he has commissioned me to form.

The first thing to be done to make it possible to carry on the necessary operations in a desert, in the mere surveying of which we four are to be accompanied by thirty-two camels laden with provisions for ourselves, servants, and animals, will of course be the making of a sweet water canal to be fed by the Nile, and which, passing Kankha and Belbeis, will follow the route of the ancient canal of the Pharaohs as far as Lake Timsah.

XI.

To Madame Delamalle, Paris.
(*Continuation of Journal.*)

December 10*th.*

I HAVE just been spending a few days with the Viceroy at Tourah, at the foot of Mokattam, where he has set up a military camp.

We are back at Cairo. When the Consuls-General called on his Highness at the Citadel, he repeated to them what he had already said to me at Tourah: " In case any foreign agent should make objections to the opening of the Suez Canal on the part of his Government, he should request that those objections be stated in *writing*, that he might be able to draw up a *document* to submit to the verdict of civilised nations." This was in reply to certain hostile expressions of the Consul-General for England, who has probably received instructions by telegraph.

I dined to-day with M. de Léon, Consul-General for the United States, who proposed a toast to the success of the Suez Canal.

XII.

To M. Arles Dufour, Paris.

Cairo, December 14th.

The Viceroy wrote by the very first mail after his arrival at Cairo to inform the Sultan of his intention to open the Suez Canal.

The Porte has recently spoken in the most complimentary terms with regard to the assistance now being rendered to its cause by the Viceroy, adding an expression of regret for the loss of two Egyptian men-of-war in the Black Sea and the death of Admiral Hassan Pacha. To this the Viceroy replied that he had nothing left to desire so long as the Sultan's own valuable life was spared, and he was able to come to his assistance; adding, that he was now more ready than ever to make fresh sacrifices for the common cause. Then followed some remarks on the railway the Viceroy proposes making between Cairo and Suez, in which England takes a great interest; and, after alluding to the unfortunate condition of the national Exchequer, as left by the late Abbas Pacha, his Highness pointed out the advantages which might ensue from the formation of international financial companies for the execution of useful works in the Ottoman Empire—the making of the Suez Canal, for instance.

He added that he had no doubt of the Sultan's acquiescence in the two schemes, for a railway and a canal.

He thought it useless to enter into longer explanations, which he is, however, prepared to give if necessary, by forwarding all the documents in support of the scheme. Such an act of respectful courtesy, to which the conventions relating to the Government of Egypt do not strictly bind

Mohammed Said, will doubtless be appreciated as it deserves at Constantinople, where the maintenance of the present friendly relations with the Viceroy is much desired.

My previsions on the subject of certain foreign susceptibilities have been soon enough realised. Influenced probably by the presence in Cairo of Mr. Murray, late English Consul-General in Egypt and now Minister in Persia, who has too long carried on the old policy of antagonism and jealous rivalry between France and England, Mr. Bruce has begun to make some opposition. For instance, he has told the Viceroy that he is in too much of a hurry about the Suez Canal affair. His Highness replied firmly that in a question of civilisation and progress he could not believe that he should meet with opposition from any European Power, but that if any foreign agent should presently have objections to make *on the part of his Government*, he should request that they be stated in writing, so that he might *draw up his document*.

The English mail is just going, so I cannot give you my ideas to-day about the formation of our company, in which the money kings of Paris and London will be able to make their profits for the common good, although it will not do to let them have their own way entirely. Subscription lists, open for a certain time, will allow of the public taking shares at par.

The survey of the isthmus is put off until the 24th, that the necessary preparations may be made. Canvass opinion in England. Heaven helps those who help themselves.

XIII.

To Madame Delamalle, Paris.
(Continuation of Journal.)

December 16th.

To-day, when I went to take my letters on board a passenger steamer, I came across my old Spanish friend General Pavia, now on his way home from Manilla, where he has been acting as Governor of the Philippine Islands for the last three years. You will remember that we knew him well at Barcelona, when he was second governor there (*Cabo Secundo*). All Spaniards, as I think rightly, consider me a fellow-countryman. We conversed in my mother tongue. General Pavia is delighted with the Suez Canal project, and says that the shortening of the distance between Europe and the Indian Ocean will lead to a time of great prosperity for the Philippine Islands, where Spain numbers some five million native subjects, and that, instead of being, as they are now, some two hundred years behind the age—one of the results of the long and tedious voyage round the Cape—they will become a source of immense wealth to the mother country.

Fearing that the Viceroy was on board the *Fernsi* (Turquoise), near the Boulac docks, I went to see him. He told me Mr. Bruce had asked him to receive Mr. Murray, whom his Highness suspects of having instigated the persecution to which he was subjected by Abbas Pacha, and that he wished to avoid the visit in question, adding: "I cannot understand how Mr. Murray can have the insolence to ask to see me."

I begged him not to hurt the English Agent's feelings in the matter, and he replied: "You don't know what insinuations have been thrown out to induce me to do honour to Mr. Murray; unless I do, they say England will take offence, comparing my treatment of him with my reception of you. But I said I did not receive you as a Frenchman or as a Minister, but as my old and well-tried friend; that, far from having done too much, I had not done enough, and that if any rooms in the Citadel had been large and comfortable enough for you, I should have made you stay with me, instead of giving you a separate palace."

"What your Highness has just said," I replied, "does but add another to my many motives for urging you to name an early day to Mr. Bruce for giving audience to Mr. Murray. If you have any grievances against him, I do not ask you to forget them; but you must remember that in exalted public positions grave interests are often compromised by a betrayal of private animosity. All this, however, need not prevent your keeping your own opinion, and giving your confidence and friendship to none but those who are worthy of them."

As usual with him, when a decided opinion of his met with dissent, the Viceroy changed the subject; but, for all that, words in season are not thrown away upon him.

Presently news was brought of the arrival near the *barrage* of the Viceroy's steamer with his sister on board, come from Constantinople at the invitation of her brother. Mohammed Said started to meet her, whilst Prince Mustapha Pacha landed with me, and drove me to the palace prepared for his aunt's reception. It was in the garden belonging to it that Kleber was assassinated. We went into the court, and saw two buffaloes tied up opposite the steps, ready for sacrifice at the ceremony of welcome. Amongst the great families of the land it is customary to slay a victim on the return of a beloved relation. The animal is killed just as the traveller crosses the threshold, the blood flowing into a trench, across which the new arrival steps, when he is congratulated and escorted to his apartments. Troops lined the road between Boulac and Cairo, along which the princess passed in an open carriage, wearing a semi-transparent veil such as is now the fashion in Constantinople.

The Viceroy had told me that he wished his "little sister," who had been exiled from Egypt by Abbas Pacha, to return in triumph; and these public honours rendered to a woman seemed to me a most significant sign of Mussulman progress.

Volleys of artillery announced the landing of the princess, and the troops presented arms. Soon the Viceroy dashed up in a phaeton, driven by himself, followed at a short distance by the great dignitaries and officers of all ranks in full uniform, riding at a foot pace in two straggling rows, a little in advance of the princess's carriage. As the latter approached, the order to present arms was passed along the line, and the soldiers cheered. The Viceroy's sister, whose eyes alone were visible, looked about her, but did not return the salutations. Behind her equipage came some ten carriages filled with veiled women, and followed by several mounted eunuchs, a squadron or two of light infantry, and a few lancers and cuirassiers wearing Saracen helmets.

At last the princess arrived at her palace on the Place

de l'Esbékie, where there will be fireworks and illuminations in the evening. Fresh volleys of artillery were discharged from the Citadel, and are to succeed each other until sunset. The same thing will go on for the next three days.

On my return to Setti Zeneb I sent a complimentary message for the princess to her first eunuch.

Sunday, December 17th.

I went to call on Father Leonardo, Superior of the Franciscan Convent, who received me in the room occupied by Murat during the French expedition in Egypt.

Later I went up the Nile on the Viceroy's steamer. As I was ascending the ladder, Kœnig Bey showed me a letter he had just written to Mr. Bruce, requesting him to come with Mr. Murray at eleven o'clock. I was about to retire when the Viceroy invited me to remain, and I guessed it was to assist at the interview, which went off capitally. His Highness shook hands with Mr. Murray when he took leave, and as soon as he was gone the Viceroy whispered to me, in a bantering tone: "I am not going to offer my hand to a friend to-day, after having giving it to an enemy. I have been diplomatic, have I not? and I have said many things I did not mean." Whilst I was with him the Viceroy received a message from M. Sabatier, asking him to name a day for his reception to present a letter from the Emperor, accompanied by the Grand Cordon of the Legion of Honour.

I congratulated the prince, who appreciates the high distinction conferred on him as it deserves, and thinks it will be an excellent moral support in his schemes of reform and progress.

I then went to thank Prince Achmet Pacha for his present of a splendid mare of the race considered the best in Arabia.

December 18th.

To-day I visited the Viceroy, who is about to return to Tourah. He had heard of my authorising Linant to draw on my banker for funds to provide the necessary outfit and provisions for our journey on the isthmus, and he told me he could not possibly allow any such thing, reproaching me in the kindest manner for having supposed it possible for him to let me incur the slightest expense whilst his guest.

This evening I was at a dinner given at Setti Zeneb, in the name of the Viceroy, in honour of Mr. Murray, who was present, with all his old colleagues, the Consuls-General, some other Englishmen, and a few Egyptian officials, making thirty in all.

December 19th.

This morning Kœnig Bey came to take me to see the Viceroy at Tourah, where I remained part of the day. We talked of the approaching survey of the isthmus, now finally fixed for the 23rd, and of the ceremony of receiving the Grand Cordon of the Legion of Honour, which is to take place at the Citadel.

December 22nd.

At half-past nine this morning all the members of the Legion of Honour now at Cairo met at M. Sabatier's, to go with him to invest the Viceroy with the insignia of their order.

His Highness sent a squadron of lancers to escort the party, together with his three best state carriages and four, to which I added mine. The cavalry led the way. I was in the first carriage, with M. Sabatier, my cousin Edmund de Lesseps, M. Delaporte, and Lubbert Bey, who was to act as master of the ceremonies. In front and on either side caracoled our mounted Chiaous and the Janissaries of the Consulate. The people drew back and saluted us respectfully as we passed, and regiments lined the road from the entrance of the Citadel to the Court. Kœnig Bey received M. Sabatier as he left his carriage, and at the entrance to the great hall we were met by Edhem Pacha, who conducted us to the chief divan. The Viceroy, attended by all the generals and chief dignitaries, advanced to the door, and the Emperor's letter was handed to him by M. Sabatier.

He remained standing whilst the French Consul handed him the insignia, with the following speech:—

I have the honour of being commissioned by the Emperor to present your Highness, in his name, with the Grand Cordon of the Legion of Honour. In conferring on your Highness this great distinction, coveted by all Europe, and which has never lost the prestige it owes to its founder, even in the most troubled times through which France has had to pass, Napoleon III. wishes not only to bestow a special mark of affection on a prince with whom he is acquainted, and whose personal qualities he appreciates as they deserve, but is also anxious by this voluntary act publicly to express his deep interest in Egypt itself, and in the glorious but arduous work of re-organisation and reform bequeathed to your Highness by your father of illustrious memory.

Your Highness is aware that in carrying out this work the encouragement and, if need be, the support of the Emperor will never fail you. I rejoice with you that this is the case, and I shall always esteem it a great honour to have been chosen to convey these assurances to your Highness on this solemn occasion, and to act as interpreter of the sentiments which, I am proud to feel, are entertained by the Government I have the honour to represent.

The prince replied in very good French, and with much earnestness of manner:—

I shall always be proud to wear this decoration, for which I have to thank his Imperial Majesty. I know full well all that I owe to the memory of my father, in whose steps I shall strive to tread. I hope to prove my gratitude by acts rather than by words.

December 23rd.

We are to start at nine o'clock, and M. and Madame Sabatier, with a few friends, will accompany us as far as Suez. We are to be attended by two mounted couriers, one for relays at the stations, the other to accompany the carriages. The road between Cairo and Suez is now macadamised, and there are fifteen relays or stations. We are to breakfast at No. 4, dine and sleep at No. 8, and shall be at Suez at noon to-morrow, having done our thirty-two leagues in the desert much as we might have gone from Paris to Orleans.

SUEZ, *December 25th.*

The beams of the rising sun streamed into my room. I opened the window and looked out. Before me lay the

Red Sea, the waves of which wash the walls of the India Hotel; on the right rose the Gebel Atâkah, and in the distance, on the left, I could see the commencement of the chain which culminates in Mount Sinai. This part of the coast has a reddish hue, which is reflected in the water, and was probably the origin of the Arabian gulf being called the Red Sea. The quay soon became animated, and boats, with oars ending in round paddles, crowded about the vessels recently arrived from or just starting for Djedda. These deckless ships, with a raised poop and tapering prow, are not unlike Chinese junks in form and rigging. The costumes of natives and foreigners alike, together with the furniture of the houses, give the traveller a foretaste of Arabia, India, and China. I notice that the people in this part move more slowly than in the rest of Egypt.

Suez is situated on an isolated angle of land, surrounded by deserts. Its inhabitants, numbering some three or four thousand, are a wretched set, who get nothing to drink but brackish water. Our canal will give them both the water and the animation they need.

I went up on to the terrace of the hotel, which commands a first-rate view of the surrounding country, as I am anxious to see everything for myself and to neglect no detail, however small; for when I understand a thing myself, I can explain it to those who are not engineers. Linant and Mougel have asked me to keep them constantly informed of my ideas and observations. I have been warned that these two engineers are not likely to agree, and the Viceroy himself advised me to take Linant only. But in an affair of such importance I prefer to have two opinions, even if they differ. Linant knows the topography of the whole country,—he has made a map of it, and has studied its geology on the spot. Moreover, the entire system of the canals of Egypt is familiar to him. Mougel, on the other hand, has executed important hydraulic works in Egypt; and although no one could be more competent than Linant to deal with all that relates to the inland portion of the Canal, Mougel's opinion will be preferable to his on the question, hitherto undecided, of the entrances from the Red Sea and the Mediterranean.

My companions not having yet put in an appearance, I went to call them, and proposed that we should make an excursion, in the course of the day, to the relics of the old canal of the Pharaohs.

We started after breakfast, some riding, others driving, escorted by fifteen mounted Bashi-Bazouks.

We soon came to the banks of the old canal, which are still distinctly visible. We measured the bed, and found it to be seventy Roman cubits across.

On our way back we rested in one of the tents provided for our journey, and Linant's steward, an old negro, Abdallah by name, served up some first-rate coffee. The renowned Ibrahim has retired into private life. The fact is, his lofty position quite turned his head, for, doubtless with a view to filling it more worthily, he invested in a fine gilded sabre, a truncheon, some patent leather shoes, a brilliant sash, &c. But where, you ask, did the base coin come from for buying all these grand things? Out of my coat pockets and my apartments in the Palace of Strangers. The facts being proved, my Ibrahim was sent about his business without more ado.

December 26th.

The journey overland from Suez to the Wells of Moses takes more than two hours. We therefore embarked on a Government steamer, which was to bring us there in an hour. Mr. Costa, owner of the largest well, was with us, and told us he had ordered a breakfast for us, which would include a sheep roasted whole. Madame Sabatier was accompanied by Mrs. Costa and her sister, both wearing the richest Oriental costumes, and with their eyelashes and eyebrows painted. We had scarcely left the port and entered the gulf when a most violent wind arose. The captain and pilot agreed in declaring that it would be impossible to land; which we could easily see for ourselves as we watched the huge waves breaking upon the beach. The hurricane was accompanied by whirlwinds of sand, which rendered the overland route impassable to ladies; so we had to give up both the Wells of Moses and the breakfast awaiting us. We tacked about, and returned to our hotel, some of the party suffering from sea-sickness.

Carriages were then ordered to take M. Sabatier back to Cairo, as he has to despatch a courier to France. He was accompanied by his wife and those who did not intend going further than Suez with us.

December 27th.

To-day has been devoted to a careful examination of the port of Suez and the mouth of the canal. We went for a long row at low tide, landing on banks and islets supposed to be rocks, but which we recognised as the remains of ancient masonry. We broke off some pieces of what probably formed the floating dock of the ancient Clysma. I intend having them analysed by Le Play, together with samples of stones, &c., from the neighbouring mountains.

On a little island near the port there is a cemetery belonging to the East India Company. It has had to be walled in, because barren Arab women try to obtain the bones of Christians, pieces of which they wear as amulets, in the hope of becoming fruitful.

We finished the day at Mr. West's, the English Consul. Dinner included mutton from Calcutta, potatoes from Bombay, green peas from England, and Egyptian poultry. We drank water from the Ganges, French wines, Mocca coffee, and Chinese tea.

December 28th.

We were on horseback at eight o'clock this morning, and wended our way towards the chief defile of the Gebel Atâkah, where St. Anthony is said to have lived in a cave, not now to be identified. From the Suez Gate the mountain looked as if it were only half an hour's distance off, but it took three hours of brisk riding to reach it. We followed the bed of a torrent, which brought us to the defile, where we proposed collecting minerals, &c. We obtained specimens of marbles, calcareous chalks, clay, &c., which we packed in our saddle-bags before setting out on our return to Suez.

We were back at the hotel at three p.m., and, after a kind of breakfast-dinner, we went to call on Mr. Costa, who took us to the house once occupied by General Bonaparte. The present proprietor, who was born in the year of the French occupation, has decorated his drawing-room with engravings after pictures of the great victories of the Emperor, in memory of the hospitality shown by his father to the leader of the French expedition.

Our vessel got up steam early this morning to take us to the further side of the Gulf of Suez, where the valley closes which begins behind Mokattam, near Cairo. Mr. Basilie Costa, who accompanied us, informed us that he had written to his father, who has a country seat near the Wells of Moses, telling him that on our return we shall land on the east of the gulf, and dine and sleep at his house, returning to Suez by land to-morrow, when we begin our caravan journey across the isthmus.

The first part of our trip went off splendidly, and at eleven o'clock we touched at the foot of the lofty mountain of Genebeh, situated on the left promontory of a large bay, of which Gebel Atâkah forms the headland on the right. Opposite to us was the valley of the Tîh, or the Wanderings, erroneously so called, as Moses and the Israelites did not land on that part of the coast. The course of the Israelites when flying with Moses from the Egyptians can be traced on the map from Lake Timsah to the Bitter Lakes, through districts then covered by the Red Sea, which, according to Linant, retain their Scriptural names. Ten leagues from Suez we cast anchor, and started for the beach in the cutter of our vessel. When it could go no farther we were carried by the sailors, who set us and our breakfast down on dry land.

We went to examine a tepid and slightly brackish spring watering an extensive plain on which flourish herbs and reeds. Some Bedouins were cutting rushes to send to the Cairo mat-makers.

We settled ourselves for breakfast beneath the shadow of the mountain, and we had fragments from veins of alabaster, marble, and other calcareous stones broken off with a hammer.

In an area of twenty leagues to the south, behind Mount Genebeh, Linant has ascertained the existence of veins of every variety of the finest marble and of verde antique. We got back to the steamer at two o'clock, hoping in a couple of hours to reach the Wells of Moses, which were really one of the stopping-places of the children of Israel after the passage of the Red Sea. We had been making head for an hour, and Mr. B. Costa was telling us of the preparations made by his father for our reception, when there was a sudden noise from the engine succeeded by clouds of steam and smoke. The stokers rushed on deck, and we thought the vessel must be on fire; but it was only the bursting of the boiler. There was no real danger, but in case of a long delay the situation might become awkward, as we had no food, water, or personal comforts on board. We were too far off to be seen either from Suez or the harbour. The fires were put out, and the tent hoisted in the bow, with the side sewn up so as to make a wind sail, by means of which we hoped to cool the boiler, as we were anxious to find out if it could be patched up. At five o'clock the engine-man had managed to stop up the hole. The boiler was refilled, steam got up, and we started again; but we soon had to put out the fires and make more thorough repairs. Fortunately the sea was very calm. Night came on, and we were obliged to lie down on deck, the steamer being unprovided with sleeping accommodation. No chance now, to Mr. Basilie's great regret, of Mr. Costa's entertainment, or of seeing the Wells of Moses. Not until three o'clock in the morning, after very hard work and a vast amount of trouble, did the sound of the paddle-wheels once more break upon our ears, and it was six o'clock before we got back to our hotel.

December 30th.

This morning we had breakfast sent up, and gave orders for our caravan of camels and dromedaries to be got ready for starting. My companions complained of being rather stiff, and Linant said the iron ring which had served as his pillow during the night had hurt his head. We soon heard that our encampment was ready, and that we might take possession of our movable apartments.

We went to our tents, which were set up between the gate of the town and the ruined citadel of the ancient Colysma, at the further end of the port. The mouth of the indispensable fresh-water canal, to be fed by the Nile, will be about here.

Here is a description of our encampment, which will be the same throughout our journey on the isthmus.

Three round tents, twenty feet in diameter, or sixty feet round. The first for Linant and myself, the second for Mougel and the young engineer Aivas, Linant's secretary and assistant, an intelligent, active and obliging young fellow, who has been brought up in Egypt and speaks Arabic like a native. The third round tent is for the servants; and there is a fourth, a long one, serving as a kitchen. Twenty barrels filled with water from the Nile are arranged between the first and second tents, and are watched over by sentinels day and night, for on their contents depend our preservation during our trip. Round the kitchen are cages, which are left open during the day, for our chickens, turkeys, and pigeons, and it is a wonder to me that they never abuse their liberty! A small herd of sheep and goats, thirty-two camels and dromedaries, looked after by some fifteen Bedouins, who lie down amongst them, and, lastly, a pair of asses and their driver, for the use of Mougel, who does not like the motion of a dromedary, complete our caravan. My tent serves as a drawing-room, Mougel's as a dining-room, and the servants' as an office. I will give you an inventory of the contents of the first. As you go in you have a clear space before you; on either side a mattress covered with a carpet, so as to serve as a divan during the day. The bedclothes are folded beneath a cushion, my pillow at night. The head of the bed is formed by the saddle of my dromedary, covered with a huge sheep-skin from Sennaar, dyed red. On either side of the head of the bed are the large saddle bags containing our personal effects, placed so as to create a draught of air; in the centre are the guns, fastened with straps to the pole supporting the tent; and between the two beds, a short distance from the pole, is a stake, with two hooks for watches, surmounted by a little iron stand, from which hangs a lantern.

We intend starting early to-morrow morning.

We got Aivas to read us the part of Linant's report

relating to the levelling executed under his direction, in 1853, between Suez and Pelusium.

December 31st.

We rose this morning at five o'clock, by the light of a brilliant moon. Men and animals were soon on foot.

The tents, barrels, cases, mattresses rolled in the carpets, cages containing the feathered fowl, portmanteaus, &c., were packed on the camels, which we sent on before us. The dromedaries were saddled, and awaited their riders in a kneeling attitude. Mounting is an operation requiring considerable agility, for the moment the right leg is flung over its back the dromedary starts up, and the best animals are those which rise the quickest. Its a good plan to throw the body a little forward and then back when the dromedary stretches its hind legs. Linant and I are very well mounted; our animals were provided for us by El-Hami Pacha, son of Abbas Pacha. I was at ease on mine directly, and as I am in good training I can accommodate myself comfortably either to the long swinging gallop or the jolting trot. There is, however, a very good pace something between these two. The other riders on dromedaries are Aivas and an Arab effendi, an assistant engineer. Our guide, the Bedouin Sheik Jaoudé, is answerable for our lives with his own. One of the two couriers, who will start with our letters when the one left behind at Cairo arrives with the mail, and the negro Abdallah complete the staff of our personal attendants.

Mougel Bey, who bestrides his donkey with conscious pride, and wears a grey coat and trousers, is the only one of the party whose costume is at all European.

We rode for three hours along the bed of the ancient canal, the banks of which are still in excellent preservation.

Before sunset we pitched our camp in the heart of the desert, in a part called Makfar (the hollow), with slight traces of vegetation here and there.

Our arrangements for the night being made, I got out my Bible, always of special interest to me when in Egypt, and which has a double attraction now that I am approaching the land inhabited by Jacob and his family, and the scene, four centuries later, of Moses's rescue of the enslaved Hebrews.

I had closed my book and was leaving my tent to enjoy a beautiful sunset, when Mougel and Aivas came up from opposite directions, both saying they had just seen a splendid luminous meteor, like a rocket, which started in the east, and after describing a semicircle sunk on the western horizon in a shower of sparks. I only caught a glimpse of the fag-end of the phenomenon, and, but for the testimony of my comrades, I should not have ventured to allude to it in my notes.

If this were the age of the giving of the law, of miracles and of omens, this apparition might be compared with that of the 15th November, the day of the great decision respecting the Suez Canal. The second phenomenon marks the 31st December, the first day of our survey, on which we have laid the first foundations of the union of the East and West.

I asked permission to read Linant's minute on the ancient as compared with the modern geography of the isthmus, and on the route followed by the Hebrews, that I might study it in connection with the important passages of the Old Testament I had just looked over.

January 1, 1855.

We were astir this morning at five o'clock.

We rounded on the west the basin of the Bitter Lakes, now dry, but which formed part of the Red Sea in the time of Moses. The ancient bed is strewn with pieces of salt, looking like broken-up ice. We rode across part of this district, leaving some quagmires on our right, which travellers do well to avoid, as they would sink in them with their animals and leave no trace. A quarter of a league to the left were the mountains of Awebet, which may perhaps yield good limestone and other building materials.

We ascended a hill retaining some blocks of granite, formerly part of the so-called Persepolitan monument. One side of one of these blocks is covered with inscriptions in the Assyrian cuneiform character; on another is carved a vulture with outspread wings, and on the corners are representations of the ancient Egyptian sceptre.

This monument is supposed to have been erected by Darius, the Persian conqueror, when he was in Egypt, either as a landmark or to commemorate the restoration of the canal of the Pharaohs, which is ascribed to him by Herodotus. The granite used was from Mount Sinai.

We still followed the desert, leaving the Bitter Lakes on our right. The ground here is not so hard as that recently traversed. The sand is finer, and retains the footprints of all the animals which pass over it. We saw the tracks of hyenas, gazelles, foxes, and hares crossing and re-crossing each other in every direction.

At four o'clock we encamped in the Wâdy el Akram (Valley of Akrams, a kind of bush).

In the evening we discussed the details of the construction of our canal from Suez to the site of our encampment. It results from our observations that the maritime canal, at its Suez entrance, may be expected to receive, in the course of twenty-four hours, a supply of about two millions of metric tons of water, due to the rise of the tide in the Red Sea; and that, by this means, as well as by the water of the Mediterranean, the basin of the Bitter Lakes will be filled, which is destined to form an immense reservoir, containing two thousand million of metric tons of water. This body of liquid will adequately supply the canal, and will produce, when not driven back by the wind, a feeble current towards the Mediterranean.

January 2nd.

We started this morning at six o'clock, the weather cloudy and the wind cold and disagreeable. We visited a second Persepolitan monument, wrongly named Serapeum, and rode along the dyke of the ancient canal, which now forms a road.

At two o'clock we arrived at the site of our third encampment, near Lake Timsah (of crocodiles), close to the Bir (well) Abou Ballah, called in the Hebrew Bible Pihahiroth, or the grassy place. The Arab name for it is Ouedbet-el-Bouze (the valley of reeds).

We are now actually in the land of Goshen.

I must now write out those verses of the Bible which refer to the land of Goshen, as we shall be passing through it to-morrow and the next day.

GENESIS XLVI.

Verse 28.—And he sent Judah before him unto Joseph, to direct his face unto Goshen; and they came into the land of Goshen.

Verses 33, 34.—And it shall come to pass, when Pharaoh shall call you, and shall say, What is your occupation? that ye shall say, Thy servants' trade hath been about cattle from our youth even until now, both we, and also our fathers: that ye may dwell in the land of Goshen; for every shepherd is an abomination unto the Egyptians.

Goshen, in Hebrew, signifies pasturage, and it is remarkable that the Arab word for pasturage is *guess*. The ancient Ethiopian word for shepherd is *Sos*, and the name of Suez is probably derived from it. So that the land of *Goshen*, the land of *Guess*, and the Isthmus of Suez would be one and the same country. We know now that the *Hykshos* dynasty signified originally the dynasty of the armed shepherds.

GENESIS XLVII.

Verse 4 . . . . Now therefore, we pray thee [said the brethren of Joseph to Pharaoh], let thy servants dwell in the land of Goshen.

Verses 5, 6.—And Pharaoh spake unto Joseph, saying, Thy father and thy brethren are come unto thee: the land of Egypt is before thee; in the best of the land make thy father and brethren to dwell; in the land of Goshen let them dwell. . . . .

Verse 11.—And Joseph placed his father and his brethren, and gave them a possession in the land of Egypt, in the best of the land, in the land of Rameses,* as Pharaoh had commanded.

EXODUS I.

Verses 7, 8.—And the children of Israel were fruitful, and increased abundantly, and multiplied, and waxed exceedingly mighty; and the land was filled with them. Now there arose up a new king over Egypt, which knew not Joseph.

Verse 11.—Therefore they did set over them taskmasters to afflict them with their burdens. And they built for Pharaoh treasure cities, Pithom and Raamses.

EXODUS VIII.—THE PLAGUE OF FLIES.

Verse 22.—And the Lord said unto Moses, ... Stand before Pharaoh, ... and say unto him, Thus saith the Lord, ... And I

---

* Rameses was the chief city of the land of Goshen.—TR.

will sever in that day the land of Goshen, in which my people dwell, that no swarms of flies shall be there. . . . .

EXODUS IX.—SIXTH PLAGUE: THE MURRAIN.

Verse 6. . . . . And all the cattle of Egypt died: but of the cattle of the children of Israel died not one.

SEVENTH PLAGUE: THUNDER AND HAIL.

Verse 26.—Only in the land of Goshen, where the children of Israel were, was there no hail.

The conclusions I draw from these verses in the Bible are, that when the land of Goshen is crossed by our fresh water canal, it will become at least as fertile as it was in olden times, and that its climate will be healthy; for in our days, as in those of Moses, the few Arab shepherds frequenting it are free from epidemics, in spite of their intercourse with the people of Lower Egypt.

EXODUS XII.

Verse 37.—And the children of Israel journeyed from Rameses to Succoth. . . . .

In Hebrew Succoth* signifies booths. At the present day the Arabs call this place Um-riam (mother of booths), or Makfar (the *hollow*, along which flowed the ancient canal).

EXODUS XIII.

Verse 20.— And they took their journey from Succoth, and encamped in Etham, in the edge of the wilderness.

Etham is situated on the borders of a vast solitude bounded by the Bitter Lakes and formerly washed by the Red Sea. We were there this morning, examining the second Persepolitan monument. The tribe which encamps there at certain seasons of the year is called the *Ethamite*.

Verse 22.—He took not away the pillar of the cloud by day, nor the pillar of fire by night, from before the people.

Moses having in his youth slain an Egyptian, who was smiting a Hebrew, had to flee to Sinai, where he married the daughter of Jethro, a priest of Midian, whose flocks he

---

* The word Succoth is the plural form of Soc, which always means a hut made of leafy boughs. See Stanley's "Sinai and Palestine," Appendix, p. 529.—TR.

tended for forty years. His brother Aaron came to seek him on the death of the Pharaoh who was on the throne when he killed the Egyptian, and whose dates coincide with those of Rameses II., the Sesostris of the Greeks. The custom of sending Machallahs, or torch-bearers, some distance in advance of caravans, which is still observed at the present day, was familiar to Moses. The torches produced the appearance of a pillar of cloud by day and a pillar of fire by night.

The Israelites crossed the last lagoons of the Red Sea by the fords, much as the Bedouins still do at low tide, near Suez. Pharaoh's generals, as those of Said Pacha now are, were ignorant of the existence of these passages.

Exodus xiv.

Verse 2.—Speak unto the children of Israel, that they turn and encamp before Pi-hahiroth [the grassy place from which I am writing] between Migdol and the sea, over against Baal-zephon: before it ye shall encamp by the sea.

Pihahiroth was situated in the midst of the former lagoons of the Red Sea, the level of which is lower than that of the sea, so that they will be flooded again when the maritime canal is opened. The Israelites, favoured by the tempest described in the Bible, had probably—it being low tide—passed the evening in the low lying districts between Lake Timsah and the Bitter Lakes, amongst the long low sand dunes, which look like white-washed walls by moonlight, and the next morning, the wind having gone down, the Egyptian troops pursued after the children of Israel, and were overthrown in the waves of the sea and the quagmires of the valley.

Exodus xv.

Verses 22, 23.—So Moses brought Israel from the Red Sea, and they went out into the wilderness of Shur [a desert of Syria, the other side of Lake Timsah and the Bitter Lakes]; and they went three days in the wilderness, and found no water. And when they came to Marah, they could not drink of the waters of Marah, for they were bitter. . .

In the desert of *Shur* there is a spring marked on all the maps under the name of *Bir-Marah*. Mara signifies *bitter*, both in Hebrew and Arabic.

Verse 25.—And he [Moses] cried unto the Lord; and the Lord shewed him a tree, which when he had cast into the waters, the waters were made sweet. . . .

Linant tells us that the Arabs of Sinai, where he has spent a good deal of time, lessen the bitterness of brackish water by throwing in branches of a shrub called Arak, a kind of thorny sorrel.

Verse 27.—And they came to Elim, where were twelve wells of water, and three score and ten palm trees: and they encamped there by the waters.

Elim is the place now called the Wells of Moses, of which there were always twelve. You will remember we made two attempts to visit them, and were to have been entertained there by Costa the elder.

EXODUS XVI.

Verse 14.—And when the dew that lay was gone up, behold, upon the face of the wilderness there lay a small round thing, as small as the hoar frost on the ground.

When the Israelites saw it they said, " Man-hu ?" the Hebrew for " What is it ? " This is the correct etymology of the word manna.

Linant has seen the Arabs of Sinai collect the manna which distils at sunrise at a certain temperature from the leaves of the tamarisk, a bush or shrub flourishing everywhere in the desert we have just traversed, as well as on the other side as far as Sinai.

This manna is a kind of jelly or scum, which forms on the leaves of tamarisks in the early morning, melting in the first sunbeams, and, falling drop by drop on the ground, is converted into a sort of paste resembling honey. Sinai manna has neither the disagreeable taste nor the purgative qualities of that found in Sicily and sold by druggists.

Linant's unpublished works will prove that the land we are now in is identical with that of Goshen.

When we arrived at our halting-place, on the borders of the valley of Pihahiroth, we held a conference to exchange ideas on the best course for our canal between Suez and Lake Timsah, examined Linant's maps and plans again, discussed the depth and breadth of the new canal, and laid down the leading principles of the report, which Linant and Mougel must agree to sign.

We were also anxious to form an approximate idea of the cost, and after many calculations we arrived at the sum total of 160 to 170 million francs. We estimated at some twenty million of francs the probable cost of the canal fed by the Nile, which is to run from Cairo to the internal port of the maritime canal, and there to divide into two branches,—one, for irrigation, going towards Suez; the other, for drinking purposes, going towards the Mediterranean port. All this, as you may imagine, will be revised, corrected, and, as I hope, slightly enlarged, with all the corroborative documents, detailed plans, &c.

January 3rd.

We started at eight o'clock on an excursion to the ruins of Rameses. We stopped a quarter of an hour on the little hillock where Succoth, the Israelites' first halting-place, once stood, and then we pressed on for the point from which their exodus was made.

Since the identification of the statues, of which I send you a sketch drawn by Linant, there can be no doubt about the site of Rameses. The hieroglyphic inscriptions on the back of the block of granite, which have been translated, say that the figures represent Rameses II. (Sesostris) and his two sons.

The ground is strewn with fragments of ancient bricks, the making of which rendered the lives of the Israelites bitter.

EXODUS I.

Verse 14—And they [the Egyptians] made their lives bitter with hard bondage, in mortar, and in brick, and in all manner of service in the field: all their service, wherein they made them serve, was with rigour.

We breakfasted in the presence of Sesostris, and returned to our camp after following part of the ancient canal connecting the Nile with the Red Sea.

January 4th.

We started at seven o'clock to go round the eastern side of Lake Timsah. We identified the site of Baal-zephon on a hill, past the foot of which our great canal will run.

The sky became clouded over and the sand began to whirl round the bushes. We were threatened with such a storm as that which enabled the Israelites to escape from the chariots of the Egyptians, so we hurried through our breakfast and hastily mounted our steeds. They had some difficulty in making head against the wind.

January 5th.

It rained nearly all night. The wind had increased in violence, and it was of no use to think of going out, still less to move a caravan through the surging ocean of sand.

Looking towards the quarter from which the wind was blowing, we saw that a regular eastern hurricane was imminent.

We accepted the situation cheerfully, and chatted together about our canal, building the most beautiful castles in the air to the accompaniment of the noise of the storm, on the subject of the smiling tracts of verdure and plantations which would perhaps some day change the aspect of the deserts around us. Suddenly an irresistible squall tore up and overturned the two tents opposite and that in which we were making *tertulia*. Then our own began to give way. The post shook, and Linant cried: "To the ropes! Abdallah, Ibrahim, Mohammed," &c. As I was farthest from the door I had the weight of the tent upon me; but I held up the pole as well as I could, and those outside raised it a little by tugging at the ropes. Then I leant in a stooping posture against the side of the tent most exposed to the squall; but the mattress on which I was standing slipped from beneath me, and I was flung across the tent on to Linant's bed, fortunately without being hurt. I obstinately resumed my position as a prop, and perseveringly pressed against the side of the tent, which was finally set up again all right. The others were also raised; and we set to work to restore order amongst our furniture and personal effects, which were strewn about, wet and covered with sand. Linant has just made a sketch of the scene in the thick of the hurricane. There you will see the ludicrous situation in which the future director of the maritime canal was placed.

We resumed the conversation so abruptly interrupted.

We estimated that the supplementary canal, in bringing the waters of the Nile to these districts, now untilled, will lead to the cultivation of about one hundred thousand hectares. *

News was brought of the appearance in the distance of a courier on a dromedary. He was bringing my letters.

Amongst them was one from Admiral Jurien, of *La Gravière*, dated, before Sebastopol, November 25th; and a very polite note from Admiral Bruat, offering me the hospitality of his vessel, if I had any fancy for seeing Sebastopol.

Kœnig Bey sent me a copy of the Viceroy's reply to the Emperor's letter, conferring on him the Grand Cordon of the Legion of Honour. I noticed one important sentence about our scheme:

> I am happy, Sire, to hear that my efforts to follow the example of my late father are appreciated by your Majesty, and that the steps I have already taken are in accordance with your views. Recognising the truth of the brotherhood of all men, and actuated by a desire to promote the interests of the whole human race, I intend uniting the Mediterranean and the Red Sea by means of a ship canal, and confiding the execution of this great work to an international company. I venture to hope, Sire, that your Majesty, whose distinguished support is given to every enterprise likely to contribute to the well-being of humanity, will deign to approve of a scheme the realisation of which will create a new outlet for the commerce and manufactures of every nation of Europe.
>
> It is true, Sire, that France is a great distance from Egypt; but at the present day what country, however remote, is not enlightened and animated by rays emanating from the lights of the civilised world?"

Señor Baguer y Ribas, Consul-General for Spain, writes to me from Cairo:

> I must tell you that an Englishman, Mr. Wilcox, one of the founders of the Peninsular and Oriental Company, has arrived in Cairo, with one of his chief colleagues, Señor Zulucta, a fellow-countryman of mine. Quite apart from my own interest, as a Spaniard, in your great scheme, I thought I owed it to my personal regard for yourself to seize this opportunity of preparing these gentlemen to join you. I think I have paved the way, and that you will not have much diffi-

---

* A French hectare represents 2 acres, 1 rood, and 35 perches of English measurement.—Tr.

culty in winning them over entirely on your return. However that may be, I consider their arrival in Egypt a providential chance in favour of your project. Señor Zulueta, whom I shall have the honour of introducing to you, is eager to make your acquaintance, as all Spaniards must be who have not the honour of knowing you. These are his own expressions.

January 7th.

The weather, which kept us shut up all yesterday, allowed of our leaving Pihahiroth to-day.

We made for the north of Lake Timsah, now the central point of the isthmus. Now I have been on the spot, I recognise the excellence of Linant's idea of making an internal port at Lake Timsah. The basin is surrounded by hills, and forms a splendid natural harbour, six times as large as that of Marseilles, and all the more convenient that it can easily be put in communication with the cultivated portions of the Land of Goshen and the interior of Egypt, by means of the junction canal fed by the Nile. Vessels anchoring in it will be able to revictual.

January 8th.

We are now beginning to come within sight of Lake Menzaleh, filled partly by the inundations of the Nile and partly by the waters of the Mediterranean. The beach of the latter affords many natural continuations for a canal between Damietta and Pelusium.

We halted for breakfast, at noon, in an oasis with shady trees; a pleasant sight, surrounded as we were by deserts stretching away as far as the eye could reach. I counted twenty-three date-trees. The Arabs call this desert Bir-el-Bourj (Well of the Tower). It contains a well of brackish water, with date-trees growing about it; and on a neighbouring hill there are the ruins of a building.

Here we waited for our caravan to come up, and then skirted along the eastern shores of Lake Menzaleh until four o'clock, noticing numerous flocks of swans, pelicans, and flamingoes, which looked like long white lines.

At last we came to the foot of a hill, the site of the ancient fortress Magdol, or Migdol, alluded to in the Bible, and called Magdolum by travellers.

Whilst our camp was being made ready, we climbed up

to the ruins of the fortress, said to have been destroyed by fire. The storeys and bricks retain traces of the action of heat. In the distance, on the right, we could see the beach of Pelusium, where Pompey was killed; and on the left, shrouded in mist, Damietta, where St. Louis landed.

January 9th.

We now turned towards Pelusium, near to which are the ruins of the modern Castle of Tineh. Tineh, the Arab word, and Pelusium, the Greek word, have the same signification, and may be translated into English as *mud*. At the present moment the place is more than muddy, for it has been swamped by the inundation of the Nile. We must, therefore, content ourselves with a view of Pelusium from a distant hill, one of the most important towns of ancient Egypt, but the ruins of which are of little interest. We just sent a passing greeting to the Mediterranean, telling her of the approaching visit of the Arabian Gulf, and then took our leave of her.

Our first survey is completed, and has convinced us of the feasibility of our scheme, which will, I hope, be shortly proved by the reports of the two engineers accompanying me.

We returned to pass the night in the oasis of Bir-el-Bourj.

January 10th.

The cold is intense, and we walked a little way to warm ourselves, leading our dromedaries by ropes. Then we mounted them again, which is rather an exciting operation. They were fresher than usual, and we soon left the caravan far behind us. Mougel and his donkeys were also distanced by a good stretch. The donkey man's terrors are very amusing: he invokes the Prophet's protection from the attacks of Bedouins; and if an Arab approaches him to ask for a little tobacco or to offer to come and have a cup of coffee in his tent, he thinks his last hour has arrived. He thumps his animals to make them go on faster, and has no peace until he has caught us up. Thinking that the poor fellow would be more uneasy than ever to-day, as we have seen several armed Bedouins tending their flocks, we halted for a short time at two o'clock.

Mougel, evidently quite absorbed in his calculations, &c., respecting the Canal, and quite unconscious of his attendant's exclamations, soon came up, and we at once remounted, skirting along Lake Menzaleh, instead of crossing the desert, as we had done on our way up.

Then we made for the entrance to El Guisr, setting up our tents at five o'clock at the foot of one of the loftiest dunes of the isthmus.

January 11th, 12th, 13th, and 14th were occupied by our return journey to Cairo. We halted by a well, and, sheltered by a clump of tamarisks, I jotted down some instructions in pencil for the engineers' report. I read them over to Linant and Mougel, who expressed themselves satisfied with the outline sketched for them to fill in. They wished me, however, to omit the clause requesting them to state their reasons in case of any difference of opinion; but I insisted on retaining it, because, this reservation being made, their agreement, upon which I rely, will have the greater weight.

January 15th.

We started early at a brisk trot, in the hope of reaching Suez at eleven o'clock. On the left we had the chain of mountains beginning with the Mokattam and ending with the Atâkah, along the base of which runs the Suez road; and on the right we could make out the minarets of Khanka, amongst its date-trees, and the winding ribbon of vegetation marking the course of the Nile. The morning seemed to me to increase in beauty, and the view spread out before me was positively lovely.

We passed Abouzambel (Ipsambul), and saw the obelisk of Heliopolis, the city of the sun, where Plato studied the archives of the Egyptian priests for seventeen years. It is a mistake to suppose that Joseph, Jacob's son, lived in this town. The Shepherd king on the throne when he was taken to Egypt ruled from San, near Lake Menzaleh, and it was there that Potiphar held the office of prime minister.

We skirted along the pretty village of Matarieh, surrounded by gardens, amongst which the so-called Tree of the Virgin could be made out. Then we passed Birket-el-Haggi (the Lake of the Pilgrims), where the large caravan from Mecca assembles every year to escort the sacred carpet to be laid upon the tomb of the Prophet.

Before us we could distinguish the massive palace of Abassieh, with its 2000 windows, built by Abbas Pacha; and a little farther, on the other side of the Nile, rose the summits of the two Great Pyramids, which have looked down on armies and travellers, not as is commonly supposed for forty centuries, but for more than sixty centuries.

And now, on the left, we catch sight of the tapering spires of the mosque, of Oriental alabaster, built by Mehemet Ali within the enceinte of the Citadel, and in which that great man intended to be buried. He had indeed a right to overshadow with his tomb a place in which heo verthrew barbarian rule and a country which he regenerated. A singular coincidence now strikes me for the first time.

In 1803 my father was Political Agent for France in Egypt, and Bonaparte, then First Consul, gave him instructions to find a Turkish chief of sufficient energy and intelligence to be proposed at Constantinople for reinvestiture with the dignity, then almost nominal, of Pacha of Cairo. Mehemet Ali, a native of Macedonia, and commander of some thousand Bashi-Bazouks, but who could neither read nor write, became the guest and friend of my father, who aided him with his advice and encouraged him to resist the encroachments of the Mamelukes, who were the enemies of France. Mehemet Ali was worthy of the future in store for him, and manifested so great a superiority to those of his own rank that the French Ambassador at Constantinople (Colonel Sebastiani) used his influence with the Sultan to obtain his investiture with the Pachalic of Cairo.

Fifty years later the son of Matthew de Lesseps, long the friend of Mehemet Ali's son, advised the latter to undertake a scheme which will render his reign illustrious, and in that very Citadel, which witnessed the violent accession to power of Mehemet Ali, through the massacre of the

Mamelukes, Mohammed Said put the finishing touch to the regeneration of Egypt, by informing the representatives of the European Powers of his intention of uniting the Red Sea and the Mediterranean and throwing open the new route to India.

I am convinced that England will profit more than any other country by this new passage; but we must not shut our eyes to the fact that a blow will be struck at the old egotistical policy of Great Britain, and of course the upholders of the time-honoured traditions are already considerably excited.

I expected no less, for, partly from my own experience and partly from what my father has told me, I am better up than most people in the policy pursued on different occasions by the English in Egypt. Why did they do all in their power to prevent the success of Bonaparte's expedition? Why, more recently, did they protect the Mamelukes, who broke up the country, suppressed foreign commerce, and condemned the fertile Valley of the Nile to sterility? Why did they unite with the whole of Europe in 1810 to check the progress of Napoleon and Mehemet Ali? Why did they uphold and encourage Abbas Pacha, that bigoted prince, the enemy of all progress, whom Providence removed just as he was about to complete the disorganisation and ruin of Egypt?

Because there was a party in England anxious to reduce the Viceroy to the condition of those Rajahs in India, whose vices are encouraged until they have sunk so low that there is nothing left for them to do but to ask for protection or to sell their States.

Fortunately everybody does not think alike in England. No; in that land of liberty there are many men of feeling and intelligence, who will sooner or later win public opinion over to their views.

My letter to Cobden will serve as a pretext, if there should be any need, to wage a crusade against the men of the past.

I have indulged in a political digression at the sight of the Citadel of Cairo; but now let us return to our dromedaries, who needed a few minutes' rest. We stopped near the tomb of Malek-Adel, and took refuge from the sun beneath its cupola. You have read Madame Cottin's romance, and will know that Malek-Adel was the brother of Salah-Ed-din (Saladdin), the Caliph reigning in Egypt at the time of the Crusade under Philip Augustus. He is much more of a hero in Madame Cottin's pages than in those of the Arab historians, for the latter do not assign him any special rôle, and do not even mention his love for the Princess Matilda or his marriage in the hermitage of St. Anthony, near Suez.

At last we arrived at the Place de l'Esbékié, and from thence we hastened to the Palace of Foreigners, where I found many friends awaiting me.

XIV.

Instructions to Linant Bey and Mougel Bey on the Scheme of a Maritime Canal between the Red Sea and the Mediterranean, and for a Fresh-water Canal fed by the Nile.

Cairo, January 15, 1855.

Now that we have completed the survey ordered by his Highness Mohammed Said Pacha, I must call the attention of Linant Bey and Mougel Bey to the chief points to be insisted on in the preliminary and provisional report, which must serve until we are able to present a more complete work, accompanied by maps, plans, sections, estimates, and other documents in support of our plan.

1. State if the present harbour can be made use of for the Red Sea entrance. What works will be necessary, such as jetties, &c.

2. Point out the precise direction of the Canal from Suez to the former basin of the Red Sea, known as the Bitter Lakes.

3. Explain how you propose to utilise these lakes, and if, in passing through them, the maritime canal will require continuous banks or none at all.

4. Give an outline of the course of the Canal as far as Lake Timsah, which is to be used as an inland harbour.

5. State what works will be required to render Lake

Timsah fit for that purpose. Give the length of quay walls. In passing through Lake Timsah the bed of the Canal will have to be wider than in other parts, to allow of vessels anchoring or lying alongside these quays without obstructing the navigation. The quays will be constructed as near as possible to the fresh-water canal.

6. Give the course of the maritime canal from Lake Timsah to Lake Menzaleh.

7. State the works to be executed on the banks of Lake Menzaleh or in the lake itself.

8. Will the mouth of the lake on the Mediterranean side be identical with that of the ancient Pelusiac branch?

9. Define exactly the nature and extent of the piers, jetties, &c., required, so as to confute the objections hitherto made, founded on difficulties said to be insurmountable, arising from the silting up of the shore and the accumulation of mud at the Mediterranean entrance to the Canal. In support of this part of the scheme, proofs, examples, and incontestable calculations must be brought forward.

10. What quantity of water will enter the maritime canal from the Red Sea at each tide?

11. How may high tides be best turned to account in the Canal itself, the basin of the Bitter Lakes, and the mouth of the Bay of Pelusium?

12. Base your calculations for the maritime canal on a width of one hundred mètres at the low-water level of the Mediterranean, with power to reduce it to sixty-five or seventy mètres in those few places where the cuttings are very heavy. The depth should be calculated at six, seven, and eight mètres below the low-water level of the Mediterranean, so that the company may choose, according to the expense, which of the three depths will best combine their interests with the requirements of navigation.

13. Answer objections founded on the difficulties of navigation in the Red Sea and the Bay of Pelusium.

14. Make a preliminary estimate of the maximum total cost, and state the probable date at which the Canal will be open to navigation.

15. Add to the scheme for the maritime canal one for a

fresh-water canal, fed by the Nile, starting between the *barrage* and Cairo, and running through the valley to Lake Timsah. The dimensions must be estimated so as to admit of a head and depth of water sufficient to allow the canal to irrigate at least 200,000 *feddans*[1] at high-tide. Near Lake Timsah, with which it will be in communication, this canal must divide into two branches for irrigating purposes — one to run towards Suez, the other towards Pelusium.

16. Ascertain if the sand of the dunes of the isthmus is likely to interfere with the construction or maintenance of the Canal, and to what advantage these dunes may be turned with the aid of the canal for irrigation.

17. Give an estimate of the maximum cost of the fresh-water canal fed by the Nile, and name the probable date of the completion of the works.

18. State the nature and quality of the materials which can be used for the works without any heavy transit dues, and name the place from which they are to be obtained.

19. Lastly, give an approximate estimate of the minimum revenues which may be expected both from the maritime and the fresh-water canal.

I do not of course pretend to limit the work of Linant Bey and Mougel Bey to this sketch.

Whilst admitting the harmony I have noticed between them, and their common conviction of the possibility of uniting the Red Sea and the Mediterranean by a Canal accessible to large vessels, I must beg of them, in case of any difference of opinion, no matter on what point, to state that difference and its grounds.

Lastly, the scheme, accompanied by an explanatory plan, should be finished as quickly as possible.

XV.

To M. Arles Dufour, Paris.

CAIRO, *January* 16*th*.

BACK yesterday from the survey of the Isthmus of Suez, ordered by and at the expense of the Viceroy, my first

[1] A feddan is 1·04 acre, English.—TR.

care is to give you a summary of the results of my interesting journey. Linant and Mougel agree in thinking it possible to make a large Canal across the isthmus, with two entrances, perfectly accessible to navigation, and a splendid port in the basin of Lake Timsah. I am confident that these two engineers have hit upon the best solution of the problem.

To their credit be it said, they placed themselves unreservedly and disinterestedly at my service; laying aside every personal consideration and uniting in an earnest wish to promote the success of the great enterprise. Not one word did they say about the conditions on which their assistance was to be given nor on the favours which the future company should concede to them.

M. Aivas, a young engineer in the service of the Viceroy, who accompanied us on our trip, deserves mention. Linant has full confidence in him, and I also think very highly of him. He will certainly not be forgotten when occasion offers.

I now come to my impressions on the European and Ottoman opinion with regard to the Canal, as illustrated in your letters and those of my other friends and of my family. It is approved of in Paris. In London, where people were as much surprised as in France, the first impression produced was not favourable, and there was a disposition to throw obstacles in our way. At Constantinople Lord Stratford de Redcliffe showed no signs of personal hostility, but said he was waiting for instructions as to the attitude he should assume. Up to the 28th December the Grand Vizier had not laid the Viceroy's communication before the Council, intending to take time to reflect. He wished to get his clue from Paris and London before committing himself. He desired to know, moreover, whether the Viceroy intended to put the question in any other form than he had done up to the present moment, that is to say, whether he would make the execution of his scheme dependent on the consent of the Porte, or, which is the same thing now, on the wishes of the great Allied Powers.

I will give you my opinion. I cannot yet let you know

that of the Viceroy, who, having been to Alexandria during my absence, is now at the *barrage*, and will not be here for two days.

I have been told that the question belonged to Paris and London. I think that it ought not to leave Egypt until further orders; and that it is not right to submit it gratuitously to outside criticism, all the elements of which are not predisposed in its favour. Our strength lies in the energetic and firm resolution of Mohammed Said. I also rely on the moral support and sympathy of the Emperor for a scheme which suits his own ideas; but in order that this support may be in the end more evident and to avoid prejudicing it, it seems to me that I should seek to preserve for our affair its character of Egyptian initiative and keep it clear of European political complications. This is what I had understood from the first; it began its success and it can secure it. Efforts have been and will yet be made to shake the courage of the Viceroy; but as he is not a man to allow himself to be intimidated, and he and I are kindred spirits in that respect, there is no fear of his being influenced by any intrigues. By continuing to maintain our position until we see our way more clearly we shall gain ground for two reasons: firstly, that even the stubborn, whose opposition arises from motives they do not care to avow, will finally have to make the best of a bad job; and, secondly, that the Porte, compelled to come to a decision, will perhaps prefer to give its adhesion to a scheme submitted to it with a deference peculiarly seasonable, as matters now stand, whereas if the Porte refused its authorisation people would be fully inclined to dispense with it.

I am now waiting to consult with the Viceroy. I suspect that he will get me to go to Constantinople before returning to France.

Now for a few words on the constitution of our company, which we shall have to see about together in France. Our friend has justly called my attention to the fact that there is no precedent in France of a joint-stock company formed for carrying out a work in a foreign land. The matter is worth the risk of its novelty, and as there is no law against it, I have no doubt we shall be able to draw up the rules so as to give the necessary guarantees to the interests of all.

The Viceroy being disposed to accept any rules for our company which I may present to him, we shall be perfectly unfettered with regard to their wording, and there will be room to introduce everything which, on account of the necessity for brevity and the absence of details, could not be included in the draught of the Firman.

The bank of the company must be in Paris, where the legal guarantees will be insured to the shareholders in respect of the company, and to the Mussulmen and European "third part" for matters of construction and working of the Canal.

In all that concerns the relations between the company and the Egyptian Government, the director of the former and the Viceroy's commissioner will be the best mediums of communication, and if there be any disputes, it will be enough to refer them to the mixed tribunal, unless arbitration should in certain cases be preferred.

Objections might be made to the fact that, up to the present moment, the director is appointed by the Viceroy without the intervention of the company, and the stipulation in the Firman with regard to that appointment might be contested. But the Viceroy made an absolute condition with regard to getting the matter in train, fixing the time for the execution of the works, as well as beginning the improvement of the enterprise; and I must say, since it is so, without assigning more merit to myself than to any other, this condition applied above all things to myself.

"There would be nothing done," said the Viceroy, "if I did not see you prepared to devote yourself to the execution of the work you have proposed to me." This excellent prince wishes to have leisure to attend to his own affairs; he has a horror of complaints, explanations, and recriminations, so he relies upon me to save him from all the worry involved in the undertaking. This is why the Firman contains no reference to financial disputes between the company and the Egyptian Government. The Viceroy, therefore, for the present, intends to have no other medium of communication with those interested in the enterprise than myself, whom he has known from childhood, and in whom he places entire confidence. You know that with the Turks personal relations and confidence are everything, and that even superior merit would not outweigh these.

It appears to me essential to tell you from this moment what I think about the question of a preliminary diplomatic act (such as that proposed when your society undertook the study of the question), to secure to the company the possession of the Viceroy's concession ratified by the Porte, and which would determine beforehand how disputes relating to that concession are to be adjudicated upon. To my mind, to revive this question would be to put the cart before the horse. On a previous occasion it was one of the causes of the failure of the scheme. Mehemet Ali, who adopted it, said he would do nothing unless an act were brought to him signed by all the Powers; and I have had to dissuade his son from something of the same kind. The Powers will accept an accomplished fact; they will never agree to provoke one.

I hold to being master of the affair, under the patronage of the Viceroy, so long as there is only trouble to be reaped. When the profits come in it will be time for me to retire voluntarily.

I have consulted no one whatsoever on the scheme, to which I am devoting all my energies, and, relying entirely upon you, though you did not know it, I should have left for Egypt, without telling you anything about it, had I not happened to meet you accidentally at the house of our mutual friend, M. Emile de Girardin, a few days before my departure.

My duties abroad long prevented me from knowing anything, except from public report, of the work of your society. I was not able to study it for myself until I did so with you and Enfantin when I recently passed through Lyons. The noble, the generous initiative taken by your society will always have a large share in the annals of the maritime canal; but that society has ceased to exist, and there is no reason for resuscitating it. There are, indeed, reasons against its reconstitution, for you know better than any one that one of the members (Stephenson) withdrew from it to devote his attention to the railway.

XVI.
To Madame Delamalle, Paris.

January 18th and 19th.

The Viceroy has come to stay two days in Cairo, and I have given him the results of our trip, with which he seems most satisfied. We talked about the intrigues set on foot during my absence. In a second interview I showed him the situation, just as I defined it in a letter to M. Arles Dufour, dated the 16th inst. His Highness sees the disadvantages of referring to the decision of European diplomatists. I added, that as Reschid Pacha will not give an answer till he gets his orders from Paris and London, it would be a good plan to strike a blow at Constantinople, where I would willingly go, backed by the Viceroy's introduction, and, without compromising him, study the situation for myself and try to get the Sultan's authorisation on my own responsibility. All I asked was a letter to the Grand Vizier in the following terms:

I have given M. Ferd. de Lesseps authority to constitute, &c, and I have requested him before availing himself of that authority to give you on my behalf a copy, in Turkish, of his minute and of my Firman. As I have no doubt that M. de Lesseps will meet with generous support from his Highness and his Ministers in the accomplishment of a work of evident importance to the interests of the Ottoman Empire in general and Egypt in particular, as well as conducive to the promotion of our mutual policy, progress, and civilisation, I recommend M. de Lesseps to you, and beg you to extend to him the confidence which he enjoys with me.

The Viceroy sent for his secretary, and told him to write such a letter as I requested to Reschid Pacha, saying to me: "I advise you to add a request that they will not make you waste your time, for you must be back in Egypt soon; as you know, fifty-three days hence, I am going to celebrate my birthday in grand style. It will be the first since my accession. I do not wish to pass that day without you."

The Viceroy then told me how some of the Consuls-General had suggested doubts of the success of the Canal on account of the cost, and how he had replied, simply, that if the money could not be raised just now for beginning it that he would supply me with the necessary funds, adding: "I already have a little reserve of 500,000 *talaris*, (£100,000), without counting what may eventually come in, as well as the help of my Government, which is no small matter, and all that that involves."

CAIRO, *January* 22, 1855.

I told you that on my return from my survey I should take counsel with my good friend the prince on the next step to be taken. I went of my own accord to visit him at the *barrage*, using the steamer he has placed at my disposal. I gave him my views on the situation in a very few words, for with him one must be brief. We decided that it was necessary to "have a pull" (*coup de collier*) at Constantinople, the Viceroy fully agreeing with my views on that subject, and promising to provide me with the most decisive letters for the proper persons, which should allow it to be supposed in terms, both seemly and dexterous, that permission could be dispensed with if withheld. "We two," he added, "can begin putting the scheme into execution just when we like, even before the company is formed."

So you see, thus supported, I can no longer be tempted to hand over this matter of mine to the vultures and lynxes of the money markets. I am not working to swell their profits. I want to do a great thing without any mental reservation or any personal *monetary* considerations. It is for this that God has permitted me to see clearly thus far and to avoid shoals. I shall *resolutely* maintain my course, and as no one will be able to turn me aside from it, so I am confident that I shall bring my bark safely to the port which we will call Said, the name of the Viceroy and Arab for *fortunate*. The most fortunate thing in connection with the end I have in view is that my acts and my measures are not, thank God, subject to the instructions or the disavowals of any Government. A burnt child dreads the fire.

I shall take care, therefore, in spite of advice from Paris, not to return to France just now. If I were to go back without having completed the preliminaries of my scheme, by obtaining the sanction or semi-sanction of Constantinople, I should be in danger of having to depend upon others. My ambition, I confess, is to pull all the strings of this immense affair *alone* until it can progress unrestrainedly. In a word, I wish to accept conditions from none, but to impose them all myself. When, as a young man, I was French agent for Mehemet Ali, that great reformer said to me one day: "If, in the course of your life, you ever have anything very important to do, remember, my young friend, that you must depend on yourself alone. *If there are two of you, there is one too many.*"

My plan is gradually unfolding itself; everything is going on as I hoped. I shall persevere. If the announcement of the power conferred on me by the Viceroy has caused surprise, people will be, perhaps, still more surprised at the simplicity of the financial organisation of the company, which is now occupying my thoughts and in which I shall try to give an example of morality.

Friends in France fear that I am contracting engagements here. Let them set their minds at rest; I am making no more engagements in Egypt than with them.

I know well that if on my arrival in Paris, with the affair an accomplished fact, I were to say to three or four great bankers, "There are thirty million francs to be made in a fortnight: take twenty; I will take ten," nothing would be easier. But, after all, who would pay those millions? The solvent shareholders, who would not then reap all the advantages I intend them to have, or, later, the credit of the scheme. It is needless to add that I shall be very firm on this point, although it has been said that I *have ended* by understanding that I ought to address myself to the great capitalists only. I have treated the givers of advice as I always do those whom I see I cannot convince: I have allowed them to talk, contenting myself with answering now and then with the "Hum! hum!" which you must know well, keeping my own opinion all the time. In a word, as I tell you everything, it is not a bad thing, as far as canvassing the affair goes, that a number of worthy people should imagine the larks will fall down all ready roasted for them, while I am more or less burning my fingers.

However that may be, I have already found, both in France and here, warm-hearted and devoted people, who have offered me their co-operation with great disinterestedness. Besides, I am confirmed more than ever in my opinion that in this world good outweighs evil. I am just starting for Alexandria, where I shall embark in the *Pharamond*, bound for Constantinople.

XVII.

To M. S. W. RUYSSENAERS, ALEXANDRIA.

ALEXANDRIA, *January* 26, 1855.

You were the first in Egypt to hear of my rough draft of proposal to his Highness the Viceroy for the constitution of the *Compagnie Universelle* of the Suez Maritime Canal. The prudence, tact, and devotion you have shown from the commencement of this important negotiation make it a duty for me, on the eve of my departure from Egypt, where our scheme is about to be put into execution, to name you the Egyptian agent *pro. tem.* of the company.

It is not as a friend that I choose you now, but as the man whom I consider best fitted to fill a difficult position, and one requiring, above all things, the honourable and disinterested qualities which I have long since appreciated in you.

Let me beg of you, when you require assistance in correspondence or accounts, to apply to M. de Bourville, of Cairo, and M. de Regny, at Alexandria. I am writing to those gentlemen to place themselves from the present moment at your service.

XVIII.

To M. Arles Dufour, Paris.

ALEXANDRIA, *January* 27, 1855.

THE Viceroy is sending me to Constantinople, where he thinks my presence necessary.

I embark to-day in the *Pharamond*, provided with the most excellent letters of introduction. That which was not opportune at the very outset is opportune to-day.

In case there should be difficulties about the actual organisation of our company, it is good for people to know that Mohammed Said is ready to put his hand to the work whenever I like, with his own resources alone and those of his country and of my friends. As I was leaving him, he said to me, "When we have made the Canal fed by the Nile, and have led the waters of the Red Sea into the basins of the Bitter Lakes and of Lake Timsah, which will certainly not be beyond our power, we shall be able to wait for people to come to us."

I can now only repeat to you, what I have said from the first, that there is no definite step to be taken in Europe before my return.

I have to acknowledge the receipt of your letter of the 2nd of January, and of those from Enfantin of the 30th of December and the 6th of January. Our friend says:

> The *Times* has already declared against us, and unfortunately it is right in treating the scheme as absolutely impossible, especially that part of it relating to the absurd idea of an entrance at Pelusium.

MM. Mougel and Linant entertain an opposite opinion. When their prospectus appears, it will undergo, in every way, the most searching examination. I will not dictate, but it seems to me that we ought to refrain from giving a formal opinion. Talabot's plan of a canal, seventy leagues long, between Alexandria and Suez, is, then, still dear to our friend's heart. You know that the Viceroy has declared for making a large maritime canal straight across the isthmus. He does not wish Lower Egypt to be cut through; and he asked me if Talabot had been to Egypt and studied the isthmus for himself before drawing up his plan. On my replying in the negative and telling him of the eminent merit of this celebrated engineer, he added that so distinguished a man could not take amiss the adoption of a course different from that suggested by himself; that he had no doubt Talabot's plan was feasible, and would have been worthy of every consideration had not more urgent reasons made him decide irrevocably on a more direct route. So that there is nothing to wound Talabot's feelings in this declaration.

In any case, you must agree with me that it is necessary in our great enterprise to put aside considerations of persons, and to do only what will contribute to its success.

With regard to Linant and Mougel, the Viceroy, in whose service they are, told them to make a preliminary survey; their scheme, therefore, is the result of an order from the Viceroy, and will be duly submitted to the approval of the company of competent men and the public of Europe.

Stephenson told you he would write to his agents in Egypt to do nothing to prejudice the interests of the Canal, but to declare in its favour. I can only conclude that he has done nothing, or that he has very untrustworthy agents, for all the English in Cairo and Alexandria, especially the railway people, have done everything in their power to injure us. It's not their fault if they have not succeeded.

For the time of my absence I have accredited M. Ruyssenaers, Consul-General for Holland, to the Viceroy. He has long been intimate with his Highness, and is in his confidence. I enclose a copy of my letter to him before leaving. The zealous and unanimous support given to me by my old friends here is entirely gratuitous. . . .

XIX.

To M. Arles Dufour, Paris.

Alexandretta, *February* 2, 1855.

I HAVE just returned from making the round of all the towns on the Syrian coast, from Jaffa to Alexandretta, whither the news has spread of the projected Canal through the Isthmus of Suez, and I have been enthusiastically received by both the Mussulman and Christian populations. It would be difficult for people in Europe to realise the way in which I have been publicly recognised by all the officials, even by the Cadis themselves, especially at Beirut, Tripoli, and Latakia. I may almost say that my journey through these towns, as promoter of the great scheme and a friend of the Viceroy, who is looked upon as the Sultan's right hand, was a triumphal progress. I hail this as a good omen for the conclusion of the business at Constantinople.

The *Pharamond*, on board which I am writing, will reach Tarsus to-morrow, and will then proceed to Rhodes, Smyrna, the Dardanelles, and Gallipoli, and drop me at Constantinople.

XX.

NOTE FOR THE VICEROY OF EGYPT AND COUNT THEODORE DE LESSEPS, MINISTER OF FOREIGN AFFAIRS.

CONSTANTINOPLE, *February* 15, 1855.

WHEN I reached Constantinople I found the ground clear. If no one had declared in favour of the scheme, no one had been able to say anything against it. I employed the first few days in getting an accurate knowledge of the situation. I learnt that the Ministers generally, and Reschid Pacha in particular, *entirely approved* of the projected Canal through the isthmus, and were ready to assist the Viceroy in carrying out his plan if they could do so without compromising themselves too much. But I discovered that pressure, not to use a stronger word, was being put upon them by the English Ambassador, who is openly called Sultan Stratford, or Abdul Canning.

I was assured of the co-operation of the Austrian Internuncio, Baron de Bruck; of the Spanish Minister, M. de Sarza; of Count de Zuylen de Nieyvelt, the Dutch Chargé d'Affairs, and of several other personages who would be able to help me in their respective positions.

I ascertained that Lord Stratford was personally most

strongly opposed to the scheme, and that although he had no official instructions from his Government with reference to it, he was acting precisely as if he had, behaving in the matter with his usual arrogance, rooted jealousy, and inveterate antagonism of everything French, and with truly British egotism. There can be no doubt that Reschid Pacha will soon throw off a yoke which is becoming unbearable.

M. Benedetti, our Chargé d'Affaires, whose local knowledge, tact, and prudence would have been so useful to me, had received a hint not to put himself too forward in the matter; but he promises to act with me in doing everything to secure the success of the negotiation, to which he knows the Emperor's Government attaches great importance. He immediately sent M. Scheffer to Reschid Pacha, knowing that he would be a most fitting person to put things in train, and would follow all the details of the affair with intelligence. By his good offices a private interview with the Grand Vizier was obtained for me, at his house on the Bosphorus, on the morning of the 12th.

I gave Mohammed Said's letter, with which I was entrusted, to Reschid Pacha, together with a copy of my report on the junction of the Red Sea and the Mediterranean, translated into Turkish, and the Viceroy's Firman, approving the scheme for which we were now asking the Sultan's consent.

He read them attentively, and we had a conference of two hours' duration, in which a confidential footing was established between us. The following is an epitome of our conversation:—

> I need not point out to you the great advantages of this undertaking, to complete which we ask the Sultan's consent, for you have already appreciated them. The only obstacle you have to fear is, I know, not the opposition of England (whose alliance I, as a loyal Frenchman, quite appreciate), but only the personal antagonism of an official who, by his flagrantly overbearing conduct, is striking a severe blow at your sovereign's authority and dignity.
>
> It is for you to consider whether you will be influenced more by such an obstacle, than by your wish to oblige an enlightened prince, who is performing an act of courtesy to his sovereign, and who is the right

hand of the Ottoman Empire, of which you are the head. Compare the interest you have in maintaining the friendly and confidential relations between you and Mohammed Said Pacha, whose honour is publicly involved in the undertaking, with the passing spleen of the representative of a foreign Court. And, further, if you consider the inclinations of such and such Powers with reference to a domestic question, in which no one can contest your right to act for yourself, do you not think that the wishes of the Emperor Napoleon, as already expressed, should also have their weight? If we are willing to wait for the Sultan's initiative, and have loyally endeavoured to prevent the smallest injury to the dignity and independence of the Ottoman Empire, we have given no cause for supposing that we have altogether abdicated our legitimate influence. I am thankful that the Emperor has never led Europe to suppose any such thing. In former times the English Government, with less delicacy than our own, first told the Porte that the Viceroy of Egypt had a right to construct a railway from Alexandria to Suez without the license of his sovereign, and, in spite of the opposition of the French Ambassador, imperatively compelled the Sultan to give his consent. There was no fear then of displeasing the French representative. We are now not only quite content that the railway favoured by England should be continued and completed, but we abstain from interfering officially in this scheme, so favourable to the development of the Ottoman Empire, and which would also promote our maritime and commercial interests, so that we may maintain the private character of the matter in hand and avoid wounding any susceptibilities. You surely will not reward such cautious conduct on our part by hindering the completion of a work applauded by all nations, and which offers so happy an opportunity of proving to the world that the Ottoman Empire is fairly embarked in the path of civilisation and progress, and retains within itself the elements of originality and vitality.

Finally, I added that I came merely as the friend of the Porte, that I was the agent of the Viceroy, and not of the French Government, from whom I had no credentials. I gathered from my own observations, and afterwards learnt indirectly, that what I said had produced considerable effect.

The next day, at a grand diplomatic dinner given by the Foreign Minister, Aali Pacha, as a farewell to Baron von Bruck, Reschid Pacha thought he might take the opportunity of telling Lord Stratford the reason of my coming to Constantinople, and met with just such opposition as we expected.

It was, therefore, necessary to act promptly and bring

the matter to a conclusion, so as to be beforehand with the Sultan, and anticipate the demands of the English Ambassador. The Austrian Internuncio, to whom I confided how things stood, told me that his personal and official support was at my service. His successor, whom he expected every day, would, of course, bring special instructions; but, in the meanwhile, he did not hesitate to pledge himself, and would do all in his power to counterbalance Lord Stratford's influence.

Whilst M. Scheffer was gone, at M. Benedetti's instigation, to induce Reschid Pacha to obtain me an audience with the Sultan, I wrote to the Grand Vizier, and received an immediate reply.

XXI.
To his Highness Reschid Pacha, Grand Vizier.
Constantinople, *February* 19, 1855.

May I request your Highness to submit the subjoined note to his Imperial Majesty's Council?

I have to thank your Highness, on M. Benedetti's behalf and my own, for the Imperial audience of which M. Scheffer will give you an account.

The kindness shown me by his Imperial Highness gives me great hopes of the success of the negotiation with which I am entrusted by Mohammed Said Pacha, who has full confidence in your Highness's support. Your noble co-operation with him in bringing about the realisation of one of the grandest schemes of ancient and modern times will add yet another signal service to those you have already rendered to the cause of the pacification of the East.

Note for the Council of his Imperial Majesty the Sultan.
Constantinople, *February* 19, 1855.

It would be superfluous for me to point out to the distinguished members of the Imperial Council the immense advantages of constructing the Suez Canal. The only obstacle consists in the personal hostility of a foreign Representative, which, should it be successful, will inflict a moral blow on your exalted authority.

I am confident that this obstacle will not prevail over the wishes I am charged respectfully to express of a noble prince who, as in duty bound, defers to his sovereign as a faithful and loyal vassal.

XXII.

To his Highness Reschid Pacha.

Constantinople, *February* 24, 1855.

After spending a fortnight in Constantinople, where I received a most friendly hearing from his Imperial Majesty the Sultan, I yesterday decided to return to Egypt, with the answer your Highness promised me for Mohammed Said Pacha. But before embarking I heard that this answer would not be such as the Viceroy is entitled to expect. I therefore postponed my departure, so that I might, to the best of my ability, avoid those untoward results of which I took care to warn your Highness at our personal interview.

I am informed that it is thought necessary to demand and wait for explanations relative to the scheme of his Highness Mohammed Said Pacha. This fresh objection, which might have been made to me the very day of my arrival, seems to me easy enough to answer.

Permit me to state the facts, and to beg you again to call the attention of his Imperial Majesty's Council to the object of my mission.

His Highness Mohammed Said Pacha wrote to your Highness in December to acquaint you with the scheme of cutting a canal through the Isthmus of Suez. Before making formal reference to the Sublime Porte he had already made known his views to all the Representatives of foreign Powers in Egypt, in order that they might apprise their respective Governments, and learn their wishes on the subject.

The Viceroy at once ordered a scientific survey of the

isthmus to be made by two engineers in his service.
When convinced that there was no physical difficulty
in the way of the success of the scheme, and having from
November 30th to February 1st received nothing but
congratulations from foreign Governments, without one
discouraging suggestion, he finally addressed himself
to the advisers of his sovereign, submitting to them the
original plan and all documents necessary to its due
appreciation, charging me with the mission of recommending it to your Highness. I was, therefore, in a
position to give every information and answer all inquiries
at Constantinople.

If you have not already done so, I beg you to inform
his Imperial Majesty's Council how matters stand, and to
call attention to the fact that my presence in Constantinople removes all ground for the unexpected suggestion
that we should wait for explanations from Egypt.

I venture to hope your Highness will shortly have the
goodness to send me a decisive answer for his Highness
Mohammed Said Pacha.

XXIII.

To HIS EXCELLENCY BARON KOLLER, INTERNUNCIO
FOR AUSTRIA AT CONSTANTINOPLE.

CONSTANTINOPLE, *February* 24, 1855.

I HAVE the honour of forwarding the documents
mentioned to you yesterday, for your Highness's private
perusal. I also enclose a copy of the letter sent to
Reschid Pacha this morning, which M. Benedetti took
charge of.

The matter is again submitted to the Sultan's Council,
and before any decision is come to, may I beg to be allowed to count on your valuable co-operation and support
for carrying through this international scheme, in which,
as you are aware, the Government of his Majesty the
Emperor of Austria has long taken the greatest interest?

ANSWER OF BARON KOLLER TO M. FERD. DE LESSEPS.

CONSTANTINOPLE, *February* 26, 1855.

I RETURN the documents you were good enough to enclose in your favour of the 24th, with many thanks for both. In an interview with Aali Pacha on Saturday, I took the opportunity of warmly recommending his Highness to bring about a prompt and favourable decision with reference to the proposed Suez Canal. Your zeal in the matter deserves the gratitude of all Europe. The interest taken in the scheme by my Government is in proportion with its immense importance.

With hearty wishes for your success,

I beg to remain, &c.

XXIV.

TO HIS EXCELLENCY LORD STRATFORD DE REDCLIFFE, ENGLISH AMBASSADOR AT CONSTANTINOPLE.

(*Letter sent the morning after a banquet at the English Embassy to which M. de Lesseps had been invited.*)

CONSTANTINOPLE, *February* 26, 1855.

I HASTEN to forward you the papers, which will at once enable you to understand my mission at Constantinople. I venture to hope that I shall no longer incur the powerful opposition of the representative of her Britannic Majesty.

Your Excellency was kind enough to say that you only wanted information, that you had not come to an irrevocable decision, or given any but a personal opinion.

The question has been in due course submitted to the Sublime Porte, without any pressure from outside. As agent of Mohammed Said Pacha it is not open to me to quit the scene, as your Excellency suggested. The Viceroy of Egypt had the right to put me here, and to keep me here.

Just as he did not desire a French or Austrian character to be given to the enterprise, neither does he wish to give it an exclusively English colour by having the question discussed in London, and made to depend on the decision of one Government. He intends the initiative in the Suez Canal scheme to be taken solely by the Egyptian and Ottoman authorities.

Your Excellency is a true patriot, and understands too well the value of a close alliance between our two countries (an alliance which I thoroughly appreciate) to promote in any way a difference of opinion between them. To wound the *amour propre* of two Governments on such a question, by any unfriendly steps that might be taken, would be deplorable.

England very rightly declares that she only drew the sword against Russia in the interests of civilisation, to insure free right of navigation, the independence of Europe, and the integrity of Turkey. Your Excellency, then, would hardly desire it to be said that England alone of all nations is hindering a work that is essentially favourable to the principles aimed at in the Austro-Franco-English treaty for the pacification of the East.

I congratulate myself, my Lord, on the interview I had the honour of having with you. It removed from my mind impressions that I do not hesitate to confess. I beg to ask your permission to renew our conversation, and will therefore come to-morrow, about one o'clock, to the English palace.

P.S.—The Viceroy, by a letter dated Alexandria, February 17th, acquaints me with the fact that up to that date Mr. Bruce had made no representation to him on the part of the English Government.

ANSWER FROM LORD STRATFORD TO M. DE LESSEPS.
(*Private.*)
HOTEL DE ANGLETERRE, *February* 27, 1855.

I WRITE early, not only to acknowledge the receipt of the documents enclosed with your note, but also to ask you to put off the visit you are kind enough to promise me till another day. Engagements which I cannot postpone prevent my accepting your kind proposal to-day.

You rightly suppose that I desire further information, and my desire is not less strong on this occasion than on any other when a great enterprise is being discussed, one which nearly concerns the interests of more than one State, which, while delighting the mind in theory, leads to difference of opinion on practical details.

You, sir, have too much knowledge and experience to object to my going no farther than this. The different considerations you have touched upon, in so delicate and flattering a way, really open deep political questions.

In my position personal independence has its limits, and cannot oppose itself to official contingencies.

XXV.

To Comte de Lesseps, Paris.

Constantinople, *February* 26, 1855.

The Sultan's Council, at a meeting held on the evening of the 23rd, to consider the Viceroy of Egypt's request, regarded it favourably till Lord Stratford, having no better plea, and being without instructions from his Government, took it into his head to produce an extract from an old letter written by Lord Clarendon to the English Consul-General in Egypt. It was somewhat doubtfully suggested in this letter that the British representative should point out to the Viceroy that his enterprise was not sure to succeed, and that it would be better, before carrying it out, to consult the opinion of all the Powers, since some of them might think their interests affected.

This communication, which at first seemed likely to be set aside, ended in causing trouble among the members of the Council. Lord Stratford's all-powerful influence again prevailed, an expedient was sought, and, as it seemed, was found—viz., to wait for further information from the Viceroy of Egypt.

The next morning, the day I intended to embark, I went to take leave of Reschid Pacha, and to ask him if his letter to Mohammed Saïd Pacha was ready, and what were its terms. He told me all, and I resolved to put off my departure.

On the 24th M. Benedetti himself took a letter from me to Reschid Pacha (copy enclosed). The same day I was invited to dine at the English Embassy. Lord Stratford, in the course of the evening, when I was alone with him and his family, began a conversation, during which he affected great friendliness, saying that there was no knowing whether, if, under other circumstances, I had expressed myself as frankly as I was doing now, many things might not have been easily arranged; that he had not taken any irrevocable decision on the question; that he only wished for further information, &c. He added that Mr. Bruce had not forwarded any of the documents, which I sent him to the Embassy at Constantinople, without having acquainted the French Consul-General with them.

It was agreed that these other documents should be sent to him on the following day. I enclose a copy of my letter to Lord Stratford, which accompanied these documents. I read it over to Reschid Pacha this morning, and he quite approved of it.

To put a stop to this ridiculous subterfuge of waiting for further explanation from the Viceroy, I showed him a letter from the prince, dated the 17th of this month, in which the following passages occur:—

Mohammed Said Pacha has done all he can to prove his interest in the matter. The Duc de Brabant has spoken to his Highness on the subject of the Canal, and expressed his admiration of the grandeur of the work; he only feared a difficulty might arise in the financial part of the scheme during a time of active hostilities. The Viceroy answered that this would be no obstacle, as he had himself sufficient funds to commence at once, and would collect more when it approached completion.

The English Consul-General remains at Cairo, seldom sees the Viceroy, and does not mention the project to his Highness. It seems, therefore, that he has no positive instructions to oppose the scheme.

I shall be obliged if you will tell Arles Dufour that I have neither time nor inclination, in the midst of my work over this negotiation, to reply to his letter, nor to Enfantin's of February 10th. I cannot take the trouble to re-read these letters, which are full of very inappropriate jokes and sarcasms. If I replied in the same strain they would probably not have the same patience that I have had, and we should quickly quarrel. What is the meaning of the scheme presented to the Emperor, of which I have never been told anything? Tell Arles that I hold more than ever to the opinions expressed in my letter of January 6th, especially on the subject of the old Societé d'Études, which as far as I am concerned, has become a purely historical matter. I can entirely agree with Baron von Bruck, who took part in that Societé d'Études.

These gentlemen need not remind me that I must not be influenced by the circumstances in which I am placed; they might know that I am not a man to be influenced or coerced when I believe I am on the right path. Let them know, in short, that I am not going to be ousted from my post, nor to follow their lead. I have no sort of connection with them, or with others, and their private arrangements, of which I know nothing, do not affect me. If they are willing to help me, and will not indulge, as they confess they do, in acts and expressions which thwart and harass me, well and good; if not, I may regret the want of their co-operation, but shall not consider the want of it fatal to my cause.

They will do well, therefore, to calm themselves, and to treat their scheme of organisation merely as a study which may be taken into consideration, like many other documents, when the company is formed by my care.

XXVI.

To the Viscount Stratford de Redcliffe.

CONSTANTINOPLE, *February* 28, 1855.

MY LORD,—There are questions which, to be properly settled, should be frankly entered into, just as there are wounds which must be laid bare in order to be cured. The straightforward manner in which you received the remarks I made in the first instance on a subject, the importance of which I do not attempt to conceal, encourages me to submit to your appreciation a point of view which, I think, it would be useful to consider with regard to the Isthmus of Suez. The great influence which your character and your long experience entitle you to exercise in the decisions of your Government in all questions concerning the East, renders it a matter of the highest importance, in my eyes, that your Excellency's opinion should be based on a full knowledge of the facts.

The results already obtained through the close alliance of France and England, prove sufficiently how beneficial it is that the two nations should be united in the interest of the balance of power in Europe and of civilisation. The future and the welfare of all nations depend, therefore, upon the perfect maintenance and preservation of a state of things which, to the everlasting credit of the Government by which it was established, can alone, with time, secure to humanity the blessings of progress and peace. Hence the necessity of getting rid beforehand of every cause of dissension, or even of coolness, between the two nations; hence, therefore, it becomes a matter of positive duty to seek in future contingencies what causes would be likely to arouse feelings of antagonism which are the growth of centuries and produce in either nation explosions against which the wisdom of Governments is powerless. Motives of hostile rivalry are gradually making way for that generous emulation from which grand results inevitably follow.

If the matter, as it stands, be looked at in a general manner, it is difficult to see any ground or motive for renewing a struggle which has cost so much bloodshed to the world. Could financial and commercial interests be a source of dissension between the two nations? But the general investment of British capital in French enterprises and the immense impulse given to international trade, create between them bonds of union which daily become closer. Can it be a matter of political interest, or of principle? But both nations have now one and the same object, one and the same ambition, viz., the triumph of right over might, of civilisation over barbarity. Can it be some petty jealousy connected with territorial aggrandisement? But it is now admitted by both that the world is large enough to satisfy the spirit of enterprise of either nation, that there are countries to be turned to account and human beings to be rescued from a state of barbarism; besides, if both flags keep together, the activity of one must profit by the conquests of the other.

Hence, at first sight, there is nothing in the general aspect of matters that would seem likely to affect our good understanding with England.

Yet, on closer inspection, a contingency becomes apparent, which, by allowing the most enlightened and moderate Governments to be influenced by popular prejudices and passions, might revive old enmities, thus compromising the alliance and its good fruit.

There is a spot in the world the free passage through which is directly connected with the political and commercial power of Great Britian, a spot which France, on the other hand, had, in days gone by, been ambitious to possess. This spot is Egypt, the direct route from Europe to India—Egypt, where Frenchmen have fought and bled.

It is unnecessary to dwell upon the motives which make it impossible that England should allow Egypt to pass into the hands of a rival Power without offering the most determined resistance; but what should also be taken into full account is that France, though not so directly interested, but acting under the influence of glorious traditions and of other feelings more instinctive than rational, and for that very reason most powerful in the case of an impressionable race, would not, on her side, allow England to assume the peaceful mastery of Egypt. It is clear that so long as the route to India through Egypt is open and safe, and that the state of the country guarantees easy and rapid communication, England will not voluntarily create for herself difficulties of the most serious nature for the sake of appropriating a territory which, to her, is only valuable as a means of transit.

It is equally evident that France, whose policy for the last fifty years has consisted in contributing to the prosperity of Egypt, both by means of advice and the co-operation of many Frenchmen distinguished in science, in matters of administration, and in all the arts of peace or of war, will not try to carry out there the ideas of another age, so long as England does not interfere.

I SUM UP ALL THE ADVANTAGES OF MY SCHEME. 93

But supposing that a crisis should occur such as those which have so often convulsed the East, that a circumstance should take place which would render it imperative for England to get a footing in Egypt in order to prevent another Power from stealing a march on her, can it be maintained for a moment that the alliance could possibly survive the complications which would result from such an event? And why should England be placed in such a position? Why should England think herself bound to be mistress of Egypt, even at the risk of breaking off her alliance with France? For the simple reason that Egypt is the shortest, the most direct, route from England to her Eastern possessions, that this route must always remain open to her, and that, as regards a matter of such vital interest, she can make no compromise. Thus, through the position which nature has assigned to her, Egypt may again become the subject of a conflict between France and England; so that this possibility of dissension would disappear if, by a providential event, the geographical conditions of the Old World were changed, and the route to India, instead of passing through the heart of Egypt, were to be brought back to the boundary, and, being open to all, were the sole privilege of no one. Well, this event, which must be within the views of Providence, is now in the power of man. It can be accomplished by human industry. It can be realised by piercing the Isthmus of Suez, an undertaking to which nature presents no obstacle, and in which available capital from England as well as from other countries will undoubtedly be invested. Let the isthmus be cut through, let the waves of the Mediterranean mingle with the waters of the Indian Ocean, let the railway be continued and finished, and Egypt, whilst acquiring more importance as a productive and commercial country, as a market and as a medium of transit generally, will lose her dangerous reputation as a means of uncertain and disputed communication. The possession of her territory being no longer a matter of interest to England, ceases to be the cause of a possible struggle between that Power and France; the union of the two nations is thenceforth assured for ever, and the world is saved from the misery which would be entailed by a quarrel between them.

This result offers such guarantees for the future that it will be sufficient to point to it, to secure for the undertaking by which it is to be obtained the sympathy and encouragement of those statesmen who are striving to place the Anglo-French alliance on an imperishable basis. You are one of those men, my Lord, and the part you take in the discussion of matters of the highest political moment, with which I am not familiar, is too important a one for me not to seek to make known to you my wishes.

In sending you, with my note of the day before yesterday, my papers relating to the Suez affair, my intention was to leave them at your disposal. I, therefore, beg your Excellency will keep them.

XXVII.

To Baron Koller, Internuncio of Austria at Constantinople.

Constantinople, *March* 1, 1855.

I HAVE to thank you for the letter which you have done me the honour to write to me on the 26th. It is a great satisfaction to me to see that you have lost no time in urging the Ottoman Government to hasten the settlement of the matter which has brought me to Constantinople. I value most highly the terms in which you are good enough to express yourself with regard to me, and I am happy to be able to include you among the most enlightened and useful supporters of the scheme to which I have devoted all my efforts.

As at present our only difficulty is English opposition, I think it my duty to put you in a position to reply to any objections which may be made, by communicating to you my correspondence with Mr. Bruce, British Agent and Consul-General in Egypt, as well as with political personages in England, and with Lord Stratford de Redcliffe at Constantinople.

XXVIII.

LETTER OF THE GRAND VIZIER TO HIS HIGHNESS MOHAMMED SAID PACHA, VICEROY OF EGYPT, DELIVERED TO M. FERDINAND DE LESSEPS.

(Original in Turkish.)

CONSTANTINCPLE, *March* 1, 1855.
(12th Djemazul Akir 1271.)

YOUR very humble servant has the honour to inform you as follows:—

M. Ferdinand de Lesseps is now returning to see your Highness. He is, indeed, as your Highness deigned to acquaint us, a guest who, in himself, deserves every respect and consideration. The object of his visit here related to the Canal business, a most useful undertaking. While he was at Constantinople I had the pleasure of seeing him on several occasions, and of conversing with him at length on many subjects. He also had the honour of being presented to his Majesty the Sultan and of receiving from him marks of the greatest esteem.

In accordance with the imperial order issued with respect to the most interesting scheme of the Canal, the question is at the present time under the consideration of the Council of Ministers. M. de Lesseps, being unable to wait till the termination of the deliberations, decided upon leaving. I shall shortly forward to your Highness a detailed account of the result.

L. S. MOUSTAFA RESCHID.

XXIX.

TO COMTE DE LESSEPS, PARIS.

SMYRNA, *March* 3, 1855.

MY note to Lord Stratford de Redcliffe, of the 26th February, was translated into Turkish and submitted on the 27th to the Council of the Sultan, to whom my letter to Reschid Pacha, of the 24th, had already been communicated. These communications produced the result I had hoped for. On the one hand it was proved that there were no further explanations to be expected from the Viceroy of Egypt; and, on the other hand, there was no longer any doubt that Lord Stratford had received no instructions from his Government, although the latter had been aware, for the last three months, of Mohammed Said Pacha's determination. Moreover, it was proved by my latest correspondence from Egypt that, up to the 17th, no official representations had been made by Mr. Bruce contrary to what the British Ambassador had given us to understand.

I was advised that Lord Stratford would strongly urge the Grand Vizier to wait for the instructions his Lordship expected from London, before giving a definite answer to the Viceroy. From the last part of his note of the 27th, of which I send you a copy, and in which there is a statement to the effect that personal independence must sometimes be sacrificed to *official contingencies*, I felt pretty sure that he meant to continue to oppose me. Lord Stratford knows that his position in England is precarious, and that several of the members of his own Government are not favourable to him. Supposing he does not go so far as to suspect that the absence of instructions, of which it is said he has complained to his Court, is a trap laid for him, still he would not allow an act to be accomplished which he thinks would create an unfavourable impression in England. Moreover, having regard to the disasters of the British army in the Crimea, he resents anything that might appear to diminish his all-powerful influence; and this feeling, for which, after all, he can scarcely be blamed, makes his English exclusiveness greater than ever, just now.

It was therefore no surprise to me to hear on the morning of the 28th—the day on which the Council was to come to a definite decision with respect to the Suez affair —that Lord Stratford had had an interview of three hours with the Grand Vizier, and that, finding it impossible to obtain a negative solution from the Council, they were conferring together with a view of hitting upon some plan which might gain time and allow of some further dilatory measure being brought forward.

Reschid Pacha is said, rightly or wrongly, to be a mere tool of the noble lord, and to fear lest his own fall should follow the decline of an influence which, it is true, he himself finds irksome at times, and from which, he secretly tells the French agents, he wishes to get rid. But, for all that, he invariably submits to the domination which he complains of and which is becoming intolerable with regard to the credit of France in the East. It would be dangerous to attach any importance to his protestations, and especially to the fact that his son is shortly to be sent as Ambassador to Paris. His vacillating nature makes him, I think, by no means fit to raise Turkey from her fallen state, and to turn to account those elements of vitality which, in my opinion, the Ottoman Empire still possesses.

The result of the understanding between the English Ambassador and the Grand Vizier was to induce the Council to defer any solution under the pretext of appointing a Commission of three members, whose mission it was, regardless of the Sultan's approval of the scheme for piercing the Isthmus of Suez, to enter with me into an elaborate examination of the articles of the Egyptian Firman. This Firman—which had been drawn up under the inspiration of the Viceroy, virtually by him, in fact, and which had been approved by the Divan at Cairo and communicated to all the Governments in Europe—was the indispensable basis of the undertaking, and was not under discussion. I was unable to follow my adversaries on such ground, and moreover it was a subject I had been specially recommended to avoid. The Viceroy considers that he is perfectly justified in not allowing an act of deference towards his sovereign to be turned into a precedent which might accustom the Porte—which so often acts under the influence of fanaticism or foreign pressure —to hinder the administration of the internal affairs of Egypt. That intelligent and enlightened prince is anxious to continue to set a good example to his country, and create resources which are as essential to the prosperity of Egypt as to the real interests of the empire. Reschid Pacha appeared to me to see the danger of the course he was about to take, and as he is very anxious to retain favour with Mohammed Said Pacha, he tried to throw all responsibility on the Council, behind which he is in the habit of sheltering himself. I did not conceal from the Grand Vizier that to decline responsibility was not sufficient to remove it, and that I considered him to be fully responsible with regard to the Viceroy and the Governments of France and Austria, of whose sympathy for the undertaking in question he was aware. I added that I had determined to return to Egypt, where the Viceroy was waiting for me to prepare the organisation of his plan; and that, pending the imperial authorisation, of which he could not doubt, I congratulated myself on having contributed, during my stay at Constantinople, to the clear definition of the question; and that I left convinced of the friendly dispositions of the Sultan and his advisers towards a scheme the execution of which was no longer to me the subject of a doubt. I promised to make known this friendly feeling at Alexandria, expressing my hope that something more positive would soon follow.

Altogether, my impressions and those of the French Embassy with regard to the period, more or less near, at which we shall obtain a result are not unfavourable. The advisability of my departure was approved by Benedetti, with whom, I am glad to say, I have cause to be greatly pleased, and who, in his position, did all he possibly could.

XXX.

To M. SCHEFFER, FIRST DRAGOMAN TO THE FRENCH EMBASSY AT CONSTANTINOPLE.

SMYRNA, *March* 3, 1855.

WHEN leaving Constantinople I regretted not having seen you, to thank you for the assistance which you constantly afforded me in all stages of my negotiations. You have aided me most intelligently and effectively. The Suez Canal owes you honourable mention.

You remember that Reschid Pasha and the other members of the Council did not appear to be very well informed as to the early antecedents of the Canal, especially as to those which concern the relations of Turkey with the holy places of Arabia. I made frequent mention of the Arabian authors who refer to the opinion existing on this subject from the earliest period of Mohammedanism, but I think it useful to submit to them the text of the passages; and for this purpose I send you several extracts, which appear interesting to me. To them I add an extract from the " Memoirs of M. de Tott," in which it is shown that Sultan Mustapha III. was very favourable to the scheme of the junction of the Mediterranean and Red seas.

CANAL OF THE PRINCE OF THE FAITHFUL.

(Extract from El Macryzy.)

THIS canal was cut by an ancient King of Egypt, for Hadjar (Agar), mother of Ishmael, whilst she was at Mecca. In the course of time it was cut a second time by one of the Greek kings who reigned in Egypt after the death of Alexander.

When the Most High sent Mohammedanism to men, and when Amrou-ben-el-Ass conquered Egypt, that general, by order of Omar-ben-el-Khatheb, Prince of the Faithful, employed himself in causing the canal to be re-cut in the year of the plague. He carried it to the Sea of Quolzum, whence vessels can go to Yemen, and India. We then pass on to the time when Mohammed-ben-Abdoullah, ben-Haçan, ben-el-Horeïn-ben-Ali-ben-abou-Thaleb revolted in the city of the Prophet (Medina) against Abou-dja-far, Abdoullah-ben-Mohammed-el-Mansour, then Caliph of Irak. This sovereign wrote to his lieutenant in Egypt to order him to fill up the canal of Quolzum, so that they should not be able to transport provisions to Medina. This command was executed, and all communication with the Sea of Quolzum cut off; and matters remained in the state in which we now see them.

Omar-ben-el-Khatheb wrote a letter to Amrou-ben-el-Ass, in the following terms:

To the rebel, the son of the rebel: whilst you and your companions were gorging yourselves, you did not disquiet yourselves as to whether I and my people were growing lean. Give us, then, assistance ! To the rescue !

I am thine, replied Amrou ; I send thee a convoy of beasts of burden, of which the first will be with thee before the last shall have left me. I hope, besides, to find a means of transport by sea.

8 *

But Amrou was not long before he repented of originating this first idea, since it was remarked to him that it was possible to spoil Egypt of its wealth, and to transfer it to Medina. He immediately wrote that he had considered on the means of transport by sea, and that he had found insurmountable difficulties therein.

Omar replied:

I have received thy letter, in which thou seekest to elude the performance of the promise contained in thy previous communication. I swear by the Almighty either thou shalt perform it, or I will turn thee out by the ears, and I will send one who will perform it.

Amrou saw clearly that he had disobeyed Omar, and he immediately busied himself about the canal. Omar enjoined him not to neglect to send him all the provisions, the clothing, the lentils, the onions, and the cattle—in one word, everything which could be found in Egypt.

El-Kendi, in his work, "Aljendi-el-Moghreby," states that this canal was dug in the twenty-third year of the Hegira (645 of the Christian era), and was finished in six months, so that in the seventh vessels could pass through and reach the Hedjaz.

Extract from the "Memoires de M. de Tott, sur les Turcs."
(Parts III. and IV.)

The Sultan Mustapha expressed great interest in the scheme for the junction of the two seas by the Isthmus of Suez. He soon wished to add to the information which I had on the subject that of various Commissioners who had been in Egypt; and it will be seen in the fourth part of these Memoirs that, if Mustapha had lived sufficiently long to undertake this enterprise, he would have found, on the spot, facilities which would have enabled him to effect the greatest revolution of which politics are susceptible. This Sultan, whose understanding was beginning to be enlightened, confided to me the preparation of a work on this important subject, the execution of which he reserved for a time of peace.

In the various works which have shed a lustre on ancient Egypt, the canal between the Red Sea and the Mediterranean would have been worthy of the first place, if the efforts of genius on behalf of public utility had been seconded by the generations destined to reap the fruits of them, and if the foundations of social welfare could obtain the same solidity as the prejudices which tend to destroy them.

This, however, is a summary of the history of this affair. It only shows us this picture,—that of all nations and of all ages. Had it not been for these continual destructions, the happiest condition would have dictated immutable laws, and the canal of the Red Sea would for ever have been the foundation of the public right of nations.

XXXI.
To M. le Comte de Lesseps, Paris.

Smyrna, March 10, 1855.

My departure from Constantinople has naturally brought about the dissolution of the Commission, which had not time to begin work. As it cannot be officially acknowledged that the delay considered necessary for the sanction of the Sultan is caused by waiting for the English instructions asked for by Lord Stratford, I have just been informed that, on the proposition of Reschid Pacha, the Divan has returned to its first determination to demand some explanations from the Viceroy. The Austrian packet, on which I embark to-day, should carry a second despatch for Said Pacha from the Grand Vizier.

My letters from Stamboul inform me that the English Ambassador has sought to arouse the fears of the Porte by representing the importance which the Canal would give to Egypt and to the Viceroy, the ideas of independence to which this scheme might give rise, and the dangers of the passage of vessels of war. All this is very perfidious, and seems to show, amongst other things, that England desires, more than any other Power, the weakening of Turkey, so as to encourage her in the idea that she only can protect her.

XXXII.
To M. Benedetti, French Chargé d'Affaires at Constantinople.

Saidie (the Barrage, near Cairo),
March 16, 1855.

Having left Smyrna on the evening of the 10th, I reached Alexandria on the 14th, and on the morning of the 15th I arrived at the residence of the Viceroy, at the *barrage,* Saidie.

At the same time as I delivered to him the despatch of Reschid Pacha—of which I send you a translation—he received by courier a letter from his brother-in-law, Kiamil Pacha, who, writing on behalf of the Grand Vizier under the form of private and confidential remarks, demanded explanations as specified in your note of the 8th.

These remarks principally concern :—

1. The guarantees to be demanded from the Canal Company as to the passage of vessels of war.
2. The concession of land to Europeans, contrary, as it is said, to ancient custom and precedent in Turkey.
3. The dangers which Egypt might incur from the hostility of England.
4. On the representations which it is pretended have been made to Said Pacha on behalf of the English Cabinet, by the British Agent and Consul-General in Egypt.

The Viceroy has made known to me his intention of replying in the following manner :—

First Question.—There will be no occasion to demand from the company undertaking to construct the Canal between the two seas any guarantee as to the national sovereignty, which remains intact in Turkey. When joint-stock companies undertake the construction of means of communication, on the same grounds as national or foreign capitalists, by means of whom railways or canals have long been constructed in England, France, and Germany, none of these countries has, in admitting capitalists, ever thought of treating with the companies concerning the interests of local sovereignty, which, being reserved, cannot be discussed, and are inalienable.

Second Question.—The concessions of land made to the Suez Canal Company in the districts now uncultivated, but which will be watered and rendered fruitful by the fertilising canal derived from the Nile, will be a blessing to Egypt, the Government of which should steadily endeavour to augment its prosperity and revenues. If such an example could be imitated in other provinces of the Ottoman Empire, where bad administration, together with prejudices destined to disappear, have impoverished and depopulated the country, instead of raising obstacles, those should be encouraged who offer in exchange for a barren and unproductive country to pay the ordinary land tax and to give up fifteen per cent. of their gains. Besides, there is nothing contrary to ordinary custom in a concession of land to a joint-stock company formed, as has already been said, by capitalists of all nations, who, consequently, do not bear the stamp of any particular nationality.

Third Question.—It appears, from the information received in Egypt from all sources concerning the reception accorded throughout Europe to the intelligence of the scheme for cutting the Isthmus of Suez, and of the advantages which must necessarily result to the commerce and navigation of Great Britain, that the hostility of England is not at all to be feared by Egypt.

Fourth Question.—The Viceroy is at last enabled to declare formally that Mr. Bruce, Agent and Consul-General of her Britannic Majesty in Egypt, who has been informed since the 27th of November last of the project of the Suez Canal, has not made any communication to him on behalf of his Government.

Such is the purport of the explanations which will be given by Said Pacha. It is now agreed upon between us that I shall be the bearer of his reply, and as I shall not probably leave here under a fortnight, I shall have time to receive your reply by the next direct packet and to know whether affairs are still in the state in which I left them at Constantinople. Besides this, time will be necessary to enable Lord Stratford to receive from London the instructions asked for, or to be decided that he is not to be allowed to make an official opposition.

I have found the Viceroy very decided in his resolutions, and, without the private letter of Kiamil Pacha, he would have considered the terms of the official communication of the Grand Vizier as the testimony of a complete approbation of his scheme. Kiamil Pacha has not managed well. He has done all he could to divert the Viceroy from his scheme. He has made himself the interpreter of all the opposing arguments raised by Lord Stratford. He has even gone so far as to recall Mehemet Ali, who, he said, would never have allowed Europeans to possess a considerable tract of country in Egypt. He has wasted his eloquence, which has produced an impression which he will regret on the mind of Said Pacha. Kiamil Pacha, then, has made a leap in the dark, and has fallen into the trap which has doubtless been set for him by Reschid Pacha. The latter would not have wished to expose himself to the displeasure of the Viceroy; and he has placed in the front the President of the Grand Council, making use of his relationship to create difficulties indirectly which he himself dare not raise.

Moreover, that which Kiamil Pacha says concerning the policy of Mehemet Ali is entirely false; for, about the year 1843, in the short space of a fortnight, he distributed to Europeans—amongst others to MM. Pastré, Larking, Thurburn, Tossitza, Zizinia, &c.—tracts of land to the extent of 25,000 feddans, and if the concession was not greater, it was because the Europeans did not wish to take more.

XXXIII.

To M. le Comte de Lesseps, Paris.

Saidie (Barrage of the Nile), *March* 18, 1855.

A SECOND letter, dictated by Reschid Pacha to Kiamil Pacha, which the Viceroy only had cognisance of yesterday, repeats and aggravates the first objections. This proceeding, in contradiction to what the Grand Vizier had said to me, and to the communication of which I was the bearer, is evidently the result of a plan arranged between the Grand Vizier and Lord Stratford. It has raised the indignation of the straightforward Said Pacha, and has only served to strengthen him in his resolution.

I have been extremely satisfied with the work of Linant and of Mougel. It is not quite finished. It is so clear and logical that it must convince.

XXXIV.

To M. HIPPOLYTE LAFOSSE, PARIS.

CAIRO, *March* 22, 1855.

I ASKED you, through Madame Delamalle, to give my best thanks to M. Thiers for the manner in which he received the news of the Viceroy's concession respecting the great undertaking of the Canal. M. Thiers has always been a staunch patriot, and it can be understood whenever one reads or hears it how it is that his heart has not been dried up by the management of public affairs. He it was who confided to me twenty years ago the management of the French Consulate-General in Egypt. It was chiefly during that time that I began those friendly and intimate relations with the young prince, the present Viceroy, which have procured me the means of carrying out the Canal. This work would be far beyond me if I could not reckon on the good wishes and co-operation of men whose decided opinion exercises an universal influence. I wished to say to M. Thiers that I hoped that he would support the Canal in his letters and negotiations with English statesmen, over whom he exercises a certain influence. Give him the enclosed copies of my letters to the English representatives in Egypt and Constantinople, from which he will see that my sole difficulty lies in England. To this point we must direct our energies, and if M. Thiers, with his extraordinary ability, will use his influence on my behalf, his opinion will bear great weight.

There is one consideration which will not escape his notice. The opening of the Suez Canal will form one of the greatest safety-valves against European revolutions. The year 1848 has shown the necessity of occupying the attention of volatile people and of opening a vent for the employment of a turbulent and idle residuum occasioned by the rapid growth of a needy population. The interest of all European nations ought, therefore, to enlist them in furthering the junction of the two seas, which opens up such a large field for speculation and enterprise. England does not dare to confess her object in opposing the scheme, but at the same time she must see that she can no longer hope for the monopoly of commerce and the dominion of the sea.

Our Continental wars and the weakness of European navies have enabled her to establish strongholds well chosen for the purpose of watching the seas and to endeavour to obstruct the commerce of other nations. But can such selfish feelings be allowed to exist at the present time? The dreams of universal dominion have passed away in every country; the downfall of the Empire of the first Napoleon has proved it. If a nation, however powerful, should wish to interrupt a great highway which will, by right, be the common property of all people in virtue of their subscribed capital, it would be condemned by public opinion, and would eventually fail in its pretentions. It would be wiser and more profitable for England to abandon designs which aim at universal power, and to participate with other nations. Its position would be most creditable with regard to commerce, industry, and navigation.

The Viceroy of Egypt has lately received a letter from Prince Metternich. In his reply, which he has read to me, he speaks of his design for piercing the Isthmus of Suez; and says that the Representatives of all the Powers at Constantinople have expressed their friendly views to the Porte; that only one Representative has opposed it, personally it is true, but not the less fatally; that the Austrian Minister, having announced an official approval, he believes he may rely upon the influence which the prince exercises amongst the diplomatists of Europe; he adds moreover that, the achievement of his enterprise being of universal interest, only selfish and narrow prejudices would try to impede it.

THE FINANCIAL PORTION OF MY SCHEME. 107

You ask me on what basis I intend to organise the finances of the company.

I have only fixed on one principle, the carrying out of which will require time and consideration. My object is to have, *in every country, the largest number possible of small shareholders, who shall be entitled to all the privileges of the company.*

What would a dozen large bankers do, with whom I could arrange to hand over the concession? They would propose that I should divide with them a certain number of thousands. They would then distribute 500-franc shares to the general public, without any expense, at a high premium, announcing—which, indeed, might be the case—that the shares will eventually yield twenty-five to thirty per cent.

Why not at once appeal to the public? The two French loans show what can be done with small capitals. When the principal is genuine, incalculable results arise from it. You will tell me that the Canal Company will not inspire the same amount of confidence which a strongly-constituted Government possesses. I think that the scheme for the junction of the Mediterranean and Indian Ocean—from which such large returns may be expected—being clearly stated, the most prejudiced minds will be convinced that no undertaking offers so great chances of profit to those who take part in it; and since no one will doubt, from the beginning, that there will not be a genuine profit, do you believe the shareholders throughout Europe, whose interests will have already been protected by those who are determined to conduct the enterprise, will fail to respond to the call? When it is known that the scheme is brought forward without any bribery, that nothing has been expended in Egypt or Constantinople to obtain or ratify the concession, and that, thanks to the generosity of the Viceroy, the plans and preliminary works have cost nothing, every one will see in the principles which we have followed the best guarantee for the future.

You reproach me for not having yet borrowed from you, who have given me proofs of your attachment and disinterestedness, which are a great comfort to those who, like myself, believe that in this world good overcomes evil. You know that I have selected a certain number of friends, who, in depositing 5000 francs each in the sole interest of the success of the enterprise, will form a common fund to defray preliminary expenses. I and my family have started it. Without the royal hospitality of *my prince* you are right in believing that my expenses would be considerable.

I thank you for having undertaken my commission with Barthélemy Saint-Hilaire, and I hope that his dear Aristotle will not be a successful rival, as he will not be compelled to leave him in giving me his assistance.

XXXV.

To His Royal Highness the Duke of Brabant,
Brussels.

CAIRO, *March* 23, 1855.

I HAVE the honour to transmit to your Royal Highness the various documents relating to the Suez Canal, for which you have kindly expressed a wish. I venture to hope that you will be pleased to call the attention of his Majesty the King of the Belgians to the importance of the undertaking, and to the interest which the enlightened prince who governs Egypt attaches to its realisation.

At the present time, when we have reason to fear that the question does not receive that consideration which it deserves from English statesmen, your royal father, whose powerful influence and judicious conciliatory disposition has so often rendered great services to Europe, might exercise the most favourable influence by the weight of his judgment.

His Highness Mohammed Said Pacha, in a reply which he recently sent to Prince Metternich, has commissioned him to thank his Majesty the Emperor of Austria for the official support given by his Internuncio at Constantinople to the Suez Canal project; and he added that this great work, being of universal benefit, could only be impeded by selfish and narrow prejudices.

Allow me to quote an extract from a publication which has lately appeared in London, which, judging the undertaking from an English point of view, appears to me to present some incontestable arguments on the interest which England ought to have in furthering the junction of the two seas.

The extract is as follows:—

Captain James Welch, of the Royal Engineers, a more recent writer than either M. Lepère or Maclaren, has discussed the question which attracts our attention. This officer stoutly asserts that the cutting of the Isthmus of Suez can only be done in a serviceable and lasting manner by English capital and labour. This is, indeed, a patriotic but bold assertion. We do not see why the capital and labour of any other great nation, if it is actuated by the same amount of interest as we have, should not be able to perform the work equally as well. In any case, the means would only differ in ratio to the interest; and if, in spite of the combination of many unfavourable circumstances, we feel confident that our country will be able to effect this junction between the two seas, it is because, sooner or later, this undertaking will become absolutely necessary for the maintenance of our Empire. Every nation would derive a great benefit from this new route opened for navigation. But the evident benefit which the European States nearest to Africa will derive has been seriously asserted as a reason for deterring England from joining an enterprise of which the result is problematic. Here, then, is an example of that old erroneous theory, which affirms that a nation can only be rich and prosperous whilst its neighbours are in a state of poverty.

Doubtless all the European countries nearest to the East will derive considerable benefit from the opening of the Suez Canal; but this ought to give us rather satisfaction than otherwise, since it cannot be denied that by the development of commerce, by whatever means, the most numerous and best invested capitals will reap in the end the greater part of the profits. Our belief is that England, and every nation like her, is called upon to assist in this great undertaking, which will far surpass anything that has yet been attempted. The making of the Panama and Suez Canals appear to us to be the greatest works of the future; they will increase and strengthen the happy bonds by which people of every clime, of every race, and of every faith, are united to England, and will for ever connect the general welfare of nations to the prosperity of our country, their safety to our power, and their independence to our liberty.—*Papers for the People*.

I beg that your Royal Highness will accept my best thanks for the encouragement which you have so kindly given me.

XXXVI.
PRIVATE LETTER TO HIS HIGHNESS MOHAMMED SAID.
BOURAJAT, LOWER EGYPT, *March* 26, 1855.

AFTER a conversation between the Emperor Napoleon and the English Ambassador, in which the Emperor highly approved of your Highness's scheme for the Suez Canal, the English Ambassador had an interview with the Minister of Foreign Affairs, and intimated to him that directions had been sent to Constantinople *only* with a view of *temporising*, and with instructions not to compromise the political situation of England and France.

It clearly shows, as we supposed, that London is not in any way disposed to compromise itself if the Sultan's sanction is given to your Highness.

It appears to me desirable that the Firman containing my power to constitute the universal company, which up to the present time has remained in possession of your Highness, should be returned to me.

Your Highness is aware that the Firman relating to the railway required by England had been issued in Egypt by Abbas Pacha without having previously obtained authorisation from Constantinople. England, however, maintained that such permission was not necessary. In the present instance you have acted with more caution, and have done wisely; but prudence has limits.

Your Highness is, moreover, convinced that I will not compromise you, as I will only make discreet use of your powers. You have been good enough to acknowledge that my mission to Constantinople has clearly defined the question, and has produced a good result. Now we must not stop half-way. France, Austria, and other Powers have supported your Highness's great scheme. England dares not openly to oppose it. Her only means of opposition is to endeavour to gain time. It would be dangerous to allow her to obtain her desire.

I repeat that the present time is a good opportunity for continuing the scheme, whilst your Highness will not cease to persuade the Porte to express its views.

Besides the powers bearing the seal of your Highness, which I shall carefully keep, and of which I shall only make use with your authority, it is desirable that I should possess the answers to the special objections raised by Reschid Pacha and Kiamil Pacha.

XXXVII.
To Comte de Lesseps, Paris.

ALEXANDRIA, *April* 5, 1855.

My last letter, of March 28th, announced to you my departure from Alexandria to meet the Viceroy, who had fixed our rendezvous on the Nile. I found the prince at Kaferleïs. We passed the evening together on board his steamer. I spent the night there, and we returned to Alexandria together by railway. From the very commencement of our interview, the Viceroy expressed himself with great warmth against his brother-in-law, Kiamil Pacha, and against the Grand Vizier, whose correspondence had just been read to him. It has not been thought sufficient to bring forward objections to his project: the most unfair and exaggerated arguments have been employed to alarm him and to intimidate those around him, and I could see that these latter were beginning to waver. He is even threatened with the displeasure of England, *whose fleets might attack him, when the business on the Black Sea is ended.*

He is told that he is very wrong to throw himself into the arms of France, whose Government, and, *still more, whose agents have but little stability; that the English agents, on the contrary, are always upheld and supported;* that their anger is very dangerous, and that they are, therefore, persons who ought to be treated with consideration. It is added that the interior tranquillity and the exterior influence of France depend upon a pistol-shot which the Emperor Napoleon may receive any day; and the whole winds up by pretending that if the Viceroy persists in his project of the Suez Canal he will lose the favour of the Sultan.

I give you the Viceroy's words verbatim. Any one who knows his character might have supposed that such a system of roguery and intimidation would produce an effect diametrically opposite to that of which Constantinople had furnished an example.

Reschid Pacha could not expect that Said Pacha, in the midst of the aberrations caused by the terror which Lord Stratford inspires in him, would have sufficient confidence in me to withdraw the veil from his disgraceful proceedings.

It must be acknowledged that the conduct of England in this case is contemptible. Lord Stratford is still permitted to entrench himself, as he did with me, behind "official contingencies," although such an attitude, suitable at the first appearance of the grant made by the Egyptian Firman, is not a fitting one four months after. To pretend now that he is waiting for instructions is, as my cousin Edmond de Lesseps wittily wrote, to ask for soup after dinner.

Can it be the case that the Cabinet in London, believing that they cannot offer opposition by bringing forward motives which they can avow, are reduced to making an opposition, as unfair as it is mysterious, through their Ambassador, who is to profess to act on his own private opinion? Such an expedient, unworthy of statesmen placed at the head of a great nation, would only serve to delay an enterprise which cannot be prevented, to lower the prestige of the Government, and to sacrifice, at a later period, a skilful diplomatist destined to be the victim of the good understanding of the two nations whose alliance is not always profitable to our sincerity. I naturally made these observations to the Viceroy. He asked me if I had heard of the arrival in Alexandria of a Turkish General from Constantinople, and if anything relating to his mission had been made public.

"There was a report," I replied, "that he has come to ask for money, horses, and corn."

When the Envoy from Constantinople arrived at Alexandria the Viceroy sent for him. He is a General named Reschid Pacha. He presented a letter from the Sultan's Minister of War, Riza Pacha, who claimed from the generosity of Said Pacha, in consideration of the urgency and gravity of the present state of affairs, an extraordinary subsidy of horses, mules, and corn. Two days later, the prince took me aside, and, with a very satisfied air, told me what follows. (I have been very careful not, inany way, to change his words, which I wrote down immediately.)

I replied to Riza Pacha that if his request had been made by the intervention of the Porte, to which I have just now but little reason to be grateful, I should have flatly refused; but that, wishing to do a kindness to the one of all the Ministers who has shown himself the most favourable to my project of making a Canal through the Isthmus of Suez, and who has not been afraid to defend it in the Council against an opposition so dreaded *by others*, I was very willing to send what he desired; but that, as every one must look to his own interests, I should at present only prepare the supplies, which would be sent off by return of the vessel which should bring the sanction of the Sultan to my project of the Canal between the two seas.

In a second letter, addressed to Kiamil Pacha, to whom I can freely tell all my thoughts, I have severely rebuked my good brother-in-law, and have reproached him for his cowardice with regard to the threats of Lord Stratford, whose tool he has become. You are, I said, like a man attacked by fever. I might be excused from replying to you in the midst of your delirium, for medicine is only administered to fever patients when the crisis is past; but as my explanations are necessary to *other persons*, I will inform you that I do not throw myself into the arms of France any more than into those of England. It might be wished that this were the case where you are. I am a 'Turco-Egyptian: my project is conceived for the good of Egypt and for the glory and profit of the Empire, and has not been influenced by any foreign Power. It is so favourable to the commerce and intercourse of the whole world, that if we did not put it into execution now, in terms agreeable to ourselves, the time would come when it would be forced upon us, upon terms which would not be agreeable to us. I have no reply to make to you on the subject of the threat respecting the English fleet: it is only the effect of your fever. As to what is said respecting the favour of my sovereign, to whom I am constantly giving proofs of devotion, I do not believe it. Yet, even if he were to be deceived, I would expose myself to his displeasure; and as I govern *hereditarily*, the difficulty would be solved by a pardon, which I would solicit, and which I should obtain. To conclude, I have given Kiamil Pacha to understand that if he continues to act and write as he has done on this occasion, my connection with him will be at an end.

The Viceroy has displayed in this correspondence a firmness, a talent, and an astuteness on which I have very sincerely complimented him. He himself dictated to his secretary his reply to Riza Pacha in the presence of the Envoy from Constantinople. This affair will prove to those at Stamboul that, when I spoke in the prince's name, I was acquainted with his wishes and intentions. He appears to me to nourish a violent resentment against Reschid Pacha, whom he considers to be, notwithstanding his reputation in Europe, a mere political cypher.

You cannot imagine, said he to me, all the money which that man has had from my father and myself, from his first embassy to Paris up to this time; but this did not prevent him from doing much injury to my father, and from endeavouring to do the same to me. By the bye, what do you think chiefly occupies the mind of this statesman in his intercourse with me? He has sent me a young female slave, whose beauty, grace, and education he praises highly. He is very anxious to know, on the one hand, whether I am pleased with her, and, on the other, whether this present has annoyed the princess. She is in my house; but I assure you that I have not yet even looked at her.

The letters which I receive from all quarters prove to me the sympathy with which the scheme of the Suez Canal is received in Europe. Here is the copy of a letter from M. Guizot to Count d'Escayrac:

I much desire the accomplishment of the design of a canal. I wish it for the benefit of the civilised world, and a little from selfish motives also. It will be the realisation of one of the schemes which, I will not say I had dreamed of, but had foreseen, and had even in some degree commenced. The present Viceroy, by carrying out this great enterprise, will gain much honour, will raise the position of Egypt considerably, and will be certain to obtain great credit in Europe. Neither I nor any other person can say what the Mohammedan East will become, in consequence of the efforts which are now being made to maintain or to transform it; but, in any case, the grand Mediterranean canal through Suez will change the relations between Europe and Asia. This is a result which is worth the trouble of being sought after, and which will perhaps be attained amidst the gloom and tempests of war.

XXXVIII.

To Comte de Lesseps, Paris.

ALEXANDRIA, *April* 8, 1853.

M. BAUDE, in an article in the *Revue des Deux Mondes*, supports Talabot's plan of an indirect course. He decides peremptorily that the Delta and the deposits on the eastern coast of Egypt are entirely caused by the slime of the Nile, which will choke up the opening of the Canal on the Mediterranean side. This is an error which will be combated by the publication of the prospectus of Linant Bey and Mougel Bey. The sediment held in suspension by the water of the river forms less than 5 per cent. of the deposit on the shores; the remaining 95 per cent. is composed of sand and shingle.

Now it is perfectly well known that the greater proportion of harbours would not be in existence if it were not very easy and very customary to execute works to prevent the deposits made by the sea. This is what will be done, at the spot which may be considered most suitable, in the Bay of Pelusium, and at much less expense and with much more benefit to navigation than would be found in the indirect course, which is 80 leagues in length, has from 18 to 24 locks, and is not sufficiently deep, on account of its crossing the Nile.

However, this question, and all others relating to the execution of the work, will be looked into and decided upon hereafter by a commission, the members of which I shall select from among the most celebrated engineers in Europe.

In the meantime I send you an analysis of the prospectus of the Viceroy's engineers, which, immediately on my arrival in Paris, I shall submit to public discussion by causing it to be translated into various languages and printed.

ANALYSIS OF THE SCHEME OF LINANT BEY AND MOUGEL BEY.
(*Dated Cairo, March* 20, 1855.)

THE Isthmus of Suez is a narrow neck of land, the opposite points of which are Pelusium and Suez. The intersection of two imperceptibly sloping plains, one from Egypt and the other from the nearest high ground in Asia, forms a longitudinal depression of thirty or forty leagues. Nature itself seems to have formed a line of communication between the two seas.

Geology would show that in early times the sea covered the valley of the isthmus. There are, in fact, vast basins, of which the principal, called the Bitter Lakes, show evident marks of the former presence of sea water.

This basin and that of Lake Timsah will be of the greatest possible assistance in forming the Canal.

The Bitter Lakes furnish at once a natural channel ready excavated, and a reservoir with an area of 330,000,000 of square mètres for its supply.

Lake Timsah, situated half way between Suez and Pelusium, in the direct route, will become the internal harbour of the Canal, where vessels may re-victual and repair, and, if necessary, warehouse their goods.

It appears certain that between Suez and Pelusium the excavations will only be in light soil, which will easily be removed by manual labour as far as the water-line, and by dredging to the bottom of the Canal.

Some people are afraid that a canal excavated across the isthmus will quickly be choked by sand, and that the cost of maintenance will be so heavy that it would be necessary to abandon the work after it was finished. Observation, however, clearly disproves this error, since in December and January last we found the remains of all the encampments of the engineers who were at work in 1847; and, to carry back the evidence for many centuries, we still find the banks of the old canal of the Pharaohs and the Caliphs.

During twelve hundred years torrential rains have certainly hollowed out gullies through these banks, obliterating or sweeping them away in places; but nowhere are they buried under the sands, and vestiges of antiquity, dating back for many thousand years, still exist on the surface of the ground.

In one part alone of the proposed Canal, nearing Lake Timsah, we meet with shifting sand-hills, which often change both their forms and positions. The long line of sand-hills between the head of the lake and Pelusium have long since become naturally fixed by the growth of various plants, under the influence of the heat and moisture.

It only remains to solve the more or less controverted question of the entrances of the Canal, both from the Mediterranean and Red Sea. Does the construction in the sea of a double line of pier at a depth of nine mètres, forming a channel wide and deep enough for the passage of every class of shipping, form an insurmountable obstacle to the formation of an entrance at Pelusium?

The proposers of the scheme reply that there is no doubt at all of the possibility of constructing these piers. They quote the examples of the *digue* at Cherbourg, which is 3768 mètres in length, in a depth of water of about fifteen mètres ; Plymouth breakwater, which is 1364 mètres long, in a depth of more than eleven mètres ; and, lastly, that at the Cape of Good Hope, which is 8000 mètres in length, in a depth of more than sixteen métres.

In all these localities the depth of water and the force of the currents have presented difficulties which will not be felt in the works on the Pelusiac coast.

It has been suggested that the shore at Pelusium was subject to the alluvium of the Nile, and that in these districts the sea held in suspension so much mud that the banks formed by the deposits at the entrance of the Canal would soon render it impassable for shipping.

The engineers have established the fact that the earthy matters held in suspension by the waters of the Nile are not in any way concerned in the formation of the deposits on the Egyptian coast, which are derived entirely from the sea. As a proof of this we find the shore at Pelusium is all pure sand. It is well known that sand-banks have long ceased to increase off the Pelusiac coast.

Also, time has preserved the ruins of Pelusium, the position of which is clearly determined.

Strabo, who lived about fifty years before Christ, states in his "Geography" that Pelusium is situated twenty stadia from the sea. Now, twenty stadia is equivalent to the 1600 *toises* measured by the engineer of the French expedition, and to the 3000 mètres which is the distance at present.

On the Suez coast, also, there is no appreciable alteration in the sand-banks. In 1847 the survey of the roadstead then made gave the same soundings as those taken by the French expedition in 1799. Both these results agree with those shown by Commodore Moresby in his fine chart of the Red Sea.

It will, then, only be necessary to construct two piers to form a channel, and to carry them out far enough into the sea to obtain sufficient depth of water for the navigation.

The roadstead of Suez is sheltered from all winds except the southeast. The scheme provides against this inconvenience by proposing an extension of the extremity of the eastern pier in a southerly direction. Besides this, up to the present time, all the vessels lying in Suez Roads have held on well in bad weather, and the store-ship of the Peninsular and Oriental Company, which has been anchored there for two and a half years, has never sustained any damage.

Now that we have proved the possibility of connecting the two seas by cutting through the isthmus, it is essential to point out our plan to place Egypt in connection with the maritime canal.

Towards Lake Timsah another valley, not less remarkable, opens out at right angles to the longitudinal depression of the isthmus, called, in Arabic, Wady Tomilat. It is in these days a waste desert, but this desert was once the Biblical land of Goshen, renowned for its fertility, which the munificence of Pharaoh allotted to the Israelites at the request of his vizier, Joseph, the son of Jacob. This valley still receives throughout its length the overflow of the canals supplied by the Nile, and thus seems to form the natural course of a connecting canal, starting from the river and joining in the centre of the isthmus the great line of maritime navigation.

The scheme proposes to excavate in this valley a canal, intended at once for the irrigation of the land and for inland navigation; at the same time it will serve to carry fresh-water to the workmen on the isthmus and to reproduce in that land the ancient fertility which obtained for it its Bible name.

Two secondary branches will leave the fresh-water canal by Lake Timsah,—one towards Suez, the other towards Pelusium.

The necessary cost of the realisation of this scheme is estimated at 185,000,000 of francs.

There can be no doubt that such a capital could easily be raised if divided amongst the richest and most powerful nations of the world, provided it can be shown that such capital will meet with a sufficient return.

This is the last question which the authors of the scheme have examined.

It is undoubted that rapidity and economy of transport always increase the development of commercial transactions to an astonishing degree. Railway traffic has, indeed, exceeded the boldest calculations. To quote only one example: the Orleans Railway has just voted a sum of 10,000,000 francs to enlarge the goods station at Ivry, through which 1,000,000 tons now pass annually.

For some years, by shortening distances, steam navigation has enormously increased the interchange of products between Europe and the distant East.

The opening of the isthmus for large vessels, without the necessity of breaking bulk, and the economy which will result from it, must, without fail, give an immense impulse to commercial relations, which already increase so rapidly.

It is evident that the communications between the two seas must bring about a complete revolution in navigation and commerce. Above all, to convince capitalists, it is no use to base calculations on the possible or the unlikely; we must stick to facts, we must even make allowance for contingencies.

It is in this manner that the authors of the scheme have calculated the certain receipts of the company. In accordance with facts which they have verified, and with recent statistical documents, they have no doubt that they are below the mark in stating that the total commercial transactions between Europe and North America and the countries beyond the Cape of Good Hope and Cape Horn would amount in 1855 to £100,000,000 sterling (or two-and-a-half milliards of francs).

In all probability this amount is already exceeded, and would be a still more insufficient estimate after the opening of the maritime canal

Now let us see what is the certain revenue this valuation would ensure to the Canal :

The two-and-a-half milliards of francs' worth of goods to be carried would represent, at an average moderate valuation of 600 francs per ton, *four million* tons.

We might, without exaggeration, maintain that the whole of this freight would, after a certain time, take the route of the maritime Canal. But the calculations of the scheme are not founded on this presumption, however certain it may be. They suppose that only one half of that quantity would adopt the route of the isthmus, and, therefore, they take only 3,000,000 tons as the amount of shipping on which they could levy tolls.

The toll will be fixed at ten francs per ton. Is the charge too much ? Can the profits of shipping easily afford to pay it ?

The authors of the scheme have proved that the total saving arising from the shortening of the route and the contingent advantages will amount to sixteen francs per ton per 1000 leagues.

This being so, the tariff is but reasonable and moderate.

Linant Bey and Mougel Bey express themselves in these terms on the subject :—

We have such a conviction that the preceding valuation will be quickly exceeded, that we propose that the company should insert in their bye-laws a clause, by which the tariff will be reduced as soon as the dividends shall exceed twenty per cent., so that the commerce of the world may participate in the advantages of this grand and useful enterprise.

XXXIX.

To Comte de Lesseps, Paris.

ALEXANDRIA, *April* 8, 1855.

I SEE that the press is already occupied with the question of the neutrality of the Canal, and inquires whether a contract to that effect is to precede or follow the last stage of the enterprise.

To endeavour to make the execution of the scheme depend on the ratification by all the Powers of the declaration of neutrality issued by the sovereign who makes the grant, would be, as I have said from the very beginning, in my correspondence with Arles Dufour, to put the cart before the horse, and needlessly to expose ourselves to the risk that its performance might be interfered with, and perhaps delayed for more than a century.

Lord Stratford said to me at Constantinople :—

Monsieur de Lesseps, all your explanations are excellent, and if you succeed, the thing is certainly sufficiently grand and important to do you the greatest honour; but it will take a hundred years to bring it about. *The present moment is inopportune.*

I replied :—

My Lord, if the affair is inopportune for you, who do not wish for it, it is opportune for me, who do wish for it; and as you yourself acknowledge that it will be useful, and will do me credit, why postpone it a hundred years? As at that period I shall not be able to witness its completion, and as I have perfect confidence in the possibility of its immediate execution, I am eager to enjoy the pleasure. You ought to be even more eager about it than I am.

To begin by throwing one's self into the arms of European diplomacy would indeed be to thrust one's self into a wasp's nest. I have just escaped one, and I am not inclined to fall into it again.

It is impossible that the whole political world should be agreed while there are opponents of the plan which is decided upon, while there exist means of any kind to gain time, and while there remains one loophole for escape. Diplomacy never decides except when it cannot possibly do otherwise.

When the execution of the Canal has become a matter of history, when no chance is left of paralysing the enterprise, either before, during, or after its execution, the general good will bring about the neutrality of the passage without many protocols.

XL.

To M. Benedetti, French Chargé d'Affaires, Constantinople.

Alexandria, *April* 14, 1855.

My letters from Constantinople háve made me aware of the fact that Lord Stratford, still contenting himself with expressing his private but very decided opinion, has not pronounced any on the part of his Government. He was questioned on the subject: he did not reply. The Porte then determined to address itself directly to London, to ascertain the feeling of the Cabinet at St. James's. The Turkish Ambassador, M. Mussurus, had a long conversation with Lord Clarendon on the project of the Suez Canal. The principal Secretary of State renewed the usual arguments of the opposition, on technical questions and on the proper opportunity. M. Mussurus brought forward, on his side, considerations of general utility; he especially insisted on the universal character of the enterprise. "If that is the case," Lord Clarendon is said to have remarked in conclusion; "if the company is to be a European one, if every one's capital is to be admitted into it, England will have her share in it, and we shall perhaps have no further objection to make."

LXI.

TO THE SAME.

ALEXANDRIA, *April* 14, 1855.

THE Viceroy did beforehand what you begged me to advise him to do. He has expressed his views very plainly by the semi-official medium which was opened to him, while, at the same time, he was deferential and respectful in his thoroughly official relations. Amongst the compliments which he addressed to the Porte, through General Reschid Pacha, he said that he was at the disposal of his sovereign, body and soul, and that, to assist him, *he would sell even his tarbouche.*

I do not intend to hurry myself. The matter will not be brought *before everybody* until it has been carefully elaborated.

The principle admitted by the Viceroy is that all countries, and the greatest possible number of small shareholders, should profit by all the advantages of the company.

The Emperor, in a notice which he published in London in 1846, of the American canal between the two oceans, says:—

> The strength of an undertaking in shares is only secured by the *bonâ fide* holders who invest their capital, and not by speculators who buy only to sell again.

We will endeavour to profit by this axiom.

XLII.
To Madame Delamalle, Paris.
(Continuation of the Journal.)

ALEXANDRIA, *April* 21, 1855.

You mention the agitation and inventions of some financiers. My chief strength in resisting them lies in my position as the Viceroy's plenipotentiary.

I shall always be seconded by this prince, who, in fact, is the head of the whole thing; whereas, if he had made me patentee before the formation of the company, he would, so to speak, have abandoned his rights, and I should have had less strength to resist the monopolies of Governments and speculators.

When I formed the plan of obtaining powers instead of a patent, I was not aware that the same idea had suggested itself to Prince Louis Napoleon (now Emperor of the French) at the time when he was seriously occupied in devising means of executing the inter-oceanic American canal.

In 1842 the attention of the prince, then a prisoner at Ham, was turned towards the plan of making this canal viâ the Lake of Nicaragua. Later on he received a visit from a French naval officer, who was about to set out for Central America. He begged him to ascertain on the spot whether the scheme was practicable. The officer's observations completed the studies of the prince, who published a very interesting notice in London, of which but a very few copies were printed.

In 1846 the prince received at Ham, from M. de Montenegro, Minister of Foreign Affairs in the State of Nicaragua, a letter which conferred upon him officially *all the powers necessary to organise a company in Europe*, and which, moreover, informed him that, by a decision of the 8th of January, 1846, the Government of Nicaragua had determined to give the name of the Napoleon Canal to the great work destined to open a new route to the commerce of the world.

Every one knows how the prince effected his escape to England, when his letter, asking permission to go to America to accomplish the mission entrusted to him, was left unanswered by the French Government. We are assured that he intended to start from London, and put himself at the head of the great undertaking which he had planned, when the Revolution of 1848 took place and opened France to him.

Those who, like myself, neither welcomed him nor voted for the Empire, cannot but acknowledge, when they travel in foreign countries, how he restored the reputation of France and must own that their prejudice against him was less justifiable than the instinct and good sense of the people.

I have now in my hands a copy of the prince's notice, written in English, and I will translate a few extracts for you:

> Central America (in the matter which is now occupying us, we may substitute Turkey) can only emerge from its present state of languor by following the example of the United States, that is to say, it must commence by borrowing workmen and capital from Europe.
>
> The prosperity of Central America (we may say the same of Turkey) is bound up with the interests of civilisation in general, and the best means of labouring for the good of humanity is by beating down the barriers which separate men, races, and nations. This is the progress pointed out to us by Christianity and by the efforts of great men who have, from time to time, appeared on the scene of the world. The Christian religion teaches us that we are all brethren, and that, in the eye of God, the slave is as good as his master; and the Asiatic, the African, and the Red Indian are the equals of the European. On the other hand, the great men of the world have, by their wars, mingled different races, and have left behind them some of those imperishable monuments—such as the levelling of mountains, the clearing of forests, the canalisation of rivers—which, by facilitating communication, serve to unite individuals and nations and bring them nearer to each other.
>
> War and commerce have civilised the world. Commerce is now continuing her conquests. Let us open to her a new route. Let us bring

the tribes of Oceania and Australia nearer to Europe. Let us cause them to participate in the blessings of Christianity and civilisation.

In order to carry out this great undertaking we appeal to all religious and intelligent men, for it is worthy of their zeal and their sympathy. We claim the support of all statesmen, since all nations are interested in the establishment of a new and easy means of communication between the two hemispheres; lastly, we address capitalists, because, in taking part in a glorious enterprise, they are certain to reap great pecuniary advantages from it.

In a few days I am going to arrange with the Viceroy for my speedy return to France.

XLIII.

CONFIDENTIAL MEMORANDUM ADDRESSED TO HIS HIGHNESS MOHAMMED SAID, AT MAREIA CAMP.

ALEXANDRIA, *April* 18, 1855.

IN order to arrange our course of action in the matter of the Canal I am about to communicate to your Highness my private information from Paris and Constantinople.

I will commence by the news from Paris. The first news of your Highness's plan was given to the Minister of Foreign Affairs, M. Drouyn de Lhuys, December 13th, by the following telegraphic despatch from Marseilles :—

> The Viceroy has given permission to M. de Lesseps to cut through the Isthmus of Suez. A canal is to be made between the two seas. Applications will be made to the capitalists of all nations for the means of executing this great work.

M. Thouvenel, the Political Director of the Ministry, communicated this despatch to my brother, the Commercial Director, adding from himself, "This is a great piece of news; I hasten to send it to you." . . .

The next day M. Drouyn de Lhuys received a visit from Lord Cowley, the English Ambassador, who arrived in a great state of agitation to ask him for an explanation of what had taken place in Egypt, and to ascertain if there had been a previous agreement between the French Government and myself. M. Drouyn de Lhuys very simply stated the truth, which was that he was entirely ignorant of what I had done in Egypt; that he had not seen me before my departure; and that it was publicly known that since my mission to Rome I had had no intercourse with the Emperor, or with his Government. He added, however, with much dignity, that should the event, which he had just heard for the first time, take place he should personally be delighted and ready to support my undertaking.

Lord Cowley then addressed himself to the Emperor, whose reserve on the subject was supposed to denote feelings favourable to the views of the English Cabinet. One of my friends was uneasy about it, and wrote to me as follows:—

The Empress says that on the last occasion of her mentioning the subject, the Emperor replied that she might make herself easy, and added these words: *the thing will be done.* She insisted on keeping the letters and documents, and said that she had determined to read them all and to understand everything.

The Emperor, who afterwards worked with M. Thouvenel during the absence of M. Drouyn de Lhuys, spoke to him in a favourable manner. He desired M. Thouvenel to write to Count Walewski, in London, to order him to bring the matter before the English Cabinet, and to express to him all the interest which he felt in it, reserving it to himself to mention it to those who had a right to hear of it during his approaching stay in England, where he is going, with the Empress, to pay a visit to the Queen.

I hear from Constantinople:

M. Benedetti has heard of the correspondence between Kiamil Pacha and his brother-in-law, the Viceroy, and he has succeeded in procuring the memoranda written by the Grand Vizier, Reschid Pacha's own hand, which were used to guide this correspondence. He commenced by having an explanation directly with Reschid Pacha, accusing him of being the inspirer of the letter in which the Emperor's name was introduced in an unsuitable manner. The Grand Vizier defended himself as best he could, which was badly enough, by throwing the blame of the proceeding on Kiamil Pacha. Instructions were asked for from Paris; the Sultan was informed of everything; and, after several meetings of the Cabinet Council, Reschid Pacha has been superseded, for the satisfaction of the natural susceptibility of the French Government.

The result of all this is that we shall be for some time quiet as far as regards Constantinople. I can, therefore, return to France, to perform my mission and to act agreeably to the programme which your Highness is pleased to approve.

Report to his Highness Mohammed Said Pacha, Viceroy of Egypt.

MAREIA CAMP, *April* 30, 1855.

I HAD the honour of submitting to your Highness the report of your engineers, Linant Bey and Mougel Bey, upon the canalisation of the Isthmus of Suez.

This work is designed to serve as the preamble to the cutting through of the Isthmus. It is accompanied by a map indicating the nature and configuration of the ground. It has merited the approbation of your Highness, who has directed me to give it the greatest possible publicity, in order to direct the attention, and to appeal to the examination and observations, of all competent men in Europe and America to a question which interests the whole world.

Your Highness decided to send immediately to the Ministers of his Imperial Majesty the Sultan the explanations which they require before ratifying the scheme of the maritime canal. For myself, I shall start for Europe directly.

I shall hasten to have the official documents connected with the proposed work printed, as well as the scheme of Linant Bey and Mougel Bey.

Arrangements will be made to obtain, within a limited time, the opinions of experts who may be willing to give the enterprise the benefit of their judgment. In the interim, your engineers will prepare the details of their definite scheme.

When this definite scheme is completed, and when the observations received from the various countries have been codified, a commission of engineers celebrated for their hydraulic works in England, France, Germany, and Holland will be named. This commission will pronounce an opinion on the scheme of your Highness's engineers, and will point out any modifications or alterations which may seem desirable. Every facility will be given to the commission to visit the Isthmus of Suez, should it be considered necessary to examine the locality before deciding.

Your Highness has now decided to circumscribe the routes to be examined within certain limits. After having deliberated on the numerous projects laid before the Government or the public during the last fifty years or more, you leave the commission quite free to adopt the best plan that science can suggest to form the communication between the Red Sea and the Mediterranean, by cutting through the Isthmus of Suez at any part of the isthmus to the eastward of the course of the Nile; but you have declared that you will not authorise the company of the great Suez Maritime Canal to adopt a route which will commence on the Mediterranean side to the west of the Damietta branch, and which will pass up the Nile itself.

It is not till after the route between the two seas has been adopted, and all the advantages and risks of those who will take part in the enterprise are well determined, that capitalists and the public will be asked to subscribe for shares, and the representatives of the interested parties will decide finally on all questions concerning the administration, execution, and performance of the enterprise.

Allow me now to explain to your Highness the preliminary works which Linant Bey and Mougel Bey will have to undertake, at once, before presenting their scheme, which are as follows :—

1. To lay out on the ground the line of the maritime canal in all its details, with all its angles and curves, and to reproduce the line so laid out on a plan.

2. To take the levels along this line, carrying them out into both seas as far as a depth of water of 10 mètres.

3. To take cross sections wherever the nature of the ground requires it.

4. To take soundings all along the line, and to carry them out to a depth of 10 mètres below low-water level in the Mediterranean.

5. To obtain samples of the different descriptions of ground discovered in the operations.

6. To fix the first cost of labour and of all the materials that will be employed in the construction of the Canal.

7. To form solid grounds for calculating the number of workmen of all classes that will be required for the execution of the work.

For my part, I shall take care to collect all the newest statistical documents, in order to fix the minimum valuation of the results.

When the time arrives to commence the construction of the maritime canal, it will be necessary to obtain from Europe a great number of engines and a large quantity of materials—wood, iron, coal, &c.

The Suez Canal Company will find the safety, economy, and facility of transport still desirable in the as yet unfinished railway to Suez, and in the establishment of the Towing Company, which has undertaken the improvement of the Mahmoudieh canal, in addition to completing its communication with the harbour of Alexandria.

The letters that I have received from Europe bear witness to the ever-increasing interest with which the scheme of the canal is everywhere received. Some persons among those who have spontaneously given their concurrence have placed considerable sums at my disposal as a contribution to the preliminary expenses of the enterprise. These offers already amount to more than 15 millions of francs. I do not think there will be any occasion to make use of them; but I have made a list of those who have made them, and your Highness will doubtless think it right to give them priority when the time comes to allot shares.

Your Highness has already agreed upon a first list of sixty foundation members, fulfilling the conditions required by the 11th Article of the Firman. Your Highness, in charging me with the duty of completing it by the addition of those who have assisted me in Europe or America in the preparation of this work, desired that, if possible, the total number should not exceed one hundred.

Your Highness has been pleased to approve the provisional nomination of M. Ruyssenaers, Consul-General for Holland, as head agent of the company in Egypt. In every sense he merits this mark of your confidence.

Such are the preliminary steps which, in your Highness's opinion, will promote the success of this great enterprise. I beg you, Sire, to inform me if I thoroughly understand your intentions.

     (Signed) Ferdinand de Lesseps.

XLIV.

To my Devoted, High-born, and Distinguished Friend, M. Ferdinand de Lesseps.

     Alexandria, *May* 19, 1855.

I have received, and approve, your report of the 30th April, which may serve you in lieu of instructions. The zeal and friendly interest you have shown in the matter are fully appreciated by me, and have given me a great satisfaction.

Ramadan 3, 1271.   Official Seal of the Viceroy.
Translation from the Turkish text.
  The Private Secretary of his Highness the Viceroy,
    (Signed) Kœnig Bey.

XLV.

To Comte de Lesseps, Paris.

     Alexandria, *May* 6, 1855.

Our correspondence from Paris and Constantinople has caused the Viceroy to decide on my departure for France.

Said Pacha is therefore going to send direct to the Porte, according to the official demand addressed to him, the explanations and information which are considered necessary for the ratification of his project. I enclose you a copy of the memorandum which I sent the prince some days ago, and which is still unpublished.

The Viceroy told me that Kiamil Pacha, in a recent letter (addressed probably to the princess, his wife, who resides at Alexandria), acknowledges the pressure put upon him by Reschid Pacha, who, to use his own expression, "*has sunk up to his beard in Lord Stratford's pool.*" He adds that, though Said Pacha may reckon on the friendship of the Grand Vizier in other matters, "*the ties he has formed leave him no liberty in that of Suez.*" The knowledge of this circumstance, and the prince's delicate feelings, which did not allow him to let himself be looked upon as the instrument of France, in the event of our Government considering itself offended by the Grand Vizier, and demanding his dismissal, caused him to give up the idea of my return to Constantinople. I shared his feelings, and told him that, for my part, it did not appear to me to be wise for me to go to Stamboul, as by going I might be a restraint on the policy of my country, which probably might not desire to exercise its power on any question but that of the Crimean War.

The matter having remained in itself Turco-Egyptian, though its results are destined to be universal, it will be for the Emperor to judge if it is wise to remove it from this ground, in case hereafter an adverse policy should endeavour to injure the interests of France, which are concerned in the enterprise.

If England is not yet persuaded, the state of affairs might become delicate, and I can conceive that there are transient diplomatic necessities which it would be imprudent in any way to ignore.

In his official despatch Reschid Pacha informed the Viceroy that Lord Stratford, whose intervention he did not scruple to publish in this manner, owned that the Suez Canal might not be free from inconvenience, and was useless, while the railway was perfectly sufficient, and that the English Ambassador had charged the Agent and Consul-General of her Britannic Majesty to make other important observations to the Viceroy.

Said Pacha, in his reply, to which are annexed the memoranda of his engineers, the maps, plans, estimates, and other documents, says that the railway, which necessitates unlading and re-lading, can never take the place of the Canal for the commerce of the world; that England will benefit by it as much as, and even more than, other nations; but that, even if she judges differently, there can be no occasion for her opinion to be shared by the counsellors and subjects of the Grand Seigneur, who, simply as good Mohammedans, ought to make a point of securing a communication between Turkey and the sacred spots of Arabia, and of saving the lives of thousands of the faithful who are destined every year to sink under the fatigues of a long and difficult pilgrimage.

The Viceroy remarks that Mr. Bruce, the English Agent, has said nothing to him on the subject.

XLVI.
To the Same.

ALEXANDRIA, *May 12,* 1855.

THE Grand Vizier, Reschid Pacha, has been dismissed. Whatever may be the ostensible reason of his disgrace, he has fallen solely in consequence of the discovery of his intrigues against France in the matter of the Canal. Thus, to commence our voyage, we have a statesman overboard; there will be others, perhaps, in the same predicament by and bye.

Kiamil Pacha writes to the Viceroy that the fall of the Grand Vizier has been caused by this fact, and that he himself, although he was spared out of consideration for his brother-in-law, felt it his duty to give in his resignation.

In case it might not suit our policy to make immediate use of all our opportunities of hurrying on the operation of the Firman of ratification, I wished to fortify the mind of the Viceroy against the impression which might be caused by our reserve. I told him that it was understood in Paris, as well as by myself, that the question ought not to be carried either to Paris or London; that, until there should be a new arrangement, it ought to remain Turco-Egyptian, and that, probably, there was, as yet, no reason for changing our friendly intervention into an official one. I added that it appeared to me essential to leave to the Egyptian prince his right of owner of the soil, and to the Porte the merit of its ratification, and not to bring on the open interference of the two Governments most influential in the affairs of the East, which, in this Suez question, would not be at all in accordance.

The persistent opposition of the English, and the opinion formally expressed by Lord Stratford that the railway ought to be sufficient for everything, or, to speak more correctly, ought to serve the English interests only, gave the Viceroy matter for reflection. He believes that there would be danger hereafter if, as he is required to do, he gave up the railway, which traverses the centre of Egypt, to a company, of which the English would be the real masters.

He has formed a resolution to complete the line of railway at his own expense, and he has announced his intention to give notice of the steps which are about to be taken, so as to give due heed to English interests; he has entered into a contract with an English firm (Messrs. Briggs & Co.) for the supply of the metals necessary for the construction of the railway, and one of his engineers (M. Mouchelet) is commissioned to commence, without delay, the surveys and the embankments on the road from Cairo to Suez.

This decision is very important, as furnishing a precedent to which to refer against the opposition of the English to our Canal.

When I told Reschid Pacha, during my stay in Constantinople, that the English Ambassador, having at one time supported the right of the Viceroy to make a railway in Egypt without even requiring the authorisation of the Porte, could not, with a good grace, prevent the making of the Canal, for which we submitted to the ratification of the Sultan; he retorted that the arrangement made by Abbas Pacha, on the request of the Consul-General of England, related to a railway between Alexandria and Cairo, and that this inland track could not be compared to the canal between the two seas. He added that there had been no idea of prolonging the line to Suez, which could alone constitute a means of communication between the two seas.

XLVII.

To the Same.

ALEXANDRIA, *May* 19, 1855.

BEFORE embarking for France I had a conversation with Mr. Bruce, the Agent and Consul-General for England. He was the first to bring forward the question of the Suez Canal: he told me that, since the month of November last, he had not received one line from his Government on this matter, not even an acknowledgment of the receipt of the documents which I had handed over to him, and which he had hastened to transmit to London. He added, that he hoped my journey to Paris, and that I proposed making to England, would contribute to bring about, if necessary, a good understanding between the two Governments, especially now that the Viceroy has determined to continue the railway to Suez, as he considers that this decision, cordially received by English politicians, removes all pretext for any opposition to the Canal project. Our conversation took place in the presence of Lord Haddo, son of Lord Aberdeen. I am very much afraid that Mr. Bruce, supposing him to be sincere, as I believe he is, will not be the representative of the English Cabinet in Egypt much longer.

I expect to find in M. Walewski, our new Minister of Foreign Affairs, one of the warmest partisans of the Suez Canal. I have a letter, written a short time ago from the Embassy in London, in which he promises me his best support in an undertaking respecting which he spoke to Mehemet Ali at the time of his mission in Egypt in 1840, and in which he feels the greatest interest.

XLVIII.

MEMORANDUM PRESENTED TO THE EMPEROR RELATING TO THE INSTRUCTIONS TO BE GIVEN TO M. THOUVENEL WHEN APPOINTED AMBASSADOR TO CONSTANTINOPLE.

PARIS, *June* 5, 1855.

THE two Governments (English and French) have, in a way, agreed not to act officially at Constantinople in the matter of the Isthmus of Suez, but to allow the question to be arranged between the Sultan and the Viceroy.

It would be necessary to keep the affair in this position for the present, or rather, to speak more clearly, for the French Ambassador to abstain from using his official weight to influence the Porte in favour of the ratification, and for the English Ambassador, on his part, to abstain from demanding of the Porte any engagement contrary to the ratification.

If Lord Stratford does not keep to this agreement, M Thouvenel will, on his side, become free.

XLIX.

Memorandum presented to Count Walewski, Minister of Foreign Affairs.

PARIS, *June* 7, 1855.

I BEG Count Walewski to do me the favour of obtaining his Imperial Majesty's commands for my journey to London, whither I am prepared immediately to proceed.

I consider that it is still wise to maintain the private nature of the Suez affair, and not to expose ourselves to the risk of letting it depend on the wishes of a Government, which would be unfavourable to the enterprise.

Supposing it necessary to reply to objections or propositions which might be made, shall I be authorised to say that the Emperor's Government will be found agreed with England from this time in declaring that commercial navigation shall at no time be hindered by a belligerent Power?

In order not to wound foreign susceptibilities it is necessary to point out, when the occasion shall present itself, that the permission to make the Suez Canal has not been granted to a Frenchman nor to a French company. M. de Lesseps, as a friend of the Viceroy of Egypt, received his plenary powers to form a universal company, to which *alone* should be granted the permission for the undertaking.

L.

Memorandum presented to the Emperor.

PARIS, *June* 9, 1855.

IN the audience which your Majesty graciously granted me on my return from Egypt, you desired me to go to England immediately, and to place myself in communication with the *Times*.

I have the honour to inform your Majesty that I am ready to start for London, and that Mr. O'Meagher, Paris Correspondent of the *Times*, with whom I became very intimate during the disturbances at Barcelona and when I was Minister at Madrid, has undertaken to send to his chief the account herewith enclosed, as his own opinion on the affair of Suez.

Communication sent to the "Times" by Mr. O'Meagher.

PARIS, *June* 19, 1855.

THE Viceroy of Egypt, in November last, caused to be communicated to the Consuls-General resident in his dominions a Firman, by virtue of which he desired M. Ferdinand de Lesseps to organise a universal company, to which should be granted permission to cut through the Isthmus of Suez. Thus the grant was not given, as has been unjustly stated, to a Frenchman or to a French company, but to a body of shareholders of all countries, which is to be formed by the care of the Viceroy, of his representative, and of his agent.

M. de Lesseps hastened at once to give this explanation to Mr. Bruce, Consul-General of her Britannic Majesty in Egypt. His letters testify to his constant desire to avoid everything which could give offence to natural susceptibility; we know that his efforts contributed not a little to persuade the Viceroy to determine on the completion of the railway from Cairo to Suez, a result which had been long desired by English politicians.

When he afterwards went to Constantinople he kept up friendly relations with Lord Stratford de Redcliffe, and although the Grand Vizier had entrusted him with an official letter to the Viceroy of Egypt, in which the scheme of cutting through the Isthmus of Suez was spoken of as most *useful and interesting*, he would not insist upon obtaining the Sultan's ratification when he became aware of the formal opposition of the English Ambassador. Lord Stratford having informed the Divan that he was about to send a report to his Government, and having requested that nothing should be decided until he should have received his instructions, M. de Lesseps, always anxious not to give any opportunity for an official manifestation of a difference of opinion between the Ambassadors of France and England, quitted Constantinople and returned to Egypt, contenting himself, for the time, with the letter from the Grand Vizier which I have just mentioned.

As soon as the Viceroy's engineers had finished a very interesting and conclusive memorial on the canalisation of the Isthmus of Suez, M. de Lesseps occupied himself, with his Highness Mohammed Said Pacha, in arranging the principal basis of the organisation of the company.

We have been assured that in the projected distribution of 200,000,000 francs to be divided among the different countries according to their present or future importance in the trade of the Indies, Great Britain is set down at 40,000,000 and France at 30,000,000.

M. de Lesseps, instead of returning to Constantinople, where he feared that he might not find, on the question of the Isthmus of Suez, the agreement which is to be desired between the Embassy of England and that of France, has to-day returned to France; where, in pursuance of the Viceroy's instructions, he will publish the official documents relating to the affair, with the engineers' memorial and plans.

We learn with pleasure that he has hitherto refused to enter into any engagement, or even to hold a conversation with any French or foreign capitalist, and that, before taking any step, he will go to London, where we hope he will find statesmen and capitalists favourable to an enterprise which, being of universal interest, seems to him to deserve our sympathy, if it is not directed by a spirit of exclusive nationality, and if it appears, from an impartial examination of the question, that the interests of Great Britain, far from being unfavourably affected by the canal through the Isthmus of Suez, will receive from it greater advantages than those obtained by any other nation. Up to this time no serious objection has been made in England to the opening of the Isthmus of Suez by a maritime canal, while many of our countrymen, among others Sir James Welch, captain in the Royal Engineers, and our celebrated author, Charles Dickens, have pointed out its usefulness.

It has been said that, in case of a war with France, England would run the risk of seeing her neighbour's fleets get ahead of her in the Indian Ocean. If the world were threatened with so great a misfortune as a collision between France and England, which we, on our part think impossible, a fleet of hostile steamships would not need to go so far to attack a Power which possesses, on the direct route to the Indies, the military chain of Gibraltar, Malta, and Aden.

We read in a recent publication : " The possessor of Aden can open and close the Red Sea at his pleasure, and if the influence of the nations and Governments of the world is to be measured principally by the good or harm they can do to their adversaries, there can surely be no small advantage to England in a change which would cause the chief part of the traffic of the globe to pass under the batteries of her forts and vessels. Is it from the Mediterranean fleets that England has most to fear an attack in India? In any case, the safety of her settlements may depend upon the lessening of the distance from her base of operation.

"India is not the only British possession the route to which will be shortened by the passage through Suez ; Australia will benefit by it no less, and it is all the more necessary to increase the defences of that country, as, if the Canal is made through the American isthmus, it will become more accessible to the ships of war of the United States.

"We may conclude from these observations that the opening of the Isthmus of Suez will involve very little risk of weakening the military power of the British Isles. It cannot compromise their commercial power, unless the diminution of 3000 miles in the distance which separates them from India should lessen the traffic between them, and unless those who produce and supply the merchandise of the extreme East should be injured by the fact that their consumption will be doubled in Europe.

"If England gains an increase of military and commercial power by the opening of the isthmus, the spirit of gain will soon triumph over her somewhat inconsiderate opposition. She will not sacrifice the absolute elevation, the base of which is enlarged with the development which surrounds it, to the relative elevation, which contents itself with lowering others, and she will no longer give any one a right to use to her, with regard to all the nations bordering on the Mediterranean, the language which is employed elsewhere respecting Greece and the East. She turns away from such a policy. Knowing that her strength lies in her power of expansion and her capacity for traffic, she seeks in the prosperity of her neighbours the enlargement of the bases of her own, and it is on this account that she has strengthened, by her assistance, so many enterprises which are highly beneficial to the Continent. She will never have encouraged one more remunerative to herself than that of a canal through the Isthmus of Suez. Her own interest is our guarantee, and as soon as she has discovered it, in spite of some deceptive appearances, we shall no longer have her opposition to fear."

We are told also that in the event of a number of European workmen being brought to the Isthmus of Suez there might be a risk that, if these workmen belonged almost entirely to one nation, the policy of another nation might be unpleasantly affected by it. This objection, which, moreover, might be set aside even if the work were going to be executed by European workmen, falls to the ground as soon as it is known that the company of the Suez Canal will have the best reasons for employing only Egyptians as daily workmen. The Fellahs of Egypt are, so to speak, born navigators. It is they alone who, under the direction of engineers and of skilful and experienced overseers, have performed all extensive works which have been undertaken up to this time. No nation can supply more easily or more cheaply a disciplined troop of active, robust, sober, and intelligent men for working at canals or at hydraulic constructions.

LI.
To M. S. W. Ruyssenaers, Alexandria.
PARIS, *June* 14, 1855.

My two former letters have informed you of the various phases of the question of the Canal from the day that I arrived in Paris.

M. Thouvenel had a farewell audience of the Emperor yesterday, and received from him his last instructions. His Majesty took the very memorandum of which I sent you a copy from one of the drawers of his writing-table. He desired the Ambassador to act in conformity with it, informing the Porte and the Sultan, however, of his wish that the ratification should be sent directly to the Viceroy of Egypt, and authorising M. Thouvenel to express his disapprobation if any hostile proceedings on the part of Lord Stratford should be taken into consideration.

I am invited to spend this evening at the Tuileries. I shall thus have an opportunity of seeing the Emperor and Empress again, and of receiving their directions for my journey to London. M. Damas Hinard, Secretaire des Commandements, who yesterday entertained at dinner the heads of the Ministry of Foreign Affairs, told me that I should be able to set out for London by the end of the week.

You see that our affairs could not be going on better. Fortunate events—connections which are formed or renewed at the very moment that it is desirable, prove to me every day more and more that the scheme of the canal between the two seas is directed by Providence and that it cannot but succeed.

M. Barthélemy Saint-Hilaire is beginning to give me his assistance in my labours.

I enclose you a note which was addressed to me by Baron James Rothschild, to whom I was able to render some services during my embassy to Madrid. We have had the conference he proposed. He asked me about my plans for the financial organisation of the scheme. I told him openly that I would not at present enter into an engagement with any one; that the matter was being investigated and negotiated; that I should bring it forward only when it was freed from every uncertainty as to its execution which might still exist in the eyes of the public; but that, the moment circumstances permitted, he would be one of the first whose useful and gratifying assistance I should seek. Baron Rothschild thoroughly approved of my plan, told me that I was taking up a very good position, congratulated me, and offered his services. Having learned that I was going to England, he sent me a letter for his firm in London, which I copy verbatim, because, bearing in mind the excellent judgment of this prince of finance, I consider it as one of the greatest encouragements. It is as follows:—

We have the pleasure of introducing to you M. Ferdinand de Lesseps, Minister Plenipotentiary, who has lately arrived from Egypt, where he has been much occupied, as you know, with the business of the Canal through the Isthmus of Suez.

We cannot doubt that you will have great pleasure in seeing M. de Lesseps, who proposes to converse with you on this subject. On our own part, we can only strongly recommend him to you, and beg you to pay the utmost attention to his interesting communications, the importance of which you, like myself, will be able to appreciate.

M. Thiers, moreover, announced to me this morning that Lord Ashburton, the brother of the Barings, the great London bankers, who is just now in Paris, has written to his family and friends in a very favourable manner of the Suez Canal, and that I shall have a warm reception from them.

Tell his Highness that one of the circumstances which has produced the most satisfactory effect on the mind of the Emperor and of our statesmen, was his resolution, as a pledge of the interest which he will take in the enterprise, to have all the surveyings, sounding, levelling, &c., completed at his own expense. It is right, therefore, that the orders which he has graciously permitted me to give on the subject should be fulfilled.

I have acquainted Khalil Bey, whose correspondence is sent direct to the Viceroy, with the principal results of my proceedings.

LII.

CIRCULAR TO THE ORIGINAL SHAREHOLDERS IN EGYPT.

PARIS, *June* 18, 1855.

THE execution of the scheme of cutting through the Isthmus of Suez can no longer, it appears, be subject to any doubt. It is therefore necessary to form, in the usual manner and in the common interest, a company of original shareholders, selected by virtue of the terms of the Firman of his Highness Mohammed Said, dated November 30, 1854, of my statement to the prince of the 30th of April, 1855, and of his order of the 3rd Ramadan 1271, informing me that my statement was to take the place of any instructions.

I have the honour to inform you that you have been chosen an original shareholder of the Universal Company of the Maritime Suez Canal, and that, in consideration of this, you are required to deposit in the hands of Mr. S. W. Ruyssenaers, of Alexandria, between this date and the 1st of September next, the sum, either of 5000 francs or of 2500 francs, according to whether you receive a whole or half share, as an original holder.

This deposit, intended to provide for the preparatory expenses, an account of which will be rendered to you hereafter, is made by each of us solely to forward the success of the enterprise, to which we intend to devote all our efforts; it does not make us responsible either to each other or to any third party; and, in conjunction with the advances so generously made by his Highness, it will enable us to bring the operation safely to maturity and to choose the most favourable moment for arranging the other shares.

In return for your deposit you will receive, later on, in case of success, and on the legal formation of the company, a number of shares in proportion to your disbursement.

LIII.

To M. Arles Dufour, Paris.

Paris, June 18, 1855.

I HAVE just received your letter of the 16th. You know that from the very beginning of my intercourse with you respecting the Suez Canal I assured you that the Universal Company, the formation of which was entrusted to me by the Viceroy of Egypt, owed no more to the Surveying Society of 1847 than to any other authors of separate or collective works, great numbers of whom have for the last fifty years occupied themselves in the survey of the Isthmus of Suez.

I had only just returned to Paris when you desired M. Girette to make a communication to me. You were made acquainted with my reply, which was as follows :—

Paris, June 1, 1855.

I have received your letter dated yesterday, accompanied by a note from M. Arles Dufour.

M. Arles Dufour is mistaken as to the nature of the assistance which I asked from him. I could not but be surprised to find that, notwithstanding the clearness of my previous letters, he should have thought it his duty to take no notice of the withdrawal recommended to him, or of my formally pronounced opinion respecting the Surveying Society of 1847, to which I have always been and have always wished to remain a stranger.

His mistake is shown in the note which you have kindly sent me, in which I hear, for the first time, of confederacy between us. I have no confederacy with any one, as I am only the representative or agent of the Viceroy, entrusted by him with plenary powers to form the Universal Company, to which has been granted the permission to make the Canal.

All misunderstanding will be at an end when I have the pleasure of seeing M. Arles. One may continue to be on friendly terms with a person without agreeing with him on certain subjects.

What I have just recalled to your memory removes the necessity for my replying in detail to your letter of the 16th.

I shall content myself with formally repudiating the idea that I could possibly endeavour in any way to detach from you any of your old associates in the Surveying Society.

I shall accept, in the name of the Viceroy of Egypt,

the co-operation of all men of honour who offer me the help of their intelligence freely and spontaneously. Being free myself from any tie of precedent, I do not think that the time has yet come for entering into an engagement with any one. I have only offered Messrs. de Bruck and de Negrelli, on behalf of the prince, whom I represent, to be original shareholders of the future Universal Company, which offer I also made to you. In acting thus I was guided simply by a feeling of justice, and I had no wish at all to interfere in *your affairs.*

As to me, I do not look upon the Suez Canal as *my business;* at present it is that of the Viceroy of Egypt, by-and-bye it will be that of every one.

LIV.

Rough Draft of a Reply to an English Memorandum, presented to Count Walewski, Minister of Foreign Affairs, at his request.

PARIS, *June* 19, 1855.

Lord Clarendon, in a despatch to Lord Cowley, which has been communicated to the French Government, announces that the Government of her Britannic Majesty foresees some inconvenience in leaving the question of the Canal through the Isthmus of Suez to be decided between the Sultan and the Viceroy of Egypt; because in that case the agents and partisans of the two allied countries, making use of their influence at Constantinople and Alexandria, might, by underhand dealing and intrigue, revive a spirit of rivalry and antagonism which has happily disappeared from the policy of the two Governments.

The question being under examination, Lord Clarendon offered the following objections:—

First Objection.

The Suez Canal is physically impossible; and if it could be executed, it would be at such an expense that no profit could be obtained from it as a commercial speculation, which proves that it could only be undertaken from political motives.

Reply.

If the Suez Canal is physically impossible, those who fear that their interests might be affected by its execution need not trouble themselves about it. If it could only be done at an expense which would not be in proportion to the profits to be gained from it, it would be equally impracticable, as the Viceroy of Egypt entrusts the task of its formation, without even guaranteeing any interest, to a company of free capitalists of all nations, without making any exceptions, without offering any special advantage to any country, and without asking for the intervention or assistance of foreign Governments. Under these conditions it is evident that private persons who are not fully convinced that it will be greatly to their interest to supply money for the work, will not do it.

The engineers of the Pacha of Egypt, who have, moreover, made known the result of their labours to her Britannic Majesty's Agent and Consul-General in Egypt, inform us, in a memorandum which will soon be published, that the projected canal through the Isthmus of Suez, with an inland harbour in the basin of Lake Timsah, projecting into the two seas by means of piers which are to stretch out as far as the depth necessary for the easy entrance of vessels, can be completed in six years, and will cost only 200,000,000 francs, half the expense of the railway from Paris to Lyons.

The Pacha of Egypt has declared to his agent that the plan of his engineers shall be submitted to the judgment of European engineers, chosen in France, Holland, and Germany, and that their scientific decision shall serve as a basis for the organisation of the Universal Company, which is to be entrusted with the execution of the enterprise.

The Governments of France and England need not, therefore, trouble themselves about the scientific question of the means of performing the work or about the material question of its execution.

What has just been said shows that the plan of the Canal, as it was spontaneously conceived and brought forward by the Pacha of Egypt, shuts out every idea of a changing policy, either on his part or on that of any European Government.

The canalisation of the Isthmus of Suez has always been looked upon as advantageous to the commercial and maritime interests of nations in general and of Great Britain in particular. Lastly, it has obtained the sympathies of the Emperor's Government, which are always enlisted in favour of every enterprise destined to increase the prosperity of nations and to facilitate international communication.

It was on this principle that the French agent in Alexandria quite recently maintained and supported the project of a railway between the Mediterranean and the Red Sea, across Egypt, which has been hitherto desired exclusively by English politicians, and which has been looked upon, erroneously no doubt, as intended to serve British interests alone.

The old policy of antagonism and of national jealousy has been nobly put aside by the Emperor's Government and by his agents, who, faithful to their instructions, have nowhere carried on that system of underhand dealings or intrigues which the despatch from Lord Clarendon to Lord Cowley seems to point out or to dread. This is proved by what has just taken place with regard to the railway from Cairo to Suez; and there is reason to hope that on every occasion when there is a step in advance to be recommended or a measure of general utility to be allowed to come into effect freely, the French agents, desirous not to give a pretext to an accusation of antagonism, will no longer find themselves in the painful position of being obliged to draw back before the formal opposition of the English agents.

Second Objection.

The project of the Canal, which, in any case, would require a very long time for its execution, would considerably retard (even if it did not entirely prevent) the completion of the railway between Cairo and Suez, in continuation of the one already established between Alexandria and Cairo. It would also certainly be injurious to our Indian interests. All that the British Government ought to seek in Egypt is a quick and easy route to India for travellers, light merchandise, and despatches. It desires neither ascendency nor territorial dominion; it requires only a free and unimpeded transit. The continuation of the railway would give us this rapid transit, and the present state of Egypt, as a dependency of the Turkish Empire, guarantees it to us freely and certainly.

Reply.

We acknowledge that the political importance of Egypt with regard to Great Britain consists in the freedom of transit to India, and that France, more disinterested than England in this respect, does not seek for an exclusive ascendency or a territorial dominion. In the intimacy of our present relations we openly admit that Egypt being the shortest and most direct route from England to her Oriental possessions, that route ought to be constantly open to her, and that in anything which relates to this important interest she can never give way.

The Government of her Britannic Majesty, which appears to attach importance only to the transit of passengers, light merchandise, and despatches, believes that the railway will suffice for all requirements, and fears that the resources absorbed in the Canal will only indefinitely retard its completion. If the two schemes were committed at the same time to private enterprise there might be reason to fear that the canal, by which will pass the commercial navigation of the whole world, would be preferred to the railway, the profits of which are very doubtful, and the first section of which was very burdensome to the Egyptian Treasury, without yielding a revenue proportionate to the expense. But, fortunately, the Pacha of Egypt has made up his mind to continue the railway from Cairo to Suez at his own expense; he has already ordered the rails from an English firm, the surveys are completed, and the work of levelling is being commenced. This arrangement has been joyfully accepted by the British Agent in Egypt; the French Agent has, on his part, congratulated the Viceroy upon it; and up to this time no one has yet remarked that the authorisation of the Porte has not been requested for this scheme, though great care was taken to solicit it for the plan of the Canal.

Thus the fear that the completion of the railway will be retarded by the making of the Canal is unfounded.

Third Objection.

The third objection to the project of the Canal is that her Britannic Majesty's Ministers cannot conceal from themselves that it is founded on an antagonistic policy on the part of France with regard to Egypt, a policy which they hoped and believed had been done away with by the happy change which has lately taken place in the mutual relations of the two countries. When the partisans of each Government believed that they could not better serve the interests of their own Government than by wounding and defeating the interests of the other, it was natural that the partisans of the French policy should consider it an object of great importance to detach Egypt from Turkey, in order to disturb the easiest means of communication between England and India. It was in this spirit and with this aim that very extensive fortifications, planned in the War Department at Paris, were constructed by French engineers on the Mediterranean coast of Egypt, to defend that country, if attacked, from any naval force coming from Turkey. It was for this purpose also that the great dam was made on the Nile, which, under pretence of irrigation, though in reality perfectly useless, furnishes the means of inundation for the military defence of a part of the Delta, and is also intended to serve as a barrier to Lower Egypt against any force approaching from the south.

It was in this spirit and with this aim that the scheme of the Canal was brought forward. Its effect would be to interpose between Syria and Egypt the physical barrier of a wide and deep canal defended by military works, and the political barrier of a strip of land stretching from the Red Sea to the Mediterranean, granted to a company of foreigners, and occupied by them. Questions of the most embarrassing and dangerous nature might arise between the Governments of these foreigners and the Porte, under the influence of circumstances which may be easily foreseen and respecting which it is not necessary to enter into details. But the policy of France at this moment, and her Majesty's Ministers trust that it may long continue so, consists in maintaining friendly relations and a close union with England, as well as in protecting and supporting the integrity of the Turkish Empire.

The present policy with regard to the Canal has survived that from which it was derived, and must give way before the new and better policy which now guides the two Governments. The physical difficulties of the proposed canal are too well known to require detailed explanation.

The sea at the two ends of the Mediterranean and at Suez is so low for a length of three miles of coast, that enormous sacrifices would be required to make a canal sufficiently deep for the passage of vessels and to keep it open, as well as to make harbours at each end for the vessels whilst waiting to enter the Canal.

To cut a canal from one sea to the other sufficiently wide and deep to allow vessels to pass would be a very expensive work, and as this canal would be constantly taking in and throwing back sand, a considerable outlay would be necessary to keep it clear. For these reasons, it may be doubted whether any expense, however great, can produce a canal which will be always open and accessible at either end; but it is almost certain that, if it could be made, it would never be a profitable commercial concern.

Reply.

If the Emperor's Ministers could believe that the present project of the Canal, the first idea of which did not originate with them, was founded on a hostile policy, they would immediately reject it; but it is not so. They rejoice with her Britannic Majesty's Ministers at the happy change which has taken place in the mutual relations of the two countries; they carry on the new policy sincerely and without any mental reservation, and nothing would appear to them more likely to maintain and strengthen the old feelings of mistrust and jealousy as an unnecessary opposition to an undertaking of universal interest.

These feelings of mistrust have disappeared from the policy of the two Governments, and the frankness of their explanations will doubtless prevent their being led astray by the prejudices belonging to a former period, and will enable them to examine impartially the question which is now brought before them.

We believe that the general opinion in England is not in accordance with the idea that the shortest route to India should only be employed for passengers and mails.

We will quote an article which was published in England in 1852, and which was very favourably received by the British press :—

Captain James Welch, of the Royal Engineers, a more recent writer than either M. Lepère or Maclaren, has discussed the question which attracts our attention. This officer stoutly asserts that the cutting of the Isthmus of Suez can only be done in a serviceable and lasting manner by English capital and labour. This is, indeed, a patriotic but bold assertion. We do not see why the capital and labour of any other great nation, if it is actuated by the same amount of interest as we have, should not be able to perform the work equally as well. In any case, the means would only differ in ratio to the interest; and if, in spite of the combination of many unfavourable circumstances, we feel confident that our country will be able to effect this junction between the two seas, it is because, sooner or latter, this undertaking will become absolutely necessary for the maintenance of our Empire. Every nation would derive a great benefit from this new route opened for navigation. But the evident benefit which the European States nearest to Africa will derive has been seriously asserted as a reason for deterring England from joining an enterprise of which the result is problematic. Here, then, is an example of that old erroneous theory, which affirms that a nation can only be rich and prosperous whilst its neighbours are in a state of poverty.

Doubtless all the European countries nearest to the East will derive considerable benefit from the opening of the Suez Canal; but this ought to give us rather satisfaction than otherwise, since it cannot be denied that by the development of commerce, by whatever means, the most numerous and best invested capitals will reap in the end the greater part of the profits. Our belief is that England, and every nation like her, is called upon to assist in this great undertaking, which will far surpass anything that has yet been attempted. The making of the Panama and Suez Canals appear to us to be the greatest works of the future; they will increase and strengthen the happy bonds by which people of every clime, of every race, and of every faith, are united to England, and will for ever connect the general welfare of nations to the prosperity of our country, their safety to our power, and their independence to our liberty.—*Papers for the People.*

M. Ferdinand de Lesseps, who is going to London, will be able, if necessary, to put M. de Persigny in a position to give the most satisfactory information on the subject of the observations contained in Lord Cowley's despatch, following the three principal objections which have just been answered.

This information establishes the following facts:—

1. That the project of the Canal is not the result of a system of antagonism and rivalry towards England.

2. That the fortifications on the sea coast of Alexandria, the plans for which, moreover, did not issue from the War Department in Paris, are not intended to secure Egypt from a Turkish invasion.

3. That the dam was not constructed as a means of defence, and that it can be used only for purposes of irrigation.

4. That Turkey, far from being uneasy about the project of the Canal, perceives, on the contrary, that it will

augment her power and prosperity by bringing Constantinople 4300 leagues nearer to the extreme East, and by facilitating communication with the sacred spots of Arabia, a great source of the Sultan's authority over Mohammedans.

5. That European colonisation is not to be feared by Egypt, where none but men of the Nilotic race can exist as labourers, and where even the Turkish race, unable to perpetuate itself, has been obliged to recruit for centuries from external sources.

6. That the sand-banks are not to be feared either in the Canal or at the two extremities.

7. Lastly, that the principle of the universality of the enterprise, which has been agreed to and recommended by the written instructions of the Viceroy, will give to England and other nations all the security they can desire.

As to the Viceroy of Egypt's state of vassalage to the Sultan, the Emperor's Government agrees with that of her Britannic Majesty in maintaining it in the state in which it has been established by treaty. The prince who is now governing Egypt is constantly giving his sovereign proof of his fidelity. Egypt is the province which, under present circumstances, provides a greater supply of money and a larger military contingent than any other in the empire. The number of soldiers sent from Alexandria to Constantinople since the beginning of the war amounts already to 42,000. The whole Egyptian fleet is in the Black Sea, and it is well known that Silistria and Eupatoria were defended by Egyptian regiments.

LV.
To Comte de Lesseps, Paris.

LONDON, *June* 25, 1855.

I AM now able to give you a sketch of my opening proceedings and their results. I have had two long conversations with the chief editor of the *Times*. He considers that England has no serious objection to offer to the Suez Canal scheme; that those hitherto brought forward have no weight, and that the article sent from Paris by Mr. O'Meagher, which was published in the *Times* of the 13th, having explained the state of the question in a favourable and very distinct manner, we ought to consult and choose the time which will be most suitable for returning to the affair. In the meantime, he promises (and that was the most important thing) not to act in opposition to the project, and as several letters, written in a spirit unfavourable to the scheme, have been sent to the managers of the journal by an English correspondent in Alexandria, this gentleman is to be written to and requested to examine the question in an unprejudiced manner, and to ascertain whether in Egypt people really believe that the project can be carried out.

On the other hand, Mr. Reeve, one of the Secretaries of the Privy Council, who has great influence over the *Times*, for which he often writes, though not always under his own name, has been very explicit. I was particularly recommended to him by Barthélemy Saint-Hilaire, his intimate friend, in whom he has the greatest confidence. He has assured me that I may be certain of not meeting in general with a prejudiced opposition.

> It would be disgraceful, said he, that England should consider it to her interest to reject a scheme which will be beneficial to the whole world. On the contrary, we shall profit by it more than any one. It is only necessary to prove to the public that the thing is feasible, that the capitalists of England will be permitted to join freely in it, as well as those of other nations, and that there will be no exceptional privileges for any country.

By the advice of the Countess of Tankerville, a friend of Lady Palmerston's, I made my appearance one morning at Lord Palmerston's house, with a letter of introduction from Paris. He received me immediately. I at once concluded that he had come to a final decision. I opened the subject frankly, begging him, if he had time, to discuss it with me, not giving me the reasons he offers to the public, but hiding none of his objections from me.

He then repeated to me, word for word, all the observations contained in Lord Clarendon's despatch to Lord Cowley, without omitting one. It was evident that he himself had dictated them, or that they had, at all events, been written under his direction. The subject was familiar to me; I had not much difficulty in replying with greater detail than I had had time to do in the memorandum presented the day of my departure. I cannot be vain enough to say that, in this first conversation, long as it lasted, I modified or shook the convictions of a man of Lord Palmerston's character, but I observed with satisfaction that my arguments remained unanswered, and that, notwithstanding his facility of speech and the clearness of his intellect, he had nothing serious to state in reply. He had evidently other objections in the background, which he had not yet produced.

> I do not hesitate, he said, with an air of cordiality, to point out to you my apprehensions; they consist, firstly, in the fear of seeing the commercial and maritime relations of Great Britain disturbed by the opening of a new route, which, by allowing a passage to the ships of all nations, will lead to the loss of advantages we now possess. I will also confess to you that I dread the uncertainty of the future with regard to France, a future which every statesman must take into his calculations as among the most melancholy possibilities, for, although we have complete confidence in the sincerity and honesty of your Emperor's intentions, the feeling of France may change after his death.

I then asked Lord Palmerston to consider, at his leisure, all the questions connected with the political aspect of the affair, being convinced that an impartial examination, free from prejudice and mistrust, would lead to the following conclusions:—

1. That England has even a greater interest than any other nation in seeing her commercial route to India shortened by 3000 leagues.

2. That it could be easily proved that if, by some almost impossible chance and to the misfortune of the whole world, the relations between France and England should ever be disturbed, the opening of the Isthmus of Suez would not be a cause of weakness to Great Britain, who is mistress of every important passage and of every maritime station from her metropolis to India. It must also be taken into consideration that,

since the use of steam, the conditions of a war between the two countries have been changed, and that the French, not a very seafaring nation, would not go to India to attack England, when she is within a two-hours' voyage from their shores. Lastly, I added that if, later on, the execution of the Canal was considered possible by scientific engineers, and if the owners of disengaged capital in all countries thought it would be greatly to their profit to engage in it, irrespective of any political influence, the Governments of France and England were in sufficiently close connection to agree upon such measures as would guarantee their mutual interests; that I had, however, no orders to enter upon the subject, and that my only object in coming to London, as agent of the Pacha of Egypt, was to ascertain the state of public opinion on the question of the Isthmus of Suez, and to endeavour honestly to give all desirable explanations and information both on the possibility and advantages of the enterprise and on the universal principle of the protection of the interests of all countries by which it was to be governed.

This first conversation was naturally only a prelude to the subject. It was very deferential on my part, and very courteous on that of Lord Palmerston, who devoted to it more time than I could have ventured to hope.

A few hours after I left him, Lady Palmerston sent me an invitation to spend the next evening at her house.

I have not yet spoken to you of M. de Persigny. He received me very cordially from the first day of my arrival. We spoke of the matter in general terms that very day, and he made me stay to dinner at the Embassy, where he was entertaining several members of the Corps Diplomatique. Neither at dinner nor during the evening was Suez mentioned but with unanimous approbation of the scheme. I took care not to introduce the subject myself, and whenever I was questioned about it I replied with reserve. I finished the evening in M. de Persigny's study, with M. Baudin, the Chief Secretary, and M. Herbet, the Consul-General.

The Ambassador continued to show himself extremely well-disposed towards me.

I went to him yesterday morning to tell him of my conference with Lord Palmerston and my conversations with other persons. He spoke to me of a despatch received from the Minister, and told me that the objections brought forward by the English Government were not their real objections; that it was therefore useless and imprudent to animadvert upon them; that he knew their true reasons, and that he had just explained his way of thinking to M. Walewski in a letter, a passage from which he read to me, and in which he requested fresh instructions before transmitting to Lord Clarendon the copy of the memorandum sent to him. He said that, in his opinion, it was necessary to use great delicacy in our proceedings with the English Government in this important matter, and he even cited my opinion as agreeing with his own. I rejoined that we did agree as to the tact required, but that an answer to Lord Clarendon's communication was nevertheless necessary. He replied that in Paris they did not seem to think so, as they ordered him to make communications which would compromise the affair. "But you ought to know something about it, for it was you who wrote the despatch." I told him that, since my return from Egypt, I had of course placed my memoranda and remarks on a subject which I had especially studied, in the hands of the Minister; that there were indeed some points on which I alone could give information, and that I could not know what had been sent to him from Paris since my departure. "The despatch," replied he, "is nothing compared to what M. Walewski writes to me privately." When he had read me a very good and sensible paragraph from the Minister's note, I ventured to remark that I saw nothing in it which was not in complete harmony with his own wish to show great consideration in his dealings with English statesmen; there seemed to me a difficulty in not answering even futile objections; that if more serious ones should be brought forward we should, doubtless, be in a position to reply to them also; and that by doing so with the moderation which forms a part of his character, he could not but gratify them by the frankness of his explanations. We parted on good terms. I assured him that he would not meet with any obstacle from me in his mission for promoting a friendly feeling with the Court of St. James's, but would find a sincere desire to assist rather than to embarrass him. He congratulated me on my views and on the agreement which existed between us.

I met him in the evening at Lord Palmerston's, and he saw that the Premier had not been otherwise than favourably impressed by me during our conference.

Yesterday I dined with Mr. James Wilson, Secretary to the Treasury, a distinguished political economist, who has offered me his services; as has also Mr. Edward Ellice, a friend of M. Thiers and a most influential member of Parliament.

Mr. Ellice has already presented me to several of his brother members of the House of Commons. He is going to invite several political and financial celebrities, who may be useful to me, to meet me at dinner on the 2nd July. His house, which is very handsome, is two doors from the one where I am lodging. I dine with him in a friendly way in the evening, and I am invited to go to breakfast with him, in his study, every morning at nine o'clock. I have had an interesting conversation with Mr. Panizzi, Librarian of the British Museum, respecting a publication I am preparing in English, and the opportuneness of which is acknowledged by every one.

LVI.

TO BARON VON BRÜCK, MINISTER OF FINANCE,
VIENNA.

LONDON, *June* 28, 1855.

ACCORDING to my instructions from the Pacha of Egypt, there is no occasion to trouble ourselves about the formation of the Universal Company as yet. When the time comes I shall put myself under your direction in everything that relates to the co-operation of Austria, that is to say, the proportion of the capital to be admitted which it will be right to allot to her, and to the meeting of those persons who will be required to give their support or to assist by their efforts.

My journey to Vienna will be a little delayed by the prolongation of my stay in London, where I have to struggle against difficulties and objections caused by an erroneous view of the affair. I must not conceal from you that the reports and speeches of a member of the Surveying Society of 1847, Mr. Robert Stephenson, and the last article in the *Revue des Deux Mondes* in favour of an indirect course by means of an aqueduct formed between the two branches of the Nile, and fed by the water of the river, have contributed not a little to mislead public opinion in England and to make some think that to cut through the isthmus is impossible, and others that it can only be done by gigantic efforts and at an expense quite disproportionate to the expected returns.

As I do not know if M. Arles Dufour has acquainted you with the opinion the Viceroy has always held respecting his proposition of making the Surveying Society of 1847 the basis of the Universal Company, to which alone the Firman of the 30th November last grants permission to make the canal between the two seas, I think I ought to send you an extract from a letter I wrote to M. Arles on the 10th July. His persistency in acting, or allowing his friends to act, as if his proposal had been accepted, and in publicly speaking or writing of the indirect course from Alexandria to Suez, of which the Viceroy disapproves, as the only practicable one, has brought about a state of things which, in spite of my moderation, necessitates a cessation of our intercourse. You know that in our enterprise there will not be what financiers call a *share of capital* for me any more than for others.

M. Arles having insinuated that I have endeavoured to bring about a break between you and him, no one can judge of the value of this accusation better than yourself. You will remember what I said to you at Constantinople on the subject of the interference of M. Arles' friends.

Be so good, if you think it wise, as to communicate what I am now telling you to the Chevalier de Negrelli, renewing to him my promise of sending him as soon as possible the preliminary scheme and the plans of Linant Bey and Mougel Bey.

The Viceroy wishes the drawing up of the final plan to be confided to a commission of engineers celebrated for their hydraulic works, and chosen in France, England, Austria, Prussia, Holland, Italy, and Spain. I shall be obliged if you will come to an understanding with M. de Negrelli, so as to be able to name, when necessary, the Austrian engineer whom you consider fittest for the business in hand.

The Viceroy continues to pay all the expenses of the surveys, and it will be only when the science of the European engineers has pronounced a decision that we shall begin to think about looking out for capital and organising the Universal Company.

LVII.

To Comte de Lesseps, Paris.

London, *June* 30, 1855.

I SAW Lord Clarendon, Minister of Foreign Affairs, the day before yesterday, and he certainly is not guided by a preconceived opinion like Lord Palmerston. I am going to tell you as exactly as possible, in the form of a dialogue, our political conversation, which was very frank and very definite, and succeeded a private conversation in which we both recalled recollections of Spain and spoke of many of our mutual friends.

F. LESSEPS.—Being commissioned by the Viceroy of Egypt to organise a Universal Company for cutting through the Isthmus of Suez, I wished to ascertain the state of public opinion in England on the subject, and to give to all who might desire to be enlightened on the matter such information and explanations as would suffice to prove: firstly, that the affair has not been undertaken by any Government, nor for the exclusive benefit of any nation; secondly, that the work is practicable from a material point of view, that is to say, that the expenses, which may be reasonably anticipated, are in proportion to the profits to be derived from it; thirdly, that we are not soliciting the intervention of the British Government, nor appealing at present to capitalists; fourthly, that the science of the engineers of all Europe will be called upon to pronounce the final decision as to the practicability of the enterprise and its maximum expenses; fifthly, that, if the enterprise is at last recognised as a feasible one, capitalists, small or great, will gladly join it, if they believe it will be to their interest to do so, without any political motive; sixthly, that as the Viceroy of Egypt has completed the railway from Alexandria to Cairo at the expense of the Egyptian Treasury, and is now finishing the last section from Cairo to Suez, he has done his best to satisfy England. He has, in fact, insured the execution of an enterprise which the British agents (in accordance, so far, with the French ones) were incessantly pressing upon him; and, seventhly, that the Suez Canal being voluntarily put by him into the hands of private individuals, there can be no fear of any injury to the resources of the country the Government of which is confided to him, and that he has had no other aim than to advance the interests of Egypt and of his sovereign.

What I ask of you now, my Lord, is to examine the question without prejudice, without a previously-formed opinion, as I am convinced that a mind so enlightened as yours cannot believe that an event beneficial to the moral and material interests of the whole world can be injurious to the power or the commercial relations of England.

LORD CLARENDON.—I will not conceal from you that the traditions of our Government have hitherto been opposed to the making of the Suez Canal. I myself, since I began to examine the question, have found my opinion to be the same, and I acknowledge that it is unfavourable.

We then commenced a discussion on the objections stated in the memorandum sent to Lord Cowley.

F. LESSEPS.—From what has lately been said on both sides it appears to me that the opinion you may have formed before you became acquainted with the new phase of the matter may, perhaps, be modified, or that, at any rate, if you are willing to examine it, you will be obliged to rest it on motives and arguments superior to your present ones. I can understand that at a period when the Governments of France and England thought it necessary to order their agents, the one to oppose the railway and the other the canal, each might hold to his opinion, however unreasonable it might be: it was a settled thing. But things have altered much during the last few years. The intimacy and sincerity of the alliance between the two countries have put an end to that antagonistic position, especially with regard to questions of progress and of the general good, which, in fact, benefit the whole world. Thus the French agents, far from opposing the English ones, supported them in the affair of the Egyptian railway, as you must know. Will England alone retain relics of that system of antagonism which has been so honourably and completely abandoned by France? The sentiments of the members of the English Cabinet are too well known for us to doubt their judgment. I repeat, therefore, that all I ask of you is an impartial examination of the matter.

LORD CLARENDON.—I am much obliged to you for speaking to me so openly. What you say deserves consideration. You may rest assured that I shall comply with your wishes by studying the question and examining it quietly and without prejudice.

Lord Clarendon then spoke of Constantinople, and said that Lord Stratford complained of Benedetti.

I replied that if Lord Stratford complained of Benedetti it was the wolf complaining of the lamb. As he told me that the English Ambassador had not taken any steps in the first instance against the Canal project, I replied that Reschid Pacha had himself informed me of his embarrassment between the active proceedings of Lord Stratford and the passive attitude of the French Chargé d'Affaires.

Well, replied Lord Clarendon, I can tell you that Lord Stratford, in his correspondence, has spoken with much pleasure of the excellent personal terms he is on with you. To return to the present relations between the English and French Cabinets: I must assure you that my colleagues and I look upon both as if they were the members of the same Government. We have perfect and unreserved confidence in the Emperor and in Count Walewski, whose uprightness has contributed so much to draw more closely the bond between the two countries.

I have much pleasure in stating that what Lord Clarendon has said is the expression of the unanimous opinion of all classes in this country.

The only fear which is generally felt in society is, that England's sincere desire for an alliance may not be generally shared in France. Fashionable men, who have lately returned from France, and who have had the *entrée* of the Paris *salons*, confirm this fear.

This is the real motive of the distrust for the future still manifested towards us by English politicians. I tell them that they are mistaken; that the alliance between the two countries is universally desired in France as well as in England; that old parties have no voice, and that any hesitation or doubtfulness caused in the policy of England by her fears for the future will bring about no other result than that of putting arms into the hands of the adversaries of the alliance, and, perhaps, of at last *denationalising* it.

LVIII.

To his Majesty the Emperor of the French, Paris.

London, *July* 4, 1855.

The interest your Majesty has been pleased to show in the great enterprise of cutting a canal through the Isthmus of Suez seems to justify this report, which I have the honour to present to your Majesty, of the result of my first proceedings in London.

The Queen's Ministers appear disposed to examine the question thoroughly. They are anxious to declare that their objections are *bonâ fide*, and devoid of any unfriendly feeling towards your Majesty's Government.

The enclosed note is a faithful report of my interviews with Lords Palmerston and Clarendon on this subject.

The editors of the *Times* and of other papers have assured me of their good intentions.

I have received sympathy and promises of assistance, and even of active co-operation, from a large number of gentlemen of influence in politics, science, trade, and commerce.

Among them I will mention Lord Holland, that old and loyal friend of France; the Duke of Northumberland; the son of the Duke of Somerset; Sir Edward Ellice, M.P.; Sir Richard Gardner, M.P.; Mr. Rendel, the first hydraulic engineer in England; Mr. Charles Manby, Secretary of the Institute of Civil Engineers; Mr. Reeve, Secretary to the Queen's Privy Council; Mr. James Wilson, Secretary to the Treasury; Mr. Morris, editor of the *Times*; Mr. Oliphant, one of the Directors of the East India Company; Mr. James Welch, captain in the Royal Engineers, Secretary to the Admiralty, and author of a treatise on the advantages of the Suez Canal from an English point of view; Mr. Panizzi, Librarian of the British Museum; Mr. Thomson Hankey, Governor of the Bank of England; Mr. Powles, Secretary of the Dock Company: Messrs. Anderson, Wilcox, and Zulueta, directors and founders of the Peninsular and Oriental Company; Sir William Gore. Ouseley, her Britannic

Majesty's Minister Plenipotentiary; Mr. Thomas Wilson, author of the scheme of a canal from the Danube to the Black Sea; and from most of the Embassies and foreign Legations.

None of the men of note with whom I have discussed the question have been willing to admit that an enterprise profitable to the interests of the whole world would damage the power of the commercial relations of England. They dismiss all idea of a preconceived opinion against the scheme; on the contrary, they affirm that, if it can be carried out, it cannot but be a gain to their country; and they regret that it should be thought in France that what is for the good of other nations should not also be for the good of England.

In short, I am convinced that the projected Suez Canal, so far from troubling in the least degree the relations between France and England, will, on the contrary, contribute, by frank and loyal explanations, to prove the sincerity of the alliance to the people of both countries.

The favour shown to the enterprise by public opinion, the publications which are being prepared, the influence of the interests of commerce and navigation, the desire to give a pledge of confidence to your Majesty, cannot fail to gain over those members of the English Cabinet whose opposition but a short time back might possibly have justified the idea of an energetic resistance, which, at the present day, appears no longer to be dreaded.

LIX.

THE SUEZ CANAL QUESTION SUBMITTED TO ENGLISH PUBLIC OPINION.

LONDON, *July* 1855.

(*Aperire terram gentibus.*)

IN the month of October 1854 I left Europe for Egypt, at the invitation of the new Viceroy, Mohammed Said, who for twenty years past has honoured me with his friendship. I had no mission from my Government, and it was in a journey made with the prince from Alexandria to Cairo, across the Libyan desert, that, for the first time, the question of cutting through the Isthmus of Suez was discussed between us. He asked me to give him a memorandum on the subject; and, having approved of my idea, he addressed a Firman to the Consuls-General of foreign Powers, destined to receive the Sultan's sanction, the object of which was to concede the scheme of the canal between the two seas, the company to be formed of capitalists of all nations, without privilege to any particular one.

Two engineers, who had executed great hydraulic works in Egypt, Messrs. Linant Bey and Mougel Bey, were nominated by the Viceroy to accompany me in an exploration of the isthmus, and, by a fresh examination of the ground, to complete the studies he had already made.

This exploration took place in December and January last. After having rendered an account of it to his Highness, I delivered to the engineers instructions from him to assist me in drawing up their report.

In March, Messrs. Linant Bey and Mougel Bey presented a rough draught, which proved conclusively to the Viceroy the possibility of carrying out his great scheme, the initiative of which came from him. They established, by reasonings and calculations that each will be able to verify, that a maritime canal direct from Suez to Pelusium, one hundred mètres wide, eight mtères deep, with an inland port in the natural basin of Lake Timsah, projecting into the two seas by means of jetties extending to the depth required for the easy entrance of vessels, would cost 160 million francs,—that is to say, half the cost of the Great Northern Railway from London to York, or the line from Paris to Lyons.

In a voyage to Constantinople I ascertained that the Sultan and his advisers were favourable to the scheme, and I brought back to the Viceroy a letter from the Grand Vizier, in which the opening of the Isthmus of Suez by means of a maritime canal was alluded to, in appropriate terms, as a *most useful and interesting* work. His Highness hastened to send the documents, charts, and plans necessary for clearly understanding the physical possibility of carrying out the project to the Divan, the sanction of the sovereign depending thereon.

I was then instructed to return to Europe to call public attention to the question and take steps to organise the undertaking on international principles and to the satisfaction of all those interests with which it has been identified from the first.

In his instructions, Mohammed Said stated that the work of his engineers should be submitted to the judgment of engineers chosen from the chief countries of Europe, and that their scientific decision should be the basis for organising the international company, to which the Canal scheme would be entrusted.

Until then there will be no call upon the shareholders for funds; and when the capitalists of all nations are allowed to share in the common work, in proportion to the commercial importance of each nation, their co-operation will only be sought when it is proved that they have a certain interest in the undertaking.

As England is evidently more interested than any other nation in the Suez Canal, my first course is to come to London, to learn the state of public opinion in England on the question, and to give to all who require information the particulars necessary to the appreciation of the moral and material circumstances of the undertaking.

Let them consult the East India Company, the merchants of Australia, Singapore, Madras, Calcutta, and Bombay; the trade of the City, the shipowners of London and Liverpool, the Manchester manufacturers, the ironmasters, machinery-makers, the Peninsular and Oriental Company, the directors of banks and large industrial enterprises, the commercial companies, the proprietors of coal pits, who, in 1854, exported 4,309,255 tons of coal, representing a value of £2,127,156 sterling, and who, by the opening of the Isthmus of Suez, will see this immense exportation increase to a yet greater extent.

I appeal to their interests and refer to their decision. Finally it has been alleged that the Turkish Government will become uneasy at the Canal scheme;

but, as in all questions where the principle being right, the foreseen consequences are unerring, from which ever side the Suez project is regarded it seems advantageous to all parties. We have already stated the Porte's opinion on the subject.

Turkey cannot extricate itself from its present state of languor without borrowing European capital and intelligence. The prosperity of the East is at the present time connected with the interests of civilisation in general. The best way to promote its well-being, together with that of humanity, is to break down the barriers still separating men, races, and nations.

LX.

To M. S. W. RUYSSENAERS, ALEXANDRIA.

LONDON, *July* 9, 1855.

I SEND you a copy of my statement, which, in my English publication, should precede the chief documents relating to the affair. This statement has been sent to Paris, for the approbation of M. Walewski, who daily takes a warmer interest in our undertaking. I am going to read it to Lord Clarendon to-day, with whom I have an appointment for the purpose. I am dealing frankly. You know that this is my habitual policy. This diplomacy is as good as any other, although it stopped my career, and I believe it will suit my business better than indirect and so-called skilful measures.

The English opposition (except Lord Palmerston's crotchet) is a phantom, which disappears as you approach it. A letter which I sent to the Emperor on the 4th of this month, and of which I sent you a copy to communicate to his Highness, gives an exact account of the situation.

Now this, in my judgment, is the plan to follow: I am simultaneously occupied with publications in London and Paris, and will take care that public opinion is directed to the question as much in England as elsewhere.

It is indispensable that the work of sounding and levelling, already agreed upon, should be executed in the Isthmus.

When these preparatory surveys are completed, it will be well for the two engineers chosen by his Highness to come to Paris, where they will be able to arrange with the European engineers appointed, and to satisfy by their judgment the interests of all those parties who will be asked to participate in the enterprise later on.

Till then *it is necessary that the Viceroy remain completely master of the affair.* The company will carry it on afterwards as it likes, when once all difficulties and doubts shall have disappeared. Our only trouble then will be to classify the applications for shares. This is the opinion of practical men in this country, where it is said that with an associate like the Viceroy, I must be on my guard against speculators, even those in high places.

I have already appointed Mr. Rendel in England, as a member of the special commission of European engineers. He is commissioned by the Government to superintend the building of piers at new harbours of refuge or at ports already in existence.

In Austria I shall choose an engineer to work with Baron von Bruck; and in Holland a Dutch engineer, to work with M. de Rochussen. The French engineer will be M. Renaud, assisted by M. Lieussou, a learned hydrographic engineer. In Prussia, Count Manteuffel and Baron von Humboldt are most willing to help us in procuring the best German engineer. In Italy we shall have M. Paléocapa, Minister of Public Works at Turin; in Spain, M. de Montesino, Minister of Public Works at Madrid.

Several of these will, no doubt, be deputed to visit Egypt in November, to examine the site. This survey will be soon over, and I shall go and return with the commissioners.

Mr. Rendel is a man as able as he is modest, and of an integrity recognised by all; his opinion will have great weight in England. So far, after the explanations I have given him, he considers this enterprise can be easily carried out. He thinks the Viceroy's engineers have worked well, and that all will be plain sailing.

The result of what has been confidentially told me is this,—that all remaining opposition in the English Cabinet arises from the fear that the Canal will interfere with the completion of the railway from Cairo to Suez, than which nothing is more desired here. His Highness guessed this with wonderful penetration, and the step taken by him is my best argument in favour of the Canal. It is, therefore, necessary that this step be followed by a result as positive as the order to take soundings for the Canal; and when M. Mouchelet has pushed forward his plans and earthworks, the Viceroy will consider whether it will not be well to order the rails for the whole line, of which Messrs. Briggs are commissioned to supply part. It would also be very judicious on his part to notify his decision officially in writing to Mr. Bruce, requesting him to communicate it to her Britannic Majesty's Ambassador at Constantinople, who, *between ourselves*, would be instructed to protest, if need be, against the Canal so long as there is no certainty that the railway is a *settled* and *irrevocable* question. "That is the question."

I am sending two English pamphlets to Mougel on the jetty works executed by Mr. Rendel, one of which runs more than a league into the sea; together with drawings of the very ingenious apparatus for carrying and sinking the blocks of stone.

LXI.

TO BARON VON BRÜCK, VIENNA.

PARIS, *July 29,* 1855.

I HAVE the honour of sending you, by favour of Baron von Hübner, two proofs, for you and M. de Negrelli, of a panoramic view of the Isthmus of Suez and the course of the maritime Canal. I also send proofs of two charts which will form part of my French publication.

I am anxious to send you the translation of my English

publication, the proofs of which I am going to correct in London two days hence.

I shall only stay in London a week, and shall return to France *viâ* Holland, where I shall make arrangements with M. de Rochussen, and the engineer Conrad, who is appointed one of the international scientific commissioners who accompany me to Egypt towards the end of October.

It will only be on my return, and after the report of the commission is published, that we shall be able to set about organising the international company.

LXII.
To Mr. Rendel, London.

LONDON, *August* 3, 1855.

I PROPOSE to Mr. Rendel that he shall be one of the chief commission of engineers chosen in Europe to examine the rough draft drawn up by the Viceroy of Egypt's engineers concerning the opening of the Isthmus of Suez by a direct maritime canal, fit for the passage of large vessels, with two entrances, one from the Mediterranean and the other from the Red Sea.

These engineers will be inscribed as founders of the maritime canal; they will receive a title which will assure to them, during the ninety-nine years concession, a right to the proportionate distribution of ten per cent. on the net profits of the enterprise, in accordance with the Firman of 30th of last November.

In addition to this their travelling expenses will be taken into consideration.

The commissioners will meet in Paris about the 15th of October, according to the latest notice which will be given; they will proceed to Egypt at once, either a few or all of them as they may consider expedient. Every preparation is made to receive them and facilitate their survey of the Isthmus of Suez.

LXIII.

Circular addressed to Members of Parliament, Merchants, Owners of Vessels for India, &c.

LONDON, *August* 8, 1855.

I HAVE the honour to send you a copy of my publication on the Suez Canal.

After having read the different documents which I bring under your notice, I trust that you will be kind enough to acquaint me with your opinion on the advantages of this important undertaking, in the success of which Great Britain has, I think, a greater interest than any other nation.

The alliance between our two countries makes me attach great importance to finding the opinion of the most enlightened men in England in accordance with that which exists in France on the subject.

You will notice that the scheme of the engineers employed by the Viceroy of Egypt must, before proceeding with the enterprise, be submitted to a commission chosen from the most celebrated engineers of Europe. Mr. Rendel, well known by the remarkable works he has executed in English ports, will be one of the commissioners.

I shall be obliged if you will let me have your reply, either addressed to my house in Paris, 9, Rue Richepance, or care of Messrs. Baring Brothers, or to the care of Messrs. Rothschild, London.

LXIV.

To his Highness Mohammed Said, Viceroy of Egypt.

LONDON, *August* 9, 1855.

SINCE my departure from Egypt I have instructed M. Ruyssenaers to acquaint your Highness with all my proceedings with reference to the Suez Canal.

At the present day no reasonable person can call in question the advantages which will accrue to the entire world by cutting through the isthmus.

The main thing now, as your Highness so well understood from the beginning, is to prove to all the possibility of carrying out the undertaking.

In conformity with your Highness's intention I have given the greatest publicity, both in France and England, to the rough draft drawn up by your Highness's engineers. The publications now appearing in London and Paris will be circulated in other countries. Moreover, I am engaged in appointing the commission of European engineers best known for hydraulic works. I have the honour to enclose a copy of the proposals I made to Mr. Rendel on your Highness's behalf. These proposals have been accepted. It has been arranged that Mr. Rendel shall meet his colleagues in Paris on October 15th. He desires before then to confer with your Highness's engineers, who must also come to an understanding with the other commissioners. Not only on their account, but also to collect materials for the definitive scheme, it will be necessary for MM. Linant Bey and Mougel Bey to come to Europe as soon as possible. I beg your Highness to be kind enough to give them instructions on this subject.

I hope your Highness will continue to approve my prudence in conducting the undertaking you have been good enough to entrust to me.

LXV.

To her Majesty the Empress.

Paris, August 17, 1855.

DURING my last stay in London, your Majesty graciously advised me to try to win over the East India Company to the Suez Canal scheme, or, at least, to weaken the opposition that it might make to the enterprise. I have the honour to submit to your Majesty—begging your Majesty to kindly communicate it to the Emperor—an account of my proceedings in this matter and their results.

I have not failed to follow your Majesty's useful advice. I hope that the Emperor will see in the written testimony of the East India Company, and also of the Peninsular and Oriental Company, a confirmation of the opinion I expressed on returning from my first journey to London.

The adhesion of the *Times* is now an acknowledged fact. The money article of that journal, which must be followed by a political leader, has produced an excellent impression on the great merchants and shipowners of the City.

I have reason to believe that Prince Albert is well disposed to the scheme; and if, during the Queen of England's stay in France, your Majesty would deign to acquaint Lord Clarendon with the interest your Majesty takes in the success of a work already favourably received by public opinion in Great Britain, your Majesty would do much to further the success of my negotiations.

LXVI.

LETTER DELIVERED BY THE EMPRESS TO THE EMPEROR.

(Report of my visit to London.)

MY first act was to come to an arrangement with Mr. Rendel, chief engineer for harbour works in England. This gentleman, who fully understands the importance which the construction of a canal through the Isthmus of Suez will be for his country, will devote his attention to the realisation of the scheme. He has agreed to join the commission of European engineers for examining the preliminary designs of the Vicoroy's engineers, and will visit Egypt in the course of two months, in order to decide on the spot on the practicability of the scheme.

I next published in London a pamphlet in English, accompanied by all the documents relating to the scheme, and supported by the opinions of English travellers and *savants* who have written on the subject. This pamphlet has been sent to the members of both Houses of Parliament, to the papers and reviews, to the merchants and shipowners connected with Indian commerce in London, Liverpool, Manchester, Glasgow, &c. It was accompanied at the same time by a circular making known the proposal for submitting the question of its execution to the decision of European science, announcing the adherence of Mr. Rendel, and pointing out that the two houses Baring Brothers and Rothschild are my London correspondents.

The *Times* of the 6th of August, in the money market article, after making a favourable digest of the pamphlet, thus expresses its opinion :—

M. de Lesseps may be assured that the national belief in the special advantages which England derives from every circumstance tending to accelerate exchanges between different parts of the world, will be favourably disposed towards all his ideas.

The following are extracts from the answers which have been sent to me by the Peninsular and Oriental Steam Navigation Company and the East India Company:

1st. By order of the Directors of the Peninsular and Oriental Steam Navigation Company :
The importance of the results, which would be attained by connecting the Mediterranean to the Red Sea by a navigable canal is so evident that there can be no two opinions on the matter, and if the scheme is realised, this company will be greatly benefited by the important results to the commerce, not only of England but of the whole world.

2nd. By order of the Court of Directors of the East India Company :
With reference to the importance of the enterprise of piercing the Isthmus of Suez, I am directed to inform you that the Court takes the greatest interest in the success of such an enterprise, destined to facilitate the means of communication between this country and India.

The replies which are daily sent to me by English statesmen and politicians all express the same opinion, of which the *Times* is the medium. This paper must shortly publish a leading article on the question. Other papers are preparing articles which will leave no doubt as to the general feeling of the country.

The Indian papers, especially the *Bombay Gazette*, have expressed their sympathy with the construction of a canal through the Isthmus of Suez.

It will be for the Emperor to decide if, as matters now stand, the English Ambassador at Constantinople can reasonably continue his opposition to the ratification of the Viceroy of Egypt's Firman, which opposition, after my correspondence from Constantinople, still remains very decided.

LXVII.

To Mr. James Wilson, London.

La Chenaie, August 31, 1855.

Since you have shown so much interest in the Suez Canal enterprise, you will be glad to hear that I have received two important documents from the Court of Directors of the East India Company, as well as from the directors of the Peninsular and Oriental Steam Navigation Company.

An article in the *Economist* of the 16th of August shows a perfect knowlege of the subject on the part of the writer. As regards the doubts expressed by him on certain questions I am glad to see them raised, since they are so candidly stated, because these observations will serve, when the time arrives for drawing up the bye-laws and forming the company, both to modify certain principles which are the object of just criticism and to enable me to give detailed and satisfactory proofs on other points which require explanation.

The allotment of 15 per cent. on the net profits to the Egyptian Government and 10 per cent. to the original members appears to me to be a fair measure. This was a spontaneous act on my part amongst the proposals which I made to the Viceroy of Egypt; and in allowing him 15 per cent. on the net profits for his generous concession, my only fear is that it is too little. As regards 10 per cent. to the original shareholders, this arrangement enables me, without affecting the present, to reserve for the future a fair return to those persons, for their anxiety and pecuniary assistance, who have made sacrifices for the realisation of the Suez Canal, and who also risk their capital for an indefinite period until the enterprise shall have become profitable. In all the recent railway concessions the French Government has demanded that after 8 per cent. has been paid to the shareholders one half of the surplus shall be handed over to it. As regards the concession of the property no one has assisted me in obtaining it from the Viceroy of Egypt. The transaction has been solely between him and myself, without any mediator, and it has been unnecessary for me to make any promises whatever on the subject. When the enterprise is offered to the commercial world, after the survey by European engineers, whom I shall accompany to Egypt about the end of October, it will be clearly shown by facts that from the commencement the enterprise has been impartially and disinterestedly conducted, and that, by avoiding the acceptance of engagements beforehand, I have wished to reserve the greatest possible advantages to future shareholders. These advantages will certainly be considerable, and I believe that few enterprises could offer the like.

The Viceroy gratuitously gives up to the company all lands necessary for the construction of the maritime canal, and *he concedes for ever*, on condition of paying the ordinary tax after ten years' possession, the vast extent of land which will be irrigated by means of the secondary canal fed by the Nile.

The ten francs per ton which is thought to be insufficient for the remuneration of the shareholders, is simply named to challenge remarks and discussion. It is expressly stated in my memorandum to the Viceroy, as well as in the report of the engineers, that the toll for transit must be definitely fixed later on; and in my opinion it cannot be drawn up with a thorough knowledge of the matter until after the works have been executed. In the meantime we must settle the sum per ton which will be saved by ships profiting by the shortening of the distance. Engineers have calculated that this saving will be about sixteen francs per ton for every thousand leagues, which gives forty-eight francs for three thousand leagues.

Ships passing through the Canal will not incur any other expense besides the toll, which will be fixed by the tariff when the company is formed. The duration of the transit can easily be calculated by the time it takes to go one hundred and sixty kilometres without any stoppage at the rate of ten kilometres per hour. There will be no locks throughout the entire length of the inland passage. Ships will enter and leave *ad lib.* without stopping.

The *Athenæum* of the 25th August contains a long article on my pamphlet. The two principal criticisms in it appear to me to be contradictory. It maintains, on the one hand, that, in consequence of difficulties and the winds of the Red Sea during certain seasons, the route by the Cape will be preferable; and, on the other hand, that the shortening of the distance, and the facilities obtained by the opening of the Canal for the benefit of commerce for all nations, will expose, in time of war, the safety of the English possessions in India. I am glad to see that these questions are discussed: truth will be elicited by them and the practical good sense of England will dispel old prejudices, jealousies, and specious reasonings, the result of a mistaken and selfish spirit.

The following is my reply to the objection raised against the decision of the Viceroy of Egypt to nominate me director of the company and president of the administrative council. He insists upon it, on account of the confidence which he has been pleased to have in my attachment to him, as well as in the success of the enterprise and my freedom from national prejudices. It has, however, always been my express intention to beg him, as soon as all difficulties have disappeared, to allow those interested themselves to nominate the person to direct and preside over their administration.

With reference to the technical part, which concerns engineers, it may be well to repeat, for the satisfaction of the *Australian and New Zealand Gazette*, that a commission of celebrated engineers, including Mr. Rendel, will shortly go to Egypt, and will assure, by its inquiry and report, every guarantee of experience and science to the enterprise.

LXVIII.

TO COMTE DE LESSEPS, PARIS.

LA CHENAIE, *September* 13, 1855.

I CONTINUE to receive very satisfactory letters and interesting communications. Tell our excellent Minister, Count Walewski, the interest which the Empress takes in the canal is, and will continue, the same. The reserve imposed upon her by politics has not changed the sentiments which she expressed to him on his entering office, in recommending him to watch over the success of our enterprise.

All the foreign Ministers have replied favourably with regard to the appointment of the first engineers in their country who are invited to take part in the international scientific commission.

I have received proposals from capitalists and contractors offering to contract for the undertaking, to advance money, and to take shares in payment, of course in consideration of a good commission. The time has not yet arrived for entering into treaties. I put them off without refusing or discouraging anybody.

I have, besides, numerous private applications for shares. I merely tender my thanks and note them.

I have not hesitated, in complying with the views expressed by the Emperor as well as those of M. Walewski, which have always been the same as mine, to do nothing in a hurry and not to give the enterprise a political aspect.

In Egypt everything goes on quietly but surely, as if the company were already formed, and the preliminary works are being prepared for our arrival with the select commission of European engineers. There is already a party of Egyptian engineers on the isthmus, assisted by half a battalion of sappers, taking the levellings for the proposed course of the Canal, also a body of engineers taking careful soundings with a view to becoming acquainted with the nature of the ground to be worked.

Tents and provisions have been conveyed to them on one hundred and twenty-eight camels.

M. de Negrelli, Director-General of Public Works in Lombardo-Venetia, has written to me that, on being informed of my correspondence with Baron von Brück, he came to Paris to come to an arrangement with me. I have asked him to call on me at La Chenaie, where I intend to remain until the 8th of October.

I am busy drawing up the bye-laws of the future company, which require great care. I have based them upon the bye-laws of all well-known companies.

I have been informed by letter from Marseilles that the General Council of the Bouches-du-Rhone has expressed an explicit wish for the realisation of the piercing of the Isthmus of Suez.

I need not, dear brother, thank you for all you have done since the beginning of my enterprise: you and Madame Delamalle have materially contributed to the success which must sooner or later be achieved.

LXIX.

To M. S. W. Ruyssenaers, Alexandria.

LA CHENAIE, *September* 24, 1855.

MY short stay in Paris was well employed in the interests of the Canal. M. de Negrelli was there. M. de Chancel's letter, of which I send you a copy, will explain to you the motive of his journey; he was summoned by the members of the Surveying Society of 1847, at the request of Stephenson, who probably wished to do again what he did once before. You know that, being sent by this Society to Egypt to speak to the Viceroy in favour of the project of a canal between the two seas, he turned against that project and obtained for himself the directorship and the contract for making the railway from Alexandria to Cairo.

However this may be, the Society, which is now dissolved, wishes to be reconstituted; it has published, in the *Revue des Deux Mondes*, articles to our prejudice which made a great sensation, and has prepared a memorial which was presented to the Emperor, at the same time asking for an audience. When M. de Negrelli heard from me all the details of what had taken place, he was not surprised that the audience had been refused. He repeated to me what he had told M. de Chancel respecting the labours of the Austrian engineers, proving that the mouth of the canal could easily be made in the Bay of Pelusium; and it was agreed between us that he should be included in the commission of European engineers, independently of the late Society, which I persisted in refusing to hear mentioned. He will embark at Trieste to join us in Egypt at the time to be appointed by me.

The French, English, Italian, Spanish, German, and American newspapers continue to entertain their readers with remarks on the subject of the cutting through the Isthmus of Suez, and speak favourably of our enterprise. My French publication produces an excellent effect. The rough draft of his Highness's engineers is appreciated as it deserves.

A personage of exalted rank, whose opinion is very valuable to me, writes as follows:—

> What strikes me most in your book is the arrangement of the business. Those who know you discover in it all the qualities which distinguish you; I see in it an assurance of success. At any rate, it will be your glory, in these days of jobbing and deceit, to have placed your confidence in means which ought to succeed, to have desired the greatest openness, to have placed money after, and made it subservient to science, and to have opposed to the intrigues of English diplomacy the uprightness of the Viceroy, an energy full of patience, and the strength of interests aware of what is due to them. To triumph by such means will be an excellent precedent. It seems to me, moreover, that everything is going on as well as possible in Egypt and at Constantinople, in London and at Paris.

The Ministry have heard from the French Embassy at Constantinople that the disposition of the Porte is most favourable, and that whenever the French Ambassador receives the order to request the ratification of the Viceroy's Firman, the business will occupy only a few days.

Some English newspapers having made observations to which I thought it necessary to reply, I have entrusted this to the care of Mr. James Wilson, M.P., proprietor of the *Economist*, the most important English weekly newspaper for industrial questions and those relating to political economy. I send you a copy of the letter I wrote him. The Viceroy and you must not be angry at my plan of entrusting the choice of the chief of the enterprise, at some distant period, to the decision of those most interested. This is done in all great undertakings with shareholders. But, in order to conform to the wishes of his Highness, our bye-laws will decree that the first council of administration, as well as its president, the choice of whom will rest with the Viceroy, shall hold office during the whole period of the works, and the same number of years after the opening of the Canal for purposes of general navigation.

Letter from M. de Chancel.

(A copy of which was enclosed in the preceding letter.)

Paris, *September* 15, 1855.

I HASTEN, according to your instructions, to acquaint you with the particulars of my conversation with M. de Negrelli.

I will repeat it verbatim :—

NEGRELLI.—I wish very much to converse with M. de Lesseps, and to consider with him if it might not be possible to put an end to the unfortunate disagreement which has arisen between him and the Surveying Society of 1847.

CHANCEL.—M. de Lesseps has had no personal disagreement with those gentlemen, but he is obliged to keep to the commission with which the Viceroy has entrusted him, the object of which is to form a Universal Company for the execution of the project by the direct route. It was the members of the Surveying Society who separated from M. de Lesseps, by adopting, in his absence and contrary to his opinion, the plan of the course by the Nile, which is formally opposed by the Viceroy, and which M. de Lesseps himself considers impracticable. Moreover, he had no sort of tie or engagement to them.

NEGRELLI.—I am of the same opinion as M. de Lesseps, and I do not despair of persuading the members of the Surveying Society to adopt the direct course, if it is proved to them that it will be a possible and advantageous one. I think Mr. Stephenson is already inclined towards it. He will not, however, pronounce an opinion, and he declares that he cannot do so until he has considered the matter on the spot. There is, therefore, no reason for the difference which exists between the Surveying Society and M. de Lesseps. In an undertaking of this importance we ought not to divide our forces. We cannot be too careful to concentrate them, and to induce all to use their influence in aid of the common object.

CHANCEL.—This is the opinion of M. de Lesseps also, and it is what he was disposed to do, but some members of the Society have (by means of strong-worded publications) pronounced so decidedly in favour of the course by the Nile, and have proclaimed in so absolute a manner the practical impossibility of insuring the flowing of the Canal into the Mediterranean by the Bay of Pelusium, that M. de Lesseps could not follow them in such a course, but has unwillingly left them to their mistake.

NEGRELLI.—The results of the surveys of my brigade, which was especially entrusted with the duty of taking soundings of the seas, leave, I am aware, no doubt as to the possibility of insuring the passage of the Canal into the Gulf of Pelusium. I have not, it is true, communicated these results to the Surveying Society, circumstances not having been favourable, but I am prepared to do so, and I am persuaded that they will come to the same conclusion as myself.

CHANCEL.—M. de Lesseps cannot but consider that, in consequence of the commission which the Viceroy has entrusted to him, the Surveying Society is no longer necessary. He has, moreover, had no connection with it, and has hardly been aware of its existence. In fact it was dissolved in 1848. M. de Lesseps has never seen, and does not now see, the necessity for its being reconstituted. The question is now placed on a fresh footing; the Viceroy's commission is the centre towards which all the great interests which are connected with the enterprise should converge. All that has hitherto been done is now objectless. The engagements which have been entered into by parties not included in the arrangements made by the Egyptian Government can, in future, cause nothing but embarrassment. They have no longer any object, and it is better for every one that they should not be revived. Of what use to our enterprise, for instance, would it be to reconstitute the old Surveying Society? It never did anything really useful; the only plan which it brought forward has been rejected as dangerous by the policy of the Egyptian Government and as impracticable by the opinion of the most competent engineers. You yourself have not hitherto thought it necessary to communicate to this Society the remarkable results of your labours, which are altogether opposed to those of the other members.

NEGRELLI.—The Surveying Society has not been dissolved; it has, during a certain period, suspended its labours until more favourable circumstances arise. The reason for not communicating to the Society the results of the observations of my brigade was simply that, before the promulgation of the Viceroy's Firman, these circumstances did not appear to me to exist, and since that time I thought it better to wait and see M. de Lesseps. At the end of 1847 we were all to go to Egypt and complete our work. The Revolution of February put a stop to this. Afterwards I believed that M. de Lesseps was proceeding in perfect unison with my colleagues, and I was fully satisfied. It is necessary, at all events, to have a society. Why not accept the one which exists, which is organised, and has established itself? I repeat, we cannot concentrate too closely the influences which are devoted to our enterprise. We have to think of acting upon the French and Turkish Governments, in order to obtain the expression of their sentiments.

CHANCEL.—M. de Lesseps does not believe that the time is come for constituting the Universal Society. He even thinks that there would be danger in doing it without having previously removed, by the decision of a commission composed of eminent engineers, whose opinion will be law, the uncertainty which the publications of your French colleagues have left on the public mind. An enterprise of this nature must not be commenced unadvisedly. We must not expose ourselves to receive a check, which would be a very likely thing to happen if we summoned capitalists at the time when the principal questions, those of the route and the execution, have been notoriously laid open to doubt. As to the political side of the matter, M. de Lesseps does not think this a fit time to take that into consideration either. The question is not yet matured. We must leave it to be acted upon by time and circumstances. It is very certain that the French and Ottoman Governments are both at heart favourable to the affair. These Governments may have reasons for delaying their official adhesion. We must respect this reserve and not endeavour to force them to a decision. The English Government, already at issue on the question, will not pronounce any decision at present. This state of things shows that the political question will not be settled until after the solution of the technical and financial ones. M. de Lesseps is to set out next month, and he hopes that you will make one of the commission of engineers who are summoned to decide on the technical question.

NEGRELLI.—Allow me again to endeavour to impress on M. de Lesseps the desirability of union and a conformity in action and in views with the Surveying Society, which cannot do otherwise than agree with the opinion you have just expressed.

CHANCEL.—There has never been any understanding, still less any conformity of action or of views, between M. de Lesseps and the Surveying Society, to which he has always been a stranger. When, in 1854, he accepted the Viceroy's invitation he intended to reconsider, on the spot, a survey which he made as far back as 1833, when he was Agent of the French Government in Egypt. It was a mere chance that, meeting M. Arles just before he started, the conversation turned upon this most interesting subject. They agreed to meet at Lyons, where M. de Lesseps, explaining his plan, showed himself inclined to accept the co-operation of sensible men who would bring to the work the aid of their intelligence, their influence, and their labours. During the first month that M. de Lesseps was in Egypt, a correspondence on this subject was carried on between him and M. Arles. This correspondence naturally ceased when the Surveying Society wished to be reconstituted without waiting for the return of M. de Lesseps, when plans of organisation appeared without his consent, and when the essential question of the route was imprudently entered upon, contrary to his wishes, by the articles in the *Revue des Deux Mondes*. This is the real state of the affair. I think it would be a very good thing for you to go and talk the matter over with M. de Lesseps, who, as I said before, hopes you will accompany him to Egypt.

NEGRELLI.—I will do so with pleasure ; but do you think he would see any objection to Stephenson, who is now in Paris, going with us ?

CHANCEL.—I think it is necessary for you to consult M. de Lesseps.

NEGRELLI.—Certainly ; but you are his friend. I want to know your opinion.

CHANCEL.—Since you ask me to give you my private opinion, I will do it frankly. I think that Mr. Stephenson does not speak out sufficiently to make his going to Egypt of any use on the conditions which circumstances dictate to M. de Lesseps. You must not forget the way in which Mr. Stephenson has once separated from his colleagues in the Surveying Society. If he went to Egypt he might a second time work for himself alone : for his own interest at first, and perhaps, afterwards, for some political interest, under the guidance of some person hostile to the Canal. M. de Lesseps owes it to the commission with which the Viceroy has honoured him not to permit any coalition which might lessen the authority belonging to his Highness in this great undertaking. I think I may assure you that M. de Lesseps will accept the concurrence of independent and enlightened men who desire honestly and without reservation to join him in this commission. The paper which he has published, and which I have just given you from him, is his programme and his standard. He must now wait for the public to respond to his call.

LXX.

TO THE BARON VON BRÜCK, VIENNA.

LA CHENAIE, *October* 28, 1855.

THE Chevalier de Negrelli will already have reported to you the conversation which I had the honour of having with him in Paris, a few hours before his departure for Vienna. The clear and exhaustive explanation which I made a point of giving him, both for his private information and your own, has led him not to insist on making me accept, as the foundation of the Universal Company, the ideas of the Surveying Society of 1847, which began to have a practical organisation in Austria only.

I think, then, that we should now hold the same opinion with regard to the Surveying Society, which, after its formation and its labours in 1847, had so little concord that its members did not publish the results of their inquiries.

I hope, also, after the explanations which M. de Negrelli will give you, we shall agree as to the necessity for not giving occasion for a diplomatic intervention on the part of the Governments of Austria, France, and England. If, ten years ago, Mehemet Ali was deterred from undertaking the cutting of the Isthmus of Suez, it was because he had been impressed with the idea that it was first necessary to obtain the sanction of these Governments. The present Viceroy of Egypt has had the good sense to begin by commencing the Canal without bringing the Governments of Europe into the affair. In not wishing to make the sanction of the Porte depend on international negotiations, the result which we should desire will be delayed indefinitely, and, may be, compromised. M. de Negrelli appeared to me thoroughly to understand what might aid or thwart the success of our great undertaking. You and Austria desire that this undertaking may attain to a successful termination; and we cannot fail to obtain it by uniting our efforts.

The most important phase of the affair will be the decision of the European scientific commission, which should be in Egypt in the beginning of November. M. de Negrelli has been good enough to inform me, as you have already stated, that he is willing to join the commission, and will leave Trieste by boat in order to come and join us. I have informed him that Mr. Rendel will be his English colleague, and M. Conrad, Inspector-General of the Water-Staat and President of the Society of Civil Engineers of Holland, will be his Dutch colleague. Count Manteuffel has informed me that the Minister of Public Works at Berlin has nominated Privy Councillor Lentzé, president of the two commissions which the Prussian Government has appointed for the hydraulic constructions and the maintenance of the dams on the Vistula and the Nogat.

Being in the country at the commencement of M. de Negrelli's visit to Paris, I commissioned one of my friends to see him. I send you a copy of the letter which he wrote to me giving an account of his interview. It shows, on the one hand, that M. de Negrelli has loyally done everything he can in favour of the Surveying Society, and, on the other, it establishes some facts of which it will be useful to preserve the trace.

LXXI.
Circular to the Members of the International Scientific Commission.

La Chenaie, *October* 11, 1855.

I HAVE the honour to inform you that the European scientific commission summoned to give its advice on the proposed scheme of making a canal through the Isthmus of Suez has to-day conpleted its labours.

The engineers of the Viceroy of Egypt, Messrs. Linant Bey and Mougel Bey, have just arrived in Paris, in order to confer with the commission, and to place themselves at its disposal.

Consequently, I beg to give you notice that the first meeting of the members of the commission will be held in Paris, on the 30th of October, at one o'clock, at No. 9, Rue Richepance. A second meeting for those members who are about to visit Egypt will be held at Marseilles, on the 6th of November, at the Hôtel d'Orient. The date of departure is fixed for the 8th of November, at ten o'clock in the morning, by the Messageries Impériales' steamboat.

His Highness Mohammed Said desires that every member of the commission may proceed to Egypt, where arrangements have already been made for receiving them. Whilst fully agreeing with him, may I add a hope that our common interest in the great enterprise you are good enough to further may lead to the maintenance of intimate relations between us?

Whilst the final preparations are being made at Cairo

for getting our caravan ready for exploring the isthmus, I think it would be useful to examine the course of the Nile as far as the first cataract. The Viceroy will place one of his steamboats at the disposal of the commission, which will enable this interesting excursion to be made in a fortnight. On returning from Upper Egypt we shall go to Suez, from thence to the port of Pelusium, where a steamboat will be waiting to take us direct to Alexandria.

LXXII.

To the Editor of the "Times," London.

Paris, October 30, 1855.

Sir,—I observe in your paper of the 25th of this month a communication from Alexandria, dated the 10th, especially devoted to criticism on my publication relative to the scheme for cutting through the Isthmus of Suez. This communication is too full of errors, both in arguments and in facts, for me to allow it to remain before the public without contradiction.

Your correspondent does not take the trouble to prove his assertions; he is content with making them. I will begin by repeating his principal arguments :

1. Every plan for a junction between the two seas in general, and the preliminary scheme prepared by the engineers of the Viceroy of Egypt in particular, must be impracticable.

2. Even if the scheme could be carried out, it would be of no advantage to commerce and navigation, which would continue to follow the roundabout route by the Cape of Good Hope.

3. Granting that the route of the Maritime Suez Canal were preferred by sailors, the enterprise would still be ruinous to the shareholders and capitalists connected with it, because the revenues would not correspond to the expenses, the valuation of these revenues by the engineers and myself being exaggerated and excessive.

4. Although there are to be no profits, yet your cor-

respondent does not fail to denounce as disproportionate the previous deduction of 15 per cent. reserved for the Egyptian Government.

If I am not mistaken, the tendency of this discussion, if not the aim of the writer of the letter, is to cause the withdrawal from the scheme of capitalists who are undecided or easily alarmed. This result, even if obtained, would not hinder the success of a great design. Europe abounds in enlightened and well-informed capitalists, who examine questions on their own merits, and who do not allow themselves to be influenced by the false alarms of hostile or prejudiced minds.

The means of raising the sum of money required by the company, the formation of which has been entrusted to me, is no longer a problem, and the spontaneous offers which have been transmitted to me up to this time from all parts of Europe by the *élite* of the intelligent classes, are more than enough to insure the success of the enterprise.

Before proceeding farther, allow me to announce to the European public, and at the same time to your correspondent, a fact that will be the best reply to his objections.

This fact is, the formation and approaching departure for Egypt of the international scientific commission, which, according to the Viceroy's instructions, is charged with the duty of examining the preparatory surveys of the preliminary scheme, of solving all the problems in science, art, and execution presented by the operation.

It will be well that the public and your correspondent should be informed how this commission was organised.

In Austria, Baron von Brück, Minister of Foreign Affairs, was requested to name the engineer who is the most capable of representing the interests of the ports of the Adriatic. The Minister's choice fell on the Court Councillor, M. de Negrelli, Director of Public Works, a very talented engineer, who, in the surveys made in 1847, was especially charged with the examination of the questions relative to the outlet of the Canal at Pelusium.

The same request was addressed to Turin, to the Hague,

and to Berlin, and the following gentlemen have been authorised by the various Governments to become members of the commission :

For Italy, M. Paléocapa, engineer, Minister of Public Works, Turin.

For Germany, the Privy Councillor Lentzé, chief engineer of hydraulic constructions in Prussia.

For Holland, the Chevalier Conrad, chief engineer of the Water-Staat.

For Spain, M. de Montesino, Director-General of Public Works.

In England public opinion has, so to speak, made its own choice. British interests and British science are represented in the commission by,—

Mr. Rendel, engineer, whose name alone gives authority;

Mr. MacClean, another engineer, equally well known in England by his hydraulic works;

Commander Harry Hewet, captain of one of the East India Company's ships, who for twenty-seven years has been making hydrographic surveys in the Red Sea and the Indian Ocean.

The commissioners for France are,—

M. Renaud, *Inspecteur-Général des Ponts et Chaussees*, and M. Lieussou, naval hydrographic engineer.

Certainly a commission composed of such men ought to remove all doubts, all mistrust, all anxiety, all timidity.

Your correspondent will surely not imagine that so many distinguished men, entrusted with such an important mission, invested with such a public character, and occupying each in his own country the highest and most honourable position, would give way before the eyes of all Europe, which are fixed upon them, to the follies or illusions of over sanguine minds, who are as careless of their own honour as of the monetary interests of the company which they call together for the completion of their mad scheme.

I will now give a programme of the labours awaiting the commissioners.

As I have already said, they will not shut themselves up in their studies; they will not keep to abstract science and theories; they will go to the spot, and will study there the problems which they have to resolve.

Between the 15th and the 20th November they will all meet at Alexandria. From thence they will proceed to Cairo, and then will go on to Suez, and will commence a complete exploration of the isthmus. They will embark at Pelusium and follow the coast as far as Gaza, in order to observe the direction of the currents and the supposed danger of alluvium; after which, they will go back to Alexandria, preparatory to returning to Europe and issuing a definitive programme of the works which have to be accomplished.

I certainly have a right to think that such a commission offers every guarantee which can be required by the most exigent distrustfulness, and I am justified in saying that the investigations and observations of its members cannot leave room in impartial minds for the gratuitous and unfounded assertions advanced by your correspondent. I have reason to hope that the Viceroy of Egypt will be able boldly to bring forward all these precautions and arrangements against the attacks, whether concealed or open, which may be made use of to bring discredit on his generous plan. I may fairly expect that England, indeed all Europe, will do justice to his pure and upright intentions and to those of his fellow-labourers.

The decisions of the commissioners will be without appeal; they will be responsible for them before the world, which is impatient to witness the commencement of a work which is no less than a pacific and beneficial revolution.

It seems to me that I have now replied to the most important objections at present advanced by your correspondent.

If the scheme is impracticable, the commissioners will not sanction an impossible undertaking.

If the plan does not offer advantages to navigation

and commerce, if it does not shorten distances, or if, in consequence of the inconveniences of this new course, it shortens them in distance but not in time, the commissioners will state the fact; and your correspondent ought to have waited for their decision before publishing insinuations the tendency of which, we are willing to believe, he had not fully calculated.

But need we wait for the verdict of the European commission to contradict, *de plano,* the allegations of the correspondent from Alexandria?

Is the execution of the projected canal from Suez to Pelusium impracticable? On one side we have the protest of an anonymous writer, who has adopted the quick and easy plan of distorting, contesting, and denying everything; on the other, we have the authority of professional men and the surveys of engineers trained to the examination of these spots and these questions.

To which side will thinking men give their confidence?

Two ideas of the same nature and of equal magnitude are at this moment occupying the scientific and commercial worlds: one is the junction of the two oceans by the American isthmus, and the other the junction of the Indian Ocean and the Mediterranean Sea by the Isthmus of Suez.

It is certain that the work of cutting through the American isthmus presents, as no one attempts to deny, far greater difficulties than that of cutting through the Isthmus of Suez; yet the former of these projects has not met with the same contradiction, the same passionate objections which are employed to impede the latter. The possibility of a maritime communication straight across from one shore of America to the other is now universally accepted. It has in its favour the assent of men of science, and, moreover, the authority of his Majesty the Emperor of the French.

I should not be surprised if your correspondent himself were to share the general opinion on this point.

Now, if the more difficult of these two enterprises is practicable, why should the easier one be impossible?

But it must be owned that it is one of the misfortunes and infirmities of the human mind that nothing good or great has ever been done on earth without coming in contact, more or less, with those jaundiced or envious, timid or discouraging natures which, by their narrow-minded and wearying resistance, would keep the world motionless.

It was against these rocks of passive resistance that our countryman Riquet wore out his genius and his life before he could enrich France with the Canal of Languedoc.

It was by the influence of these narrow-minded systems that Fulton's discovery—which is now the great support of war, of civilisation, and of commerce, by land and sea —was for a time rejected.

The communication *viâ* the isthmus, according to your correspondent, will not be advantageous to commerce, which will continue to follow the route of the Cape of Good Hope. He thinks, then, that it makes no difference as to the time, expense, and safety of the sailor who has to navigate between two given points, whether he has to go 3000 leagues or between 5000 and 6000; more than that, he believes that he *will prefer* the passage of 5000 or 6000 leagues to that of 3000. And yet, at this very time, your mails, your despatches, your passengers, and your light and valuable goods are always sent to the Indian Ocean *viâ* Suez, notwithstanding the inconvenience of a double trans-shipment and the fatigue of the journey across Egypt and the desert. And when these inconveniences are done away with; when, by a wide and short canal, ships, passengers, and goods of every kind, can be conveyed safely and rapidly from one sea to the other; is it likely that they will refuse to adopt the shortest way, the way, even now, preferred by all who are able to make use of it?

Navigation and commerce will not accept the Suez Canal route! Has your correspondent, then, heard nothing of the thousand echoes of the European press, of the solicitude with which all maritime nations are watching the progress of our work? has he not discovered the sympathy of science and of British opinion? Does he know nothing of the interest which your East India Company was the first to take in the execution of this project? But let this pass.

According to him, the operation will be disastrous and the shareholders will be ruined.

This is not the opinion of the most eminent, the most powerful, and the most enlightened financiers of England and of all Europe, for they have offered the most important and efficacious assistance to the enterprise, and, as I have already said, as far as its finances are concerned, the success of the undertaking is certain.

The feasibility of the execution of the Canal once granted, the benefits are self-evident; they require no discussion. They are proved by the intelligence and consciousness of the world in general.

They rest:

Upon a grant of ninety-nine years;

Upon the increase of the navigation and traffic already existing between the two richest and most populous parts of the globe;

Upon the commercial progress which necessarily results from the rapid and more easy connection between Western civilisation and populations of more than 7,000,000 of souls, which have been hitherto left in their solitude and barbarism;

Upon the importance of the lands granted to the company, the natural and well-known fertility of which requires, for its renewal, only the irrigating canals which are included in the expenses of the estimate;

Upon the value of the building lands at each end of the Canal and around the interior port of Timsah, which will some day become another Alexandria.

In declaring that there is an excess in the previous deduction of 15 per cent. from the net profits conferred upon the Egyptian Government, your correspondent appears to me to be a little inconsistent. What is the use of disputing about profits when he says that there is no possibility of there being any profits? What matters the share of each individual if the total be a chimera?

Why, indeed, should he urge these idle objections unless his object is to frighten away capitalists from this dreaded performance?

Or is not your correspondent as certain of his facts as he wishes to appear? And do these so-called chimerical profits really seem to him sufficiently real and important to be worth the trouble of foreseeing and measuring their distribution?

The Egyptian Government has reserved to itself a fixed and invariable share of 15 per cent. on the net profits. Firstly, it was its right. It was at liberty to attach to the grant such a reciprocity of advantages as it considered just or useful. Has it made a bad use of this right? Let us take France, for example. In making grants to companies for railways the French Government reserved to itself a share in the profits, whatever they might be, from the time that they should exceed 8 per cent. I do not hesitate to declare that, so far as concerns the Suez Canal, I prefer the Egyptian conditions.

But these very advantages yielded by the company are far from being without compensation, for if, on the one hand, the Egyptian Government shares in the profits, on the other hand, it lavishes gifts upon them, besides the grant of a privilege for ninety-nine years.

It secures to them the gratuitous possession of all the land which the course of the Canal will cover and of all the land near its banks.

It grants them the possession of all Government lands which will be watered, that is to say which will be brought to their utmost state of fertility by the two branch canals, from the Nile to Lake Timsah and from Timsah to Suez.

It guarantees to them the free admission of all instruments, materials, machines, and articles of every kind necessary for their work.

It takes upon itself the greater part of the expenses connected with the surveys and the preliminary operations; it has made, and continues to make, important advances.

Are so many privileges and favours recompensed too highly by the association of the giver, even to the amount of 15 per cent., in the net profits of the enterprise which owes to him all these abundant germs of a future harvest?

I go farther still, Mr. Editor. I declare that the value of the land which has been granted will alone, after the establishment of fresh-water canals, which is to be the first work, represent a capital corresponding at least to the collective funds which are to be supplied for the performance of all parts of the plan.

The company, therefore, receives from the Egyptian Government much more than it gives, and owes to the Viceroy thanks, and not reproaches.

I believe, Mr. Editor, that I have now replied to every essential or important point in the assertions which have been sent to you. Your correspondent endeavours also to make war upon my publication respecting the Isthmus of Suez in trivial matters of statistic detail. I really cannot lengthen a discussion already too long by engaging in these uninteresting skirmishes. I content myself with adhering to my calculations. If he insists on an examination, I am ready to prove that the error is not on my side.

There are still, however, some other considerations mentioned by your correspondent which, I think, require a passing mention and contradiction.

Among the reasons which he brings forward to prove the impracticability of the enterprise, he declares that in the plans no arrangement has been made for supplying food and water to the body of workmen who are to be placed upon the barren and unpopulated isthmus.

It is evident that your correspondent has read neither my prospectus nor the preliminary plan prepared by the engineers, MM. Linant and Mougel, otherwise he would have seen that this necessity was, on the contrary, the first to be thought of and provided for. The plans for the work clearly announce that the first operation to be undertaken is to commence the cutting which will put the Nile into navigable communication with the isthmus, and thus secure to the whole line not only fresh water and necessary provisions, but also the means of inland navigation, which will facilitate arrangements and labour.

Your correspondent, who appears to enjoy and to seek occasions for displaying his hostility to the Egyptian Government, draws a very dark, but, I should say, a very untrue, picture of the fate of the native workmen under the power of the Administration and through the negligence of the Ministers. What is the use of this digression? The Egyptian Government will have nothing to do with the matter. The workmen will be paid under the superintendence and on the responsibility of the Universal Company, managed by Europeans.

Your correspondent, still full of the desire of finding that the cutting is impossible, forces himself to fear that, though the soil of the isthmus is light on the surface, it may change, lower down, into limestone and beds of flint. Even that would not be an insurmountable difficulty. But on what reason or what probability does this supposition rest? On none at all. Nay, I am mistaken, it rests on one. He declares that no borings have been made in the isthmus, and if none have been made, evidently their results could not be favourable *to the purpose of the projectors*.

The reply is easy, and it will be decisive.

Numerous borings have been made in the isthmus at various times. It is well known that M. Figari, a distinguished Italian geologist, has been employed many years in works of this kind, and I have in my possession an interesting memorandum from him on this very question.

Besides this, the Viceroy's engineers have proposed to renew these experiments. There are in consequence at this moment three brigades of engineers in the desert. The first is making borings on the intended line of the Canal, the second is occupied in marking this line on the ground, and the third is taking the various levels of the line. The works are being carried on in such a way as to enable the engineers to lay before the scientific international commission, on the spot, the whole series of operations and of the results obtained from them.

Will your correspondent be reassured now? But might he not have been reassured much sooner if, as he is in the country, instead of sounding an alarm, he had endeavoured to obtain information?

Nor are these the only errors with which I have to reproach him. This is not the first time that he has made use of the enormous circulation of your journal to propagate false ideas respecting questions and facts of great importance.

He wrote to you, for instance, on the 9th September last, that the Viceroy of Egypt was going to Europe, in order to combat in Paris and London the bad effects of the complaints made of him by the Sultan to the Western Powers.

The Sultan has never expressed to the Western Powers, or to any Court, the sentiments towards his Highness Mohammed Said Pacha which are ascribed to him. I have many proofs of this; I may without impropriety mention some which have come under my own knowledge.

A short time ago I had the honour of a private audience of his Majesty the Sultan; and I am quite in a position to declare that his Majesty looks upon Mohammed Said Pacha as one of the most devoted supporters of his Crown, and that this opinion is shared by all the members of his Council.

I can safely affirm that never was a vassal on better terms with his suzerain, and that your correspondent's account is an invention not only without foundation, but even without probability.

In fact, does not this whole tale rest on the pretended indifference displayed by the Viceroy as to supporting his sovereign in the present war?

It will be sufficient to call to mind what Egypt has done on this occasion.

Immediately on his accession to power, Mohammed Said Pacha hastened to send to Constantinople 10,000 of his best troops. Since the commencement of the war in the Crimea the Egyptian contingent has been gradually increased to 37,000 men. The Viceroy at the same time joined his fleet to that of Constantinople; and the disaster at Sinope proved to the world the courage of his sailors, even before the defence of Silistria and Eupatoria had earned admiration for the discipline and devotion of his soldiers. The orders of the day issued by Omar Pacha, and the proclamations of the Sultan himself, did justice to the services of this army. The French and English press have spoken more than once in high terms of its exploits. Even quite recently an Egyptian corps supported General d'Allonville's cavalry in their brilliant encounter with the Russian cavalry.

The sending of 30,000 picked men, the aid of a fleet, the payment of tribute in advance, these are the efforts which have been made by Egypt under her present Government to support the honour and independence of the Ottoman Empire. The Divan has, therefore, nothing to complain of; and, I repeat, it is perfectly satisfied.

It would be a great misfortune, Mr. Editor, if the European press were to be deceived as to the intentions and actions of the enlightened prince who governs Egypt, not like a simple Pacha of Damascus or Smyrna, as your correspondent pretends, but by virtue of an hereditary right guaranteed by international treaties.

Your correspondent, who says nothing about the wrong-doings of the present Viceroy's predecessor, about the disorders and irregularities of his Government, seems to have made it his task systematically to decry the prince who is now labouring to repair these faults. An enumeration of the improvements and reforms which have already marked his short administration will suffice for his defence. From the first year of his government he has restored freedom to commerce; he has done away with inland custom-houses; he has destroyed the tax upon natural productions, the chief source of the oppression of the Fellahs; he has restored the balance of the finances; he has religiously fulfilled all obligations entered into by the former Government; he has satisfied the claims of foreign agents; he has ordered the completion, at his own expense, of the railway from Alexandria to the Red Sea; and he has proposed to Europe to cut through the Isthmus of Suez. Results such as these may defy the attacks of censoriousness or of ill-humour.

To hinder is the strength and resource of vulgar natures; to advance and to give assistance to well-disposed persons is the instinct of noble and generous minds.

I owe, sir, a public acknowledgment to your highly esteemed journal for having been the first to aid, by its sympathy and its approbation, an enterprise which will be one of the grandest claims of our age upon posterity, and the eternal glory of the prince who conceived it and is about to carry out its execution.

The opinion of all Europe is now in favour of the success of this work; it will certainly honour you for the impartiality and intelligence displayed by you in seconding it, and I know that this will be your best recompense.

Accept Mr. Editor, &c.

LXXIII.

To Madame Delamalle, Paris.

(Continuation of the Journal.)

Malta, *November* 13, 1855.

WE embarked at Marseilles, in the *Osiris*, a name of good omen in Egypt, for in old times it represented the prosperity and fecundity of the land, through the regular inundations of the Nile.

The following are the members of the party:

Messrs. MacClean, Conrad, Renaud, Lieussou, Larousse, Barthélemy Saint-Hilaire, Linant and Mougel, my son Charles Aimé, M. and Madame Lafosse, Mr. Senior (a friend of the Mr. Ellice who received me so kindly in London), Mrs. Senior, and MM. Jobez and Jacquesson, friends of Saint-Hilaire.

I have received the following letter from M. Ruyssenaers:

As soon as you arrive in the harbour of Alexandria, Hafouz Pacha, Minister of Marine, Kœnig Bey, Private Secretary to his Highness, and I, will come alongside with Government boats to receive and escort the commissioners, your travelling companions, to land. On the quay you will find his Highness's carriages to take you all to the hotel, where apartments have been prepared by order of the Viceroy. Preparations are being made at Cairo and Suez for your reception, and everything is being arranged for your journey into Upper Egypt and the desert. Lastly, orders have been given that a special train should be prepared for you on the day of your arrival, as the Viceroy wishes to see you first in private, probably that he may come to an understanding with you before receiving the commissioners.

<p style="text-align:center">ON THE NILE, DAMIETTA BRANCH, November 19, 1855.
(<i>My Fiftieth Birthday.</i>)</p>

AT three o'clock yesterday I left Alexandria by railway and at seven arrived at Kaferleïs, where I found a steamboat waiting to take me to the *barrage*.

This morning I met the Viceroy, who was coming to welcome me with his little squadron of steamers. He stopped them, sent his boat for me, and when I went on board threw himself into my arms and embraced me cordially. He was visibly affected, and spoke to me most affectionately.

I breakfasted with him, and we remained four hours in conversation. The whole plan of our future operations was arranged exactly according to my wishes. He is anxious for my companions, the members of the commission, to be his guests, and he will give them a hearty welcome and splendid hospitality.

During our excursions he will send a confidential agent to Constantinople to press for the ratification. He approves of my plan as to contracts and bye-laws. In short, he is very much pleased with all that has been done. All is, therefore, going on well.

<p style="text-align:center">LXXIV.
To M. THOUVENEL, FRENCH AMBASSADOR AT CONSTANTINOPLE.
CAIRO, <i>November</i> 22, 1855.</p>

I SEND you a memorandum of the proceedings of the international commission since its arrival in Egypt. We set off to-morrow in a steamer to ascend the Nile as far as the first cataract.

The Viceroy has informed me that as soon as the commissioners have brought their investigations to a close, and are in a position to lay before him their final opinion as to the possibility of the junction of the two seas, (reserving to themselves the power of drawing out a complete plan of the works in Europe), he intends to send Edhem Pacha, Minister of Foreign Affairs, to Constantinople, whom he proposes including amongst the international commissioners, and who will watch all their operations. Edhem Pacha is not unacquainted with the art of engineering, which he studied in England and France. For the last thirty years he has been successively at the head of the management of Public Instruction and of Public Works in Egypt. His mission to the Porte will be to hasten the Sultan's ratification of the grant in favour of the Suez Canal, which is to be executed by a company of capitalists of all nations.

The Viceroy has already given verbal instructions to Edhem Pacha, in my presence, in the following terms:

> When you have presented my official letters to the Porte you will state how important it is for the dignity of the Empire, and as a proof of its resolution to maintain its internal independence, that I should receive the authorisation I have now been soliciting for a year, and which has been agreed to in theory by the Divan. This just desire of displaying internal independence cannot reasonably meet with any serious obstacle from the Powers which have combined to defend the exterior independence of the Empire. I do not ask that the approbation I seek should be sent me clandestinely. I am but a simple Pacha, but for all that, after having publicly announced my plan to the Representatives of all the foreign Powers, no one has raised any objections; on the contrary, I have nothing but congratulations. Let the same line of conduct be pursued at Constantinople; and if, by chance, any opposition should be raised, let the Government ask to have the reasons for such opposition formally expressed in writing. We must have done with delays; and when once European science has proved the possibility of the enterprise we must not wait until the opinion of Europe rises up against unjustifiable resistance, or against a passive attitude calculated to justify those who refuse to believe in the existence amongst us, either now or in the future, of elements of national progress and vitality.

You will, doubtless, think it wise to inform the Emperor's Government (at the same time stating your own opinion) of the new phase about to be entered into by the Suez Canal affair. For my part, I shall acquaint Count Walewski with it through our friend M. Sabatier.

MEMORANDUM JOINED TO THE ABOVE LETTER.

THE international commissioners for surveying the Isthmus of Suez left Marseilles on the 8th of November. Having reached Alexandria on the 18th, and spent three days in that town, they made excursions to the east and west, to study the nature of the rocks, as well as of the sands which stretch along the whole shore as far as the mouths of the Nile. The commissioners have chosen M. Conrad, a Dutch engineer, as their president. On the 23rd they were received with distinction and cordiality by his Highness the Viceroy of Egypt at the camp near the *barrage*, where the Egyptian troops (whose manœuvres were excellent) are trained under the personal direction of the prince. Having been consulted by him respecting various works which he is executing or planning for the internal canalisation of the country, the commissioners must first proceed to Upper Egypt, and ascend the Nile as far as the First Cataract. They will then descend as far as Cairo, and go from thence to Suez, in order to commence the scientific exploration of the isthmus as far as Pelusium. In the meantime special agents are continuing the necessary taking of levels along the line of the maritime canal, the placing of stakes and borings, which are already completed in the greater part of the route, and of which the present results are most satisfactory. Other agents are working at the hydrographic exploration of the Gulf of Pelusium, into which the Canal is to flow. In a word, the international commission, aided by the munificence of Mohammed Said Pacha, who has spared no expense to facilitate their surveys, are working as earnestly as could be desired, and the time is not far off when they will be in a position to pronounce their final decision with regard to the undertaking which has so justly excited the interest of Europe.

LXXV.

To Madame Delamalle, Paris.

Cairo, *November* 27, 1855.

After I had written to you on the 19th, and had told you about my first interview with the Viceroy, we went together to his country residence near the *barrage*. He has had two rooms prepared for me in his own apartments. We were together three days from morning till night. You will believe that the time was usefully employed, and that we had leisure to pass and repass in review all questions concerning the present and the future of the Canal. This excellent prince, whose knowledge is most varied and who has a wonderful memory, has also said a great deal to me about the details of his Government and all that he has done for the benefit of the country since my departure, of his personal administration and the difficulties he meets with from those who serve him, most of whom, instead of doing their duty, seek only to enrich themselves. He confessed to me that he has often been overwhelmed by discouragement, and had thought of giving up his power. " Think how grievous it is," said he, "to be in the position of a man who wishes to do right, but yet, from actions of the subordinates he is obliged to employ, is aware that history may one day justly accuse him of having done wrong. It is of no use to lecture my Turkish functionaries: very few of them believe that they ought to identify themselves with the country to the prosperity of which they owe their own well-being. They still want to milk the cow without taking care of her, and without being willing to give her anything to eat. Nothing is ever too good for them; but when some poor Fellah is in question, it is quite another thing. I have just turned off one of my Turkish secretaries. Will you believe me that the knave, to whom I had given an order to write a decree granting a modest pension to an Egyptian soldier who had been maimed in the East, had the audacity to tell me that the sum was too great for the man? The other day, too, I was informed that an old master-blacksmith of the arsenal, who has served for forty years, and has trained a great number of excellent workmen, was reduced (on account of having been blind ten years) to owe his subsistence to the charity of his former pupils. He asked for a pension, which was never granted him. The President of the Council at Cairo, my representative, that traitor Hassan Pacha, considered that the poor fellow had no right to one, because during the time he was in the service he had received daily wages, and not an annual salary!"

I comforted the dear prince by reminding him of all that he has done within the last year, and mentioned some honest, modest, and energetic men who might assist him. "With such noble intentions and such an excellent object," I added, "you cannot but succeed. You cannot do everything at once; but with perseverance you will soon get out of the position which now appears difficult and complicated."

At dinner, in the evening, he remarked that I eat very little, so I told him that I had been thinking of all that he had told me, and that I much regretted the periods of depression he had mentioned to me.

It was now his turn to reassure me. He resumed his former vivacity. What I had told him of the fame which would from henceforth be attached to his name on account of the great enterprise of the Suez Canal, and the arrival of the international commissioners, who had come to Egypt on his summons, had, he said, quite restored his spirits. He continued to show me the most touching marks of confidence during the ensuing days.

I enclose a copy of the letter I am about to send to M. Thouvenel at Constantinople. I shall also communicate it to my brother Theodore, so that he may acquaint Count Walewski and M. Benedetti with the Viceroy's resolution.

I presented the commissioners to the Viceroy on the 23rd. He could not have welcomed them more graciously. They were all enchanted with their reception. The Viceroy's conversation with them was very full of witty remarks. When I remarked to him that he treated them liked crowned heads, he replied immediately, "So I ought: for they are heads crowned by science." He invited them all to breakfast with him. He also begged Kœnig Bey, his former tutor, now his private secretary, to sit down at table, and presented him to them with the remark, "He has often put me upon bread and water; but I do not treat him so in return."

We embark to-morrow for Upper Egypt in a very comfortably furnished and well provisioned steamer.

ON THE NILE, *November* 27, 1855.

THE reception given by the Viceroy to the members of the commission, and the noble liberality with which he has provided all that could aid our voyage or make it agreeable, surpassed all my hopes. This reception, besides the comforts which it procures for us, has the best possible moral effect with regard to our enterprise, for it makes the warm support of the Viceroy clear to every one. The progress made in one year is immense; you will understand the satisfaction I feel when I see the various phases of the plan I have formed gradually and successfully unfolding themselves.

We are all pleased with our new fellow-traveller, M. de Negrelli. He is a gentleman and a man of the world; we are on pleasant terms with him. He has shown me the letters he has already written to his Government from Cairo. He insists upon the necessity of not allowing diplomacy to interfere further than by volunteering its good offices and encouraging the Porte to give its distinct approbation to the Viceroy's project. The work of the engineers sent by him to the Gulf of Pelusium in 1846 is very interesting. It consists of a dozen highly elaborate plans, giving the soundings, the inclinations and the declivities of the soil under the water, from the shore to a certain distance in the sea. He is convinced, from observations made during several consecutive months, that there is but little movement of the land in the bay, where the anchorage is very good, as it enabled the man-of-war which brought the Austrian engineers to remain anchored there throughout March, April, and May without any inconvenience. Their operations are now found to be correct, and are being completed by the exertions of M. Larousse, a hydrographic engineer in our navy, who has been placed at my disposal by his Minister; and by those of M. de Hommet, a naval lieutenant, a clever and distinguished officer, whom M. Albert Rostand, director *des Servicee Maritimes des Messageries Impériales*, has permitted me to employ. Thus the further we advance in the examination of the questions bearing upon the great work of cutting through the isthmus, which appears impossible to so many persons, the greater are the facilities afforded to us by beneficent nature.

A fresh report, which has been sent to us by the engineers appointed to make soundings along the intended course of the Canal, again gives us most favourable results, which are moreover conformable to the opinion expressed beforehand by M. Elie de Beaumont.

Mr. MacClean, the English engineer, who replaced Mr. Rendel (invalided), and whose scientific knowledge and uprightness do justice to the recommendation of Mr. Charles Manby, is not the most backward of our engineers in enthusiasm for the success of the enterprise.

M. Conrad, the Dutch engineer, has been elected president of the commissioners by his colleagues. He is an excellent and very well-informed man, and we think very highly of him.

I need not speak to you of our countrymen MM. Renaud and Lieussou, with whom you are acquainted. We might have looked a long time before we met with better men.

BEFORE THEBES, *December* 1, 1855.

THIS morning we visited the ruins of Dendera. The temple is dedicated to Hathôr, the Egyptian Venus. It is modern in comparison with the other monuments of Egypt, as it only dates from Cleopatra and the Roman period. Champollion said, when he saw it,—

> I shall not endeavour to describe the impression made upon us by the propylæon, and, above all, by the portico of this great temple. It

is easy enough to measure it; but to give an idea of it is impossible. In it grace and majesty are equally combined.

We experienced the same feeling.

The portico, or vestibule of the temple has eighteen columns, each sixty feet high and twenty-one feet in circumference. From the base to the capital each is covered with hieroglyphics, as are also all the walls, both external and internal. From the vestibule you pass into the principal hall, into which, on the right and left, open chambers, passages, and staircases leading to the platform. Beyond the principal hall you come to another, a smaller one, corresponding with the choir of our cathedrals, enclosed by walls covered, like the others, with hieroglyphics, and with a passage running round them. Behind this passage are narrow corridors, with carvings, in splendid preservation, and a portrait of Cleopatra on every stone. In one of these sculptures she is represented recumbent, having just given birth to Cæsarion, her son by Julius Cæsar. The face of Cleopatra does not belie her reputation for beauty; and one can understand how, after being the widow of her two brothers, she made a conquest of the all-conquering Cæsar, and afterwards reigned supreme in the heart of Antony, whose misfortunes and death were the cause of the tragical end of this queen, so frequently represented by our painters. The engraving in my study at La Chenaie gives a very unworthy idea of the famous and last descendant of the Ptolemys.

We are now before Thebes, a short distance from Luxor. After dinner I landed alone on the bank of the river. In the shadow I saw colonnades and porticoes, and I could not resist an inclination to go nearer. I was thus able, by the light of the stars, to admire a row of columns loftier and more massive than those of Dendera, porticoes, temples, and the *brother* of the Obelisk in the Place de la Concorde. I went on board again, to give an account of my excursion to my fellow-travellers. My son, Charles Aimé, immediately went with them to enjoy the sight. We shall go and see it all again early to-morrow morning. We shall then breakfast on board, after which, at about eleven o'clock, horses will be brought for us to ride to Karnac, where there is a great deal to be seen.

M. and Madame Lafosse are still in raptures with their journey. Madame Lafosse is very much pleased with the horses of the country; she greatly enjoyed her ride this morning to Dendera. Mrs. Senior will not be perfectly happy until she has seen a crocodile; we have several times passed places where they are generally seen in great numbers, but unfortunately it appears that the paddles of the steamer frighten them and drive them to seek a refuge at the bottom of the Nile. Modern civilisation terrifies this sacred animal of the Old Egyptians, and it is no wonder that it should prefer the food thrown to it by the priests of the temples of Thebes to the sharp whistle of the steamboat, announcing our appearance this evening at one of the hundred gates of the oldest city in the world.

We laugh at Mrs. Senior about her intense wish for a crocodile. Madame Lafosse, who in some degree shares this wish, has promised the pilot five francs for the first crocodile he shows her. The ancient Egyptians called this amphibious creature *champsah;* the Arabs call it *timsah* (that, you know, is to be the name of our future internal harbour on the Suez Canal). Dendera and Thebes do not make me forget the dear Canal, for I am perfectly mad on that subject.

OFF THEBES, *December* 4, 1855.

OUR first day at Thebes (the 2nd) was devoted to visiting the monuments of antiquity on the right bank, at Luxor and Karnac. Those at Luxor consist of a succession of temples or palaces, founded by Pharaoh Amenophis-Memnon III., about 3500 years ago. The dedication of these temples as translated by Champollion will give you an idea of the hieroglyphic style; it is as follows:

Hail! the powerful and temperate Hôrus, reigning by a just claim: the organiser of his country, he who keeps the world in tranquillity, because in the greatness of his strength he has vanquished the Barbarians; the royal Lord of Justice, the Well-beloved of the Sun, Child of the Sun, Amenophis, governor of the Pure Region [Egypt], has raised these buildings, consecrated to Ammon [the principal Egyptian divinity], the Sovereign God of the Three Zones of the Universe, in the Oph of the South [that is the southern part of Thebes]. He has caused them to be executed in good and hard stone, in order to erect a durable edifice: this is what has been done by the Child of the Sun, Amenophis, the cherished of Ammon Ra.

The original monuments of Luxor were added to or restored by the successors of Amenophis III. until the commencement of the Greek domination under Alexander, son of Alexander the Great.

In one of the halls are a series of bas-reliefs representing the wife of Pharaoh Thoutmosis IV. In the first the god Thoth is seen announcing to her that Ammon has granted her a son; then the same queen, whose situation is clearly indicated, is conducted by Hathôr (Venus) to the lying-in chamber (the Mammisi); farther on she is represented on a bed giving birth to King Amenophis; women are supporting her, and divine genii, who support the bed, raise the emblem of life towards the new-born child. In another, the queen is nursing the young prince. In another, the god Nile, painted blue (the period of low water), and the god Nile, painted red (the period of high water, or inundation), are presenting the little Amenophis, together with other divine children, to the chief divinities of Thebes; the royal infant is in the arms of Ammon Ra, who is caressing him. Then, again, the young king is being instituted by Ammon Ra; the goddesses who protect Upper and Lower Egypt are offering him crowns, the emblems of his rule over the two countries. And in the last bas-relief Thoth is selecting his great name: *Sun*, Lord of Justice and Truth.

Some buildings behind the grand colonnade, which I mentioned in my last letter, and especially the great pylons and the two obelisks (one of which is in Paris), date from the period of Rameses the Great (Sesostris)—that is to say, about 3200 years ago. The pylons are immense stone walls of from fifty to sixty feet high, the pictures on which, representing Sesostris fighting and conquering his enemies, have been frequently reproduced.

We went on board again at ten o'clock. We had as many as thirty horses, collected from all parts, to take us to Karnac in the afternoon. After half-an-hour's journey we filed through the great avenue of Sphinxes, most of which are mutilated; passed under the immense sculptured gateway, the general appearance of which, though they cannot be compared, coincides with that of the Arc de l'Etoile; and found ourselves opposite a succession of monuments, of which no description can give you any idea. How, indeed, can it be possible to convey the impression produced by the Great Hall of Karnac, where assemblies were held? This hall has a hundred and forty columns, sixty feet in height and twenty-seven in circumference. The sculptures and colours are admirably preserved. Of this scene Champollion wrote:

> I shall take care not to describe anything, for either my words would fail to express the thousandth part of what ought to be said in describing such objects, or if I were to make a faint outline of them, even a very imperfect one, I should be taken for an enthusiast, perhaps even for a madman.

He adds, however:

> In this marvellous palace I contemplated the portraits of the old Pharaohs, famous for their great actions; and they are real portraits. Though carved a thousand times in the bas-reliefs in the external and internal walls, each preserves his own physiognomy, which is quite different from that of predecessors and successors; there, in colossal representations, sculptured in a manner more perfect than any one in Europe could conceive, we see Madoueë fighting against the enemies of Egypt, and returning triumphant to his country; farther on are the campaigns of Rameses-Sesostris; in another place, Shishak is dragging to the feet of the Theban Trinity the chiefs of more than thirty conquered nations, amongst which I discovered (by the letters composing the name), Iouda-hamalek, the king of the Jews, or of Judea. Here is a commentary on the fourteenth chapter of the First Book of Kings, which relates the arrival of Shishak in Jerusalem and his successes.

The kingdom of Judea is personified by the portrait of King Rehoboam, the same who is mentioned in the Bible.

The resemblance of this portrait to the face of Isaac Pereire struck me very much; he must be descended in a direct line from King Rehoboam, who lived a thousand years before Christ.

Mr. MacClean has calculated that the extent of the palace of Karnac is equal to two-thirds of the railway station at Birmingham; each side appears to be a thousand mètres, or a quarter of a league, in length. From it a view is obtained, in the plain on the other side of the Nile, of the two colossal statues of Memnon, and the temples on the left bank which we are to visit to-morrow.

Mr. MacClean has made another calculation: he says that he would undertake to erect a monument in Europe resembling the largest pyramid of Gizeh for 25,000,000 francs, and that the Suez Canal will represent an amount of labour—in removing soil and carrying materials—thirty times as great as that of the pyramid, and that it will cost only eight times as much as the latter would cost to build now, that is to say, 200,000,000 francs.

We left the palace of Karnac by a second avenue of Sphinxes opening on to the ruins of a little temple, which was, and still is, surrounded by a large circular pool formed by the hand of man. There the ground is covered with colossal fallen figures and basalt statues, in perfect preservation; from this place most of the statues now in the museums of Europe were taken.

We paused on our return under the colonnade of Luxor, where some Arab sellers of antiquities were awaiting us. We each purchased something. I bought twenty-four sheets of thick grey paper, for Victorinet, on which were impressions of Egyptian sculptures, representing them very correctly, and three pieces of cloth of palm fibre found in the tombs. Last year eight hundred pieces of this cloth were found in one tomb. It is the same as was used for making bandages to bind up the mummies.

After dinner we found that the Governor of the place had prepared a ball-room for us on the shore, near the spot where our steamer was anchored. This ball-room consisted of a carpet spread upon the ground: it was lighted by four machallahs, or torches made of resinous wood. In the background were squatting Arabs, to the left were the musicians, near them five dancing girls with their clown, and on the right were arranged folding-chairs ready for the European public.

As soon as we left the dinner-table and appeared on deck, the dancing commenced. M. Lafosse and M. Barthélemy Saint-Hilaire, accompanied by the commissioners and Mr. Senior, took their places on the chairs. I remained on deck with Mrs. Senior and Madame Lafosse. I thought the dresses of the dancing girls and the light of the torches reflected in the water would have a better effect from that distance than from a closer position. Mrs. Senior did not think the dance *very shocking;* but, as you will suppose, it had been requested that there should be no improprieties in the performance.

The next morning (the 3rd) we were all on the alert at five o'clock. Our horses had been assembled the evening before on the other bank, and as soon as we found they were ready we embarked for the eastern side of Thebes.

The first monument to be visited when you approach Thebes from this side is that of Koorneh. This edifice, though very inferior in extent to the grand and important buildings of Karnac, strikes the eye equally with them, by its magnificence, the profusion of its sculptures, and the solidity of its materials. It belongs to the age of the Pharaohs, and carries us back to the most glorious epoch of which Egyptian annals have preserved the memory. Much *débris* is scattered about on the ground near, pointing to the existence of other and still more ancient monuments.

The bas-reliefs which adorn the interior of the portico and the exterior of the three doors leading into the palace apartments, represent Menephta I., and, more frequently, Rameses the Great, doing homage to the divinities of Egypt, or receiving from the bounty of the gods the regal power and the other blessings which were to embellish their mortal life. We remarked a series of small designs in which the presiding gods of the Nile and protecting goddesses of Egypt are represented presenting Rameses the Great with all the products of land and water, in monthly rotation.

The central door opens into a hall fifty feet long by thirty-five wide; a great part of the ceiling, which is supported by columns, still remains, with its coloured hieroglyphics.

Champollion says that one of the inscriptions contains the dedication of the palace by Menephta I. A second inscription informs us that this hall was the place where religious and political assemblies were held and where the courts of justice sat. It was intended, though on a smaller scale, for the same purposes as the vast halls of the great Theban palaces, supported on many rows of columns. Champollion tells us that they all have the name Manôskh in the inscriptions carved on the ceilings, that is to say, *the place of harvest*, meaning, of course, *the place where grain is measured*, which name was always reserved by the Egyptians for the largest halls in their public edifices.

We had the opportunity of seeing that Government corn is still measured under the colonnades of the old palace of Luxor.

One of our guides, an old man who had accompanied Champollion, and who showed me a recent certificate given him by M. Mimaut, pointed out to me the sculptures on the walls which had been especially studied by our illustrious countryman, whose premature death was a great loss to science. He showed me one where the childhood of Rameses the Great is represented. The young king is being embraced by the divine mother Mouth, who offers him her breast.

The inscription is as follows, verbatim:—

> Thus speaks Mouth, the Lady of Heaven: My cherished and loving son, Lord of Diadems, Rameses, the beloved of Ammon, I, thy mother, rejoice in thy good deeds; feed on my milk.

Another corresponding composition is sculptured on the opposite wall: the goddess Hâthor (Venus) is nursing the King Manephta I., and addressing him in the same words.

After our visit to Koorneh we remounted our horses and entered the valley leading to the tombs of the kings, hollowed out under the mountain. It is indeed the valley of death and desolation; there is not one blade of grass nor one living creature to be found there. Masses of rock, stones detached from the mountains, were strewn on either side, whilst overhead shone a sun which was hardly bearable even in the month of December. After an hour's journey we were amply rewarded by a visit to the tomb discovered by Belzoni in 1815. We all declared it to be the most interesting thing we had yet seen. After this exploration we found an excellent breakfast awaiting us at the entrance of another tomb; and when the meal was ended I read a chapter from Champollion to my companions, from which I give you some extracts:—

> The topographical details given by Strabo do not permit us to seek the tombs of the ancient kings anywhere but in the valley of Biban-el-Molouk. This was the royal necropolis, and the place selected was perfectly suitable to its sad destination. . . . No order was observed, either as to dynasty or succession, in the choice of the position of the different royal tombs. Each king caused his own to be hollowed out in the spot where he thought he had found a vein of stone suitable for his burial and for the size of the intended excavation. It is difficult to repress a certain feeling of surprise when, after passing under a very simple doorway, one enters wide galleries or corridors, covered with sculptures in perfect preservation, leading in succession to halls supported by pillars still more richly decorated, until at last one reaches the principal hall, called by the Egyptians the Gilded Hall, which was larger than any of the others, and in which reposed the mummy of the king in an enormous granite sarcophagus.

I will now give you a description of the first tomb we saw, that of Pharaoh Rameses, the son and successor of Meïamoun, who lived 3100 years ago.

I am still quoting Champollion:—

> The string-course of the outer door is ornamented with a bas-relief which is, in most respects, the same as all the decorations of the tombs of the Pharaohs. It is a yellow disk, in the middle of which is the Sun, with the head of a ram (that is to say, the setting sun), entering the southern hemisphere, and adored by the kneeling king; on the right of the disk, that is to say, on the east, is the goddess Nephtys, and

on the left (the west), the goddess Isis, occupying the two extremities of the sun-god's course in the northern hemisphere; by the side of the sun, within the disk, is sculptured a large beetle, which here, as elsewhere, is the symbol of regeneration or of successive transmigrations: the king is kneeling on the celestial mountain, on which rest the feet of the two goddesses.

The sculpture I have described is always accompanied by an inscription, of which the following is a literal translation: " Thus speaks Osiris, the Lord of the Amenti [the western region inhabited by the dead]: I have granted to thee a dwelling in the sacred mountain of the west, as I did to the other great gods [the kings who preceded him], to thee, Osiris, king, Lord of the World, &c., still living." This last expression would prove, if it were necessary, that the tombs of the Pharaohs, enormous undertakings which required lengthened toil, were commenced while they lived, and that one of the first cares of an Egyptian king was, in conformity with the well-known custom of this singular nation, to provide immediately for the execution of the sepulchral monument which was to be his last asylum.

This is still more plainly demonstrated by the first bas-relief which meets our eyes on entering the tombs. On the ceiling of the first corridor we read magnificent promises made to the king for this mortal life and a list of the privileges reserved for him in the celestial regions.

Immediately after this sculpture, a very delicate sort of oratorical prologue, the matter is more fully entered upon by a symbolical carving: the disk of the Sun has set out from the East and is advancing towards the frontier of the West, which is distinguished by a crocodile, an emblem of the darkness into which the sun and the king are about to enter. . . .

These general representations are followed by a development of details. Some of the walls of the succeeding corridors and halls are covered with a long series of sculptures representing the journey of the Sun through the northern hemisphere (an emblem of the king during life), and on the opposite walls is portrayed his progress through the southern hemisphere (an emblem of the king after death).

The numerous sculptures relating to the journey of the sun-god above the horizon and in the luminous hemisphere, are divided into twelve series, each separated from the rest by a richly-carved door and guarded by an enormous serpent. These doors represent the twelve hours of the day. Near the door of the first series, that of sunrise, we find the twenty-four hours of the astronomical day typified by human forms, each, with a star on its head, walking towards the centre of the tomb, as if to watch the direction of the sun-god's course. In each of the twelve hours of the day is represented the barque of the god floating on the celestial river. . . .

By the first Hour the *bari*, or barque, is beginning to move, and receives the worship of the spirits of the East. Among the sculptures of the second Hour is seen the great serpent Apophis, the

brother and enemy of the Sun, watched by the god Atum. At the
third hour the sun-god arrives in the celestial zone, where the fate
of souls is decided with regard to the bodies they are to inhabit during
their fresh transmigrations; we see the god Atum seated on his
throne, weighing in the balance the human souls which present
themselves one after the other; one has just been condemned; we see
it being reconducted to earth in a *bari*, which advances towards the
gate-way guarded by Anubis (with the head of a wolf or jackal), and
then driven along with rods by Cynocephali (dogs' heads), emblems
of celestial justice; the guilty soul being represented under the form
of an immense trout, over which is carved in large letters, *greed*, or
gluttony.

The sun-god at the fifth Hour visits the Elysian fields of Egyptian
mythology, inhabited by happy souls, resting after their transmigrations on earth; on their heads they wear the ostrich feather, the
emblem of their upright and virtuous conduct. We see them presenting offerings to the gods, or, under the inspection of the Lord of
Joy, they are gathering the fruits of the celestial trees of Paradise.
Farther on some are holding sickles in their hands: these are the
souls who cultivate the fields of truth. Elsewhere we see them bathing,
swimming, and sporting in a large basin filled with heavenly and
primordial water, all under the inspection of the god of the Nile. In
the following Hours the gods are preparing to fight the great enemy
of the Sun, the serpent Apophis. They are arming themselves with
hunting spears and loading themselves with nets, because the monster inhabits the waters of the river on which the vessel of the Sun
sails; then they stretch out cords, Apophis is taken; he is bound.
They take the immense reptile out of the river by means of a cable
which the goddess Selk attaches to his neck, and which is drawn by
twelve gods, assisted by a very complicated machine worked by the
god Sev (Saturn), assisted by the genii of the Four Cardinal Points.
But all these preparations would be useless against the efforts of
Apophis but for an enormous hand (that of Ammon), which, appearing from below, seizes the cord and stops the dragon's violence. At
the eleventh Hour of the day the captive serpent is strangled, and soon
after the sun-god arrives at the extreme point of the horizon, where he
disappears. . . .

The Sun's journey through the southern hemisphere (that of darkness) during the twelve hours of the night is sculptured on the walls
of the royal tomb opposite to those of which I have just given you a
short account. There the god, who is always painted black from head
to foot, passes through the seventy-five circles, or zones, which are presided over by the same number of divine personages of all shapes,
armed with swords. These circles are inhabited by guilty souls, who
are suffering various punishments; it is, indeed, the original idea of
Dante's hell, for the variety of torments is truly astonishing, and I am
not surprised that some travellers, horrified at these scenes of carnage,
have thought that they found in them a proof of human sacrifices in

ancient Egypt; but the inscriptions remove all doubt on this head: these are the proceedings of another world, which have nothing to do with the manners and customs of this one.

The guilty souls are punished in different ways in most of the infernal zones visited by the sun-god; these impure spirits are almost always represented under a human shape, but sometimes under the symbolical form of a crane or a sparrow-hawk with a human head, painted black all over, to indicate at once their perverse nature and their dwelling in the abyss of darkness. The souls are firmly bound to stakes, and the guardians of the zone, brandishing their swords, reproach them with the crimes they have committed on earth; some are suspended head downwards; some, with their hands bound upon their breasts and their heads cut off, are walking in a long file; others, with their hands tied behind their backs, are dragging their hearts, which have been torn from their breasts, along the ground. Living souls, in great caldrons, are being boiled, either in a human form or in that of a bird; in some cases only their heads and hearts are represented. I also remarked some souls thrown into the caldron with a fan, the emblem of happiness and celestial repose to which they had lost all right.

On each zone, near the victims, is inscribed their condemnation and the penalty they are suffering. *These hostile souls*, it is written, *do not see our god when he darts rays from his disk; they no longer inhabit the terrestrial world, and they do not hear the voice of the great god when he passes through their zones.* While, on the contrary, near the representation of the happy souls on the opposite walls one reads: *They have found favour in the eyes of the great god; they inhabit the dwellings of glory, where a celestial life is theirs; the bodies which they have quitted will repose for ever in their tombs, while they themselves will enjoy the presence of the supreme god.*

I wished to copy these details, with which I was much struck, because they show that this old land of Egypt is the mother of everything—of religion, arts, and sciences. How great is the analogy between the Egyptian system of rewards and punishments after this life and our hell and the paradise where *the elect shall rejoice in the presence of the Lord!*

Moses was instructed in the mysteries of the Egyptian priests revealed to us by Champollion. Plato, another of the initiated, taught his disciples the immortality of the soul; and, later, Christianity, relying upon this great truth, purified all previous doctrines by one simple rule never before practised and but little heeded now: *Love one another.*

In the second tomb visited by us, that of Rameses Meïamoun, we observed eight small halls, opening on the right and left from the entrance passage, before we arrived at the large halls. On the walls of one of these little apartments is represented the mode of kneading bread, roasting, and other culinary operations; another reproduces all the furniture used by the Pharaohs—capital arm-chairs *à la* Voltaire, couches, with animals' feet, covered with rich stuffs; whilst another portrays a complete collection of the arms and military ensigns of the Egyptian legions. On the walls of another are to be seen carved and painted boats and royal barges, with their decorations. In one of these rooms two harpers are depicted, whose instruments exactly resemble modern harps, &c.

At about two o'clock we determined to attempt the passage of the valley, beneath a cloudless sky and under the influence of the sun-god in the upper hemisphere. We arrived, in the midst of a general silence, at the temple bearing the name of Rameseum, because Thebes owed it to the munificence of Rameses the Great (3200 years ago).

I again quote Champollion:—

The imagination is overwhelmed, and one feels a very natural emotion in visiting these mutilated galleries and beautiful colonnades, when one remembers that they were the work, and very frequently the habitation, of the best and most celebrated of the princes whom Egypt counts in her long annals, and to the memory of Sesostris I pay the same kind of religious veneration which all antiquity has surrounded him with. No part of the Rameseum remains complete; but what has escaped the barbarity of the Persians and the ravages of time is sufficient to give us a very exact idea of the whole. The Rameseum is perhaps the finest and noblest of the monuments of Thebes. . . .

The colonnades which laterally enclosed the first court no longer exist. The vast space formerly comprised between these galleries and the two pylons is encumbered by the enormous *débris* of what was probably the largest and most magnificent colossus the Egyptians ever raised, I allude to that of Rameses the Great.

This colossal statue of a seated man is broken into three pieces; it cannot have been less than thirty-five feet high, and was hewn from one piece of fine granite.

Numerous bas-reliefs, representing the king, Rameses, adoring the great divinities of Thebes, cover three sides of the pillars forming the gallery in front of the pylon; on the fourth side of each is sculptured a colossal figure of the king, about thirty feet high.

Some pillars adorned with colossal figures, and the columns which formed the second court of the palace, are also remarkable for the richness of their sculptures.

Farther on is the hypostyle hall (the hall of meetings), thirty columns of which still exist. At the entrance of this hall, to the right, is a bas-relief representing the mother of the conqueror; her name was Taouaï.

Leaving the hypostyle hall by the central door we entered another hall with columns, the decorations of which, like all the rest, are magnificent.

Farther on begin the king's private apartments.

The rest of the palace, which extended as far as the foot of the mountain, is completely destroyed.

We passed through the ruins, and took our way towards the two famous colossal statues of Memnon, which, rising from the midst of gigantic *débris*, still overlook the plain of Thebes; these *débris* occupy the space where formerly stood the palace of Memnon, so named by the Greeks, but which the Egyptians called Amenophis. This Amenophis, the third of his name, lived 1680 years B.C., according to Champollion.

The two statues are about sixty feet high; they both represent the monarch seated in an attitude of repose, with his hands on his knees. One of them was highly celebrated, because at one time it was supposed to emit sounds when struck by the first rays of the sun. At the foot of the statue are some old inscriptions of Greek and Roman tourists, declaring that they had really heard its accents. Since, either purposely or by accident, a cleft has been made in the entire length of this statue; a man, by climbing up to the part behind the chest, can produce a sound similar to that of a bell by striking with a hard stone on a certain point. I have heard it myself by making an Arab take in a stone; indeed, he even brought back a fragment from the part he had struck.

From thence, still keeping across the plain, we reached the hill of Medinet Habou. Here, half-buried under rubbish and heaps of earth, are a series of magnificent monuments, in no way inferior to those we had just visited. Champollion, who studied them carefully, discovered from them the state of the arts in Egypt in each of the principal periods, and obtained, so to speak, a summary of all the monuments of Egypt. We find here, he says, a temple belonging to the most brilliant Pharaonic period, that of the first kings of the Eighteenth Dynasty (which lasted nearly 4000 years); an immense palace of the period of the conquests; an edifice of the first decadence under the Ethiopian invasion; a chapel, erected under one of the princes who threw off the yoke of the Persians; a propylæum of the Greek dynasty; some propylæa of the Roman period; and, lastly, in one of the courts of the palace of the Pharaohs, some columns which once supported the coping of a Christian church.

This last visit, and certainly not the least interesting, terminated our explorations in Thebes. The day had been fully occupied. At sunset we re-embarked, with our horses, to return to the right bank of the river, and went on board our steamer, where we found a good dinner awaiting us, and our beds, of which we were very glad to avail ourselves.

This morning we took a distant farewell of the monuments of Thebes. Before the day broke, or we had risen, the motion of the paddles announced our departure.

We arrived at Esneh early. While we were "coaling," a word which sounds very inappropriate after poetical recollections of antiquity, but which will in reality enable us to surpass all its marvels, we landed, and went to visit a *modern* temple (hardly 2000 years old). Champollion is very hard upon this temple, the hieroglyphics of which are perhaps faulty in orthography; but we, ignorami, thought them very beautiful. The temple is in perfect preservation. The great pillared hall is uninjured, and the capitals, all different, and still retaining their original colouring, struck us as very charming. It seems that the inscriptions on the walls relate to Ptolemy Epiphanes, Claudius, Titus, Domitian, Trajan, Antoninus, and Septimus Severus.

We then walked in the gardens of a palace belonging to the Viceroy, and afterwards rested in a large hall, reclining on luxurious divans.

When we returned on board we continued our course up the beautiful Nile, which the ancient Egyptians were quite justified in deifying.

M. Renaud, being blessed with very long sight, soon announced that he saw a crocodile basking in the sun on a little flat island. At this news we all rushed on deck. Mrs. Senior jumped for joy; she had an excellent view of the creature, which, on turning its head towards us, seemed terrified and plunged into the river. Two other crocodiles we saw during the day did the same thing. It was fortunate that we did see them, as Mr. Senior was going to assert in his journal that this monster was a fabulous animal, like the phœnix.

December 5th.

We landed at Edfou at seven o'clock this morning. We visited the great temple, a magnificent monument dating from about the same time as that of Esneh. We returned to breakfast on board, and as we continued our voyage we saw four crocodiles one after the other.

As soon as it was dark we anchored in the middle of the river, to avoid shoals or sand-banks.

December 6th.

We started again at five o'clock, and at seven o'clock began to distinguish the rocks forming the passage between Assouan (Syene) and the island of Elephantine. The view is charming, set in a framework of trees and verdure. The motley population of Assouan followed the authorities down to the quay: the different shades of complexion, from deep brown to ebony black, contrasting with their white or brilliantly-coloured costumes. Here we found a population differing entirely from that of Egypt, whose frontier we have now reached; we are already in Nubia.

After receiving the authorities on board, and still before breakfast, we went to walk on the island of Elephantine, the sacred isle of the Pharaohs, where there were, a Nilometer,[1] in which the land tax was assessed, and temples, which now no longer exist; the last of the latter was destroyed thirty years ago, that the materials might be used in constructing some buildings in the neighbourhood of Assouan. At Elephantine all the inhabitants seem to be Nubians; the boys are all naked; the little girls wear a belt with a fringe, such as you have seen; the men and women are wrapped in cotton stuffs; the women show their faces, and their physiognomy is in general noble and agreeable. Herodotus says that this population, which did not belong to Ethiopia (Nubia), spoke the Ethiopian language; the same is the case now, 2300 years later. They were called Ichthyophagists, because they lived on fish.

In the afternoon we went to the First Cataract, some on dromedaries and others on horses or donkeys. This cataract is about an hour and a half's journey from Assouan. A most curious sight was awaiting us.

We embarked above the cataract in a good-sized barge, which had been prepared for us. The rowers sang in chorus at every stroke of the oars, to the accompaniment of the *tarabouk*. For a quarter of an hour we followed the course of the Nile on this side of the rocks, then we landed on the opposite bank, at the spot where the river becomes a cataract. There our boat was surrounded by thirty young men, looking like Florentine bronze statues, who had been following us for some time, either swimming or floating on thick planks four or five feet long. They waited till we had taken our station on a sort of promontory overlooking the cataract, and then threw themselves fearlessly into the strongest part of the current, appeared and disappeared in the whirlpool formed by the waves, which were dashing furiously over one another;

---

[1] The Nilometer (or measurer of the Nile) at Elephantine consists of a walled-in staircase leading down to the Nile, on one of which is marked a series of lines marking the various heights to which the river rose under the Cæsars.—TRANS.

and, after incredible evolutions, regained the shore and came round us to receive their baksheesh. All this did not take longer to do than I have taken to relate it, yet these Hercules, with figures like that of Apollos, had been careful to bring back their heavy pieces of wood on their shoulders, and had hastily draped themselves before appearing before the ladies of our party.

We re-entered our barge, putting off our visit to the island of Philæ to the next day, the temples of which we could make out; and on landing we mounted as before, and returned to Assouan.

On the 7th the hammocks on our boat were down at half-past four in the morning. We were on horseback before the rising of the sun, which is even hotter here than on the plain of Thebes, for we are now only ten leagues from the tropic zone.

We first visited the granite quarries of Syene, from whence so many colossal monuments, obelisks, and statues formerly came. We saw an obelisk, sculptured on three sides, which had been cut, and still attached to the rock on which it rests. Passing through a winding valley, intersected by other valleys, leading across this chain of granite and basalt, the piled-up blocks of which are the very picture of chaos, a ride of two hours brought us on to a plain, surrounded by magnificent verdure, near the Nile and the monuments of the lovely island of Philæ.

Our barge of the evening before was waiting to take us to the sacred island of Isis, Osiris, and Horus. These names recall the fabulous period of Egyptian mythology. It was in Philæ that Isis hid her divine husband to save him from the attacks of Typhon, the god of evil; that is to say, from sickness or from the attacks of the Arabs of the desert. It was in a little neighbouring islet that she had her young son Horus buried.

Champollion writes as follows of the monuments still existing:—

The small southern temple was dedicated to Hathor, and was built by Pharaoh Nectabenes, the last king of the Egyptian race, dethroned by the Persians in their second invasion. The great gallery, or covered portico, leading from the pretty little building to the principal temple, dates from the time of the Roman Emperors. The sculptures were executed during the reigns of Augustus, Tiberius, and Claudius.

The first pylon is of the period of Ptolemy Philometor, who has fitted a propylæum into it, dedicated to Isis by Pharaoh Nectabenes. The existence of this propylæum proves that, before the great temple of Isis still existing, there was another, which must have been destroyed by the Persians under Darius Ochus. This would account for the presence of relics of more ancient sculpture, employed in the construction of the columns of the pronaos of the present great temple.

It was Ptolemy Philadelphus who constructed the sanctuary and the adjoining halls in this monument. The pronaos was built by Evergetes II., and the second pylon by Ptolemy Philometor. The sculptures and bas-reliefs of the whole edifice were executed under Augustus and Tiberius.

Between the two pylons of the great temple of Isis, one on the right and the other on the left, are two fine edifices of a peculiar style. The one on the left is a temple dedicated to Hathor, in gratitude for the safety of Isis in bringing Horus into the world. The oldest part of this temple was built by Ptolemy Epiphanes, or his son Evergetes II. Evergetes claims the honour of its construction in the dedication on the interior frieze.

The same king appropriates, by a similar inscription, the edifice on the right, built almost entirely by his brother Philometor.

Some drawings by Linant will make you better acquainted with the pretty scenery of Philæ and Assouan, than I can.

We returned to our steamer before ten o'clock. The preparations for departure were made while we were at breakfast, and we again went down the Nile, stopping only at the coaling stations, and arriving at Cairo on the 11th. We looked eagerly forward to reaching Keneh, where M. Ruyssenaers had agreed to send our letters from France. We arrived there on the 8th, and joyfully received our letters. I must interrupt this account to answer them, and to prepare some work which must be done before we make our excursion to the Isthmus of Suez.

LXXVI.

Message sent to the Members of the International Commission at Suez in the name of his Highness the Viceroy of Egypt.

Suez, December 16, 1855.

Gentlemen,—In the tour through Egypt just completed by you, you have studied the canal system of the country. Now that you are about to commence your important labours on the Isthmus of Suez, I think it right to remind you that his Highness Mohammed Said does not wish to bind you to any programme whatever. In desiring me to ask you to assemble, chiefly with a view to the examination of the proposed scheme of his engineers, Linant Bey and Mougel Bey; in giving preference to the direct line from Suez to Pelusium, rather than to another route submitted to the public in an article written by M. Paulin Talabot; and in considering it desirable for the interests of the Ottoman Empire to impose certain restrictions upon the company in this respect, it is on the understanding that he assigns no limits to science. He wishes the international commission to devote itself, without the least reserve, to investigating all the routes known for the last fifty years, so that its final decision may be delivered with perfect freedom, and there may be no doubt in future as to the best means of connecting the Mediterranean with the Arabian Gulf.

LXXVII.

Condensed Report of the International Commission to his Highness the Viceroy of Egypt.

Alexandria, January 2, 1856.

Your Highness summoned us to Egypt to study there the Suez Canal question.

In furnishing us with the means of judging on the spot the merits of the various solutions that have been proposed, you invited us to submit to you the easiest and safest route, and that which would be most advantageous to the commerce of Europe.

Our exploration, favoured as it has been by unexceptionally fine weather, and facilitated by the ample means placed at our disposal, is now completed.

We have found numberless obstacles, or rather impossibilities, to cutting the Canal viâ Alexandria, and unexpected facilities for forming a harbour in the Bay of Pelusium.

A direct Canal from Suez to the Bay of Pelusium is, then, the only solution of the problem of the junction of the Red Sea and the Mediterranean; its construction is easy, its success certain.

It is our unanimous conviction that the results to the commerce of the world will be immense.

We will explain our reasons in a detailed report, supported by hydrographic plans of the bays of Suez and Pelusium, sections giving the relief of the ground, and borings indicating the nature of the ground to be traversed by the Canal.

The compilation of the report, and of the plans, sections, and borings, which will accompany it, is a work of time, with which we shall be actively employed in Europe, so that in a few months we shall be able to submit them to your Highness. For the present we hasten to submit to you our conclusions:—

1. The route viâ Alexandria is inadmissible, both from an engineering and a commercial point of view.

2. The direct route offers every facility for the construction of the Canal properly so-called, with a branch to the Nile, and presents no extraordinary difficulties in the creation of two harbours.

3. The harbour of Suez opens into an immense and safe roadstead, accessible in all weathers and with nine mètres of water at 1600 mètres from the shore.

4. The harbour of Pelusium, which the scheme placed on the further side of the gulf, will be located about twenty-eight kilomètres more to the west, where there are eight mètres of water at 2300 mètres from the shore, where the anchorage is good and getting under sail easy.

5. The cost of the Canal between the two seas, and the

works in connection with it, will not exceed the 200 million francs mentioned in the proposed scheme of his Highness the Viceroy's engineers.

The members of the International Commission of the Suez Canal,

(Signed)   CONRAD, *President*.
A. RENAUD.
D. NEGRELLI.
MACLEAN.
LIEUSSOU, *Secretary*.

LXXVIII.

MEMORANDUM SENT WITH THE SUMMARY OF THE REPORT OF THE INTERNATIONAL SCIENTIFIC COMMISSION TO THE FRIENDS AND SUPPORTERS, WHOSE NAMES ARE GIVEN BELOW.

ALEXANDRIA, *January* 4, 1856.

JOMARD, Member of the Institute, Paris.
MORRIS, *Times*, London.
THOUVENEL, Constantinople.
BRUSI, Barcelona.
ERLANGER, Frankfort.
COUTURIER, Marseilles.
CHARLES MANBY, London.
THEODORE PICHON, Smyrna.
EDMOND DE LESSEPS, Beyrout.
REVOLTELLA, Trieste.
FLURY HERARD, Paris.
Comte DE LESSEPS, Paris.

Count WALEWSKI, Paris.
DAMAS HINARD, Paris.
DE CHANCEL, Paris.
MARCOTTE, Marseilles.
SENIOR, London.
ELLICE, London.
JAMES WILSON, London.
THIERS, Paris.
The Archduke MAXIMILIAN, Vienna.
Baron VON BRÜCK, Vienna.
Duc DE BRABANT, Brussels.
Lord HOLLAND, London.

The International Suez Canal Commission have just finished the explorations in Egypt, and have transmitted their conclusions and report to the Viceroy.

Starting from Suez on the 21st of December, and after making a study of the roadstead they crossed the isthmus from south to north, taking note, *en route*, of the soundings and levels which had been going on for the past three months, and which allowed them definitely to fix the route of the maritime canal in the depression of the valley.

On the 28th of December they encamped on the shore at Pelusium, whence they embarked, on the 31st, on board the Egyptian steam frigate the *Nile*. This vessel has been for the last month either anchored or cruising about in the bay, with a sailing corvette serving as a coal hulk.

The commission, when it first passed through Alexandria, left instructions with M. Larousse, naval engineer, who has surveyed in detail forty-four kilomètres of the shore with remarkable activity and intelligence. Assisted by D'Arnaud Bey, the Viceroy's engineer, and M. Cianciolo, Italian engineer, M. Larousse has made a detailed plan of that part of the bay which he was requested to study.

Their observations have furnished the following favourable, and somewhat unexpected, results.

Opposite the ruins of Pelusium the soundings have shown a depth of eight mètres at a distance, already mentioned, of 7500 mètres from the shore. But in going westward the depth of eight mètres gradually nears the shore, till at a distance of 2350 mètres it continues parallel to the shore for a distance of twenty kilomètres. This was a great gain, and the European engineers could not fail to profit by it in determining the spot where the future canal should enter the Mediterranean. In nearing the shore along this line of twenty kilomètres, between the Oum Fareg and Gemileh mouths, the soundings gave excellent and solid bottom, with a depth of five mètres at 750 mètres from the shore, of six mètres at 1600 mètres, and eight mètres at a distance of 2300 mètres. The depth of nine, ten, and twelve mètres were successively obtained at distances of 3000 to 6000 mètres.

It results from these important facts that the piers of the Canal in the Bay of Pelusium, where the water is always clear, will not require to be half the length originally supposed. It will be the same in the roadstead of Suez, which was nearly as imperfectly known as that of Pelusium.

The international commission, in their report to the Viceroy, declares in favour of the direct route, as being the only solution of the problem of the junction of the Red Sea and the Mediterranean. They have unanimously declared that the execution is easy and the success certain.

LXXIX.

CIRCULAR TO THE MEMBERS OF THE COMMISSION WHO HAVE NOT ARRIVED IN EGYPT: MESSRS. RENDEL, HARRY HEWET, CH. MANBY, LENTZÉ, PALEOCAPA, AND TO M. SABATIER, CONSUL-GENERAL FOR FRANCE IN EGYPT.

ALEXANDRIA, *January* 4, 1856.

THE majority of the international commissioners who, as agreed among you, proceeded to Egypt to study the Suez Canal question on the spot, have concluded their work. Your honourable colleagues charge me to send you a copy of the short statement they are about to send to the Viceroy, as requested by him.

You will observe that these gentlemen, having their attention confined to the sole question of the possibility of the scheme—a question that observations on the spot alone could solve—have said nothing of any arrangement of detail, or of the execution of the necessary works.

They intend drawing up a sketch of a detailed report when they shall have received the necessary documents, about to be forwarded to them by the Viceroy's engineers. This sketch will be submitted to you, and I shall take care to let you know the place fixed upon for a general meeting, where the report will be discussed before being finally approved.

LXXX.

TO CHEVALIER REVOLTELLA, BANKER AT TRIESTE.

ALEXANDRIA, *January* 5, 1856.

M. NEGRELLI informs me that Baron von Brück, in accordance with the choice reported to me, has suggested you as representative at Trieste of the future interests of the International Suez Canal Company.

The conversations you will have with M. de Negrelli and his colleagues, who are about embarking for Trieste, and whom I commend to you, will obviate any necessity for me to enter into details on beginning our relations with each other. In sending you the decisive and final report of the international commission, I confine myself to offering you, in the name of his Highness the Viceroy, the appointment of agent to the scheme, in which your friends Messrs. von Brück and de Negrelli have already played an important part.

LXXXI.
To Madame Delamalle, Paris.
(*Continuation of Journal.*)
Alexandria, *January* 6, 1856.

The members of the commission left to-day for Trieste. Barthélemy Saint-Hilaire and my son have sailed for Marseilles in the *Calcutta*.

The Egyptian expedition was really wonderful. A combination of most favourable circumstances contributed to bring about the result, and, as a final stroke of luck, to the important discovery of a maritime basin close to the shore in the well-known Bay of Pelusium.

You foretold the return of the rainbow of November 15, 1854. Well! when our labours were so happily brought to a close, when we were about to bid farewell to the Pelusian shore, on December 31, 1855, and as we took our places in the boats, we saw the *sign of the covenant* appearing in the east, the tender colours becoming more and more clear and getting gradually higher and higher till a perfect bow was formed. Without being superstitious, one could not help being vividly impressed by such a sight at such a solemn moment, especially when it awakened such memories for me as you will understand.

We embarked on the Nile, where the captain received us, the guard being under arms. We again found a body of stewards, cooks, and servants on board, placed there by the Viceroy's order, whose splendid hospitality is with us at sea just as it was in Upper Egypt and in the desert.

We entered the port of Alexandria on the 1st of January, all the ships' flags flying to celebrate the new year.

We were hardly at anchor before a boat from the Viceroy came to fetch me. One of his Highness's officers had orders to take me at once to the Raz-el-Tin Palace, at the entrance of the harbour, where the Viceroy, who had arrived from Cairo two days before, was waiting for me.

The commissioners disembarked at the same time, and were welcomed by a salute of seventeen guns.

The prince was most impatient to know the result of the labours of the commission. As soon as he saw me, he knew by the expression of my face that it was a happy one, and at my first words he embraced me.

After the *Calcutta* left, the Viceroy wanted to have his pretty water residence, in which I stayed last year, fitted up for me; but I told him that, till he went back to Cairo, whither I should accompany him, I should stay at my friend Ruyssenaers' country seat.

Thither I retire for my *veillée d'armes*, which does not prevent my seeing the Viceroy every day. I am arranging my correspondence and employ my time of rest usefully.

LXXXII.

To M. DE CHANCEL, FORMERLY IN THE FRENCH NAVY, INSPECTOR-GENERAL OF THE ORLEANS RAILWAY.

ALEXANDRIA, *January* 10, 1856.

WHEN you receive this letter you will already have seen the report of the international commission.

You will soon see M. Barthélemy Saint-Hilaire in Paris; and he will tell you all that has taken place in Egypt. I have told him at once to collect all the correspondence relating to the affair, ready for my return. He will concert with you on all that must be prepared beforehand. There will be nothing else to decide upon with regard to the financial or administrative organisation of the future company.

I send you the decisive Firman of concession and the conditions, together with the bye-laws approved by the

Viceroy. You must thank your coadjutors MM. Denormandie, Marc, and Mocquard, for the care they have taken to complete these documents.

I have not adopted the plan of a concession in *perpetuity*, of which I was unwilling to speak to the Viceroy. A concession for ninety-nine years has been decided on, and has been known to everybody for the last year.

If we were again to raise so important a question, it would be impossible to foresee the discussions and difficulties to which it might lead. For my part, I expect they would be very weighty, both on the part of Constantinople and of England. For last year the Ministers of the Porte told me they thought the concession of ninety-nine years too long, and that it would perhaps be better to reduce it to sixty. I had to tell them that it was not for them to dispute the details of the Viceroy's Firman, the articles of which had been approved by the Grand Council at Cairo, but that they had simply and solely to decide whether they should or should not grant the ratification asked for.

Moreover, the scheme for a concession in perpetuity, asked for by an English company for the canal from the Danube to Kustandjé, had only been granted by the Sultan for a limited period.

The limit of ninety-nine years cannot, in my judgment, re-open the question of the declaration of neutrality, which has been made by the Viceroy, and must be approved by the Porte. You defined this neutrality very well in an article you sent to the *Patrie*; but I notice that in general it is not well understood.

A concession made to a company to open and work a passage across Egyptian territory, with a declaration of neutrality, does not *denationalise* that passage. This must not be lost sight of whenever a neutrality agreed on by international conventions is discussed.

The Viceroy told me that, in a recent correspondence with Constantinople, it was said that at the expiration of the concession of the Canal it would be well to agree that it should become the property of the Empire, and not of Egypt. He replied, with spirit, that he wondered at the distinction they were anxious to make, and that he had till now always believed that Egypt formed part of the Ottoman Empire.

The only article in which I have suggested any considerable change in the draught of the bye-laws is that which fixes an annual assignment to the council, instead of 3 per cent. on the profits, till they shall be able to collect the revenues. As I am personally interested in the question, you will understand why I do not wish to settle the matter single-handed. It seems to me best to leave its decision to the first general meeting of shareholders. You were quite right in abolishing the entrance tickets.

You can, therefore, get the documents printed and send me two hundred copies. Translations are now being completed in Cairo.

In case the discussion on the course of the Canal should be re-opened, in spite of the decision of the international commission, I have given M. Barthélemy Saint-Hilaire a copy of the *procès verbal*, in which the scientific commission condemn the indirect course. It is not intended to be made public, but it will supply unanswerable arguments if the partisans of the curved direction require explanations.

LXXXIII.

To M. Barthélemy Saint-Hilaire, Paris.

Alexandria, *January* 14, 1856.

Whatever may be the political tendencies which letters from Paris and Constantinople notify to us as a result of the impression produced by the report of the international commission, we will manage that they shall not stop our proceedings, and continue to press on.

If the ground is clear at Constantinople, if circumstances permit French policy to agree with our allies, or if they disagree to pronounce openly in our favour to the Porte, it will be very easy to make straight for, and reach the desired end.

But if it should be otherwise, we must meet the objections, and attain our end more slowly, but still surely, by other means. Accordingly I propose the following plan to the Viceroy:

Up to this time what are the objections seriously made, and in more or less good faith by our opponents? They say the enterprise is impracticable, and if it were practicable that we could not find the money to carry it out.

The first objection has been completely answered. The other has not been so yet; and we must not leave this weapon in the enemy's hand, although it seems to me to be a very blunt one.

As soon as we think the time has come, his Highness will send me an authentic copy of the new Firman of concession, containing the conditions and bye-laws. Armed with these documents and with the report of the international commission, I shall set out for Europe, and beginning with Austria, Russia, and Germany, I shall unite the interests of all, and summon the subscribers whilst waiting for the Sultan's ratification, which is already admitted in principle and only considered as a matter of form.

When once we have got the necessary capital the enterprise will be in a fair way to be carried out; we shall have accomplished facts on our side, and we shall be impregnable.

I cannot yet fix the date of my leaving Egypt. I must pay every respect to the Viceroy's desire not to be hurried in the matter. The confidence he places in me obliges me not to involve him more deeply in the affair than he already is. Moreover, I find that the prudent principles I have from the very first adopted are the best means of pleasing him.

It is well that you should have by you the letter that I sent from Suez to the members of the international commission, suggesting to them, in the Viceroy's name, not to limit themselves to consider one course only, but to pronounce an opinion on all. I enclose a copy. It will always be the best answer to those who accuse us of having been exclusive.

LXXXIV.

To M. DE NEGRELLI, VIENNA.

ALEXANDRIA, *November* 19, 1856.

LEST the impression produced in Europe by the report of the commission should not bring about the Sultan's ratification as its immediate result, I think it best not to stay longer in Egypt. We have got to a point where, without deciding hastily, we must not let our opponents have the chance of successfully intriguing whilst we are idle.

Should a time of inaction supervene, the result of the natural or acquired slowness of all Eastern negotiations, it would perhaps give a dangerous appearance of hesitation to the affair.

We have arranged with the Viceroy that Edhem Pacha shall not be sent to Constantinople before it is quite certain that the English Ambassador will not oppose his mission.

The result of this is, that I should lose time if I waited here for the answer from Constantinople.

If this answer is too long delayed, the Viceroy, whose position is much improved by the measures taken during the past year; by a letter from the Grand Vizier acknowledging the utility of the scheme; and by the support and sympathy of all Europe, will begin to doubt whether he will obtain the authorisation, which we all know ought to be accorded to him as soon as the French and English Governments agree. Up to this time his loyalty has prevented him from too clearly revealing the weakness of Constantinople, and showing too openly how powerless it is to take the initiative.

While we steadily press on towards the realisation of our project, subject only to a purely formal ratification, every adherent we can get is a new argument and fresh power in its favour. When the company is formed and the capital subscribed, save for waiting for the Imperial *Tradeh* as the final stroke, the enterprise will change from a project into a matter of fact. We must reckon on this, and, under the patronage of the Viceroy, we shall be in a position to negotiate with the different Powers to defend their respective interests.

Might and right, for right only is not enough, will be on our side. Do not let us forget the words of the Emperor Napoleon when I told him about the Firman of concession:

"You have *done well*," he said to me, "in not admitting other Governments to your enterprise; and you will do well not to relinquish this plan. If I assist you now, *there will be war with England;* but when the interests of European capital, and especially of French capital, are engaged, every one will assist; and *I first of all.*"

I refer these reflections to you for consideration, and before I leave Egypt shall be very glad to have your opinion on them, or that of Baron von Brück and Prince Metternich.

I intend embarking from Alexandria for Trieste in a month's time. Until then I shall be actively employed in getting ready and despatching to M. Lieussou all the information required by the commission.

I send you a copy of the Firman and the bye-laws as amended by the notes and suggestions of a commission of lawyers and financiers to whom I entrusted them in Paris.

LXXXV.

PUBLIC NOTICE IN THE EUROPEAN AND AMERICAN JOURNALS.

ALEXANDRIA, *January* 20, 1856.

THE international commissioners for the making of the Suez Canal, viz., Messrs. Paleocapa, Conrad, Negrelli, MacClean, Rendel, Harry Hewet, Manby, Montesino, Renaud, Lentzé, and Lieussou, will meet in two months' time to consider and definitely settle what works are to be carried out.

Persons desirous of submitting plans, or of offering suggestions, are requested to communicate with M. Barthélemy Saint-Hilaire, Member of the Institute, General Secretary of the Suez Maritime Canal Company, at No. 9, Rue Richepance, Paris.

LXXXVI.

To Madame Delamalle, Paris.
(Continuation of Journal.)

ALEXANDRIA, *January* 20, 1856.

THE Viceroy has been suffering with his eyes for some days. He keeps his room, where I pass a few hours with him daily. He is better to-day, and, for change of air, we are going this morning to Tantah (the most important town on the Delta), whence we proceed next week to Cairo.

In accordance with Count Walewski's advice, communicated to me by my brother, I am going to get Barthélemy Saint-Hilaire to go to London.

LXXXVII.

To M. Barthélemy Saint-Hilaire, Paris.

CAIRO, *January* 25, 1856.

IT appears that the English Minister expects to be questioned in the House of Commons on the Suez question. As I cannot be in London during the first few days after the opening of Parliament, it would be well for you to be present. You had better get up the subjects which will be discussed with your friends' assistance. Among the English, who are a practical people, there is much astonishment, and there will be more, at their Government taking part in the matter. It is not necessary that they should think we protest against this interference; on the contrary, what we do want is, that, in accordance with public opinion as already expressed, and the feeling in Parliament itself, it should be determined that the Viceroy in coming to an understanding with the Sultan, as he has a right to do, should no longer meet with opposition from the English Ambassador, as has been the case up to the present time. Bearing in mind the Anglo-French alliance, it becomes more and more important that London should be in agreement with Paris, and that all chance of a contest should be avoided between the two Ambassadors, one of whom could scarcely help supporting Mohammed Said's just demand, if the other persisted in opposing it.

That is the point at issue. Do all you can to get it settled. You are exactly fitted to act in London in a matter which M. Walewski will point out to you himself, or which will be pointed out to you by my brother. Your friends, and those of M. Thiers, will assist you. I enclose you letters for mine, and for those who helped me last time I was in England.

I do not mention Sir Cornewall Lewis, Chancellor of the Exchequer, brother-in-law to Lord Palmerston; nor Mr. Reeve, because you yourself recommended me to them; nor Mr. Ellice, M. Thiers's friend; nor Lord Lyndhurst, Lord Derby, and the Marquis of Lansdowne.

The Viceroy bade me beg you to tell M. Thiers how sensible he is of the interest that illustrious statesman has shown in him.

Mr. MacClean, who is a great authority as an engineer, will not fail to be useful to you.

LXXXVIII.

To Kœnig Bey, Private Secretary to his Highness the Viceroy, Alexandria.

Cairo, *January* 26, 1856.

His Highness begs me to ask you to send me, as soon as possible, a Turkish translation of his Firman of January 5th, containing the conditions and bye-laws of the international company. You are to add at the end of these despatches the following appendix:

To my devoted friends, &c., (according to the protocol already used in the copy of the Firman of November 30, 1854, which was delivered to me the 3rd of Ramadan 1271).

Before the concession given to the International Suez Canal Company is ratified by his Imperial Majesty the Sultan, I send you the authenticated copy, in order that you may be able to constitute the said financial company. As far as the works themselves of the Suez Canal are concerned, they can be proceeded with now as soon as the authorisation of the Sublime Porte shall have been delivered to me.

LXXXIX.
To M. Mougel Bey, Alexandria.

CAIRO, *January* 28, 1856.

THE Viceroy has acceded to my request to send you to Europe to assist in preparing the final report of the international commission, as well as to assist, in the name of his Highness, the European engineers in discussing and drawing up a list of the works to be carried out. Linant Bey will remain in Egypt to continue the surveys and preparatory works.

I have already had several conferences with Edhem Pacha. He has sent for the contractors of the Tourah quarries. The markets are falling, and until you can come here we shall strictly define the quantities of materials to be prepared, both of freestone and ashlar, bricks and lime, as well as decide on depôts.

We shall not have the drainage pumps for the excavation of Lake Mensaleh, which are entrusted to M. Noetinger, till to-morrow. The Nazir of the *barrage* has refused to give it up, on the sole order of Edhem Pacha. To avoid such delays under other circumstances, I have begged the Viceroy to send the formal orders of his Cabinet direct to all the Administrations and Governors of provinces adjoining the site of the works, so that whatever Edhem Pacha requires may be given him at once.

A note in Turkish, written in my presence, has been forwarded by the Viceroy himself to Talat Bey, with orders to despatch this circular.

XC.
To the Chevalier de Negrelli, Vienna.

CAIRO, *February* 3, 1856.

YESTERDAY I received your favour of January 25th. I hastened to read it to the Viceroy, who is very anxious to become acquainted with all that his friends of the international commission write to me. He was very happy to learn the deep interest taken in him and his scheme by his Imperial Majesty your Emperor, by his Highness the Archduke Ferdinand Maximilian, by Prince Metternich, Baron von Brück and his colleagues the Austrian Ministers.

It is a great satisfaction to him to learn that his efforts in the interests of the civilisation of Egypt, of its prosperity and its friendly relations with Europe, not only with regard to international commerce, but still more with regard to the maritime junction between one part of the world and the other, are appreciated by the most powerful sovereigns, the most enlightened princes, and the most illustrious statesmen. He congratulates himself, in short, that an engineer so famous as yourself should have studied on the spot, the country he rules with a view to constant progress. This aim, which the hereditary Constitution of the Egyptian Government alone enables him to carry out in the true interests of the Ottoman Empire and of European politics, could not be pursued with more intelligence and energy than by the prince whose good feeling, loyal character, and desire to do right you have been able personally to judge of.

He is convinced, moreover, that his personal position, that of his family, and the interests of Egypt, so far from losing can only gain while the diplomatic discussions are going on; and on this account he has learnt with pleasure the suggestion, made by his Highness Prince Metternich and his Excellency Baron von Brück, to include the Suez question in the treaty of peace. You will remember that I shared this opinion from the beginning, and that if up to the present time I considered it dangerous for European politics to interfere between the Sultan and the Viceroy on the question of the Imperial ratification of the Firman of concession, I thought that when once the principle of the scheme had been acknowledged and accepted, no matter by whom, it was much to be desired, for the safety of Egypt and the peace of Europe, that the great channel of commerce should be guaranteed by the maritime Powers.

I intend leaving for Trieste on the 17th of this month. Together with Baron von Brück we will discuss matters concerning our enterprise, and the financial and political questions connected with it.

I forward you the Viceroy's decree relating to the workmen employed by the Universal Company. This will allow the commission to fix its labour estimates exactly, and when the company is formed it will be an indispensable guide should it be thought advantageous to have the work done by contract.

XCI.

To Madame Delamalle, Paris.

(*Continuation of Journal.*)

Cairo, *February* 4, 1856.

I told you of my leaving Alexandria with the Viceroy, who was suffering with his eyes, and of our stay at Tantah, where I occupied a room next his own. While his illness continued, which it did for more than twenty days, I read and acted as eyes to him part of every day. On our arrival at Cairo, and as he alighted, in the presence of the great dignitaries assembled to receive him, he took me by the hand, and made me go with him in his carriage. When we reached the Kasr-el-Nil Palace he gave orders for the private rooms he occupied last year to be got ready for me, while he lived in part of the harem, its inhabitants being now in Alexandria. After being present at the ceremony of kissing hands by the Cairo authorities, Ministers, Generals, and officers of the household, I was conducted with much ceremony to the wing of the palace reserved for me. This wing, situated between the garden and the Nile, opposite the Isle of Boulac, consists, on the ground floor, of a large and beautiful gallery opening on to the reception-rooms. On the first floor is another gallery, with recesses for sofas and windows at intervals, and a white marble fountain in the centre. The galleries are paved with marble, and the walls ornamented with gilding and landscape paintings. On one side my bedroom has six large windows overlooking the Nile, from which you can see the Pyramids as if they were but a few yards off. The three other sides are covered with mirrors. The ceiling consists of thirty squares of glass with gilt framing. It is here that old Mehemet Ali used to come to rest from the cares of power, and at that time no human eye but his own was allowed to see this residence. A handsome saloon, opening out of the bedroom, serves me as a dining-room when I do not breakfast and dine with the Viceroy, which is however seldom. I have sometimes very long interviews with him. Two days ago he would not let me leave him from six o'clock in the morning till eight at night. The more I see of him, the more I am struck by his friendship, his noble feelings, and loyal character. As is the case with most princes, he improves on acquaintance. His mind is full of resources, but his hasty temper, amusing enough in private, sometimes becomes terrible when he is obliged to be severe, although he is always just.

Even after my departure the Viceroy waited for me to tell him the proper time for sending Edhem Pacha to Constantinople. When the prince, of his own free will, and for the first time, spoke to me of a mission to be sent when the international commission shall have completed its surveys, I was careful to let people in Paris and Constantinople know beforehand, so that they might be able to declare themselves.

I would not let the Viceroy's envoy run the risk of being thwarted by the English, and not sufficiently supported by the French, Ambassador. Till I know what course to pursue I wait, and shall continue to wait.

Yesterday the Viceroy received a letter, very favourable to the Canal, from the Archduke of Austria, Ferdinand Maximilian, as much in his own name as in his brother's, the Emperor. The letter ends thus :—

> I have no doubt that the eminent men who are engaged in this great enterprise, in which your Highness is so much interested, will overcome all obstacles and bring it to a happy issue, and thus advance the interests of the world and the glory of him who so happily governs Egypt.

As Kœnig Bey was at Alexandria, the Viceroy asked me to write an answer, that he might sign it at once and send it by this mail. Here it is :—

I am very glad to hear, on your Highness' own authority, that your health is re-established, as you inform me in your kind letter of January 9th. I am delighted at your promise of an early visit to Egypt. It will give me great pleasure to renew relations that have always been so friendly.

The interest your Highness has shown in me and my scheme, and that which his Imperial Majesty the Emperor, your august brother, has condescended to evince, are greatly valued by me, and encourage me to proceed on that path of progress and social improvement which has obtained for me such exalted sympathy.

You tell me of fresh publications by the partisans of an indirect course for the maritime canal to be fed by the Nile. All they have found to say against me is that I am *simple and candid* (not enough so, however, to be misled by them); moreover, they denounce me for having a monomania for the straight course. If there be any monomania, mine at least is as good as their's—for mine has succeeded.

XCII.
To Comte de Lesseps, Paris.

Cairo, *February* 10, 1856.

A few months back the Egyptian Government received some propositions from Mr. Leon Gisborn, representative of an English company about to be formed for establishing telegraphic communication between England and India *viâ* Alexandria, Suez, Massowah, and Aden. These proposals were recommended by the Ottoman Government, by Mr. Frederick Bruce, her Britannic Majesty's agent in Egypt, and were supported by Lord Canning, Governor-General of India. I hear that Mr. Gisborn complains of being sent from one Minister to another without obtaining any answer. I mentioned it to the Viceroy. His Highness asked me if I thought there would be any danger in letting a telegraphic wire between England and India pass through Egypt without his knowledge of the messages passing from one point to the other. I told him I thought all opposition to such a scheme mere prejudice, and that, in any case, if he did foresee inconvenience, he should say so frankly, and not keep the petitioner in uncertainty.

The next day I was asked by his Highness to go down to his Divan, where I found Mr. Bruce and Mr. Gisborn, whom he had invited to meet me. "I appoint my friend M. de Lesseps," he said to them, "to discuss and examine your project with you. Go with him to his apartments. I will approve what he does, and will give orders to have the convention to be arranged between you translated into Turkish, that it may be submitted to me for my signature."

In two hours the treaty was discussed, drawn out, and signed.

Mr. Bruce can now see that so far from imitating the example of some of his fellow-countrymen, isolated heirs of a policy of exclusion and antagonism, who have been trying for a year past, and are trying now, to hinder the world-wide enterprise of the Suez Canal, I, on the contray, have used all means in my power to promote the liberal principle of free telegraphic communication between England and its Eastern possessions across Egyptian territory.

I enclose herewith the project that has been agreed to and approved by the Viceroy. It will be well for M. Walewski to know the details, which I leave him to use as occasion dictates.

XCIII.

To Madame Delamalle, Paris.
(Continuation of Journal.)
Cairo, *February* 7, 1856.

I propose leaving for Trieste in ten days. All my documents, sealed by the Viceroy, are ready. Tell M. Chancel this, when you acknowledge the receipt of his letter to me of January 25th. All his correspondence is excellent; he has good judgment. I do not entirely share his anxiety on what may happen in the English Parliament on the Canal question. If the subject is introduced, whether by independent question, which we should avoid provoking, or by the Government itself, it seems to me it would be difficult for any open declaration to be made against the proposed Canal. I admit that we must allow a great deal for English conceit. But John Bull generally sees how the land lies, and as matters now stand, he can't put himself in direct opposition to the public opinion of Europe, and openly give the lie to his supposed programme of progress and commercial liberty, or remove the mask from his political exclusiveness.

Let us imagine the worst, and suppose that Lord Palmerston and his agents, who have general instructions from him to thwart the policy of France, succeed in keeping up the state of affairs at Constantinople to which the Sublime Porte rather disgracefully submits, his success would soon come to an end, because it could not prevent our forming our company; having time to thwart him; and agitating everywhere, without stopping our preparations or losing a moment in pressing forward the enterprise.

XCIV.

To M. BARTHÉLEMY SAINT-HILAIRE, PARIS.

TRIESTE, *February* 28, 1856.

You will know by this time that I left Egypt with all my arrangements in perfect order.

Tell M. Chancel that I was in time to get Article 17 of the conditions withdrawn as well as the following clause in the tariff: "The ratification of which we reserve." In the future this alteration will be very useful, for Mohammed Said will not always be here, and with Oriental Governments, who never give a distinct answer, it is necessary that the company should be free to modify its tariff at any time according to its interests and requirements. Otherwise Oriental decision on the question, backed by English influence, might at some time damage the interest of the shareholders, if, as I foresee will be the case, the shareholders were not Englishmen.

None of my papers received the Vice-regal seal till the eve of my departure for Alexandria. It was impossible to get it done whilst the Viceroy was ill.

They say peace will be proclaimed. I hope I shall reach

Paris before they are occupied in inserting clauses in the treaty referring to the isthmus. If, however, there should be any danger in the delay, I beg you to send to my brother, asking him to communicate the enclosed note to Count Walewski, and if need be to the Emperor. If there is no need to hurry, wait for my arrival. I think I shall submit the note in question to Baron von Brück, on my way to Vienna, and to Prince Metternich, for as Austria takes the initiative in proposing a general peace, she should do the same in proposing the neutrality of the isthmus. Moreover it is probable, after what has been written to me, that she has already given instructions to her Plenipotentiaries with this object.

Tell my brother that the clauses proposed for insertion in the Treaty of Paris are the result of notes that I took down from M. Thiers's dictation in his room, in the Place Saint George, on the 14th June 1855.

Clauses Proposed for Insertion in the Treaty of Paris.

The signing Powers guarantee the neutrality of the Suez Maritime Canal for ever.

No vessel shall at any time be seized either in the Canal, or within four leagues of the entrances from the two seas.

No foreign troops shall be stationed on the banks of the Canal without the consent of the territorial Government.

XCV.

To M. DE NEGRELLI, VIENNA.

PARIS, *March* 21, 1856.

I MUST begin by telling you that though I was spoiled by the hearty welcome at Trieste and Vienna, I have had much to make me vain in that received by me at Paris from their Majesties and all influential persons.

I have been *authorised* during the last few days to request Count von Buol to be kind enough to take the initiative at the Conference in the name of Austria, after coming to an understanding with Lord Clarendon, and to inform him that he may count on the thorough support of the French Plenipotentiaries. Moreover, I am charged to give Count von Buol, as the basis of his proposals, the scheme that you know of; its adoption or modification is left to him.

Count von Buol, in accordance with a hint from me, ought to concert with Count Walewski. I have no doubt but that he is authorised by his instructions to move in the matter, and I have good hope that after my own proceedings with the Russian, Prussian, and Sardinian Plenipotentiaries, their co-operation will be as sure as that of France.

In case you have not already noticed it, I call your attention to the following passage in the speech to the Emperor by the President of the Senate, at the birth of the Prince Imperial:

"The East and the West, who have been searching for each other ever since the Crusades, and are only now beginning to find each other, will join their two seas and their sea-shores and cause the beneficent stream of thought, wealth, and civilisation to flow."

The Emperor's answer to the Plenipotentiaries at the Peace Conference is also noteworthy. It concludes with a significant phrase to the address, *degli nostri cari amici*:

"I shall educate my son in the opinion that nations ought not to be *self-seeking*, and that the peace of Europe depends on the prosperity of each nation."

The press in Paris and London continue to give capital articles. Our friend Barthélemy Saint-Hilaire has laid his pen down for a little, and I see with great satisfaction that the question is getting more and more to be considered as a fact that must be accomplished.

P.S., 23*rd*.—As I did not send my letter the day before yesterday, I can now tell you that yesterday I had an important talk with Baron Manteuffel and Count Cavour, who promised me positively the co-operation of Prussia and Sardinia. This morning I met the Grand Vizier, Aali Pacha. One is always satisfied with what the Turks say; but there is often a reverse to the medal. Aali Pacha told me he remembers the conversation he had with Prince Metternich about the Suez Canal, and that he considered the enterprise entirely favourable to the Ottoman Empire. As I knew Lord Palmerston had made him promise to go to London after the peace was signed and before his return to Constantinople, I sought to forewarn him against the trap the English Plenipotentiaries were laying, by trying to prepare him to oppose the difficulties of detail, or the reasons of delay which seemed to come from Constantinople. In short, I left nothing undone to secure the result. If that result is not immediate, it cannot be very long in coming, for nothing can stop us now.

XCVI.

REPORT TO HIS HIGHNESS THE VICEROY OF EGYPT.

PARIS, *March* 25, 1856.

THE unanimous welcome accorded to the scheme, the great and universal interests represented by it, seem to make it necessary for the enterprise of making the Suez Canal to have direct and constant communication with public opinion by a special, and in some sort an official, organ.

By means of such an organ, the company entrusted with managing this powerful element of civilisation and wealth for two worlds would have periodical and regular relations with its shareholders. While keeping public opinion on the alert, it would acquaint all with its progress and work; it could appeal to all trades when their co-operation was wanted; it could ventilate problems which might arise, and would have to be solved by elevating public opinion and promoting wider sympathies.

From this point of view alone the advantages and influences of such a publication cannot be disputed.

17 *

The Mediterranean will become the queen of commerce and navigation, the great route of nations and of their commerce.

The organ of the International Company, if edited with intelligence and spirit, neither extravagant nor exclusively national, should become the organ of the whole commercial interest in the Mediterranean. It ought to cross the isthmus and unite the interests of East and West in its sheets.

Egypt would naturally become one of the chief objects of its interest and solicitude; for there can be no assured prosperity, and no security for the future of the Company, if Egypt is wretched and its position precarious.

The Canal through the Isthmus of Suez is an event pregnant with political consequences to the ancient country of the Pharaohs. She will hold the key of the world; she will play an important *rôle* among the Powers; by the force of circumstances she will affect the equilibrium of Europe; she will compel nature to make her straits as important as those of the Dardanelles.

The site of the town on the shores of Lake Timsah is not inferior to that of Alexandria itself. Henceforth all nations will be interested in the prosperity and the future of Egypt. But intellectual intercourse must be established; Europe must know Egypt better; it must be made familiar with her efforts and difficulties in order to understand the obstacles she has already overcome and those she has yet to conquer.

Egypt in the future must become what she was in the past, — the leading Power of the East. The International Canal Company is henceforth answerable for the progress or decline of Egypt; there must be reciprocity of co-operation and defence between them. A newspaper, the company's organ, would fail in its object if it did not understand that one of the chief objects of its publication is to help Egypt to develop her internal resources and make herself popular in the outer world. As the means of making public the most useful of modern enterprises it should include all questions that affect its particular object, but should not go beyond them. It should always be a means of peace-making, of union, and of good-will to all; and should make a rule against admitting anything that would embitter, disturb, or divide the great interests which it is its aim to promote on behalf of industry and of peace.

XCVII.
MEMORANDUM FOR THE EMPEROR OF THE FRENCH.

PARIS, *March* 29, 1856.

EUROPEAN Science, by the organ of its most celebrated engineers, has declared that to cut a canal across the Isthmus of Suez is a work easy of accomplishment, sure of success, and one which will not cost more than two hundred million francs.

The Viceroy of Egypt has already began preparatory works.

Public opinion in England is favourable.

The Porte, before it sanctions the Firman of the Viceroy of Egypt, which it has already affirmed in principle, is waiting for the French Government to give its approbation officially and to guarantee assistance against the English Ambassador's opposition.

In the present state of affairs it remains for your Majesty to choose the time when you shall think fit to overcome the last resistance of the English Cabinet.

You will judge whether it is possible, in the diplomatic documents which will follow the declaration of peace, to introduce a clause to guarantee for ever to the traders of all countries a free passage for their ships and the neutrality of the maritime canal.

Subjoined is an extract of correspondence from Pera, which reveals the state of affairs at Constantinople.

PERA, *March* 16, 1856.

You will find the Grand Vizier, Aali Pacha, very much in favour of the scheme of the Suez Canal. The only thing he waits for is the publication of a diplomatic document to guarantee the neutrality of the Canal by all the European Powers.

Your adversaries of last year have not changed their opinions.

Lord Stratford deplores the infatuation which has seized opinion in London in favour of your canal, and makes it no secret that he still considers the scheme hostile to the true interests of England. The past teaches us that if he received official orders to act, he would quietly take no notice of his instructions, and try to promote his personal opinion, encouraged by private letters from Lord Palmerston. His opposition cannot be overcome unless the French Ambassador receives orders from his Government to declare its intentions.

LXXXVIII.

To M. Thouvenel, French Ambassador at Constantinople.

PARIS, *April* 4, 1856.

SINCE I came to Paris I have delayed writing to you till I could tell you exactly how matters stand. I now repeat to you what I told the Emperor when he summoned me on the very day that peace was signed. I enclose a copy of my note.

All the Plenipotentiaries have, in my presence, declared most favourably for the Suez enterprise, with the exception, of course, of the English.

Count von Buol, who was authorised by his Government to take the initiative and propose that the Conference should consider the question, now that he has had a conversation with Lord Clarendon, is afraid that he will meet with decided opposition from him, and will take no further steps till he is assured of the support of the French, Russian, and Sardinian Plenipotentiaries. He acted wisely in so doing, for opinion in England is becoming so much more favourable that I cannot doubt but that this political resistance must die a natural death without any need of fighting it. Accordingly it will be better not to force Lords Palmerston and Clarendon to give a decided opinion, which it will be difficult for them to retract later on, if they remain in office.

Now, therefore, the Emperor holds the key of the position, and he will know the right moment to act. I, for my part, being certain of his interest in our success, leave him alone, doing all I can meanwhile to accomplish our end, with his full approval.

XCIX.
Memorandum for His Highness the Viceroy of Egypt.

PARIS, *April* 8, 1856.

I MUST not conceal from your Highness that Lord Palmerston and his agents are trying to spread the opinion that the Suez Canal will be a source of great embarrassment to Egypt, and that the question may possibly revive the union of the Powers which, in 1840, opposed the Vice-royalty of Egypt, again leaving France isolated.

But, on the other hand, your Highness kows that you will improve your personal position and guarantee Egypt from future ill-fortune by carrying out your scheme of the Suez Canal. The liberal-minded way in which this project was first conceived, and in which it is now being prosecuted, is gradually drawing all Europe over to the interest of Egypt.

By still pursuing this policy and by keeping true to the ties of vassalage, secured as they are by treaty and by custom, your Highness will increase your fame.

Without the Suez affair, and the sympathies it has aroused in your favour, your enemies in Europe, and those who intrigue against you, could easily have profited by the Peace Conference, based on the integrity of the Ottoman Empire, to decrease your personal importance and strengthen Constantinople at the expense of Egypt.

Your adversaries say that your administration has been undeservedly praised since you have taken possession of the Government of Egypt; that you are not a friend to civilisation and progress, as you try to make people believe; that you are in reality more opposed to Europeans than Abbas Pacha was; in a word, that you are a Turk like the rest, and perhaps more so than the rest. As for this grand Suez enterpirse, they affirm that you have not the perseverance to carry it out.

This last exaggeration will confute itself.

Our friends have used it to show how false the other statements are. In short, if your Highness were not as resolute as you are able, intelligent, and liberal in your relations to Europe, you would not for the last fifteen months have undertaken, without support, the initiative and the responsibility of the great scheme which now places you in such high estimation, and you would not have gone so far in the matter to give it up just when all is going well, and when all European interests are concerned in it.

Such being the case, you will feel that to draw back would be dishonourable, a sign of weakness and instability of character which you would not contemplate for an instant.

If an accusation is to have any weight, it should have some probability in it. If your Highness, like every one else, has faults, you will never break your word or compromise your dignity, and you certainly will not err by a want of self respect and proper pride.

But when one has to govern others, and is placed in a public position where it is impossible to escape criticism, it is necessary not only to be right, but to seem so too: you must be careful in conversation, circumspect in public, and avoid wounding public opinion.

Your Highness must not forget that if Turkey is saved from ruin, it will be because she mixes in European affairs, and does so *bonâ fide* and without mental reservation. Egypt must not fail in the course she has now been pursuing so long; she must not waver in the enterprise of the Suez Canal. The large and liberal-spirited concessions already made in this matter are the best answers to accusations of barbarism and prejudice against European civilisation.

Your Highness, foreseeing the difficulties you are likely to meet, well understood from the outset that you must go steadily on till the end is accomplished, interesting in the enterprise as many countries of the world as possible. Its success, however, will be a sure means of profit for you, and of maintaining and increasing your position.

In the actual state of affairs, in what we may call a crisis or general movement drawing nations together in the interests of peace, the making of the Suez Canal was inevitable; and if your Highness had not had the foresight to propose it to the world and begin to carry it out, you would at last have had to propose it to the Porte under conditions unfavourable to your dynasty in Egypt, when perhaps those who are now trying to oppose you would have tried to help you against your own interest, with a view to attempting to carry out the scheme without reference to you. You must not conceal from yourself that if they are trying to make you appear feeble and unstable, on the other hand, they represent the scheme of the Canal as hostile to your safety, because they wish you to draw back, so as to deprive you of the means of protecting yourself legally and popularly.

Thus far public opinion in England is favourable in that it is useless to force the hand of English statesmen whose resistance is declared. Politics will reveal the right moment for action to us.

It will therefore be no matter of surprise if the Suez Canal is not mentioned in the diplomatic documents which will follow the proclamation of peace. We had better wait than run the risk of not appearing unanimous, since the ultimate result is in no way doubtful.

Beginning the preparatory works and making the auxiliary canal fed by the Nile will keep up the interest in Egypt, reply by work done to hostile suggestions, and without losing time will allow the political difficulties in the matter to be settled naturally without offending anybody.

While waiting, I am going to make a few days' stay in England. The publications are proceeding. The international commission, whose official report is getting ready, will meet and draw up a detailed programme of the works to be carried out. The financial interests will gather around us. In short, we shall prove that we exist, and are advancing towards our goal under the patronage and with the assistance of a friend who would find it difficult to place himself in a higher position at the outset of his career.

C.

MEMORANDUM FOR COUNT WALEWSKI, MINISTER OF FOREIGN AFFAIRS, PARIS.

EPITOME of a conversation I had with Lord Clarendon on April 13, 1851.

DE LESSEPS.—You know that a commission of the most skilful engineers for hydraulic works in Europe unanimously decided that to make a canal through the Isthmus of Suez was easy, sure to succeed, and would not cost more than 200 million francs.

After this declaration the Viceroy of Egypt confirmed by a new concession the old one he accorded to me on November 30, 1854; and when he was assured that the Porte would offer no obstacle to the realisation of the enterprise, he approved the conditions and bye-laws of the International Company, which he entrusted to me to organise.

This organisation is approaching a happy conclusion. As I was certain of success in France, I went to London, where I intended to form an English committee to distribute a sum of 40 million francs appropriated to English capitalists in the general subscription-list, drawn up with the Viceroy's sanction.

Now, since the English Ambassador at Constantinople interfered last year to prevent the Porte ratifying the Viceroy's concession, I ask you what I am to inform English capitalists, and whether your Government intends to put obstacles in the way of the realisation of the enterprise?

LORD CLARENDON.—If we have thrown doubts on the opportuneness of your scheme, we have not done so in consideration of English commerce, but solely from a consideration of Ottoman policy; because we feared that opening the isthmus, by giving too much importance to Egypt, would disturb its relations with Turkey. As much in my own name as in that of the English Cabinet,

I formally repudiate the idea which has been attributed to us, that we fear commercial competition, and wish to oppose, in our own interests, a maritime advantage by which we should be the first to profit. Such sentiments are contrary to the principles of my whole political life, and to those which are the economic basis of English Government. What was in our minds, I repeat, was the authority of the Porte over Egypt, which the Viceroy does not seem to hold in sufficient account, as he has pursued his project without first obtaining the Sultan's ratification.

DE LESSEPS.—I am delighted to find that the question is cleared of the greatest difficulty of all, viz., the fear that British interests would suffer by a canal through the Suez isthmus. Although Lord Stratford has shown this fear, to my own knowledge, I have constantly declared for twelve months past that such was certainly not the opinion of England. I have said so in several pamphlets both in Paris and London, and recently at a public meeting at Trieste, reported in French and foreign newspapers.

As for the Porte, it, no doubt, can better judge of what is advantageous to it in its relations with Egypt than can any foreign Power: moreover, I am in a position to state that it has never shared any of the prejudice towards the Viceroy gratuitously attributed to it. I had the honour of a personal interview with the Sultan and his Council on the subject of the Suez Canal; and as long ago as the beginning of last year, I should have reported the Imperial ratification to Alexandria had it not been for the gratuitous interference of the English Ambassador.

Nevertheless, the principle of the scheme was accepted by the Sultan; moreover this was stated in a letter from the Grand Vizier to the Viceroy, and made public.

Ever since then the Viceroy has been patiently waiting for the good-will of England.

It should be known, as a further proof of the Viceroy's condescension and caution, that the conventions regulating his Government and the succession in Egypt do not lay the least obligation on him to go to Constantinople for authorisation to carry out the canal work, or any other. What he is not allowed to do is formally expressed in those conventions; and when he has fulfilled all statutable charges and paid his tribute punctually, he is not forbidden to carry out any works of public utility, and certainly not an enterprise which will be not the less profitable to his sovereign than to his subordinates.

It is noteworthy that this very argument was used a few years back by the English Ambassador at Constantinople with reference to the Egyptian railway between Alexandria and Cairo.

At the present time Mohammed Said Pacha is carrying the works for the railway as far as Suez, and it will probably be successfully completed at the end of this year. Neither the Porte nor even England thought of raising the smallest objection to the absence of Imperial authorisation in this matter. But this does not apply to the Suez Canal question, because the authorisation in this case *has* been asked for; and I, for my part, insisted particularly on the formality being attended to, in order to give every guarantee that could be desired by the European capitalists who intend engaging in the enterprise.

Now, as I cannot believe that the Ministers of a great and powerful nation are trying to shelter their private opposition behind the weakness of the Porte, I set myself to refute the only objection which seems to me to exist, viz., that which is alleged in simple solicitude for the authority and sovereignty of the Sultan.

The Viceroy of Egypt, since his accession, has always proved himself the faithful and devoted vassal of his Grand Seigneur. It has never entered his mind to break, in the least degree, the conventions that regulate his Government. His relations with his sovereign are as cordial as could be wished, notwithstanding the attempts made, from time to time, to inspire distrust between them; the sacrifices made by Egypt in the late war have strengthened the bonds. It is difficult to conceive in what respect the opening of the Suez Canal will disturb these relations.

As I am allowed to express my mind freely at this interview, I will say that, in my opinion, it will be a very dangerous and very impolitic thing to create a distrust, that does not now exist, between a sovereign and his vassal.

The friends of the Anglo-French alliance should not forget what passed in 1840.

At that time a policy hostile to France profited very cleverly by the distrust excited against Mehemet Ali, and England headed a league against Egypt, whose weakness materially helped the scheme of the enemies of Turkey.

Mehemet Ali, with whom, as French Agent, I was then living, tried to establish the heriditary right of his family, in order to give Egypt a settled Government. The intention to substitute himself for his sovereign is most untruly attributed to him; nothing was further from his thoughts. He saw the decline of Turkey, and had no other ambition than to be the right arm and best support of the Ottoman Empire, for he feared its disintegration. With the aim of strengthening the Empire, he wished to civilise Egypt, where a tractable and homogeneous people enabled him to introduce successively those reforms which would otherwise have met with difficulties and resistance.

If the Allied Powers sincerely wish Turkey to rank with European Powers, it will be better done by deeds and practical examples in the means they took to become so, than by *hatti-scherif* or *hatti houmayoum*.

Egypt is a country where you can easily plant the seeds of civilisation without serious obstacles, whereas Turkey must necessarily borrow them from Europe to spread them over the East.

Let me count on your well-known loyalty and your exalted character to make your Government understand the situation, which must engage its attention, and cannot remain in uncertainty much longer.

In a word, may I hope that the ratification asked for by the Viceroy of Egypt at the Sultan's hands will no longer be opposed by her Britannic Majesty's Ambassador at Constantinople?

LORD CLARENDON.—I do not see any reason why we should not come to an understanding. When you go to

London, pray have an interview with Lord Palmerston on the subject of our conversation. I will discuss it with him immediately, for I return to London in a few days.

CI.

To M. DE NEGRELLI, VIENNA.

LONDON, *April* 17, 1856.

I SEND you an official report, drawn up for Count Walewski, of an important conversation I had with Lord Clarendon the very day I left for London. When you have read it, you will understand why I came to England. I got here eight days ago, but have not yet had an interview with Lord Palmerston, owing to the sudden death of his son-in-law, Lord Cowper. But I have not lost time, for I have been carefully organising an English committee of trustworthy people, who will do here what you and Baron von Brück have done so well in Austria.

From all this it results that, as I foresaw, we must not count too much on active diplomatic co-operation, and that we must proceed diligently with the works, which policy will have to recognise later on, because they will affect political interests. Till then rest assured that it will be dangerous for any one to meddle in the business. The danger I should most dread would be that the Viceroy should be scared at such interference, and that this would be a means of strengthening a policy unfavourable towards Egypt, under the pretext of guarantees against her. This question of guarantees was already mooted at the Conference, because it was feared that the completion of the Suez Canal might increase the Viceroy's power. This, I repeat, is the greatest difficulty I have to contend with, and one that requires great caution and serious consideration.

As matters now stand, our great aim is to prevent any Power, and above all England, putting any obstacle in the way of the ratification the Viceroy asks from the Sultan, and which the latter is inclined to give.

When once we have obtained this, we shall be masters of the situation and shall avoid the danger alluded to above. Talk it over carefully, then, with Prince Metternich and Baron von Brück. Rest assured that if the Viceroy had the least suspicion that any Power intends to diminish his proper influence, he would renounce all European aid in completing the Canal. For my part, I am too great a friend of his not to follow his example. Our base of operation and our protection are in Egypt. If, for the last fifteen months, I had sought my inspiration from any other quarter I should have done nothing, and matters would not have been as far advanced as they are.

Whatever progress has been made it depends on the Viceroy whether it is carried on to completion or not. There is no need for me to enlarge at greater length on the subject, for you are well aware how serious it is; you know Egypt and Mohammed Said sufficiently well to agree with me.

I broke off in this letter to go and meet Lord Palmerston. The English Premier, entirely supporting his colleague at Paris, persists in his opposition and does not conceal from me that Lord Stratford will continue to act against us, not now in the interests of England, but in the pretended interests of the Ottoman Empire. These tactics are the last resource of the enemies of the Canal. I am about to re-commence, and shall prudently follow up, my work, but with more perseverance and vigour than ever, in influencing English public opinion. Another campaign does not discourage me. Meanwhile the affair will ripen, become more important, and gain a consistent strength that will make us triumph.

Pray convey my thanks to the Ministers von Toggenburg and von Brück, and also to Prince Metternich, for their kind welcome when I last passed through Vienna, and for their continued kind interest.

Mr. MacClean is quite convinced of the success of the enterprise. In accordance with the expressed wish of all the members of the international commission I shall go with him and Mr. Rendel to the general meeting about to be held in Paris.

CII.

To M. Barthélemy Saint-Hilaire, Paris.

LONDON, *April* 7, 1856.

I FOUND Lord Palmerston just as he was in 1840, defiant and prejudiced against France and Egypt. He was exceedingly polite, and not without a certain frankness of manner; but after he read the account of my interview with Lord Clarendon he became, on the Suez Canal question, more contradictory, more incoherent, and, I venture to say, more foolish than one could have imagined. He believed France had for a long time been carrying on a Machiavellian policy against England in Egypt, and that it was money from Louis Philippe, or his Government, that paid for the fortifications of Alexandria. In the Suez Canal scheme he saw the result of this policy. Then, taking another line, he persisted that it was impossible to make the Canal, and that he knew more about the question than all the engineers in Europe, and their opinions will not shake his. Then, forgetting how thoroughly he had proved its impossibility, he delivered a long tirade about the inconveniences that would result, both for Turkey and Egypt, if the Viceroy's demand were conceded and the enterprise carried out. He concluded by telling me frankly that he opposed me. As I listened to him I asked myself from time to time whether the man before me was a maniac or a statesman. Not one of his arguments was worth a minute's serious discussion. I answered all his objections as he brought them forward; but as I was arguing with one who had made up his mind, I found it only waste of time to prolong the interview. As I like things to be perfectly clear, I am glad to know what to think of it. I shall, therefore, prepare myself accordingly.

Let M. Thiers know all I have told you, and send me

word what he thinks of it. I should not be surprised if Lord Palmerston, his old opponent of 1840, believes him to be the author and continuer of the Machiavellian policy aforesaid.

CIII.

To M. S. W. RUYSSENAERS, ALEXANDRIA.

LONDON, *April* 21, 1856.

WE now know the real motive of Lord Palmerston's opposition. He is afraid of assisting the development of Egypt's prosperity and power. Happily his motive will not discourage the Viceroy in pursuing his noble scheme.

I have suspected this a long time, and drew his Highness's attention to it a year ago, when I was speaking to him about a despatch from the last Governor-General of India but one, in which he said that if England should one day take possession of Egypt, as she had done of India, she would be mistress of the world. Moreover, his Highness will not forget that in a document, published in 1840 by Mr. Urquhart, First Secretary of the British Embassy at Constantinople, Lord Ponsonby wrote to the Grand Vizier that the policy of England and the Porte should be to send Mehemet Ali and all his descendants back to the desert destitute.

We cannot but see that, although this idea cannot be realised now, and can only remain in the wooden heads of some stubborn and insular politicians, it accounts for the irritation produced at the approaching execution of an enterprise that will render such a theory powerless. As long as a partisan of the policy of weakening Egypt remains at the head of the English Ministry we must paralyse his evil intentions by agitating with great prudence, by continually enlightening public opinion, and by advancing slowly and quietly towards the accomplishment of the work.

The Viceroy will see by my advice and my conduct how desirous I am not to compromise him. If I thought more of the Canal than I do of him, nothing would be easier than for me to give up the scheme into the hands of great capitalists, who would quickly carry it out by absorbing him; but I want him to remain master of the situation, and for the Canal to be a means of consolidating and strengthening his political position.

Even without the Canal, which I have pointed out is the cause of some Englishmen traducing him, the Viceroy may be quite sure that they would have done just the same under some other pretext, and that soon it will be the Canal which will be his protection.

Since I have been in England I have constantly been rectifying the wrong impressions they have here about Egypt; these impressions are spread by the ill-will of certain newspapers.

The day before yesterday, Mr. MacClean gave a banquet in my honour, which has not been without importance, in the great hall of the Trafalgar Hotel at Greenwich. He asked about thirty to meet me, among whom were the best known engineers, manufacturers, merchants, and bankers in England. Mr. MacClean, in proposing my health after dinner, spoke of the gratifying and hospitable reception accorded to him and his colleagues of the international commission in Egypt, and expressed, in his own name and that of the company present, the desire they had in England that the Suez Canal scheme should be realised and my efforts crowned with success. This toast and my reply were received with hearty approval.

My object is to make English public opinion declare in favour of the Suez Canal, and then the English Government will be obliged to follow the same policy as that of the French.

A Mr. Wylde, geographer to the Queen, formerly M.P., and the proprietor of the "Great Globe" in Leicester Square, dilates three times a-day, at his establishment, on the advantages that the passage through the isthmus would have over the long voyage round the Cape. To illustrate his public lecture, he has now had made a plan in relief, the same size as the one of Sebastopol, which has attracted many people. This popular propagandism is excellent.

In my conversation with Lord Palmerston, of which you will see an account in the copy of my letter to Barthélemy Saint-Hilaire, the Premier confessed that the English Ambassador at Constantinople had maintained that the Viceroy could proceed with the railway from Alexandria to Suez without the Sultan's authority, but that the case of the Canal was different. To this I replied that the only difference I could see was that the English Government supported the railway and opposed the canal.

In conclusion, tell the Viceroy that this opposition must end in defeat, and that with his perseverance and continued support these obstacles and difficulties will but serve to better his position and make success more complete.

CIV.

To M. THOUVENEL, CONSTANTINOPLE.

LONDON, *April* 22, 1856.

HEREWITH I send you information which will be interesting to you, and useful also if occasion requires; you may rely on its being correct.

On the day that the Emperor gave a banquet to the Ministers Plenipotentiary at the Peace Congress, and when dinner was over, Aali Pacha, the Turkish Plenipotentiary, approached his Majesty and asked him what he thought of the Suez question, adding that his master considered it very important in all respects, but wished to know the intentions of the Emperor of the French. The Emperor answered that he took the greatest interest in the matter; that it seemed to him useful for all the world; that he had considered it in all its bearings; that he was acquainted with all the documents connected with it, and that he greatly hoped it would be carried out; that grand as it was it had aroused some objections and opposition, especially in England; but that, for his part, he did not think the objections urged against it were valid, and he trusted they would be removed; that, meanwhile, he did not at all wish to hurry matters, for fear of entangling them, and that having regard to the happy alliance between the two peoples, he waited for the time to arrive (which could not be far distant) when they would come to an agreement on this question.

Aali Pacha answered that his master would be pleased to learn the sympathy the Emperor had expressed, and that he himself was very favourable to the scheme, although there was some difference of opinion on matters of secondary importance, and certain precautions must be taken in the interest of the suzerainty of the Porte; but that whatever objections there might be in points of detail, the Porte was none the less friendly to this great work, which would be so advantageous to Egypt and in which it might also hope to have some share of profit.

The Emperor appeared to agree with all Aali Pacha said.

Then, leaving the Grand Vizier for a moment, he turned to Lord Clarendon, and asked him what he thought of the Suez business, telling him what he had heard from Aali Pacha and what he had answered. Lord Clarendon, a little surprised at this sudden attack, replied that it was a very serious matter; that he had not sufficiently considered it to give an answer on the spur of the moment; that he ought to refer to his Cabinet; and that, besides, the scheme was one which it was impossible to carry out. The Emperor, while quite agreeing that the matter required reflection, maintained that it could be carried out, and that science had declared for it. When Lord Clarendon insisted, the Emperor said that he accepted the hypothesis that the Canal was possible, and, arguing from this, he asked the opinion of England. Lord Clarendon then stated that, in the interests of English trade, there was no objection to make, and that England would greatly profit by it; but that with regard to the relations of Egypt and Turkey, it was a very delicate matter, and that the Viceroy had no right to make the Canal without the authority of the Porte.

The Emperor expressed his friendliness to the Sublime Porte, and the conversation dropped.

Now this conversation seems to me decisive; and the lessons to be drawn from it are the following:—

1. To treat the susceptibilities of the Porte with the greatest care. To find out exactly what are the objections *on points of detail*, in which we shall of course trace the influence of Lord Stratford de Redcliffe.

2. We must treat with no less care the susceptibilities of the Viceroy, as the opponents of the Canal would not be sorry to bring him into hostility with his suzerain.

3. The opinion expressed by the Emperor of the French will have great weight with the Porte and even with England.

4. After Lord Clarendon's declaration, we must apply to public opinion in England and engage English interests in the enterprise.

CV.

To M. S. W. RUYSSENAERS, ALEXANDRIA.

PARIS, *May* 6, 1856.

I HAVE prolongéd my stay in London, and shall not set out for Paris for another two days. This visit to England will bear fruit, for I have formed some excellent connections.

I have been presented to the Queen, and have seen Prince Albert privately, when I had a long interview in his study, about the Canal; he is quite *au courant* of the projected works. He told me that the Duke de Brabant, who is interested in the enterprise, called his attention to it. I received a hearty welcome from the Duke of Cambridge, who very frankly and unreservedly expressed a hope that the scheme would succeed. In short, on several occasions I have not hesitated to speak my mind, so that no further support might be given to the plan of depreciating the Viceroy, which some correspondents have been trying to do for a long time. I have brought forward positive facts, putting the matter in its proper light and enabling people to judge Mohammed Said as he deserves, in spite of faults and errors of detail, such as are not easily avoided in a country where the organisation of the Government is not yet complete.

The Royal Geographical Society of London, composed,

as you know, of highly-influential men, gave me a very significant demonstration. I was invited to dine at the Society's rooms. Lord Sheffield was in the chair. My health was proposed in a speech eulogising my efforts to realise the Suez Canal scheme. Then Mr. Gladstone, a cousin of the Minister (*sic*), said, in very good French: "M. De Lesseps, if we have not been so prompt to welcome your enterprise as others, it is because of our disposition of character; but when once we are convinced, we go further, and perhaps persevere more, than other nations do. For my part, I have had doubts about the principle of the scheme; I have them now; but I ask nothing better than to be convinced, and I give you my sincere wishes for your success."

I thanked my entertainers for the interest shown by so distinguished a meeting of travellers and learned men in an enterprise which would certainly increase the study of geography and facilitate its discoveries. As I was informed that several of the members present could not attend the meeting of the Society and desired to learn particulars, I gave a complete account of the exploration by the international commission and of the result of their labours. Questions were put to me about the danger from sand and on the objections raised by the *Edinburgh Review*. My replies seemed to give satisfaction.

I was then taken to the meeting of the Society. The president, Sir R. Murchison, wanted to introduce the question of the Isthmus of Suez as an extra subject, for it was not on the orders of the day. After several speeches, in which the speakers insisted, one after the other, on the necessity of opening prompt and easy communication between nations, the president asked me to speak on the Isthmus of Suez. The hall was full, many ladies being present, and as I rose I received rounds of applause. These again greeted me at the close of my speech, which the secretary begged me to write out and send him, that it might be entered in the minutes of the Society. I have done so. The following is a copy:

Captain Fitzroy, when speaking of a canal through the Isthmus of Darien, said just now, in eloquent language, that many great enterprises which seem chimerical before you study them, are found by all to be quite practicable when they have been seriously examined on the spot. I hope this will be the case with the inter-oceanic canal, which has been under discussion, and I pray it may be realised. As for cutting a canal through the Isthmus of Suez, on which the president has asked me to speak, I can assure you that the scheme is perfectly practicable.

A few months ago I called together a commission of the engineers of Europe who are most famous for harbour and canal works. The larger part of this commission went to Egypt, and declared unanimously that to cut through the isthmus, and establish two seaports in the Mediterranean and Red seas, would be easy of accomplishment and certain of success.

The Suez roads are large and safe. More than five hundred vessels can find room there; the depth is from five to thirteen mètres, with a capital anchorage. The English corvette *Zenobia* has been kept there for three years as a coal magazine for the India mail boats. She is in a position much exposed to winds; but in the course of these years her anchors have not given way, her cables have not suffered the least damage, and her communication with the shore has never been interrupted for a day,—a thing which does not always happen even in harbours that are considered good. Two deep and sound channels, about twenty mètres deep, so large that vessels can always tack, form the entrance to the anchorage.

From these data the commission concluded that the Suez roads had every qualification for forming the entrance of the maritime canal.

Throughout their survey from Suez to Pelusium, the international commission met with no obstacle to cutting or to preserving the canal in a smooth soil, which geologically was very favourable. It discovered, by soundings, that the soil of the isthmus consists in general of, first, a layer of agglutinated sand, then a layer of clayey earth, then one of calcareous chalk, till they reached a plastic clay, about eleven or twelve mètres below the level of the sea.

During an excursion on the isthmus, the Viceroy of Egypt sent the steam frigate *Nile* into the Bay of Pelusium, where M. Larousse, the hydrographic engineer, instructed by the commission, made several soundings, and drew up a hydrographic plan of the bay. It was found that a belt of fine sand stretched in front of the coast line like that of the shore, which ended at a depth of ten mètres; and then began a belt of mud, making good anchorage for ships, and stretching out into the depths of the Mediterranean. The part of the bay where there is the greatest depth, is round the hill at Tannis. There are eight mètres of water here, at a distance of two or three hundred mètres from the shore, and this depth is continuous for five leagues from the mouth at Oum Fareg to that at Gemileh. Here the commission decided to fix the entrance to the canal from the Mediterranean. Piers of two or three thousand mètres are nothing uncommon, and in the place where they will be fixed will afford every facility for the ingress and egress of ships.

I am now bringing out a pamphlet, which will contain the official report of the investigations of the engineers of the commission made during their survey of the isthmus, and will also answer the erroneous notion the *Edinburgh Review* has put forward about the practicability of the scheme. The errors into which the *Review* has fallen, however, are excusable, because at the time when the article was written, nothing was known of the engineers' explorations.

In a country where there is perfect freedom of discussion, a good cause is sure to triumph.

The English publication which I mentioned is just coming out.

Before leaving London I got together a local committee, composed of a member of the East India Company, a member of the Bank of England, two well-known financiers from the City, Mr. Powles, general secretary of the Dock Company, and the two English members of the international commission. But this committee is not to act till the Sultan's ratification has been obtained.

We must now wait for the meeting of the commission of engineers, and for the opinion of the City of London to develop, to make a new chapter in the history of the business. The ground is well prepared, and we have nothing to do now but to wait patiently for the harvest, not ceasing, however, to watch the crop.

CVI.

To his Highness Mohammed Said, Viceroy of Egypt.

PARIS, *May* 20, 1856.

ALTHOUGH I acquaint your Highness with all that could interest you by every mail, I cannot but write at once to say how much I was touched by your affectionate letter of April 26th. I do not need fresh evidence to make me confident of the continuation of your friendship.

I have long noticed that your Highness's enemies are also those, either secretly or openly, of the Canal, and, remembering this, I was not surprised to hear what they had attempted after my departure from Egypt. But we can often learn from our enemies, when we are not afraid of knowing the truth and have spirit enough carefully to notice the attacks made on us; and when we have a sufficiently clear conscience to know how much is slander and how much is calumny, our enemies, instead of injuring us, really do us good service. We answer the slander by rectifying the error that gave rise to it, and we can always upset calumny by the evidence of positive fact and by perseverance in irreproachable conduct.

I can assure your Highness that all you have done is thoroughly appreciated in Europe, and that you must not judge of public opinion by the ridiculous statements made by some evil-disposed or discontented people who are trying to act against the Egyptian Government by calumny and fault-finding. The truth gets stronger day by day. Flatterers may tell your Highness that you have no need to justify your conduct; but it is always well loyally to explain our actions, for if we do not, rogues, who are always active, have a good handle against honest men, who are not officious and do not suspect evil. I have arranged so as to keep the press of all countries *au fait* of our news, and the relations thus formed are entirely disinterested.

CVII.

To M. ELIE DE BEAUMONT, PERMANENT SECRETARY OF THE ACADEMY OF SCIENCES.

PARIS, *June* 13, 1856.

I HAVE the honour to forward to the Academy of Sciences a number of samples of the soundings taken in the Isthmus of Suez.

These soundings were taken in order to learn through what strata the maritime canal would have to pass between Suez and Pelusium.

Together with these I enclose,

1. A book giving the thickness of the seams crossed in each boring, and their relative level to the Mediterranean.

2. A map of the isthmus, on which is shown where the different borings were made.

3. The official report of the international commission of engineers, giving the results of their survey of the isthmus.

4. A horizontal section of the projected canal from Suez to Pelusium.

Although the principal object of the commission was to ascertain the course the maritime canal should take between the Mediterranean and the Red Sea, I thought it would be a pity to lose so precious an opportunity for scientific research. The geology of the country, if not entirely ignored, is certainly little known, and the samples I send you will assist in making it understood.

Later on, when the works of the great Canal are in full progress, I shall take care to have everything preserved that may be discovered in the cuttings. But till that time I am anxious not to lose information that can be obtained now, and I am glad to submit it to the Academy, by the hands of one of the most distinguished geologists of our day.

Memorandum.

At a meeting on Monday, June 16th, the Academy of Sciences appointed a committee to examine M. de Lesseps's different communications. The following are the members: MM. Cordier, Charles Dupin, Elie de Beaumont, Dufrénoy, and Admiral Dupetit Thouars.

CVIII.

An Account given at the Opening of the General Meeting of the Engineers of the International Scientific Commission, at Paris, June 23, 1856.

I wish to point out to you, in a few words, the reasons for the special object of this meeting, to which you have been good enough to come from all parts of Europe with a readiness for which I tender you my best thanks.

Your are, by the aid of science and your own experience, to solve all the technical questions relating to the canal which is to join the Mediterranean and Red seas. The scientific solution also of this great enterprise is entirely in your hands, and you are to decide conclusively what are the practical conditions necessary to carry it out.

I shall not now go into more details, which you all know sufficiently well; but it will be useful, I think, before you begin your deliberations, to give a short account of the works which up to this time have been put in hand, in readiness for your decision.

In November last the majority of your commissioners went to Egypt, to judge on the spot of the merits of the rough draft of the scheme, drawn up by the Viceroy's engineers, MM. Linant Bey and Mougel Bey.

The commissioners began their investigation at the port of Alexandria, and going thence to Cairo, were able to form an impartial opinion on the indirect channels suggested for the Canal.

The commission then visited Suez and its roads; it recognised their natural capabilities, and fixed the general direction of the outlet of the Canal.

Leaving Suez, a thorough investigation was made of the isthmus itself. The course marked out for the Canal was followed, and the borings, which had been ordered and carried on for some months, were verified. A complete set of samples of those borings are here for your inspection; they were submitted last Monday to the Academy of Sciences, by the illustrious permanent secretary, M. Elie de Beaumont.

When they reached Pelusium, the commissioners examined the results of more than 500 soundings that had been made with much intelligence and energy by the young hydrographer, M. Larousse, and gained information about this part of their work, as they had done about the Suez roads.

On their return to Alexandria the commissioners sent a short report to his Highness the Viceroy, in which they briefly stated the result of their labours. They stated the reasons on which their opinion was founded at greater length in the series of official reports with which you are acquainted.

When they got back to Europe, the commissioners had

need to complete the papers already in hand by fresh documents from the Viceroy's engineers, and these required long research.

These deeds, which are indispensable to your decision, are now all complete. Their absence delayed your meeting, which otherwise would have been called earlier.

You have now everything in hand necessary to assist your judgment.

Some of your colleagues, who were able to be in Paris eight days ago, held meetings to prepare beforehand the bases of your discussions. The English engineers took part in these preliminary arrangements, although at a distance, and have sent their colleagues notes which will be very valuable to you.

The following is an exact account of all the documents that I have had collected, as the commission suggested, and which are henceforth at your disposal:

1. Chart of the Isthmus and cross sections.
2. Plan of the Isthmus, with the suggested course of the Canal.
3. Plan of the soundings on the coast, and in the Pelusian Roads.
4. Plan of Suez Harbour and Roads.
5. Horizontal section of the Maritime Canal.
6. List of borings made in the Isthmus, and sketch showing the water level in each boring made in the course of the Canal.
7. Chest of samples from the borings.
8. Tidal courses observed at Suez.
9. Abstract of observations on the tide taken at Suez.
10. Abstract of observations on the tide taken at Pelusium.
11. Comparative results of the different levellings taken between the Mediterranean and Red seas.
12. Account of experiments on evaporation made at the mouth of the Nile.
13. Investigations and calculations on the management of the water in the Maritime Canal.
14. Table of levels taken in the Isthmus of Suez, and observations of the tides in the two seas.
15. Estimate of earthworks in the horizontal and cross sections of the bed of the Canal.
16. Inquiries into the produce of the country, and the cost of the necessary materials for the work.
17. Geological account of the Isthmus.
18. Plan of the proposed piers at the mouth of the Canal in the Pelusian Roads.
19. An important minute by M. Paléocapa, with maps and plans.

Such, gentlemen, is the list of subjects for investigation at your present meeting and the documents which will be at your disposal.

The international scientific commission on the Suez Canal, which you represent, consists, when complete and with some additions, of the honourable members whose names I subjoin:

For England, Mr. MacClean, as chief engineer; Captain Harris, of the British Navy, who was chosen because of of his special study of the Suez Canal question and his practical knowledge of the Red Sea; Mr. Chas. Manby, secretary of the Institute of Civil Engineers in London; and Mr. Rendel.

For Holland, Mr. Conrad, chief engineer of the Water Staat.

For Austria, Mr. Councillor Negrelli, Inspector-General of the Railways of the Empire.

For Prussia, Mr. Councillor Lentzé, Chief Engineer of the Works on the Vistula.

For Italy, the engineer M. Paléocapa, Minister of the Public Works at Turin.

For Spain, Don Cipriano Segundo Montesino, Director-General of Public Work at Madrid.

For France, M. Renaud, Inspector-General and Member of the General Council *des Ponts et Chaussées;* Rear-Admiral Rigault de Genouilly, Captain Jaures, and M. Lieussou, Hydrographic Engineer to the Navy.

Moreover, you have among you the respected M. Jomard, one of the last representatives of the Egyptian Scientific Commission of 1798, who was anxious to assist at your first meeting last year; and his co-member of the Institute, M. Barthélemy Saint-Hilaire; who followed the labours of your colleagues in Egypt, and who since then has never ceased to afford me his wise and useful co-operation in the task I have undertaken.

The section of the commission that went to Egypt nominated M. Conrad as its president and M. Lieussou as its secretary. These gentlemen consider that their offices, which they have held with so much zeal and distinction, conclude to-day. Some of your colleagues thought it would be fitting to offer the presidency of your general meeting to M. Paléocapa, who seems called to the office by his age, his consummate experience, and the high position he occupies in the councils of his Government.

M. Paléocapa, however, although much gratified by the overtures officially made to him, has thought it best to decline this mark of confidence in him, excusing himself on the plea of his health, which however allows him to take part in your deliberations. The assembly will therefore proceed, after hearing M. Conrad, to elect a president and a secretary.

M. Mougel Bey, who is present, and has come from his Highness the Viceroy, is ready to give you any information and explanation you may require of the documents that his colleague Linant Bey and himself have drawn up and arranged with great care. He will explain, if need be, the general idea and chief data on which their rough draft, which is submitted to you, was based.

In concluding the remarks I have offered, gentlemen, and before you begin your important deliberations, I congratulate myself on seeing you thus happily assembled to promote the great work which has so powerfully excited the sympathies of Europe.

CIX.

SUMMARY OF RESOLUTIONS PASSED BY THE INTERNATIONAL SCIENTIFIC COMMISSION AT SIX MEETINGS HELD ON THE 23RD, 24TH, AND 25TH OF JUNE, 1855.

(*Forwarded to the different correspondents of all countries, till a Report, to be drawn up by a special commission, shall be translated and published.*)

PARIS, *June* 25, 1856.

1. The commission has rejected the plan of an indirect channel across Egypt, and has adopted the principle of a straight channel from Suez to the Mediterranean.

2. It has rejected the proposal of feeding the maritime

canal by water from the Nile, and adopted that of filling it from the sea.

3. It has discussed the advantages and disadvantages of having the Canal banked the whole way from one sea to the other; and finally decided that the Canal should not be banked where it crosses the Bitter Lakes.

4. These Bitter Lakes, being left open, will have the the effect of weakening the force of tidal current; and the commission considers that locks at the two entrances to the Canal, at Suez and Pelusium, will not be necessary. It reserves the right, however, of making them later on if required.

5. It decides on a width of 100 mètres at the water line, 46 at bottom throughout the whole course of the Canal, 20 kilomètres of which must be walled between Suez and the Bitter Lakes. It has reduced the width of the rest of the Canal to 80 mètres at the water line and 36 at bottom.

6. The plan of the proposed scheme drawn up by the engineers of his Highness the Viceroy is maintained.

7. With reference to the entrance from the Mediterranean (Port Said), the commission adopt the plans of piers for Port Said which the members who went to Egypt drew up, only the width of the channel will be 400 mètres, instead of 500, and an inner dock will be added.

8. With reference to the port at Suez on the Red Sea the commission adopt the site and direction of the channel. The width will be 300 mètres, instead of 400, and an inner dock will be added.

9. The commission hold that when the Canal is opened, the shallows on the Egyptian side and on that of the Red Sea should be marked by powerful lights.

10. A port for victualling purposes and for repairs will be made on Lake Timsah.

11. As regards auxiliary fresh water canals fed by the Nile, the commission leave the engineers who carry out the works to decide on the best way of making them, with the sanction of the Viceroy's Government.

12. Finally, it appears from detailed information supplied by the naval officers who are members of the com-

mission that the navigation of the Red Sea is as good as that of the Mediterranean and the Adriatic. This conclusion, which the commission endorse, is the result of the opinion of Captain Harris, who has made seventy voyages from Suez to India.

CX.

To Comte de Lesseps, Paris.

Vienna, *July* 8, 1856.

When the labours of the international commission were over, it was my duty to go and acquaint the Viceroy with the definite result of their deliberations. But I thought that when I told him the scientific opinion of engineers, it would be a good thing to take him the political opinion of a veteran European diplomatist.

I want you to show Count Walewski the opinion of Prince Metternich, which I committed to writing when I left him, and he has admitted that my report is correct.

The Opinion of Prince Metternich.

His Highness Mohammed Said had the right to carry out the Suez Canal. Every step he has taken in this matter deserves the assent of European statesmen; but in a question of so much importance, in which he could foresee that foreign politics would be engaged, he was very wise to apply for the ratification of the Porte.

Official approbation for an enterprise so manifestly advantageous to the Ottoman Empire, as also to all other nations, cannot be withheld since science has given a favourable opinion and sufficient capital is forthcoming to carry it out.

Thus, then, while the Sultan has begun by agreeing with his vassal's proposal, his Highness will take up an excellent position with regard to Europe by proposing that the friendly or Allied Powers, in order to avoid all difficulties with them or with Egypt in the future, should send Plenipotentiaries to guarantee by convention the perpetual neutrality of the Suez Canal, which has been admitted in principle, as far as the Ottoman Empire is concerned, in Article 14 of the Act of Concession.

In this way the domestic question of how to make the Canal is separated as it ought to be from the foreign question of neutrality. By this means the prerogatives of territorial sovereignty remain intact, and the Ottoman Empire by taking, for the first time since the conclusion of peace, a position of influence which is fitting in a negotiation that affects the public rights of Europe, gives satisfaction to the political and commercial interests of all Powers, at the same time obtaining by their consent a fresh guarantee of its own integrity and independence.

The Viceroy of Egypt, who served his suzerain so faithfully in time of war, will render him no less a service by his conduct in this work of peace, and thus Napoleon I.'s prediction will be fulfilled, for, from the beginning of this century, he regarded the opening of a canal between the two seas as a means of contributing to the glory and strength of the Ottoman Empire.

CXI.

To Madame Delamalle, Paris.
(Continuation of Journal.)

Alexandria, *July* 16, 1856.

I REACHED the port of Alexandria this morning, and I could not have arrived at a better time, for when the ship cast anchor the guns of the port proclaimed the Viceroy's birthday. When I learnt that the Consular corps and other authorities were going to congratulate his Highness at eight o'clock, I took care no one should tell him I was on board the mail boat from Trieste; and going to the palace without stopping in the town, I entered the Viceroy's room: we embraced, and I was the first to offer my felicitations.

I shall conclude my business and leave for Paris on the the 22nd, going *via* Trieste, Vienna, Milan, Genoa, and Marseilles.

CXII.

To M. Thouvenel, Constantinople.

Alexandria, *July* 20, 1856.

PUBLIC opinion here is engrossed with the official mission of Nedjib Bey, the envoy from the Sultan, who brings magnificent presents to his Highness the Viceroy. The autograph letters by which the Grand Seigneur accredits him were read with great ceremony in the presence of all the functionaries, Ulemas, Christian Patriachs, and Rabbis.

Nedjib Bey, whom I knew in Constantinople and with whom I had private interviews, seems well satisfied with the reception, and declared himself convinced that the Porte ought to ratify the Viceroy's concession of the Canal.

In this matter Mohammed Said has evinced a temper, perseverance, and tact worthy of the greatness of the enterprise. He understands that France is not willing to take the initiative at Constantinople, and that it is not considered well to oppose the more influential voice of the French Ambassador to the prejudices of the English Envoy, and in the present state of the affair he does not think he ought to let the matter remain any longer in this vicious circle, after the feeling manifested in England and in the rest of Europe. He asked my opinion: what that is you know, and it is now confirmed by that of Prince Metternich, with whom I had a long interview as I passed through Vienna on my way to Egypt. That illustrious veteran diplomatist, who, in spite of his eighty-four years, recalled with wonderful clearness all the circumstances in the history of the scheme and the situation of each of the Powers interested in it, authorised me to write down his opinion, and begged me to send it to the Viceroy *as his political testament.* These are his own words.

I have just been making arrangements with the Viceroy for beginning to cut the auxiliary canal, which is to take the Nile water into Lake Timsah at the close of the year. We are anxious that the affair shall not suffer from these political delays. We are making head, and shall accomplish the work.

CXIII.

Report to his Highness the Viceroy of Egypt on the Fellah Workmen to be Employed by the International Suez Canal Company.

Alexandria, *July* 20, 1856.

The Act of Concession for the Suez Canal gives complete authority to the International Company to obtain the artisans necessary to carry out the work. Article 2 provides that, in every case, four fifths at least of the hands employed shall be Egyptians. Article 22 promises the company the loyal and hearty co-operation of the Government and its officers. It enrols the two chief engineers of the Viceroy in the company, who are to manage the works, superintend the workmen, and carry out the regulations relative to the work in hand. The practical application of this principle, and adhering to the conditions and clauses attached to its execution, is most essential to the company's interest and the surest guarantee that the work will be promptly and economically executed.

The company has now to secure for the works a sufficient number of efficient, strong, and acclimatised hands, and to fix the maximum of wages, that the estimate of expenses the engineers of the international scientific commission are going to draw up may be complete and accurate.

In order to be quite sure of enough men, it must also concentrate the labourers in one place, under regulations for their order, discipline, and welfare, which will allay all apprehensions and present reciprocal advantages to labour, on the one hand, and capital on the other.

With reference to this matter, Mohammed Said has entrusted me to draw up a decree, which I think it will be well to publish, in order to reassure all interests and answer many of the objections raised against the feasibility of making the Canal without difficulty.

Thanks to the decree, the company will henceforth have at its disposal such workmen as the chief engineers shall think necessary, without resorting to large importations from the European labour market; to which we ought never to have recourse, although our so doing has been gratuitously suggested as a material difficulty and political inconvenience.

In the interest of the company the rate of wages should be two-thirds less than those given in similar enterprises in Europe.

In the interests of the men, it should exceed by one-third the daily pay they are now receiving in Egypt.

Besides cash payment, food and shelter are guaranteed to the hands, as well as free medical attendance in case of illness or accidents. Moreover, the sick and wounded are to receive an indemnity equivalent to half a day's pay daily. We believe this to be the first time that such a thoughtful and humane measure has been officially introduced in workshops (*sic*) even in Europe.

The solicitude shown by the Viceroy in this important particular in favour of the labouring classes, who up to this time have been too little considered in the East, with the guarantees insisted on for their protection and assistance, will perhaps be the best proof, to those who know the old customs of the East, of the progress that Egypt, under a generous impulse, has made in the ideas of Western civilisation. Mohammed Said, who is as well acquainted with his own religion as he is with European learning, well knows that the Mussulman law in no way opposes progress; he often says that it is the bad government, evil customs, and bad habits of the East that want reform more than the laws. In short, the book which proclaims love as the rule of life, and says that in the eyes of God the best man is he who does most good to his fellows, can never oppose measures taken in the interests of the highest civilisation.

We, MOHAMMED SAID PACHA, Viceroy of Egypt, anxious to assure the execution of the works for the Suez Maritime Canal, to arrange that the Egyptian working men who shall be employed shall be well treated, and anxious at the same time to protect the interests of the cultivators, proprietors, and contractors of the country, have drawn up, in conjunction with M. Ferdinand de Lesseps, founder and president of the International Company of the said Canal, the following code:

ARTICLE 1.—The men to be employed on the company's works shall be supplied by the Egyptian Government, when applied for by the chief engineer, as they shall be required.

ARTICLE 2.—Fixed pay will be allotted to the workmen, according to the average pay fixed in private undertakings, at from two and-a-half to three piastres a day, not including food, which shall be paid in kind by the company, to the value of one piastre. Hands under twelve years of age will only receive one piastre, but full rations.

The rations shall be given out every day, or every two or three days, in advance; and in cases where it shall be found that the workmen are in a position to provide their own food, the value of their rations shall be given in money.

The money payments shall be made every week.

The company, however, will not give out more than half-pay for the first month, till it has accumulated a reserve of fifteen days' pay, after which full pay will be given to the men.

The care of providing plenty of drinkable water for all the wants of the men is undertaken by the company.

ARTICLE 3.—The task imposed on the men shall not exceed that fixed in the Egyptian *Ponts et Chaussées* contract, which has been adopted in all canal works undertaken in the last few years.

The number of men employed will be regulated with reference to seasons, and agricultural pursuits.

ARTICLE 4.—The police in the workyards will be Government officers and agents, acting under the chief engineer's orders, in accordance with regulations approved by us.

ARTICLE 5.—Workmen who shall not have completed their task will have their pay reduced by not less than a third, and in proportion to the amount of work left undone.

Defaulters will entirely lose the fifteen days' pay in reserve. Their share will be devoted to the hospital, which is treated of in the next article. Men giving any trouble in the workyards will be docked of a proportionate part of the fifteen days' pay in reserve; they will also be liable to a fine, which will go to the hospital fund.

ARTICLE 6.—The company will find shelter for the workmen, either in tents, sheds, or suitable houses. It will provide a hospital and ambulances, with all necessary appliances for treating the sick, at their expense.

ARTICLE 7.—The travelling expenses of the men engaged and their families, from the time of their leaving home till they arrive at the workyards, will be defrayed by the company.

Every workman who is ill will receive, whether in the hospital or in the ambulances, besides everything to restore his health, a pay of one and-a-half piastre during the whole of the time he is unable to work.

ARTICLE 8.—Artisans, such as masons, carpenters, stonecutters, blacksmiths, &c., will receive the usual pay the Government allots for their work, exclusive of food, or its equivalent.

ARTICLE 9.—When soldiers of the line are employed on the works, the company will give each of them a sum equal to the pay of civilians at the works, on account of the high rate of their ordinary pay, and of their dress.

ARTICLE 10.—Everything necessary for the transport of soil, materials, or powder for blasting purposes, will be supplied by the company or the Government, at net cost, which will be demanded three months (at least) in advance.

Our engineers, Linant Bey and Mougel Bey, whom we place at the disposal of the company to direct and conduct the works, will superintend the workmen, and act in concert with the administrator appointed by the company to remove any difficulties that may arise in carrying out this decree.

Given at Alexandria July 20, 1856.   (L. S.)
Viceroy's Signet.

(Translated from the Turkish.)

CXIV.

Extract from a Report presented to the King of Holland, in July 1856, by M. Simons, Minister of the Interior.

We owe the larger part of our commerce to our vast possessions in India and to their rich productions. We also owe to them our mercantile marine, for which these possessions offer so wide a scope, and the increase of our revenue since the principle of free trade has been so happily established among us. The opening of the proposed canal through the Isthmus of Suez, which would so greatly shorten the voyage to India, will necessarily have an immense influence on our commerce, and, for this reason, is a matter of the first importance to us. The Netherlands will certainly lose nothing by this great step; on the contrary, everything suggests that they will greatly gain; but in either case we must at once take steps for our security when the event takes place.

I am convinced that we ought at once to call the attention of our traders to the proposed change.

I therefore take the liberty of suggesting that your Majesty should appoint a commission of inquiry.

This commission should discuss the following questions:—

1. What influence will the Suez Canal have on commerce and navigation in general, and on Dutch commerce in particular?
2. Means suggested for preserving and increasing our commerce in case the proposed change takes place.
3. What steps should the Government take to maintain and encourage the exertions of our manufacturers in this enterprise?

Text of the Royal Order issued in Accordance with M. Simons's Report.

We, William III., &c.

Whereas the projected Canal through the Isthmus of Suez must bring about great changes in all commerce; and whereas it is of great importance to call the attention of the trade of Holland to the changes contemplated, and to the means to be employed to profit advantageously by the said changes, or at least to avoid suffering in any way; and whereas we have seen the Report of our Minister of the Interior, dated July 8, 1856.

We have ordered, and do order,—

1. That a commission shall examine into the matter and present a report thereon, which shall contain all acts and documents which will be useful to trade, to navigation, and to the State.
2. The following shall be members of this commission:

E. P. de Monchy, President of the Dutch Commercial Company at Amsterdam, President of the Commission.

J. D. Spengler, President of the Chamber of Commerce and Manufacture at Amsterdam.

A. Van Rijckevorsel, H. son, President of the Chamber of Commerce and Manufacture at Rotterdam.

J. Buys't Hooft, President of the Chamber of Commerce and Manufacture at Dortrecht.

G. de Clercq, Secretary to the Commercial Company.

L. M. F. Plate, ex-President of the Commercial Factory at Batavia.

F. W. Conrad, Chief Engineer of the Water and Dyke Department, President of the International Commission on the Suez Canal at the Hague.

P. Van Vlissengen, Manufacturer and Ship-owner at Amsterdam.

Van Oordt, Director of the Steam Ship Company at Rotterdam.

G. J. Sprenger, President of the Chamber of Commerce and Manufacture at Middelburg.

J. Van Hulst, President of the Chamber of Commerce and Manufacture at Harlingen.

S. Vissering, Rector of the Leyden University.

M. A. M'sGravesande Guicherit, Professor of Commercial Law at the Royal Academy at Delft, secretary.

3. The Commission shall meet at the Hague.

WILLIAM.

The Minister of the Interior,
SIMONS.

Loo, *July* 10, 1856.

CXV.

REMARKS ON THE OFFICIAL INQUIRIES RELATING TO THE PIERCING OF THE ISTHMUS OF SUEZ.

PARIS, *August* 10, 1856.

THE scheme for cutting through the Isthmus of Suez is engaging the attention of several Governments—viz., those of England, Sardinia, Holland, Austria, Venice, and Rome, each looking at the matter from its own point of view.

Sardinia, Austria, Holland, Venice, and the Pope already consider the undertaking to be definitive, and are preparing, with laudable foresight, for the results it must produce. Some are enlarging their old harbours, with a view to the expected increase of their trade; others are making new ones. Some are situated on the Mediterranean, on the Adriatic, others on the North Sea, and for them the distance which separates them from wealthy colonies, the principal source of their wealth and power, will be lessened by one half.

It is, therefore, no exaggeration to say that our great undertaking is becoming a subject of interest to the official world. This is quite a new phase.

The English Government has despatched a cruiser off Pelusium to test the soundings of the international commission.

Thus different Governments, without having recourse to diplomatic action and each on its own account, are taking notice of our undertaking. All these inquiries can only tend to promote the scheme, and we confidently await the approaching result.

CXVI.

REMARKS ON EGYPT PUBLISHED IN THE "ISTHMUS DE SUEZ" NEWSPAPER, PARIS, AUGUST 25, 1856.

IF the special condition of each of the several countries which compose the Turkish Empire be attentively considered, it is impossible not to be struck by the exceptional circumstances in which Egypt is placed.

The population of Egypt has nothing in common with that of the remainder of the Empire. It is neither Turkish, nor Greek, nor Arab. The inhabitants of the Valley of the Nile are the same as the Egyptians of Pharaoh. To any one who has lived among them, there can be little doubt on the subject. In body and in mind, in their habits and in their prejudices, they are the faithful representatives of the old race; and the revolutions which have wrought so many political changes in Egypt do not seem to have produced any material alterations in the primitive type of the native population.

Hence it may be said that the modern Egyptians have inherited the good and bad qualities of the Egyptians of old. Indeed, in every historical record, from Holy Writ downwards, the salient features of the national character are invariably marked with the same stamp.

The Egyptian has one characteristic in common with other races of Ethiopian origin, inasmuch as, though usually thoughtless, indolent, and gentle, he will at times give proofs of obstinacy and energy, and yield to the most violent passions.

He is made up of strange contrasts : great intelligence, with an improvidence and carelessness of his own interests which often pass all bounds, an easy-going and, as a rule, sociable disposition, with instinctive repugnance to all that is foreign; almost passive submission to direct control, with a decided tendency to disregard authority when it cannot be enforced at once.

History, both ancient and modern, testifies to the fact that by their innate hardiness, their aptitude for works of the most varied description, and their activity in executing them, the Egyptians are capable of great things ; but this is only on condition that they be subjected to treatment suited to their nature and under firm and able guidance. If left to their own resources, they have not initiative, dash, and enterprise enough to better themselves, and with them it is very rare that a sense of duty makes up for the absence of those good qualities.

In close proximity to the native population, and on all sides of it, are the Arabs of the desert. This vicinity is often the cause of sanguinary encounters and of ruin to the bordering districts, whenever Government is unable to protect them against the incursions of the roving tribes.

Thus an improvidence and thoughtlessness, which render control and guidance a matter of constant necessity ; traditional submission to an authority which seems devoid of real strength and spontaneous means of action ; some evil propensities which require checking ; such are the data which should be taken into careful consideration in dealing with the moral and social state of the Egyptian population.

The physical circumstances affecting Egypt are no less remarkable.

Egypt, as we know, is one of the most fertile countries in the world. The abundance and variety of her natural products are proverbial ; and for many centuries her political standing was due in a great measure to her importance as a productive country. But, unlike other regions favoured by nature, the fertility of the soil is dependent, in the case of Egypt, on a single fact,—the existence of the Nile, by whose annual overflow the earth is refreshed and rendered fertile. Were it not for these floods Egypt would be a mere desert ; were it not for the Nile she would be nothing ; her existence depends on the phenomenon of the periodical floods, the recurrence of which is fortunately as regular as are the revolutions of the celestial bodies.

But the river does not of itself extend these beneficial effects beyond its banks, and the portions reached by its waters are naturally very restricted. Hence the necessity of having recourse to artificial means to husband and guide the waters so as to reach the most distant parts of the territory, and the urgency of creating a vast system of canals, embankments, and dams, to neglect the maintenance of which for a single day would be to render barren and lay waste a more or less extensive portion of Egypt. Now it may be looked upon as certain that these works, which necessitate a general knowledge of the requirements of the country, great means of execution, and much ready money, will never be carried out if left to the carelessness of private individuals, whose resources in every respect are, moreover, too limited to admit of their executing the works. It is, therefore, for the Government to undertake them.

Thus, we see a great, a rich country, whose prosperity, nay, whose very existence, is wholly dependent on the favourable or unfavourable disposition, the strength or the weakness of its rulers. It is easy to infer what must result from such a state of things.

For the present we shall confine ourselves to remarking that under the Mamelukes, whose authority was first shaken by the French expedition, and whom Mehemet Ali finally crushed, most of the canals of Egypt became choked up, irrigation works were almost destroyed, population decreased, and the sources of production were pretty nearly exhausted.

Lastly, the geographical position of Egypt gives her, in the eyes of the world, an importance which no other fraction of the Ottoman Empire possesses. Situated on the extreme boundaries of Africa and Asia, with the Red Sea on one side and the Mediterranean on the other, Egypt is the shortest, the most direct, route between the West and the far East, the central point of the vast traffic of Europe, India, China, and Oceania. After a rival means of communication had been opened by the discovery of the passage round the Cape of Good Hope, the route discovered by Vasco de Gama, deprived Egypt for a long time of the trade with China and the Indies. But then the way round the Cape was only preferred because it obviated trans-shipment, and was to the old navigators a means of saving time and money. However powerful these considerations may have been they did not alone determine the selection. It had, apart from this, become a matter of necessity for traders, for the simple reason that the route across Egypt was no longer practicable.

The state of anarchy in which, with rare intervals, Egypt had been plunged since the beginning of the fifteenth century, the conflicts of which she had constantly been the field, the fanaticism and inhospitable habits of the rulers, had raised a barrier over which trade, alarmed by the absence of security, had ceased to attempt to pass.

Egypt, by her geographical position, is the most natural and advantageous means of transit between West and East; and this is a privilege which cannot be lost so long as the internal state of the country does not destroy the work of nature. The proof of this is, that as soon as order was re-established and foreign interests became the object of a wise and steady protection, the route through Egypt was again opened to the trade of the whole world. In this respect Egypt has already partly recovered the importance she had lost; and the easier and safer transit becomes under the auspices of an enlightened and competent Administration, the greater will be this importance, as well as the guarantees offered to commercial nations.

From the fact that Egypt may be noted as having a special and characteristic population, with physical conditions of existence which are unique, and a geographical position which is the converging point of the most important commercial interests, it may be inferred that there are in that country elements of strength, together with causes of prostration, wants, social conditions: a system of life, in fact, essentially peculiar to it. This explains why Egypt never permanently remained a mere province, whatever may have been the power of the conqueror.

Whenever it has happened that Egypt has been reduced to the state of a mere province, that is to say, placed under a form of government common to other dependencies, the following alternative has invariably presented itself: either the principles of her prosperity have been stifled by a system of administration unsuited to her requirements, or she has recovered her independence through the weakness and incapacity of the central authority, or through the defection of governors who knew how to turn the resources of the country to account with a view to their own greatness.

What took place, for instance, after the conquest of Egypt by Sultan Selim in 1517? His son and successor, Soliman the Legislator, was undoubtedly a prince of consummate ability and experience. He was judicious enough to see that Egypt had to be governed in a peculiar manner. But he made one mistake. By imposing too great restrictions on the authority of the Pachas sent to Cairo as governors, and by only giving them a precarious and unstable position, he deprived them of the influence and consideration necessary to cope with the intrigues and the factious and rebellious spirit always smouldering somewhere in Egypt. The Mamelukes took advantage of this to seize the power, and became the real masters of the country. The Turkish governors soon became mere prisoners in their hands; and the Porte, unable to take any part in the administration of Egypt, and obliged to content itself with the promise of a small tribute, which was never paid, retained nothing, for more than two hundred years, than a purely nominal authority over the conquest of Selim.

At the foot of the Pyramids General Buonaparte struck the first blow against the domination of the Beys, the worst to which Egypt was ever subjected. On the departure of the French army, the Ottoman troops, with the help of the English, placed Turkish governors in the towns. But the Sublime Porte had not yet really recovered possession of the country. Things were in such a state of disorder that the representatives of the sovereign were powerless. It is to Mehemet Ali that the Sultan may be said to be indebted for the recovery of Egypt, and for her recovery in a position of such prosperity and social importance as to enable her to afford valuable assistance in men and money to the central Power.

But can we believe that Mehemet Ali, notwithstanding his rare ability, could have accomplished his task had he been invested only with a temporary and limited authority? Could he, in his mere capacity as the Governor of a province, have succeeded in crushing the still formidable remnants of the Circassian levies; in quelling anarchy in all its varied forms; in putting a stop to the depredations of traditional brigandage; in overcoming the formidable insurrection which in 1824 set Upper Egypt in a blaze; in restoring the holy cities to the veneration of the Mussulmen; in bringing back the order and industry, which had so long been lost; in repairing and extending to a degree hitherto unknown the water system of the valley of the Nile ;· in giving to agriculture an impulse which has increased tenfold the commercial importance of Egypt ;—in a word, could Mehemet Ali, had he merely been the Governor of a province, have been able to create that active and vigilant administration which, by establishing on a solid basis internal tranquillity and public security, has once more opened Egypt to the explorations of travellers, to the investigations of science, to foreign commercial enterprise, and to an important traffic between England and India?

To obtain such wonderful results, Mehemet Ali required, besides his own genius, permanent and undisputed authority, complete freedom of action, and forty years of work and efforts all tending to the same object. Nay, he required something more than all this. Why conceal it? He required the assurance that his undertaking would be continued by his family, and that he was working for his descendants.

From the facts we have just set forth, and their consequences, it is plain that the only conditions on which Egypt can secure internal tranquillity, fully develop her resources, and really belong to, or usefully form part of, the central power, are that she should possess institutions in conformity with her moral condition, a system of administration specially fitted to her requirements, and a Government which shall combine relative independence with guarantees of strength and stability.

The exceptional position of Egypt and the consequent necessity of constituting an equally exceptional local authority, have already been acknowledged by the statesmen of Europe and of Turkey. Imperial wisdom has found expression in the Hatti-Sherif of 1841, issued, by the advice of the great Powers, with a view to the practical carrying out of the principle.

The Hatti-Sherif, indeed, clearly decides the question. Without affecting the rights of the sovereign it makes large concessions to Egypt and her vassal prince, as may be seen from the following quotation :

1st. The Government of Egypt is made hereditary, in favour of Mehemet Ali and his descendants.

2nd. The Viceroy of Egypt may maintain a native army.

3rd. In consideration of a fixed annual tribute to the Sultan, the Viceroy has the right to levy and administer the whole of the revenues of Egypt.

With the exception of a few imperfections, which must no doubt be attributed to a feeling of distrust, the result of a comparatively recent crisis, it is only fair to acknowledge that the Imperial decree of 1841 has so constituted authority in Egypt as to conciliate the most varied interests. This record of the generous ideas of the reigning Sultan secures to Egypt the free development of those germs of prosperity innate in her, and to the Sublime Porte the possession of advantages lost through the policy of the Emperor Soliman. A

conflict of interests is no longer possible, nor are the calamities which
resulted from them to be feared if both parties honestly conform to the
spirit in which this great work has been conceived. Thanks to the
loyal conduct of the Vassal on the one hand, and the wisdom of the
Sovereign on the other, the weak points of the Hatti-Sherif just
mentioned have not hitherto been practically felt. Whenever the
Viceroy has explained to the Sultan the inadvisability of carrying
out to the letter certain matters of detail which were useless or
prejudicial to the real interests of Egypt and the Empire, such representations have been favourably received. On the other hand,
the Viceroy has readily and spontaneously increased the tribute
originally agreed upon, or under certain circumstances granted extraordinary subsidies.

By the Hatti-Sherif the number of Egyptian troops was limited to
18,000. But, as a matter of fact, the Porte has allowed the successors
of Mehemet Ali to raise their military forces to a much higher figure;
and this has turned out to her own advantage, as, when the last war
broke out, Turkey was supplied with nearly 40,000 out of the 60,000
men forming the total strength of the Egyptian army.

By the Act of 1841 it was decreed that Egyptian troops should
wear the same uniform as Turkish. How could this regulation be
carried out when it is well known that the climate of Egypt renders
such an uniform irksome, and even unhealthy, for the men? The
gallant Zouaves, who planted the standard of France on the walls of
Sebastopol, wear the Turkish dress,—the *chirwal* (wide trousers) and
the turban; does that in any way prevent them from holding first
rank among the soldiers of France? There were Mamelukes in
Napoleon's guard; the Emperor of Russia has his squadron of Cir-
cassians. Dress has nothing to do with courage and devotion, and it
would have been childish to make it a test of loyalty.

The Hatti-Sherif further enacts that the laws and regulations
issued by the Sublime Porte with regard to public administration
shall be applicable to Egypt. Had these enactments been fully
carried out they might have served as a pretext for cancelling part of
the essential concessions stipulated for, with a view to securing a
good system of administration in Egypt.

Under the Government of Abbas Pacha, predecessor of Mohammed
Said, negotiations took place between the Imperial Divan and the
Viceroy with respect to certain clauses of the *tauzimat*, to the carrying out of which the Viceroy feared there would have been very
serious objections in Egypt. Without entering into the arguments put
forward on either side, it will be sufficient to state that, thanks to the
wise intervention of statesmen devoted to the interests of their respective countries, among whom was Fuad Pacha, now Minister for
Foreign Affairs in Turkey, the Sultan, acting in a spirit of profound
justice, decided in favour of Egypt. A special exception to the
articles in question was made in favour of the local government, and
the difficulty was thus got over.

The debates which took place on this occasion revealed the existence of a party viewing with disfavour the creation of a special Administration for Egypt, and which would not be unwilling to distort in its application the spirit of the Act of 1841. We allude to certain reformers, who are perfectly sincere no doubt, but who are so imbued with their theories that they insist on putting them into practice on every occasion, at the risk of committing the most serious mistakes. The principle they go upon is the uniform organisation of the Ottoman Empire, on the pattern of the system of administrative centralisation prevailing in France. They do not reflect that France, with her eighty-six adjacent departments, and her compact, homogeneous population, is a very different thing from the Turkish Empire, made up of such varied countries and nationalities. Because unity exists in France, and centralisation has produced excellent results, French centralisation and unity are to be applied to Turkey! Starting with these data, and impatient to carry out their hobby, no obstacle, no danger would be too great to prevent them from placing the Empire under one sweeping system of uniform administration. As if, in the case of a State composed of such dissimilar elements, true unity, perfect unity, did not consist in the uniformity of results rather than of means; as if, for a monarchy so constituted, true centralisation did not result from the active and ever-ready co-operation of all the elements of national strength, developed in accordance with their nature and the laws necessary to their existence.

If an attempt were made to diminish the share of authority justly allotted to the Government of Egypt and to shackle its freedom of action, that Government would not suffer alone; the central authority itself would have cause to regret any imprudent action in the matter.

For if the ruler of Egypt be conscious of his duties and of his responsibility in the eyes of the world and of his sovereign, if he reflect on the important and numerous interests depending on the preservation of order and tranquillity in the country entrusted to his care, he will deem it imperative not blindly to accept any measures which might injuriously affect the rights whence he derives the authority necessary to enable him rightly to fulfil his mission. He will, therefore, morally resist any measures tending to weaken the means of action which it had been previously considered advisable and useful to place at his disposal. This would not in any way affect his loyalty, and, so far from the integrity of his intentions being questioned, his resistance would in itself be the best proof of his devotion to the common cause. But, for all that, the fact remains that if a disagreement were to occur between the central authority and Egypt, if there were a momentary break in the combination of elements constituting the Ottoman Power, if harmony of views and action ceased to exist, nothing could have a more injurious effect on public welfare in Turkey.

We could, to a certain extent, understand uncompromising partisans of centralisation being prepared to run a certain amount of risk for the sake of carrying out their system, if great benefits were to accrue therefrom to the Ottoman Empire, and if, by means of a more direct intervention in the administration of Egypt, the Sublime Porte could obtain greater resources than those derived under the present system. But experience has proved that such a result is not even to be hoped for. We know what Turkey used to derive from Egypt when the latter was under the rule of Pachas from Constantinople; the reckoning would not take long to make up.

As regards military forces, it would have been hopeless to expect anything from a population whose only motive for taking up arms was to pillage travellers or fight amongst themselves.

Indeed, at the present time this very same country pays into the Imperial Treasury, at regular intervals, and sometimes in advance, an annual tribute which, all administrative expenses deducted, amounts to no less than twelve million francs. This large sum is increased on many occasions by valuable presents. Moreover, in the last war Egypt was able, without weakening the public forces necessary for her own protection and the preservation of order at home, to contribute to the army of the Sublime Porte a large number of brave and disciplined soldiers, who fought nobly on the banks of the Danube and in the Crimea, together with a naval force composed of several frigates and vessels, some of which shared the disaster of Sinope. This was not all; 40,000 muskets, and supplies of every description were furnished to the sovereign power from the stores and arsenals at Cairo and Alexandria.

In every mosque throughout Egypt prayers are said in the name of the Sultan; his cypher is on the standards of the native army. The Canal from the Nile to Alexandria, the greatest work of modern Egypt, the *barrage* of the Nile, are, by the names they bear, sufficient tributes to the memory of the sovereigns under whose reign they were executed. And actual and compulsory homage to the Sublime Porte are external indications which, like everything else now, point to and confirm the Sultan's claim to sovereign power over Egypt.

This renewal of affinity between the past and the present is conclusive, and we need no further commentary.

True friends of Turkey, those who believe that the welfare of Egypt is inseparably connected with the regeneration of Turkey, should therefore devote themselves to maintaining the principles which found expression in the Hatti-Sherif of 1841. The friends of the generous Abdul-Medjid clearly saw that the only means of completing this work of regeneration would be to enlighten the Sublime Porte as to the steps to be taken to sift the elements of vital strength inherent to the Empire from those pernicious influences which paralyse their development.

Already, by their advice, wise reforms are on the eve of being carried out, and important means of communication are to be opened with the interior of the Empire, thus affording those facilities of intercourse so essential to the development of commerce and of agriculture, and enabling foreign capital to turn to account the natural resources of the country. Egypt had the honour of originating this movement. For the last quarter of a century the Egyptian Government has shown the greatest tolerance in religious matters, and long before the principle of the equality of rights had become law in Turkey, Christians were enjoying in Egypt the same privileges as Mussulmen in all relating to rank and position.

If, leaving questions of principle, we come to persons, it can easily be shown that there is not the slightest danger for the interests of Egypt, so intimately connected with those of Turkey, under the administration of a prince like the present Viceroy, who, of his own free will, renounced the traditional claim of his predecessors to the leadership of agricultural interests in Egypt, who has freed commerce from its shackles, and who, the day after his accession, gave orders that the railway should be continued from Alexandria to the Red Sea, and at the same time resolved to open to the world the most important of all routes of communication by the making of the Suez Canal.

CXVII.

To M. THOUVENEL, CONSTANTINOPLE.

LA CHENAIE, *August* 28, 1856.

YOUR kind letter of the 7th of August reached me in the country, where I am staying for a few days.

According to my idea I cannot allow the question to be transferred to Paris and London, whilst Paris does not express its views more decidedly than it has done up to the present time, and whilst the English Government maintains its opposition, that is to say whilst Lord Palmerston is the head of the Ministry. As this state of affairs might be prolonged for an indefinite period, the plan devised by Metternich appears to me to have the great advantage, by leaving the Porte to deal direct with the Viceroy, of not placing the French and English Governments in opposition to each other. But it is evident that if you are convinced that the Porte will not act in concert with the Viceroy without first obtaining the permission of England, the plan in question falls to the ground, unless you receive orders to support the request of the Viceroy. For this I have exerted myself since my arrival in Paris. I have informed the Emperor of the situation, and Count Walewski is also well aware of it. It will be for them to decide. In England I have done everything that man can do; and the results obtained have surpassed all my hopes; but it is useless for the press of the United Kingdom to be almost unanimous, as Lord Palmerston is perfectly resolved not to let himself be influenced by any consideration, and, from his inveterate jealousy towards France, it cannot be supposed that public opinion and judgment can exercise any influence on his mind in this matter.

In this position what can I do?—warn the French Government; regret not seeing it come to a decision, but conceal the situation as much as possible from the eyes of the public, and continue to carry on the scheme in Egypt, where I have always found the most firm and, I might add, the only foundation for my operations.

During my last journey in Egypt I settled with the Viceroy the important question of employing native workmen on the works of the canal.

Since my return to Europe I have been actively engaged on the approaching publication of the general report of the engineers of the international commission, containing an estimate of the cost. This estimate is very satisfactory.

I shall return to Egypt at the beginning of November, to see the work put in hand.

The longer the Porte puts off its ratification, which has been requested rather out of deference than from necessity, the more will it diminish its own position in the transaction and increase that of the Viceroy.

As regards the enterprise itself, no intrigue can any longer succeed in frustrating it, supported as it is by the decision of science, by the interest of the whole commercial world, and, what is perhaps still more decisive, by the fact that the funds will exceed the requirements of the undertaking.

September 3, 1856.

On the suggestion of M. Baruffi, Professor of the Royal University, Turin, the Scientific Congress of France, which met this year at La Rochelle, has unanimously expressed the following resolution:

The Scientific Congress,—

Considering that the piercing of the Isthmus of Suez, projected by M. de Lesseps, under the auspices of his Highness the Viceroy of Egypt, would be extremely useful to all nations without injuring any one,—

Considering that this enterprise is one of the most important means of civilisation that Providence could put into the hands of man,—

Expresses a desire that the Isthmus of Suez may be shortly opened for navigation for all countries.

The Bishop of La Rochelle was president of the congress, and, as he has done each year, M. de Caumont prepared the preliminaries of the meeting with a devotion to science worthy of all praise.

CXVIII.

MEMORANDUM FOR THE EMPEROR.

PARIS, *October* 12, 1856.

AT the time of M. Thouvenel's departure for Constantinople in June 1856, it had been agreed that the two Ambassadors of France and England should abstain from intervening with the Porte for or against the question of the Suez Canal.

If one of the two agents failed in keeping to this arrangement on his part, his colleague was to be at liberty to act as he saw fit.

Up to this time Lord Stratford has never ceased to make use of his influence to inspire the Ministers of the Porte with prejudices against the plan of cutting through the Isthmus of Suez, and to prevent the ratification of the grant regularly and legally made by the Viceroy of Egypt.

It is, moreover, certain that the English agent in Egypt has endeavoured to influence the Viceroy with a view to dissuading him from a project which excites the warmest sympathy in France as well as in the rest of Europe. But although the schemes of English policy have been completely foiled in Egypt, the energy and intelligence of Mohammed Said, who, in reality, confides in the support of your Imperial Majesty, the same could not be the case at Constantinople, where the Turkish Government, weak as it now is, yields only to force. Thus the Turks, placed between the powerful threats of Lord Stratford and the scrupulous silence which our Ambassador has been ordered to maintain, are naturally changing their attitude, and testifying feelings hostile to the Canal, to which they were at first favourable.

This state of affairs alone would be detrimental to our dignity in the East; but Lord Stratford has lately complicated it, to the injury of our legitimate influence and our interests. In order plainly to show that he had the power to hinder a measure connected with a very important French interest, and that it would be easy for him at the same time to satisfy English interests even in those matters in which they are most exclusive and domineering, he has obtained the consent of the Porte to the formation of an *English Company*, which is to have a grant for the construction of a railway, 350 leagues in length, from the Mediteranean to the Persian Gulf. In the contract the Sultan will guarantee an interest of six per cent. on the money invested in the undertaking. This railway, the surveys for which are not yet commenced, is to-day quoted at a premium in the London money market. It will cost from four to five millions sterling, and it will expose Turkey to an annual charge of thirty million francs for the sole profit of English capitalists and British influence; for it is impossible not to see that, hereafter, the British Euphrates Valley Railway will, as it were, take possession of the centre of Syria and of the countries bordering on the Valley of the Euphrates.

However this may be, it is probable that should the enterprise succeed, which I doubt, it would decidedly advance civilisation and human progress. It would not, therefore, be right for us to oppose it; but should not what has lately taken place serve in some sort as an example to us, and make us feel that it is time to send instructions to our Ambassador, so that the Suez Canal scheme may no longer be impeded at Constantinople, and that the formal ratification may be granted?

In concluding this memorandum it is only right to add that the Suez Canal enterprise has demanded no guarantee of support, that it does not aid the exclusive policy of any Power, and that, far from imposing a burden upon Turkey, it yields Egypt a privilege of 15 per cent. upon its revenue.

In writing this memorandum for your Majesty, who alone can judge of what ought to be done at Constantinople, I have limited myself to an exact account of the state of affairs.

I shall still endeavour to assist the progress of affairs in Egypt, persevering in that line of conduct which I am happy to find has procured me the approbation of your Majesty.

CXIX.
To M. S. W. Ruyssenaers, Alexandria.

PARIS, *November* 5, 1856.

I LEARN that the Viceroy is much annoyed by all the intrigues which are carried on against him on account of the Canal scheme. All my correspondents agree on this point, and those at Constantinople mention particularly the efforts made by the English Embassy to establish a state of mistrust and bad feeling with regard to Egypt.

As the general report of the international commission is already in the press, and M. Barthélemy Saint Hilaire undertakes the corrections and the publication, I see that it will be well for me to go to Egypt as quickly as possible, to assist in reassuring our prince. I shall be able to embark at Marseilles on the 12th of this month.

The report of the commissioners will have a very good effect: it will be an historical document. Herewith is a summary of its contents:

FIRST PART.

Sec. 1.—Preliminary considerations.
Sec. 2.—Description of Egypt and the Isthmus of Suez.
Sec. 3.—Indirect routes.
Sec. 4.—The direct route.

Sec. 5.—Of the level of the two seas.
Sec. 6.—Of the cutting and the geology of the Canal through the Isthmus of Suez.
Sec. 7.—The Canal at the summit-level.
Sec. 8.—The question respecting locks at the ends of the Canal.
Sec. 9.—Depth and width of the Canal.
Sec. 10.—On the opening of the Canal into the Red Sea and the Mediterranean.
Sec. 11.—Interior port of Timsah.
Sec. 12.—Light-houses on the shores of the Red Sea and the Mediterranean.
Sec. 13.—As to boats on the Canal.
Sec. 14.—Electric telegraph.
Sec. 15.—Fresh-water canal for junction and for irrigation.

SECOND PART.

Sec. 16.—Details of the route.
Sec. 17.—Preliminary measurements.
Sec. 18.—Analysis of prices.
Sec. 19.—Estimate of expenses.
Sec. 20.—Means of constructing harbours.
Sec. 21.—Calculation of the cost of keeping up the maritime canal.
Sec. 22.—Conclusion.

You must read this remarkable report in all its details, in the third volume of the documents published since the grant was made ; and in the meantime I will communicate to you the parts which will be most interesting to the public, namely, the first, second, and sixth paragraphs.

First Part.

SECTION I.

Preliminary Conditions.

We have been requested by his Highness Mohammed Said, Viceroy of Egypt, to give our opinion on the preliminary plan for the junction of the Red Sea and the Mediterranean presented to him by his engineers, MM. Linant Bey and Mougel Bey, in accordance with his orders, and on the proposal of M. Ferdinand de Lesseps. When his Highness the Viceroy confided to us the special examination of this preparatory work, and desired us to elaborate a definite project, he would not in any way limit our researches into this great question, which will affect the commerce of the whole world. On the contrary, he has declared to us several times, through M. Ferdinand de Lesseps, the *concessionaire* of the enterprise, " that he dictated no programme of any kind to the international commission charged with so important an inquiry; that, although the principal aim he proposed to our labours was the examination of the preliminary plan of his engineers, he imposed no limits on science; that he, therefore, beggéd us to investigate all the plans which have been proposed during the last fifty years for opening communication between the Red Sea and the Mediterranean, so that no doubt may be left as to the best means of uniting them; in short, that what he expected from us was a statement of the easiest and safest solution of this problem, and the one most advantageous to Europe, to Egypt, and to general commerce."

The first care of the international commissioners, after having accepted this mission, was, of course, to hasten to the spot, and to judge by actual surveys what were the difficulties or facilities presented by nature to the realisation of this project. Five of the members, Messrs. Conrad, MacClean, de Negrelli, Renaud, and Lieussou, went to Egypt in November 1855, and, after an exploration extending over two months and a half, they brought back, in addition to their personal observations, the greater part of the documents necessary for forming a final judgment and verifying its correctness. With regard to such documents as they were not able to procure for themselves, they had them prepared, according to directions, by special agents; and after more than eight months spent in making surveys of every kind, the international commissioners found themselves in a position to draw up the scheme required.

The Suez Canal question can be traced back to the most remote antiquity. But it has several times changed its object, according to the necessities of the times. The original idea was to join the Valley of the Nile to the Red Sea, in order to facilitate the traffic between Egypt and Arabia; but it is now proposed to make a communication between the Mediterranean and the Red Sea, to facilitate navigation between Europe and the Indian Ocean.

As Egypt had continuous intercourse with Arabia before the elements of a traffic transit existed between the Mediterranean and the Red Sea, the idea of connecting the Valley of the Nile with the basin of the Red Sea naturally preceded that of joining the two seas. The Pharaohs and the Kings of Persia only cared to facilitate the carriage of the produce of Egypt to the Red Sea. It was with this limited view that they put the Valley of the Nile in communication with the Arabian Gulf by a canal from the Pelusian branch, the waters of which naturally flowed across the wâdy (valley) as far as Lake Timsah. But in thus supplying, in the simplest manner, the only requirement of their age, they in fact opened a navigable route between the two seas. So long as the largest ships could pass along the Nile, this solution of the problem of the junction of the Mediterranean and the Red Sea was the most suitable, as it satisfied at once the requirements of the commerce of Egypt and the small traffic transit then existing.

The Ptolemys were not likely to dream of cutting directly through the isthmus to enable ships going from one sea to the other to avoid a detour. It would have been a considerable work for that period, and would not have done away with the necessity for a branch towards the Valley of the Nile. By restoring and enlarging the canal of the Pharaohs they satisfied fully, and at a much smaller expense, the commercial requirements of their times.

Under the Cæsars much the same thing was required, but the silting up of the Pelusian branch and the increase of the draught of vessels having rendered the navigable route between Bubastis and the Arabian Sea dangerous, the Emperor Adrian increased the depth of the canal, and secured its being kept full by fixing the place for the water to enter at the head of the Delta, near the spot where Cairo now stands.

At the time of the invasion of the Arabs, Amrou, Omar's lieutenant, conceived the idea of joining the two seas by a canal going straight from Suez to Pelusium. The waters of the Nile, brought from Cairo by the old canal of the Cæsars, would have fed this canal; but Omar opposed the plan, fearing to open the way to Arabia to Christian vessels. The fanaticism of the Caliphs closed Egypt itself to the commerce of Europe. The Suez Canal no longer had for its sole object the private commerce of Egypt and Arabia, as had been the case under the Pharaohs and the Kings of Persia; it was made subordinate to the political relations of the two countries. Whilst Omar re-established the canal of the Cæsars to carry provisions into Arabia, El Mansur, a hundred and fifty years later, caused it to be filled up, in order to starve Mecca and Medina.

The conquest of Egypt by the French revived the question of the Suez Canal, which had been forgotten for ten centuries. M. Lepère, chief engineer *des Ponts et Chaussées*, having examined it with a view both to Egyptian commerce and to the navigation of large vessels, pointed out two solutions:

1st. For the commerce of Egypt, a canal with a small water-way from Suez to Alexandria, crossing the central region of the Delta, and fed by the Nile.

2nd. For the through navigation, a canal with a large water-way, fed by the waters of the Red Sea.

This second solution, a desirable rather than a feasible plan, had never before had a chance of being seriously considered. We believe it is the only one which can satisfy the requirements of the great commerce now carried on between Europe and the Asiatic seas, where several of the European nations have wealthy colonies, the progress of which becomes every day more rapid.

It is the prodigious development which has taken place during the few last centuries, and especially in the nineteenth, in the navies and the commerce of all civilised nations which has caused the urgent necessity for this new and shortened communication to be felt. Antiquity was not likely to feel this want, for it had not the same requirements.

Commerce and navigation, limited as they were until modern times almost entirely to the Mediterranean, were not of sufficient importance to require more facilities and a greater extension. The somewhat rare intercourse then carried on with Asia generally required only an overland route, and Europe had not at that period the immense establishments she now possesses in India and China. Moreover, even if the ancients could have conceived this idea, which will be an honour to the nineteenth century, they would probably have been incapable of executing it.

Since the discovery of the Cape of Good Hope things have changed very much. But the route which that discovery opened to navigation, dangerous as it was, was for some time all that was required. It was not until intercourse with Asia had continuously increased during three hundred years, and with no prospect of its again lessening, that a fresh improvement became indispensable. England, which is the country most interested in these questions, as it is the one possessing the richest and most extensive provinces in Asia, was the first to inaugurate this step; and, thanks to steam, she established, eighteen years ago, a route, *viâ* the Red Sea and the Isthmus of Suez, which conducts travellers and despatches in less than a month from the Indian ports to those of the United Kingdom.

It is, therefore, a canal of international utility which his Highness the Viceroy of Egypt wishes to make.

This important destiny of the new canal shows us plainly in what spirit the labours which it will necessitate should be undertaken; and it appeared to us that these considerations, general as they are, ought to form the ruling idea of our report. We shall, therefore, in the various divisions of which it will be composed, never lose sight of the fact that it is a great maritime canal, easy to pass through, always open and always safe, which is required by civilisation in the present state of the commercial relations of the world.

SECTION II.

A brief Description of Egypt and of the Isthmus of Suez.

It is well known that the territory of Egypt is that part of the basin of the Nile comprised between the cataracts and the sea. Shut in between almost parallel chains of mountains, which separate it from the Libyan desert and from the Red Sea, it forms, above Cairo, a very narrow valley, 200 leagues in length and only three or four wide, constituting Central and Upper Egypt. It afterwards stretches out between the hills which continue towards the north-west and north-east, the two chains of mountains, the direction of which until then has been due north and south, and it forms, between Cairo, Alexandria, and Pelusium, an immense triangular plain, with an area of 1375 leagues, which constitutes Lower Egypt.

The Nile had formerly seven branches, the two outermost of which, flowing at the foot of the hills, emptied themselves respectively near Alexandria and Pelusium, and embraced the whole plain.

It now parts below Cairo into two branches, which empty themselves at Rosetta and Damietta, and which thus divide Lower Egypt into three provinces—Béhéré to the west, the Delta in the centre, and Cherkié to the east. These three provinces are furrowed by a multitude of canals. They are off-shoots from the two branches of the river which lose themselves in the series of lagoons extending along the sea coast between Alexandria and Pelusium. These canals, made for the irrigation of the land, are generally navigable during the season of the inundation, and, after having fertilised the soil, they facilitate the transport of produce. But the only canal the character of which is essentially commercial is the Mahmoudieh, which joins the Nile to the port of Alexandria

The chain of mountains lying eastward, between the Valley of the Nile and the Red Sea, is a solid mass with abrupt declivities, which maintains a great elevation until it reaches the line between Cairo and Suez. After passing that line, this mass becomes suddenly lower, and extends, by calcareous hills, in a north-east direction to the other side of Lake Timsah, and as far as Lake Menzaleh by table lands of sand and gravel, which form part of the soil of the isthmus.

This calcareous spur may originally have been a cape jutting out between the Mediterranean and the Red Sea. It still clearly separates the Valley of the Nile, which forms the cultivatable soil of Egypt, from the basin of the Isthmus of Suez, which is a mere desert. This separation, however, is not now quite perfect, and in great inundations the waters of the Nile spread into the isthmus, towards the north by Lake Menzaleh, and towards the central part by the valley of Wâdy Toumilat, which is formed by a slight depression of the land between the calcareous hills and the table-lands of sand and gravel.

The waters of the Nile have covered all the soil, which they overflow in great inundations, with a layer of slime, the thickness of which generally diminishes in proportion to its greater distance from the river. This superficial deposit, which forms the cultivatable soil of Egypt, rests upon a thick layer of sea-sand, still impregnated with salt.

The bed of the Nile, looked upon as a general hollow in the ground, everywhere shows this division of the subsoil into two distinct layers. The line of demarcation forms a level, slightly inclined towards the sea, and following pretty nearly the level of the water at low tide. The filtration of the water into the sea-sand maintains in the subsoil a permanent humidity, which, rising to the surface through the layer of vegetable earth, covers it with saline particles. This tendency of the salts with which the subsoil is impregnated to rise is increased in summer by the great heat, and by the fact of the water of the river remaining above low-water mark. It would render the soil sterile if it were not washed every year by the fresh water of the Nile. The washing of the ground is thus the primary condition of all cultivation in Egypt. Hence arises the necessity for that number of canals which intersect Lower Egypt in every direction, in order to convey to every part of it water, that is to say, vegetation and life.

These canals serve at once to inundate the land and to dry it after it has been washed. To cut off the supply of water obtained by these canals from the river, or to intercept their passage to the sea, would be measures equally certain to render all cultivation impossible in Lower Egypt.

The canals formed to receive the inundations, in the layer of vegetable earth, are easily kept up; but those which are dug in the layer of sea-sand, for irrigation during the time of low water, are incessantly encroached upon by the sand from the heaps which are drawn in by the water which filters through, and they are blocked up even more rapidly in the place where the water flows in from the river. A canal of eight mètres in depth must necessarily reach the layer of sand, and there would be great difficulty in making and maintaining it.

From the cataracts to the sea, a distance of three hundred leagues, the Nile receives no tributary; its bed presents for that distance a uniform width, which may be calculated at twelve hundred mètres in Upper and Middle Egypt, and six hundred mètres in Lower Egypt, where it is divided into two branches. It flows tranquilly, and without winding, from south to north, through a smooth plain covered with its deposits and sloping slightly towards the sea. The general inclination of this plain is one mètre in a kilomètre from the cataracts to Cairo, and half a mètre only from Cairo to the Mediterranean.

The Nile increases and decreases slowly and regularly. Its waters after having gradually risen from June to September, sink as gradually from October to May. The height of the inundation, which naturally diminishes towards the mouth of the river, varies from one year to another, but only in a limited degree. The least inundation is about two-thirds of the greatest.

This sort of annual tide to which the river is subject gives it a periodical height, which is expressed in the following chart for Cairo :—

	Level above the Mediterranean.	Swiftness on the Surface.	Amount passing in 24 hours.
Minimum height at the time of decrease ...	14m. +0.00	0m. 50	50,000,000 m.c.
Maximum height during the inundation	14m. +8.00	1m. 50	800,000,000 m.c.

The waters of the Nile are always thick, principally during the inundation; they contain on an average 0.004 of slime. A very small part only of this slime remains deposited on the flooded land and raises the soil; almost the whole of it is taken into the sea. The river rolls down also the sand which the wind carries into its bed and that which the current detaches from the shores. This sand, which in the Upper Nile forms a number of banks, ceases at a considerable distance from the sea. At twenty kilomètres from the mouths of the river the soil of its bed presents only a small quantity of sand, which is, to a certain degree, lost in the mass of mud, and the alluvium carried on to the sea is almost entirely composed of mud.

The mouths of the Nile at Rosetta and Damietta are barred by sand-banks, which are exceedingly variable, and on which there is scarcely from one to two mètres of water when it is low, and from two to three at the time of the increase.

These details of the configuration and nature of the soil of Lower Egypt, formed upon the scale of the waters of the Nile, were necessary, in order to form an estimate of the relative fitness of the different routes which we had to examine. We must now present to you a general idea of the Isthmus of Suez.

Without entering here into geological details, which will be more suitable elsewhere, we must give a hasty description of the whole isthmus.

Lying directly between the end of the Arabian Gulf and the Mediterranean, this slip of land is a hundred and thirteen kilomètres long, that is to say, a little less than twenty-nine leagues. Suez is in 29° 58′ 37″ north latitude, while Tineh, the ancient Pelusium, is 31° 3′ 37″. The difference of latitude is therefore only 1° 5′. The topographical chart joined to this report will suffice to show at a glance the configuration of the isthmus. Between the Red Sea and the Gulf of Pelusium, from south to north, there is a depression which is very evident, especially in the passage of the Bitter Lakes and Lake Timsah. This depression has indeed some undulations between the Bitter Lakes and Lake Timsah, and, farther on, between Lake Timsah and Lake Menzaleh. But with the exception of two ridges, which rise from twelve to fifteen mètres, and are very short, there is a sort of almost horizontal valley along the whole length of the isthmus.

Towards the middle of this longitudinal depression, that is to say at Lake Timsah, is another depression, which is almost perpendicular to the first, and which extends from the centre of the isthmus to the alluvial lands of the Delta. This second depression, which is less marked than the other, lies from west to east. This is what is called Wâdy Toumilat, the ancient Land of Goshen, where the Israelites came to establish themselves under Jacob, when they were summoned by Joseph, and from whence they were led out by Moses about the seventeenth century before the Christian era.

It results from this external configuration of the isthmus that the direction of the Canal is marked by Nature herself; secondly, that the other depression, which extends from Timsah to Belbeys, the ancient Bubastis, might with equal ease connect the interior navigation of Egypt with the maritime navigation which passes along its frontier. Wâdy Toumilat, when the increase of the Nile is great, is filled by the waters of the river, which reach as far as Lake Timsah, and which formerly, perhaps, reached as far as the the Bitter Lakes themselves, going round the ridge which separates it from them. Our colleagues who went to Egypt found the slime of the Nile in the bogs of Lake Timsah to be similar to that which covers the plains of Lower Egypt and the bottom of the Valley of the Nile.

The solution of the problem, thus considered, appears very simple, and if there is anything to be surprised at, it is that, in the face of indications so precise and so striking to all who have visited the localities, any one should have taken the trouble to seek for a more complicated solution without having first ascertained the impracticability of the other.

SECTION VI.

Borings, and the Geology of the course of the Canal through the Isthmus of Suez.

Now that we are acquainted with the surface of the isthmus, it is necessary to discover the nature of the soil which the Canal will have to pass through in sinking to the minimum depth of eight mètres. The labours of the Egyptian commissioners are not very satisfactory in that respect. The memorandum of M. Lepère does indeed furnish some curious facts as to the surface of the isthmus. But they paid hardly any attention to the subsoils; and they only made two examinations of the bed of the old canal, one at Station 16, and the other at Station 21. These borings did not go very deep, and appear to have been made rather to satisfy curiosity than as part of a systematic plan of investigation. They were not carried lower than four or five feet at the utmost, and the indications of the two were very similar.

In the first station (16) they found a rich, argillaceous, salt, and very damp sand. In the second, which was a little deeper (Station 21), they discovered gypsum in banks, and loam, tolerably compact, mixed with sand, and with a saline dampness in it.

This is all the geological information which M. Lepère has collected. It is very easy to understand that he did not feel the want of more. As he proposed to re-open the old canal, and to follow its course as much as possible, he was very certain that the ground was fit to contain the water, as it had done it formerly. The banks (still existing) of the canal of the Pharaohs were a sufficient and indisputable proof of this.

But with us it could not be the same, and one of the principal cares to which we had to give our attention, was that of borings. We have had nineteen made from the Red Sea to the Mediterranean: first in the roadstead of Suez, then in the ridge which separates Suez from the Bitter Lakes, in the basin of these lakes, in the ridge of Serapeum, in the ridge of El Guisr, the highest point of the isthmus, and, lastly, in Lake Menzaleh. The sheet of instructions for borings joined to this report will show, as a whole and in detail, the operations which we have caused to be performed. We will now make only a slight mention of them.

The entire soil of the Isthmus of Suez belongs to the Tertiary formation, like Lower and Middle Egypt and the great plateau of the Libyan desert.

Two borings were first made in the roadstead of Suez in the course of the future channel; one on the bank which is to the left on entering the harbour; and the other, more to the north, on the isolated bank which is opposite Suez on the left. The former, eleven mètres in depth, produced, from the surface to the bottom, yellow agglutinated sand, coarse and somewhat muddy sand, very fine ochreous sand, and yellow argillaceous sand. The second, twelve mètres deep, produced shells, gravel, and coarse agglutinated sand, which forms a hard rock of $3\frac{1}{2}$ mètres in thickness; fine yellow sand slightly agglutinated, coarse red sand, and tolerably firm sand and gravel.

Such is the nature of the soil which the dredging-machine is to hollow out to form the channel in the roadstead of Suez. There will be no real difficulty except in the $3\frac{1}{2}$ mètres of thickness, where the agglutinated sand has almost attained the hardness of stone. It is not coral, as has sometimes been said; but it is a very hard substance, the excavation of which will cost a greater amount of labour than will have to be expended on any other part of the line.

To the north and west of this town extends a plain, which presents a slight declination at once towards the isthmus and towards that part of the gulf which is comprised between Suez and the mountains of Attaka. This perfectly arid plain is composed of sand and shingle, the sand forming by far the larger proportion. Setting out from Suez, and following the shore of the gulf to the north, the sand which occurs appears to consist of the deposit left by high tides. It is impregnated with a damp salt which makes it compact.

The third boring, undertaken at $8\frac{1}{2}$ kilomètres from Suez, on the first traces of the canal of the Pharaohs, on the track of the caravans from Egypt to Mecca, gave ten mètres of clay, more or less sandy, under a thin bed of slightly agglutinated sand. The two banks of the ancient canal, in some places fifty mètres apart, are more and more conspicuous as we advance towards the north; and occasionally their height is not less than five or six mètres. We begin to find some appearance of crystallised sulphate of lime and some pebbles, a very small number of which have made their way into the mass of sand.

Boring No. 4, at about twenty kilomètres from Suez, yielded scarcely anything (after 2·30 mètres of red sand) but clay, sometimes compact, sometimes sandy and foliated, and sometimes brown and very rich. This boring went down almost 16 mètres. In this part there are, here and there in the soil, some calcareous substances of different sizes. But these disappear as soon as we arrive at the Salt Lakes.

Borings 3 and 4 therefore, show plainly the nature of the land which will have to be excavated in the ridge which separates the Red Sea from the Bitter Lakes. It consists almost entirely of clay, more or less compact, which will be able to resist the action of currents strong enough to undermine embankments of sand. Towards the highest part of this ridge gravel is pretty abundant and tolerably coarse; but it diminishes towards the basin of the lakes, and then disappears entirely.

The Bitter Lakes, the length of which is not less than forty kilomètres, and which have long been dried up, are divided into two basins, first a small one, and then a larger one, which is both deeper and longer. The depression which forms them is not very evident to the eye at first sight, and there is some difficulty in distinguishing it. But the appearance of the soil is no longer the same. The bottom is soft sand impregnated with salt. To the right and left, a horizontal ridge indicates the old course of the water. Shells, which ceased on leaving Suez, are now numerous; and vegetation, which was also wanting, begins to be seen at intervals; it is scanty at first, but becomes more and more abundant as far as the southern extremity of the isthmus. Small rhomboids of sulphate of lime cover the bottom of the lakes, in greater or less quantities, and in the little basin especially, this sulphate of lime is crystallised into needles.

Four borings made in the little basin, the superficial soil being on the level of the Mediterranean, or 4·63 mètres, 4·50 mètres, and 5·40 mètres, below it, yielded, besides sulphate of lime, sand and shells, and light brown clay, more or less sandy. This clay has occasionally the appearance of the slime of the Nile.

The great basin is about twenty-five kilomètres long. The bottom, near the edge, is covered with sand, shells, and crystallised sulphate of lime. The deepest part is occupied by a thick bed of sea salt. Ridges of little pebbles and shells, similar to those of the sea, point out the old shore. These ridges, three in number, are placed one behind the other, and are of different heights.

Two borings have been made in the most depressed part of the Bitter Lakes: these are the 9th and 10th. One, at the depth of 2·20 mètres, presents only agglutinations of shell, more than 20 centimètres in thickness, and after these, sulphate of lime in very fine needles, and salt. The other, which is 3·50 mètres deep, shows nothing but sea salt, which, at this place, appears to be from 7 to 8 mètres in thickness, and would furnish the material for an easy and profitable speculation. At these two borings, the surface of the soil is 6·69 mètres and 7·35 mètres below the lowest level of the Mediterranean. These masses of salt are sometimes placed on deposits of mud from the Nile, and it is probable that they were produced by salt springs.

As soon as we have passed the great basin of the Bitter Lakes we come to the ridge of Serapeum; and starting from this point, which is almost the middle of the isthmus, we find nothing but sand as far as the Mediterranean, except at Boring 19, where there is marl. This is proved by all the other borings. Thus, a first boring (No. 11), made at the boundary between the lakes and Serapeum, produced only sand and fine gravel for 8 mètres, and sand varying in coarseness and a little clayey and tolerably compact for 3·50 mètres. The elevation of the soil above the low levels of the Mediterranean was, at this place, 3·40 mètres. A second boring (No. 12), made at the other end of Serapeum, and on the slope which leads to Lake Timsah, also produced only sand mixed with fine gravel; sand, more or less fine; and white or red sand.

After having passed over the ridge of Serapeum we find, to the north, above Lake Timsah, the point called Scheik-Ennédek. This is a tomb of a santon of that name. This point deserves to be noticed, because there seemed for a moment reason to believe that it would furnish materials useful in the construction of the Canal. But it is not so. It is true that there is in this place a bank of calcareous stones. But it is only half a mètre thick. It is at the top of a hillock of stratified sand, which has no solidity. These stones, specimens of which were shown to the international commissioners, might do very well to make the heap which is dignified by the name of a tomb. But, then, as they are, they could not be used for any work of art. The most they would be fit for would be to wall the banks of the Canal. There is also limestone exactly similar to that of the elevation, which occupies nearly the middle of the lake. But this second limestone is no better than the former; and we must give up all hope of finding in the middle of the isthmus materials of which we can make any other use than that which we have already pointed out.

When our colleagues visited Lake Timsah, the southern part was dry. There was a little water only in the northern part. This was because the inundation of the Nile was not very great last year, and the river did not then reach the lake. But the signs of its presence could be seen everywhere, at the foot of the sand hills and the tamarisks, by the slime which had been previously left there, similar to that of the plains of Upper Egypt.

The sand hills which intersect the lake must be very old, as on one of them, where our colleagues stopped, a great quantity of antique pottery is found. The water which we find in Lake Timsah is much salter than that of the sea, and it exhales that odour of sulphuretted hydrogen which is perceived in harbours where the sea is stagnant and without a tide. This excessive saltness, which, however, does not prevent reeds from growing in abundance on the shores, is caused, no doubt, by banks of salt below, which are dissolved by the Nile water.

The shores of Lake Timsah seem to be quite firm along their whole extent. But it is probable that formerly the Red Sea stretched even as far as this, for we find here, under the slime, shells of that sea, which do not exist in the Mediterranean. To the west there is a succession of movable sand flats stretching over about two kilomètres, and 400 or 500 mètres distant from the lake.

Two soundings (Nos. 15 and 16) made in Lake Timsah, towards the extremities, yielded only sand of different colours, and somewhat argillaceous.

To the north of Lake Timsah the ridge of El Guisr is, as is well known, the highest point of the isthmus; it is 16 mètres above the lower level of the Mediterranean.

Like the whole of the slightly elevated plateau which stretches to the north of the wâdy, it consists of a great deposit of sand, protected by plants and small gravel from the action of the wind. It has clearly every appearance of complete solidity, and it in some sort connects the plateau of the wâdy with the deposits of sand which extend towards the east and Syria as far as the Arabian chain, of which it seems to form an integral part.

The boring made in the ridge of El Guisr was naturally the deepest of all that had to be executed. It goes down 23·35 mètres (boring No. 18). We find there, going from the surface to the bottom, sand alternating with little beds of clay and of sulphate of lime; small gravel; a great deal of fine sand; and, in the last four mètres, sand hardened almost into stone and shingle.

On the higher part of Serapeum we distinguished traces of old earthworks for a canal; it must have connected the Red Sea with the Pelusiac branch; and the communication between the two seas would thus have been more direct. We may suppose it to have been the one called the Canal of Necho. We do not know historically to whom to attribute this experiment. But it is certain that it was made either by the Pharaohs or by Amrou. The banks of this canal are as apparent as those which we find to the north of Suez, as far as the Bitter Lakes, and they prove, in the same way, that the soil possesses the most complete solidity in its present state, which has existed for so many centuries.

From the ridge of El Guisr to Pelusium, that is to say, for a distance of about thirteen leagues, the whole ground presents great undulations, with very gentle declivities. It is nowhere hilly. The gravel, which has been getting finer and finer, now entirely disappears. The sand, which is tolerably firm under foot, is by no means inclined to shift, on the line of the canal. All around we find the vegetation of the desert, and the bushes form thickets which it is impossible for camels to get through. This vegetation might be employed as fuel.

Two borings were made in Lake Menzaleh: one at the southern extremity, and the other, eight leagues farther on, at the point at which the canal is to open into the Mediterranean. The former, made on the level of the sea, yielded a little Nile slime and sandy clay, and a great deal of sea sand. The second yielded sea sand, muddy sand, and, after that, sandy mud.

To recapitulate, we find that the Maritime Canal of Suez, in its whole course of 157,956 mètres, will have to pass through two principal kinds of soil: first, clays, from Suez to the Bitter Lakes; and then, firm sand, from the Bitter Lakes to its termination in the Bay of Pelusium.

As to the shifting sand, which, according to the general opinion, was to threaten the preservation and duration of the Canal, this is a chimera which has not the slightest foundation. The direct observations made by our colleagues upon the spot prove that the whole soil of the isthmus is perfectly fixed, either by the gravel which covers it, or by the vegetation. What shows it more plainly than anything else is the appearance, after so many centuries, of such considerable traces left there by the old works of canalisation. If the movement of the sand had the effect which it is supposed to have upon the soil of the isthmus, these traces would have disappeared long ago; instead of being, as they still are, five or six mètres high, they would be buried and invisible, as so many monuments are in several other parts of Egypt. Even the existence of the immense depression of the Salt Lakes proves that the displacement of sand carried by the wind is very trifling; for if it were what it is supposed to be, this depression, vast as it is, would have been filled up by this time and long before. Another fact, equally significant though small in itself, which has been mentioned by our colleagues is, that the traces of an encampment made last year near ancient Migdol, have remained perfectly uninjured, and that the slight ridge raised around the tents, far from having disappeared, had as sharp edges as if they had been made the day before.

Thus, neither the surface of the soil nor the nature of the subsoil presents the smallest obstacle to the formation or preservation of the canal.

CXX.

Opinion of General Albert della Marmora with regard to the Geology of the Isthmus.

November 9, 1856.

GENERAL ALBERT DELLA MARMORA, Senator of Piedmont, brother of the general of the same name who commanded the Italian army in the Crimea, is a very distinguished geologist. He has devoted thirty years to the study of the soils composing the island of Sardinia and the western coast of the Mediterranean Sea and its various islands, and he has analysed the works of M. Renaud and M. de Negrelli, members of the international commission. In the exact details contained in their observations, M. Albert della Marmora finds very striking points of resemblance with the facts he has himself observed both in Sardinia and in other parts of the coast of the Mediterranean. These facts may, he believes, throw a good deal of light on what, at some very remote period, caused the drying up of the Isthmus of Suez. In Sardinia, near Cagliari, a large valley called Campidano presents dried-up lakes which very much resemble the Bitter Lakes, and the bottom of which is covered, in the same way, with a thick crust of salt. It appears that the drying-up of this lake is traced back to the time of the great geological phenomenon which geologists designate by the name of the Upheaval of Tenarus. It is to an upheaval of this kind that M. Albert della Marmora thinks we should attribute the drying-up of the isthmus, which was formerly covered by the sea, like the lakes of Campidano. M. Albert della Marmora believes that the soil of the Isthmus of Suez does not belong entirely to Tertiary deposits properly co-called, but to a somewhat more recent epoch, that of the particular upheaval to which he alludes.

CXXI.

To Madame Delamalle, Paris.

(Continuation of the Journal.)

CAIRO, *November* 22, 1856.

I ARRIVED to-day at Alexandria, where the Viceroy had given orders that I should be received, and sent on to Cairo by a special train. The prince was awaiting me at his palace of Kasr-el-Nil, where he made me stay with him. His first words when he saw me were, "*Your coming puts me into good humour with the world.*" He confided all his troubles to me. His greatest annoyance is that emissaries have been sent into Egypt, who try to lower him in the eyes of the people and to act upon the minds of the soldiers. I endeavoured to lessen his vexation by representing to him that the reports made to him were certainly exaggerated. He then spoke of his plan of leaving Egypt for a time, and visiting the people of Soudan and Sennaar, who, far from the centre of Government, have been for forty years groaning under the most cruel oppression. I congratulated him upon the idea, and promised to accompany him as far as he wished to go. The journey is decided upon. It will be of use to the

Canal. Make yourself easy, and tell Saint-Hilaire that I count upon him to take my place. M. Ruyssenaers will watch over our interests in Egypt.

CXXII.
To Mr. Richard Cobden, M.P., London.

CAIRO, *November* 22, 1856.

Two years ago I announced to you the resolution formed by Mohammed Said, Viceroy of Egypt, to open the Isthmus of Suez by a maritime canal. It was at the time when our two countries were united for purposes of war that I called your attention to a work of peace, progress, and civilisation. I requested the aid of your influence and your talents, in case some members of the aristocracy who have the power of directing affairs should be blinded by old prejudices, by narrow sentiments of exclusiveness or rivalry, and should endeavour to oppose the execution of an enterprise of universal interest.

Since that time I have had an opportunity of discussing this interesting question with you in person. I informed you that the opposition which I had expected had made its appearance, but that in a country like yours, where all subjects are freely discussed, I thought the first thing to be done was to enlighten the public mind, which was still very badly informed, and to prove plainly the practicability of the enterprise.

This action on public opinion has taken place. The most experienced engineers of Europe have visited the isthmus, and have published their definitive report; funds have been offered to commence the execution of the project; the Viceroy of Egypt has put himself at the head of an enterprise supported with unanimity and energy by the press of Europe and America; and, lastly, the adhesion of the Governments has gone hand in hand with public feeling.

Only one difficulty has presented itself: this is the opposition of your Government, which, through the influence of its Ambassador at Constantinople, has succeeded in delaying the formality of the ratification required by the Viceroy from the Porte, with respect to a grant legally made by him.

In so just a cause I shall not be in want of resources to overcome this obstacle, against which I have hitherto thought it useless to struggle, because it was too soon for it to hinder the progress of the enterprise, and because, all the preliminary surveys not being completed, we were not ready to proceed to the execution of the work.

In a short time the state of things will be different; but in the meantime, in order to avoid as far as possible the inconveniences which would result from a dispute, you will not be surprised that I wish to continue to address myself to the intelligence of the public.

My opinion is that all this is likely to rekindle a bad feeling between France and England at the very time when it is important that a sincere union between the two nations should take the place of the uncertain and already wavering alliance between the two Governments. If, on the one hand, the country which has proclaimed freedom of commerce is so little consistent with herself in a matter of freedom in international transactions, and, on the other hand, France comes to the conclusion that her old allies have two modes of weighing and measuring for her, it is evident that all the efforts of reasonable men will fail, sooner or later, before a fresh outbreak of the old prejudices which for so long a time separated the two nations.

Indeed, how can we on the Continent believe in the sincerity of England, in her love of universal improvement, of civilisation, and of the general welfare, when it is declared that England, where public opinion is supreme, permits her Government to maintain its incredible opposition to the Suez Canal, a private undertaking, which cannot, either by its origin, its plan of formation, or its aim, justify any dread of a rival policy? How can the apostles of free trade and competition propagate their doctrines when the two most important members of the Cabinet, who but a short time ago were in their ranks, are prevented by fear and horror of competition from consenting to the demolition of a slip of land separating the two most important seas and presenting a feeble barrier to all the navies of the globe?

One of your greatest Ministers pronounced the following words in a sitting of the House of Commons, which covered itself with glory by its vote :

> You have to pronounce between an advance towards liberty and a return to prohibition ; you must choose the motto by which the commercial policy of England is to be known : shall it be *Forward* or *Backward?* Which of these two words best suits this great empire? Consider our position, the advantages granted to us by God and by Nature, and the destiny awaiting us. We are placed at the extremity of Western Europe, as the chief link connecting the Old World with the New. The discoveries of science and the improvements in navigation have already brought us within ten days of St. Petersburgh, and will soon bring us within ten days of New York. An extent of sea-coast, larger in proportion to our population and the superficial area of our soil than that of any other nation, secures to us maritime strength and superiority. Iron and coal, those sinews of industry, give our manufactures a great advantage over those of our rivals. Our capital is greater than that which they have at their command. In inventions, in skill, in energy, we yield to none. Our national character, the free institutions under which we live, our liberty of thought and action, an unfettered press, which spreads with rapidity the news of all discoveries and improvements ; all these circumstances place us at the head of the nations which are developing themselves naturally by the free exchange of their produce. Is this a country which can fear free trade—a country which can only prosper in the artificial atmosphere of prohibition? Choose your motto : *Forward,* or *Backward.*

It was on the 27th March 1846 that Sir Robert Peel expressed himself thus, and when the Bill for Free Trade was afterwards brought back to the House of Commons, having passed the House of Lords, the celebrated Minister added :

> The name which ought to be, and which will be, mentioned in connection with this success, is neither that of the noble lord (John Russell), the leader of the party which supports us, nor mine ; it is that of a man who, by the purity of his motives and his indefatigable energy, has appealed to the reason of every one of us, and has forced us to listen to him by an eloquence so much the more admirable that it is without pretension and without ornament : it is the name of RICHARD COBDEN.

It is now for you (armed with the experience of the last ten years of prosperity and progress, secured to the British Empire by the triumph of your system) to maintain the principle of free competition, deserted by some of your former companions in the strife, and to offer to your countrymen once more the choice between the two mottoes — *Forward* or *Backward*. The strength of your own convictions and of public opinion will not fail to insure you a success in which the honour and interests of England are certainly concerned.

I have no doubt that the question I have submitted to you will be brought before the British Parliament. If you will undertake the office of its advocate, my friend and fellow-labourer, M. Barthélemy Saint-Hilaire, Member of the Institute, will give you every information that you may require; he will act in accordance with your opinion, and, when the proper time arrives, will work in accord with you and other friends.

I have requested him to deliver this letter to you, and to commence an acquaintance which you will, I am sure, find pleasure in continuing with so honourable and distinguished a man.

CXXIII.

MEMORANDUM FOR HIS HIGHNESS THE VICEROY OF EGYPT RESPECTING THE VESSEL WHICH IS TO REMAIN ANCHORED ALL THE WINTER IN THE ROADSTEAD OF PELUSIUM.

CAIRO, *November* 24, 1856.

AGREEABLY to the instructions of the naval members of the international commission, a captain in the merchant service, M. Philigret, was engaged at Marseilles, and is now at Alexandria, on his way to the Bay of Pelusium, there to take charge of the vessel which is to remain at anchor for six months on a spot indicated to him.

His Highness is requested to desire that orders may be given to the Minister of Marine at Alexandria to furnish, on the request of M. Ruyssenaers, all that Captain Philigret may require to fulfil his mission. Mougel Bey has already communicated with the Minister of Marine on the subject.

Memorandum.

November 25, 1856.

THE Viceroy's orders were immediately given, and will be executed during our journey into Nubia, both those relating to Captain Philigret's business and those concerning the continuation of the operations on the isthmus.

March, 1876.

AN ALPHABETICAL LIST
OF
HENRY S. KING & CO.'S
PUBLICATIONS.

ALLEN (Rev. R.), M.A.
>   ABRAHAM: HIS LIFE, TIMES, AND TRAVELS, as told by a Contemporary 3800 years ago. With Map. Post 8vo. Cloth, price 10s. 6d.

AMOS (Professor Sheldon).
>   THE SCIENCE OF LAW. Second Edition. Crown 8vo. Cloth, price 5s.
>   Vol. X. of the International Scientific Series.

ANDERSON (Rev. Charles), M.A.
>   NEW READINGS OF OLD PARABLES. Demy 8vo. Cloth, price 4s. 6d.
>   CHURCH THOUGHT AND CHURCH WORK. Edited by. Containing articles by the Revs. J. M. Capes, Professor Cheetham, J. Ll. Davis, Harry Jones, Brooke, Lambert, A. J. Ross, the Editor, and others. Second Edition. Demy 8vo. Cloth, price 7s. 6d.
>   WORDS AND WORKS IN A LONDON PARISH. Edited by. Second Edition. Demy 8vo. Cloth, price 6s.
>   THE CURATE OF SHYRE. Second Edition. 8vo. Cloth, price 7s. 6d.

ANDERSON (Colonel R. P.)
>   VICTORIES AND DEFEATS. An Attempt to explain the Causes which have led to them. An Officer's Manual. Demy 8vo. Cloth, price 14s.

ANSON (Lieut.-Col. The Hon. A.), V.C., M.P.
>   THE ABOLITION OF PURCHASE AND THE ARMY REGULATION BILL OF 1871. Crown 8vo. Sewed, price 1s.
>   ARMY RESERVES AND MILITIA REFORMS. Crown 8vo. Sewed, price 1s.
>   THE STORY OF THE SUPERSESSIONS. Crown 8vo. Sewed, price 6d.

ARCHER (Thomas).
>   ABOUT MY FATHER'S BUSINESS. Work amidst the Sick, the Sad, and the Sorrowing. Crown 8vo. Cloth, price 5s.

ARGYLE (Duke of).
>   SPEECHES ON THE SECOND READING OF THE CHURCH PATRONAGE (SCOTLAND) BILL IN THE HOUSE OF LORDS, June 2, 1874; and Earl of Camperdown's Amendment, June 9, 1874, placing the Election of Ministers in the hands of Ratepayers. Crown 8vo. Sewed, price 1s.

ARMY OF THE NORTH GERMAN CONFEDERATION.
: A Brief Description of its Organization, of the Different Branches of the Service and their *rôle* in War, of its Mode of Fighting, etc., etc. Translated from the Corrected Edition, by permission of the author, by Colonel Edward Newdegate. Demy 8vo. Cloth, price 5s.

ASHANTEE WAR (The).
: A Popular Narrative. By the Special Correspondent of the Daily News. Crown 8vo. Cloth, price 6s.

ASHE (T.) Author of "The Sorrows of Hypsipyle."
: EDITH; OR, LOVE AND LIFE IN CHESHIRE. Sewed, price 6d.

ASHTON (John).
: ROUGH NOTES OF A VISIT TO BELGIUM, SEDAN, AND PARIS, in September, 1870-71. Crown 8vo. Cloth, price 3s. 6d.

AUNT MARY'S BRAN PIE.
: By the author of "St. Olave's," "When I was a Little Girl," etc. Illustrated. Cloth, price 3s. 6d.

: SUNNYLAND STORIES. Illustrated. Fcap. 8vo. Cloth, price 3s. 6d.

AURORA: A Volume of Verse. Fcap. 8vo. Cloth, price 5s.

AYRTON (J. C.)
: A SCOTCH WOOING. 2 vols. Crown 8vo. Cloth.

BAGEHOT (Walter).
: PHYSICS AND POLITICS; or, Thoughts on the Application of the Principles of "Natural Selection" and "Inheritance" to Political Society. Third Edition. Crown 8vo. Cloth, price 4s. Volume II. of the International Scientific Series.

: THE ENGLISH CONSTITUTION. A New Edition, Revised and Corrected, with an Introductory Dissertation on Recent Changes and Events. Crown 8vo. Cloth, price 7s. 6d.

: LOMBARD STREET. A Description of the Money Market. Sixth Edition. Crown 8vo. Cloth, price 7s. 6d.

BAIN (Alexander), LL.D.
: MIND AND BODY. The Theories of their Relation. Fifth Edition. Crown 8vo. Cloth, price 4s.
Volume IV. of the International Scientific Series.

BANKS (Mrs. G. Linnæus).
> GOD'S PROVIDENCE HOUSE. Crown 8vo. Cloth, price 3s. 6d.

BARING (T. C.), M.P., late Fellow of Brasenose College, Oxford.
> PINDAR IN ENGLISH RHYME. Being an Attempt to render the Epinikian Odes with the principal remaining Fragments of Pindar into English Rhymed Verse. Small quarto. Cloth, price 7s.

BARLEE (Ellen).
> LOCKED OUT; A Tale of the Strike. With a Frontispiece. Cloth, price 1s. 6d.

BAYNES (Rev. Canon R. H.), Editor of "Lyra Anglicana," etc.
> HOME SONGS FOR QUIET HOURS. Second Edition. Fcap. 8vo. Cloth extra, price 3s. 6d.
> *** This may also be had handsomely bound in Morocco with gilt edges.

BECKER (Bernard H.)
> THE SCIENTIFIC SOCIETIES OF LONDON. 1 vol. Crown 8vo. Cloth, price 5s.

BENNETT (Dr. W. C.)
> SONGS FOR SAILORS. Dedicated by Special Request to H.R.H. the Duke of Edinburgh. With Steel Portrait and Illustrations. Crown 8vo. Cloth, price 3s. 6d.
> An Edition in Illustrated Paper Covers, price 1s.
>
> BABY MAY. HOME POEMS AND BALLADS. With Frontispiece. Crown 8vo. Cloth elegant, price 6s.
>
> BABY MAY AND HOME POEMS. Fcap. 8vo. Sewed in Coloured Wrapper, price 1s.
>
> NARRATIVE POEMS AND BALLADS. Fcap. 8vo. Sewed in Coloured Wrapper, price 1s.

BENNIE (Rev. Jas. Noble), M.A.
> THE ETERNAL LIFE. Sermons preached during the last twelve years. Crown 8vo. Cloth, price 6s.

BERNARD (Bayle).
> SAMUEL LOVER, THE LIFE AND UNPUBLISHED WORKS OF. In 2 vols. With a Steel Portrait. Post 8vo. Cloth, price 21s.

BETHAM-EDWARDS (Miss M.)
    KITTY. With a Frontispiece. Crown 8vo. Cloth, price 3s. 6d.
    MADEMOISELLE JOSEPHINE'S FRIDAYS, AND OTHER STORIES. Crown 8vo. Cloth, price 7s. 6d.

BISCOE (A. C.)
    THE EARLS OF MIDDLETON, Lords of Clermont and of Fettercairn, and the Middleton Family. Crown 8vo. Cloth, price 10s. 6d.

BLANC (Henry), M.D.
    CHOLERA: HOW TO AVOID AND TREAT IT. Popular and Practical Notes. Crown 8vo. Cloth, price 4s. 6d.

BLUME (Major William).
    THE OPERATIONS OF THE GERMAN ARMIES IN FRANCE, from Sedan to the end of the war of 1870-71. With Map. From the Journals of the Head-quarters Staff. Translated by the late E. M. Jones, Maj. 20th Foot, Prof. of Mil. Hist., Sandhurst. Demy 8vo. Cloth, price 9s.

BOGUSLAWSKI (Captain A. von).
    TACTICAL DEDUCTIONS FROM THE WAR OF 1870-71. Translated by Colonel Sir Lumley Graham, Bart., late 18th (Royal Irish) Regiment. Third Edition, Revised and Corrected. Demy 8vo. Cloth, price 7s.

BONWICK (James).
    THE TASMANIAN LILY. With Frontispiece. Crown 8vo. Cloth, price 5s.
    MIKE HOWE, THE BUSHRANGER OF VAN DIEMEN'S LAND. With Frontispiece. Crown 8vo. Cloth, price 5s.

BOSWELL (R. B.), M.A., Oxon.
    METRICAL TRANSLATIONS FROM THE GREEK AND LATIN POETS, and other Poems. Crown 8vo. Cloth, price 5s.

BOTHMER (Countess Von).
    CRUEL AS THE GRAVE. A Novel. 3 vols. Cloth.

BOWEN (H. C.), English Master Middle-Class City School, Cowper Street.
    STUDIES IN ENGLISH, for the use of Modern Schools. Small Crown 8vo. Cloth, price 1s. 6d.

BOWRING (L.), C.S.I., Lord Canning's Private Secretary, and for many years Chief Commissioner of Mysore and Coorg.
    EASTERN EXPERIENCES. Illustrated with Maps and Diagrams. Demy 8vo. Cloth, price 16s.

BRAVE MEN'S FOOTSTEPS. By the Editor of "Men who have Risen." A Book of Example and Anecdote for Young People. With Four Illustrations by C. Doyle. Third Edition. Crown 8vo. Cloth, price 3s. 6d.

BRIALMONT (Colonel A.)
> HASTY INTRENCHMENTS. Translated by Lieut. Charles A. Empsom, R.A. With nine Plates. Demy 8vo. Cloth, price 6s.

BRIEFS AND PAPERS. Being Sketches of the Bar and the Press. By Two Idle Apprentices. Crown 8vo. Cloth, price 7s. 6d.

BROOKE (Rev. James M. S.), M. A.
> HEART, BE STILL. A Sermon preached in Holy Trinity Church, Southall. Impl. 32mo. Sewed, price 6d.

BROOKE (Rev. Stopford A.), M.A., Chaplain in Ordinary to Her Majesty the Queen.
> THE LATE REV. F. W. ROBERTSON, M.A., LIFE AND LETTERS OF. Edited by Stopford Brooke, M.A.
> I. In 2 vols., uniform with the Sermons. Steel Portrait. Price 7s. 6d.
> II. Library Edition. 8vo. Two Steel Portraits. Price 12s.
> III. A Popular Edition, in 1 vol. 8vo. Price 6s.
> THEOLOGY IN THE ENGLISH POETS.—COWPER, COLERIDGE, WORDSWORTH, and BURNS. Second Edition. Post 8vo. Cloth, price 9s.
> CHRIST IN MODERN LIFE. Sermons Preached in St. James's Chapel, York Street, London. Eighth Edition. Crown 8vo. Cloth, price 7s. 6d.
> FREEDOM IN THE CHURCH OF ENGLAND. Six Sermons suggested by the Voysey Judgment. Second Edition. Crown 8vo. Cloth, price 3s. 6d.
> SERMONS Preached in St. James's Chapel, York Street, London. Eighth Edition. Crown 8vo. Cloth, price 6s.
> SERMONS Preached in St. James's Chapel, York Street, London. Second Series. Third Edition. Crown 8vo. Cloth, price 7s.
> FREDERICK DENISON MAURICE: The Life and Work of. A Memorial Sermon. Crown 8vo. Sewed, price 1s.

BROOKE (W. G.), M.A., Barrister-at-Law.
> THE PUBLIC WORSHIP REGULATION ACT. With a Classified Statement of its Provisions, Notes, and Index. Third Edition, revised and corrected. Crown 8vo. Cloth, price 3s. 6d.
> SIX PRIVY COUNCIL JUDGMENTS—1850-1872. Annotated by. Third Edition. Crown 8vo. Cloth, price 9s.

BROWN (Rev. J. Baldwin), B.A.
> **THE HIGHER LIFE.** Its Reality, Experience, and Destiny. Fourth Edition. Crown 8vo. Cloth, price 7s. 6d.
>
> **THE DOCTRINE OF ANNIHILATION IN THE LIGHT OF THE GOSPEL OF LOVE.** Five Discourses. Second Edition. Crown 8vo. Cloth, price 2s. 6d.

BROWN (John Croumbie), LL.D., etc.
> **REBOISEMENT IN FRANCE**; or, Records of the Replanting of the Alps, the Cevennes, and the Pyrenees with Trees, Herbage, and Bush. Demy 8vo. Cloth, price 12s. 6d.
>
> **THE HYDROLOGY OF SOUTHERN AFRICA.** Demy 8vo. Cloth, price 10s. 6d.

BROWNE (Rev. Marmaduke E.)
> **UNTIL THE DAY DAWN.** Four Advent Lectures delivered in the Episcopal Chapel, Milverton, Warwickshire, on the Sunday evenings during Advent, 1870. Crown 8vo. Cloth, price 2s. 6d.

BRYANT (William Cullen).
> **POEMS.** Red-line Edition. With 24 Illustrations and Portrait of the Author. Post 8vo. Cloth extra, price 7s. 6d.
> A Cheaper Edition, with Frontispiece. Post 8vo. Cloth, price 3s. 6d.

BUCHANAN (Robert).
> **POETICAL WORKS.** Collected Edition, in 3 Vols., with Portrait. Price 6s. each.
>
> CONTENTS OF THE VOLUMES.
>
> I. "Ballads and Romances."   II. "Ballads and Poems of Life."
>   III. "Cruiskeen Sonnets;" and "Book of Orm."
>
> **MASTER-SPIRITS.** Post 8vo. Cloth, price 10s. 6d.

BULKELEY (Rev. Henry J.)
> **WALLED IN**, and other Poems. Crown 8vo. Cloth, price 5s.

BUNNETT (F. E.)
> **LEONORA CHRISTINA, MEMOIRS OF**, Daughter of Christian IV. of Denmark; Written during her Imprisonment in the Blue Tower of the Royal Palace at Copenhagen, 1663-1685. Translated by F. E. Bunnètt. With an Autotype Portrait of the Princess. A New and Cheaper Edition. Medium 8vo. Cloth, price 5s.
>
> **LINKED AT LAST.** 1 vol. Crown 8vo. Cloth.
>
> **UNDER A CLOUD; OR, JOHANNES OLAF.** By E. D. Wille. Translated by F. E. Bunnètt. 3 vols. Cloth.

BURTON (Mrs. Richard).
>THE INNER LIFE OF SYRIA, PALESTINE, AND THE HOLY LAND. 2 vols. Demy 8vo. Cloth, price 24s.

BUTLER (Josephine E.)
>JOHN GREY (of Dilston): MEMOIRS. By his Daughter. New and Cheaper Edition. Crown 8vo. Cloth, price 3s. 6d.

CADELL (Mrs. H. M.)
>IDA CRAVEN: A Novel. 2 vols. Crown 8vo. Cloth.

CALDERON.
>CALDERON'S DRAMAS: The Wonder-Working Magician—Life is a Dream—The Purgatory of St. Patrick. Translated by Denis Florence MacCarthy. Post 8vo. Cloth, price 10s.

CAMDEN (Charles).
>HOITY TOITY, THE GOOD LITTLE FELLOW. With Eleven Illustrations. Crown 8vo. Cloth, price 3s. 6d.

>THE TRAVELLING MENAGERIE. With Ten Illustrations by J. Mahoney. Crown 8vo. Cloth, price 3s. 6d.

CARLISLE (A. D.), B.A., Trin. Coll., Camb.
>ROUND THE WORLD IN 1870. A Volume of Travels, with Maps. New and Cheaper Edition. Demy 8vo. Cloth, price 6s.

CARNE (Miss E. T.)
>THE REALM OF TRUTH. Crown 8vo. Cloth, price 5s. 6d.

CARPENTER (E.)
>NARCISSUS AND OTHER POEMS. Fcap. 8vo. Cloth, price 5s.

CARPENTER (W. B.), LL.D., M.D., F.R.S., etc.
>THE PRINCIPLES OF MENTAL PHYSIOLOGY. With their Applications to the Training and Discipline of the Mind, and the Study of its Morbid Conditions. Illustrated. 8vo. Cloth, price 12s.

CARR (Lisle).
>JUDITH GWYNNE. 3 vols. Second Edition. Crown 8vo. Cloth.

CHRISTOPHERSON (The late Rev. Henry), M.A.,
Assistant Minister at Trinity Church, Brighton.
> SERMONS. With an Introduction by John Rae, LL.D., F.S.A. Crown 8vo. Cloth, price 7s. 6d.

CLAYTON (Cecil).
> EFFIE'S GAME; HOW SHE LOST AND HOW SHE WON. A Novel. 2 vols. Cloth.

CLERK (Mrs. Godfrey), Author of "The Antipodes and Round the World."
> 'ILAM EN NAS. Historical Tales and Anecdotes of the Times of the Early Khalifahs. Translated from the Arabic Originals. Illustrated with Historical and Explanatory Notes. Crown 8vo. Cloth, price 7s.

CLERY (C.), Captain 32nd Light Infantry, Deputy Assistant Adjutant-General, late Professor of Tactics Royal Military College, Sandhurst.
> MINOR TACTICS. Second Edition. With 26 Maps and Plans. Demy 8vo. Cloth, price 16s.

CLODD (Edward), F.R.A.S.
> THE CHILDHOOD OF THE WORLD: a Simple Account of Man in Early Times. New Edition. Crown 8vo. Cloth, price 3s. A Special Edition for Schools. Price 1s.

> THE CHILDHOOD OF RELIGIONS. Including a Simple Account of the Birth and Growth of Myths and Legends. Crown 8vo. Cloth, price 5s.

COLERIDGE (Sara).
> PRETTY LESSONS IN VERSE FOR GOOD CHILDREN, with some Lessons in Latin, in Easy Rhyme. A New Edition. Illustrated. Cloth, price 3s. 6d.

> PHANTASMION. A Fairy Romance. With an Introductory Preface by the Right Hon. Lord Coleridge, of Ottery St. Mary. A New Edition. Illustrated. Cloth, price 7s. 6d.

> MEMOIR AND LETTERS OF SARA COLERIDGE. Edited by her Daughter. Third Edition, Revised and Corrected. With Index. 2 vols. With Two Portraits. Crown 8vo. Cloth, price 24s. Cheap Edition. With one Portrait. Cloth, price 7s. 6d.

COLLINS (Mortimer).
> **THE PRINCESS CLARICE.** A Story of 1871. 2 vols. Cloth.
> **SQUIRE SILCHESTER'S WHIM.** 3 vols. Cloth.
> **MIRANDA.** A Midsummer Madness. 3 vols. Cloth.
> **THE INN OF STRANGE MEETINGS, AND OTHER POEMS.** Crown 8vo. Cloth, price 5s.
> **THE SECRET OF LONG LIFE.** Dedicated by special permission to Lord St. Leonard's. Fourth Edition. Large crown 8vo. Price 5s.

COLLINS (Rev. Richard), M.A.
> **MISSIONARY ENTERPRISE IN THE EAST.** With special reference to the Syrian Christians of Malabar, and the results of modern Missions. With Four Illustrations. Crown 8vo. Cloth, price 6s.

CONGREVE (Richard), M.A., M.R.C.P.L.
> **HUMAN CATHOLICISM.** Two Sermons delivered at the Positivist School on the Festival of Humanity, 87 and 88, January 1, 1875 and 1876. Demy 8vo. Sewed, price 1s.

CONWAY (Moncure D.)
> **REPUBLICAN SUPERSTITIONS.** Illustrated by the Political History of the United States. Including a Correspondence with M. Louis Blanc. Crown 8vo. Cloth, price 5s.

CONYERS (Ansley).
> **CHESTERLEIGH.** 3 vols. Crown 8vo. Cloth.

COOKE (M. C.), M.A., LL.D.
> **FUNGI;** their Nature, Influences, Uses, etc. Edited by the Rev. M. J. Berkeley, M.A., F.L.S. With Illusrations. Second Edition. Crown 8vo. Cloth, price 5s.
> Vol. XIV. of the International Scientific Series.

COOKE (Professor Josiah P.), of the Harvard University.
> **THE NEW CHEMISTRY.** With Thirty-one Illustrations. Third Edition. Crown 8vo. Cloth, price 5s.
> Vol. IX. of the International Scientific Series.
> **SCIENTIFIC CULTURE.** Crown 8vo. Cloth, price 1s.

COOPER (T. T.)
> **THE MISHMEE HILLS:** an Account of a Journey made in an Attempt to Penetrate Thibet from Assam, to open New Routes for Commerce. Second Edition. With Four Illustrations and Map. Demy 8vo. Crown 8vo. Cloth, price 10s. 6d.

CORNHILL LIBRARY OF FICTION, The. Crown 8vo. Cloth, price 3s. 6d. per Volume.
    HALF-A-DOZEN DAUGHTERS. By J. Masterman.
    THE HOUSE OF RABY. By Mrs. G. Hooper.
    A FIGHT FOR LIFE. By Moy Thomas.
    ROBIN GRAY. By Charles Gibbon.
    KITTY. By Miss M. Betham-Edwards.
    HIRELL. By John Saunders.
    ONE OF TWO; OR, THE LEFT-HANDED BRIDE. By J. Hain Friswell.
    READY-MONEY MORTIBOY. A Matter-of-Fact Story.
    GOD'S PROVIDENCE HOUSE. By Mrs. G. L. Banks.
    FOR LACK OF GOLD. By Charles Gibbon.
    ABEL DRAKE'S WIFE. By John Saunders.

CORY (Lieutenant-Colonel Arthur).
    THE EASTERN MENACE; OR, SHADOWS OF COMING EVENTS. Crown 8vo. Cloth, price 5s.

COSMOS. A Poem. Fcap. 8vo. Cloth, price 3s. 6d.
    SUBJECTS.—Nature in the Past and in the Present—Man in the Past and in the Present—The Future.

COTTON (Robert Turner).
    MR. CARINGTON. A Tale of Love and Conspiracy. 3 vols. Crown 8vo. Cloth.

CUMMINS (Henry Irwin), M.A.
    PAROCHIAL CHARITIES OF THE CITY OF LONDON. Sewed, price 1s.

CURWEN (Henry).
    SORROW AND SONG: Studies of Literary Struggle. Henry Mürger—Novalis—Alexander Petöfi—Honoré de Balzac—Edgar Allan Poe—André Chénier. 2 vols. Crown 8vo. Cloth, price 15s.

DAVIDSON (Samuel), D.D., LL.D.
    THE NEW TESTAMENT, TRANSLATED FROM THE LATEST GREEK TEXT OF TISCHENDORF. Post 8vo. Cloth, price 10s. 6d.

DAVIES (G. Christopher).
    MOUNTAIN, MEADOW, AND MERE: a Series of Outdoor Sketches of Sport, Scenery, Adventures, and Natural History. With Sixteen Illustrations by Bosworth W. Harcourt. Crown 8vo. Cloth, price 6s.
    RAMBLES AND ADVENTURES OF OUR SCHOOL FIELD CLUB. With 4 Illustrations. Crown 8vo. Cloth, price 5s.

DAVIES (Rev. J. Llewelyn), M.A.
> **THEOLOGY AND MORALITY.** Essays on Questions of Belief and Practice. Crown 8vo. Cloth, price 7s. 6d.

D'ANVERS (N. R.)
> **LITTLE MINNIE'S TROUBLES.** An Every-day Chronicle. Illustrated by W. H. Hughes. Fcap. Cloth, price 3s. 6d.
> A Simple Chronicle of a Child's Life.

DE KERKADEC (Vicomtesse Solange).
> **A CHEQUERED LIFE,** being Memoirs of the Vicomtesse de Leoville Meilhan. Edited by. Crown 8vo. Cloth, price 7s. 6d.
> Containing many recollections of the First Emperor Napoleon and his Court.

DE L'HOSTE (Colonel E. P).
> **THE DESERT PASTOR, JEAN JAROUSSEAU.** Translated from the French of Eugène Pelletan. With a Frontispiece. New Edition. Fcap. 8vo. Price 3s. 6d.

DE LIEFDE (Jacob).
> **THE GREAT DUTCH ADMIRALS.** With Eleven Illustrations by Townley Green and others. Crown 8vo. Cloth, price 5s.

DE REDCLIFFE (Viscount Stratford), P.C., K.G., G.C.B.
> **WHY AM I A CHRISTIAN?** Fifth Edition. Crown 8vo. Cloth, price 3s.

DE TOCQUEVILLE (Alexis).
> **CORRESPONDENCE AND CONVERSATIONS OF, WITH NASSAU WILLIAM SENIOR.** 2 vols. Post 8vo. Cloth, price 21s.

DE VERE (Aubrey).
> **ALEXANDER THE GREAT.** A Dramatic Poem. Small crown 8vo. Cloth, price 5s.
> **THE INFANT BRIDAL, AND OTHER POEMS.** A New and Enlarged Edition. Fcap. 8vo. Cloth, price 7s. 6d.
> **THE LEGENDS OF ST. PATRICK, AND OTHER POEMS.** Small crown 8vo. Cloth, price 5s.

DE WILLE (E.)
> **UNDER A CLOUD; OR, JOHANNES OLAF.** A Novel. Translated by F. E. Bunnètt. 3 vols. Crown 8vo. Cloth.

DENNIS (John).
> **ENGLISH SONNETS.** Collected and Arranged. Elegantly bound. Fcap. 8vo. Cloth, price 3s. 6d.

DOBSON (Austin).
> **VIGNETTES IN RHYME AND VERS DE SOCIÉTÉ.** Second Edition. Fcap. 8vo. Cloth, price 5s.

DONNE (Alphonse), M.D.
> **CHANGE OF AIR AND SCENE.** A Physician's Hints about Doctors, Patients, Hygiene, and Society; with Notes of Excursions for Health in the Pyrenees, and amongst the Watering-places of France (Inland and Seaward), Switzerland, Corsica, and the Mediterranean. A New Edition. Large post 8vo. Cloth, price 9s.

DOWDEN (Edward), LL.D.
> **SHAKSPERE:** a Critical Study of his Mind and Art. Second Edition. Post 8vo. Cloth, price 12s.

DOWNTON (Rev. Henry), M.A.
> **HYMNS AND VERSES.** Original and Translated. Small crown 8vo. Cloth, price 3s. 6d.

DRAPER (John William), M.D., LL.D. Professor in the University of New York; Author of "A Treatise on Human Physiology."
> **HISTORY OF THE CONFLICT BETWEEN RELIGION AND SCIENCE.** Seventh Edition. Crown 8vo. Cloth, price 5s. Vol. XIII. of the International Scientific Series.

DREW (Rev. G. S.), M.A., Vicar of Trinity, Lambeth.
> **SCRIPTURE LANDS IN CONNECTION WITH THEIR HISTORY.** Second Edition. 8vo. Cloth, price 10s. 6d.
>
> **NAZARETH: ITS LIFE AND LESSONS.** Third Edition. Crown 8vo. Cloth, price 5s.
>
> **THE DIVINE KINGDOM ON EARTH AS IT IS IN HEAVEN.** 8vo. Cloth, price 10s. 6d.
>
> **THE SON OF MAN:** His Life and Ministry. Crown 8vo. Cloth, price 7s. 6d.

DREWRY (G. Overend), M.D.
> **THE COMMON-SENSE MANAGEMENT OF THE STOMACH.** Second Edition. Fcap. 8vo. Cloth, price 2s. 6d.

DURAND (Lady).
> **IMITATIONS FROM THE GERMAN OF SPITTA AND TERSTEGEN.** Fcap. 8vo. Cloth, price 4s.

Du Vernois (Colonel von Verdy).
> STUDIES IN LEADING TROOPS. An authorized and accurate Translation by Lieutenant H. J. T. Hildyard, 71st Foot. Parts I. and II. Demy 8vo. Cloth, price 7s.

E. A. V.
> JOSEPH MAZZINI : A Memoir. With Two Essays by Mazzini—"Thoughts on Democracy," and "The Duties of Man." Dedicated to the Working Classes by P. H. Taylor, M.P. With Two Portraits. Crown 8vo. Cloth, price 3s. 6d.

Eden (Frederic).
> THE NILE WITHOUT A DRAGOMAN. Second Edition. Crown 8vo. Cloth, price 7s. 6d.

Edwards (Rev. Basil).
> MINOR CHORDS; OR, SONGS FOR THE SUFFERING: a Volume of Verse. Fcap. 8vo. Cloth, price 3s. 6d.; paper, price 2s. 6d.

Eiloart (Mrs.)
> LADY MORETOUN'S DAUGHTER. 3 vols. Crown 8vo.

English Clergyman.
> AN ESSAY ON THE RULE OF FAITH AND CREED OF ATHANASIUS. Shall the Rubric preceding the Creed be removed from the Prayer-book? Sewed. 8vo. Price 1s.

Epic of Hades (The).
> THE EPIC OF HADES. By a New Writer. Author of "Songs of Two Worlds." Fcap. 8vo. Cloth, price 5s.

Eros Agonistes. Poems. By E. B. D. Fcap. 8vo. Cloth, price 3s. 6d.

Evans (Mark).
> THE STORY OF OUR FATHER'S LOVE, told to Children; being a New and Enlarged Edition of THEOLOGY FOR CHILDREN. Fcap. 8vo. Cloth, price 3s. 6d.
>
> A BOOK OF COMMON PRAYER AND WORSHIP FOR HOUSEHOLD USE, compiled exclusively from the Holy Scriptures. Fcap. 8vo. Cloth, price 2s. 6d.

Eyre (Maj.-Gen. Sir Vincent), C.B., K.C.S.I., etc.
> LAYS OF A KNIGHT-ERRANT IN MANY LANDS. Square crown 8vo. With Six Illustrations. Cloth, price 7s. 6d.
> Pharaoh Land. | Home Land. | Wonder Land. | Rhine Land.

Faithfull (Mrs. Francis G.)
> LOVE ME, OR LOVE ME NOT. 3 vols. Crown 8vo. Cloth

FARQUHARSON (Martha).
> I. **ELSIE DINSMORE.** Crown 8vo. Cloth, price 3s. 6d.
> II. **ELSIE'S GIRLHOOD.** Crown 8vo. Cloth, price 3s. 6d.
> III. **ELSIE'S HOLIDAYS AT ROSELANDS.** Crown 8vo. Cloth, price 3s. 6d.

FAVRE (Mons. Jules).
> **THE GOVERNMENT OF THE NATIONAL DEFENCE.** From the 30th June to the 31st October, 1870. The Plain Statement of a Member. Demy 8vo. Cloth, price 10s. 6d.

FISHER (Alice).
> **HIS QUEEN.** 3 vols. Crown 8vo. Cloth.

FORBES (Archibald).
> **SOLDIERING AND SCRIBBLING.** A Series of Sketches. Crown 8vo. Cloth, price 7s. 6d.

FOTHERGILL (JESSIE).
> **HEALEY.** A Romance. 3 vols. Crown 8vo. Cloth.

FOWLE (Rev. T. W.), M.A.
> **THE RECONCILIATION OF RELIGION AND SCIENCE.** Being Essays on Immortality, Inspiration, Miracles, and the Being of Christ. Demy 8vo. Cloth, price 10s. 6d.

FRASER (Donald), Accountant to the British-Indian Steam Navigation Company, Limited.
> **EXCHANGE TABLES OF STERLING AND INDIAN RUPEE CURRENCY,** upon a new and extended system, embracing Values from One Farthing to One Hundred Thousand Pounds, and at Rates progressing in Sixteenths of a Penny, from 1s. 9d. to 2s. 3d. per Rupee. Royal 8vo. Cloth, price 10s. 6d.

FRERE (Sir H. Bartle E.), G.C.B., G.C.S.I., etc.
> **THE THREATENED FAMINE IN BENGAL:** How it may be Met, and the Recurrence of Famines in India Prevented. Being No. 1 of "Occasional Notes on Indian Affairs." With 3 Maps. Crown 8vo. Price 5s.

FRISWELL (J. Hain).
> **THE BETTER SELF.** Essays for Home Life. Crown 8vo. Price 6s.
> *Contents:*—Beginning at Home—The Girls at Home—The Wife's Mother—Pride in the Family—Discontent and Grumbling—Domestic Economy—On Keeping People Down—Likes and Dislikes—On Falling Out—Peace.
> **ONE OF TWO; OR, THE LEFT-HANDED BRIDE.** With a Frontispiece. Crown 8vo. Price 3s. 6d.

b

GARDNER (John), M.D.
> LONGEVITY; THE MEANS OF PROLONGING LIFE AFTER MIDDLE AGE. Third Edition, revised and enlarged. Small crown 8vo. Cloth, price 4s.

GARRETT (Edward).
> BY STILL WATERS. A Story for Quiet Hours. With Seven Illustrations. Crown 8vo. Cloth, price 6s.

GIBBON (Charles).
> FOR LACK OF GOLD. With a Frontispiece. Crown 8vo. Cloth, price 3s. 6d.
>
> ROBIN GRAY. With a Frontispiece. Crown 8vo. Cloth, price 3s. 6d.

GILBERT (Mrs.)
> MRS. GILBERT, FORMERLY ANN TAYLOR, AUTOBIOGRAPHY AND OTHER MEMORIALS OF. Edited by Josiah Gilbert. New and revised Edition. In 2 vols. With 2 Steel Portraits and several Wood Engravings. Post 8vo. Cloth, price 24s.

GILL (Rev. W. W.), B.A., of the London Missionary Society.
> MYTHS AND SONGS FROM THE SOUTH PACIFIC. With a Preface by F. Max Müller, M.A., Professor of Comparative Philology at Oxford. Post 8vo. Cloth, price 9s.

GODKIN (James).
> THE RELIGIOUS HISTORY OF IRELAND: Primitive, Papal, and Protestant. Including the Evangelical Missions, Catholic Agitations, and Church Progress of the last half Century. 8vo. Cloth, price 12s.

GODWIN (William).
> WILLIAM GODWIN: HIS FRIENDS AND CONTEMPORARIES. With Portraits and Facsimiles of the handwriting of Godwin and his Wife. By C. Kegan Paul. 2 vols. Demy 8vo. Cloth, price 28s.
>
> THE GENIUS OF CHRISTIANITY UNVEILED. Being Essays never before published. Edited, with a Preface, by C. Kegan Paul. 1 vol. Crown 8vo. Cloth, price 7s. 6d.

GOETZE (Capt. A. von), Captain of the Prussian Corps of Engineers attached to the Engineer Committee, and Instructor at the Military Academy.
> OPERATIONS OF THE GERMAN ENGINEERS DURING THE WAR OF 1870-1871. Published by Authority, and in accordance with Official Documents. Translated from the German by Colonel G. Graham, V.C., C.B., R.E. With 6 large Maps. Demy 8vo. Cloth, price 21s.

GOODMAN (Walter).
: CUBA, THE PEARL OF THE ANTILLES. Crown 8vo. Cloth, price 7s. 6d.

GOSSE (Edmund W.)
: ON VIOL AND FLUTE. With Title-page specially designed by William B. Scott. Crown 8vo. Cloth, price 5s.

GOULD (Rev. S. Baring).
: THE VICAR OF MORWENSTOW: a Memoir of the Rev. R. S. Hawker. With Portrait. Post 8vo. Cloth, price 10s. 6d.

GRANVILLE (A. B.), M.D., F.R.S., etc.
: AUTOBIOGRAPHY OF A. B. GRANVILLE, F.R.S., etc. Edited, with a brief account of the concluding years of his life, by his youngest Daughter, Paulina B. Granville. 2 vols. With a Portrait. Demy 8vo. Cloth, price 32s.

GRAY (Mrs. Russell).
: LISETTE'S VENTURE. A Novel. 2 vols. Crown 8vo. Cloth, price 21s.

GREEN (T. Bowden).
: FRAGMENTS OF THOUGHT. Dedicated by permission to the Poet Laureate. Crown 8vo. Cloth, price 7s. 6d.

GREENWOOD (James), "The Amateur Casual."
: IN STRANGE COMPANY; or, The Note Book of a Roving Correspondent. Second Edition. Crown 8vo. Cloth, price 6s.

GREY (John), of Dilston.
: JOHN GREY (of Dilston): MEMOIRS. By Josephine E. Butler. New and Cheaper Edition. Crown 8vo. Cloth, price 3s. 6d.

GRIFFITH (Rev. T.), A.M., Prebendary of St. Paul's.
: STUDIES OF THE DIVINE MASTER. Demy 8vo. Cloth, price 12s.

GRIFFITHS (Captain Arthur).
: MEMORIALS OF MILLBANK, AND CHAPTERS IN PRISON HISTORY. With Illustrations. 2 vols. Post 8vo. Cloth, price 21s.
: THE QUEEN'S SHILLING. A Novel. 2 vols. Cloth, price 21s.

GRUNER (M. L.)
: STUDIES OF BLAST FURNACE PHENOMENA. Translated by L. D. B. Gordon, F.R.S.E., F.G.S. Demy 8vo. Cloth, price 7s. 6d.

GURNEY (Rev. Archer Thompson).
> **WORDS OF FAITH AND CHEER.** A Mission of Instruction and Suggestion. 1 vol. Crown 8vo. Cloth, price 6s.
>
> **FIRST PRINCIPLES IN CHURCH AND STATE.** Demy 8vo. Sewed, price 1s. 6d.

HAECKEL (Professor Ernst), of the University of Jena.
> **THE HISTORY OF CREATION.** A Popular Account of the Development of the Earth and its Inhabitants, according to the Theories of Kant, Laplace, Lamarck, and Darwin. The Translation revised by Professor E. Ray Lankester, M.A., F.R.S. With Coloured Plates and Genealogical Trees of the various groups of both plants and animals. 2 vols. Post 8vo. Cloth, price 32s.

HARCOURT (Capt. A. F. P.)
> **THE SHAKESPEARE ARGOSY**: Containing much of the wealth of Shakespeare's Wisdom and Wit, alphabetically arranged and classified. Crown 8vo. Cloth, price 6s.

HAWEIS (Rev. H. R.), M.A.
> **SPEECH IN SEASON.** Third Edition. Crown 8vo. Cloth, price 9s.
>
> **THOUGHTS FOR THE TIMES.** Ninth Edition. Crown 8vo. Cloth, price 7s. 6d.
>
> **UNSECTARIAN FAMILY PRAYERS,** for Morning and Evening for a Week, with short selected passages from the Bible. Square crown 8vo. Cloth, price 3s. 6d.

HAWTHORNE (Julian).
> **BRESSANT.** A Romance. 2 vols. Crown 8vo. Cloth, price 21s.
>
> **IDOLATRY.** A Romance. 2 vols. Crown 8vo. Cloth, price 21s.

HAWTHORNE (Nathaniel).
> **NATHANIEL HAWTHORNE.** A Memoir, with Stories now first published in this country. By H. A. Page. Post 8vo. Cloth, price 7s. 6d.
>
> **SEPTIMIUS.** A Romance. Second Edition. Crown 8vo. Cloth, price 9s.

HAYMAN (Henry), D.D., late Head Master of Rugby School.
> **RUGBY SCHOOL SERMONS.** With an Introductory Essay on the Indwelling of the Holy Spirit. Crown 8vo. Cloth, price 7s. 6d.

HEATHERGATE. A Story of Scottish Life and Character. By a New Author. 2 vols. Crown 8vo. Cloth, price 21s.

HELLWALD (Baron F. Von).
> **THE RUSSIANS IN CENTRAL ASIA.** A Critical Examination, down to the present time, of the Geography and History of Central Asia. Translated by Lieut.-Col. Theodore Wirgman, LL.B. In 1 vol. Large post 8vo. With Map. Cloth, price 12s.

HELVIG (Captain Hugo).
> **THE OPERATIONS OF THE BAVARIAN ARMY CORPS.** Translated by Captain G. S. Schwabe. With Five large Maps. In 2 vols. Demy 8vo. Cloth, price 24s.

HINTON (James), late Aural Surgeon to Guy's Hospital.
> **THE PLACE OF THE PHYSICIAN.** Being the Introductory Lecture at Guy's Hospital, 1873-74; to which is added ESSAYS ON THE LAW OF HUMAN LIFE, AND ON THE RELATION BETWEEN ORGANIC AND INORGANIC WORLDS. Second Edition. Crown 8vo. Cloth, price 3s. 6d.
>
> **PHYSIOLOGY FOR PRACTICAL USE.** By various writers. With 50 Illustrations. 2 vols. Second Edition. Crown 8vo. Price 12s. 6d.
>
> **AN ATLAS OF DISEASES OF THE MEMBRANA TYMPANI.** With Descriptive Text. Post 8vo. Price £6 6s.
>
> **THE QUESTIONS OF AURAL SURGERY.** With Illustrations. 2 vols. Post 8vo. Cloth, price 12s. 6d.

HOCKLEY (W. B.)
> **TALES OF THE ZENANA;** or, A Nuwab's Leisure Hours. By the Author of "Pandurang Hari." With a Preface by Lord Stanley of Alderley. 2 vols. Crown 8vo. Cloth, price 21s.
>
> **PANDURANG HARI;** or, Memoirs of a Hindoo. A Tale of Mahratta Life sixty years ago. With a Preface by Sir H. Bartle E. Frere, G.C.S.I., etc. 2 vols. Crown 8vo. Cloth, price 21s.

HOFFBAUER (Captain).
> **THE GERMAN ARTILLERY IN THE BATTLES NEAR METZ.** Based on the official reports of the German Artillery. Translated by Capt. E. O. Hollist. With Map and Plans. Demy 8vo. Cloth, price 21s.

HOLROYD (Major W. R. M.), Bengal Staff Corps, Director of Public Instruction, Punjab.
> **TAS-HIL UL KĀLĀM;** or, Hindustani made Easy. Crown 8vo. Cloth, price 5s.

HOPE (Lieut. James).
> **IN QUEST OF COOLIES.** With Illustrations. Crown 8vo. Cloth, price 6s.

HOOPER (Mrs. G.)
> THE HOUSE OF BABY. With a Frontispiece. Crown 8vo. Cloth, price 3s. 6d.

HOOPER (Mary).
> LITTLE DINNERS: HOW TO SERVE THEM WITH ELEGANCE AND ECONOMY. Ninth Edition. Crown 8vo. Cloth, price 5s.
>
> COOKERY FOR INVALIDS, PERSONS OF DELICATE DIGESTION, AND CHILDREN. Crown 8vo. Cloth, price 3s. 6d.

HOPKINS (Manley).
> THE PORT OF REFUGE; or, Counsel and Aid to Shipmasters in Difficulty, Doubt, or Distress. Crown 8vo. Cloth, price 6s.

HOWARD (Mary M.), Author of "Brampton Rectory."
> BEATRICE AYLMER, AND OTHER TALES. Crown 8vo. Cloth, price 6s.

HOWARD (Rev. G. B.)
> AN OLD LEGEND OF ST. PAUL'S. Fcap. 8vo. Cloth, price 4s. 6d.

HOWE (Cupples), Master Mariner.
> THE DESERTED SHIP. A real story of the Atlantic. Illustrated by Townley Green. Crown 8vo. Cloth, price 3s. 6d.

HOWELL (James).
> A TALE OF THE SEA, SONNETS, AND OTHER POEMS. Fcap. 8vo. Cloth, price 5s.

HUGHES (Allison).
> PENELOPE, AND OTHER POEMS. Fcap. 8vo. Cloth, price 4s. 6d.

HULL (Edmund C. P.)
> THE EUROPEAN IN INDIA. A Handbook of Practical Information for those proceeding to, or residing in, the East Indies, relating to Outfits, Routes, Time for Departure, Indian Climate, etc. With a MEDICAL GUIDE FOR ANGLO-INDIANS. By R. R. S. Mair, M.D., F.R.C.S.E., late Deputy Coroner of Madras. Second Edition, Revised and Corrected. Post 8vo. Cloth, price 6s.

HUMPHREY (Rev. W.), of the Congregation of the Oblates of St. Charles.
> MR. FITZJAMES STEPHEN AND CARDINAL BELLARMINE. Demy 8vo. Sewed, price 1s.

INTERNATIONAL SCIENTIFIC SERIES (The).

I. **THE FORMS OF WATER IN CLOUDS AND RIVERS, ICE AND GLACIERS.** By J. Tyndall, LL.D., F.R.S. With 14 Illustrations. Sixth Edition. 5s.

II. **PHYSICS AND POLITICS**; or, Thoughts on the Application of the Principles of "Natural Selection" and "Inheritance" to Political Society. By Walter Bagehot. Third Edition. 4s.

III. **FOODS.** By Edward Smith, M.D., LL.B., F.R.S. Profusely Illustrated. Fourth Edition. 5s.

IV. **MIND AND BODY:** The Theories of their Relation. By Alexander Bain, LL.D. With Four Illustrations. Fifth Edition. 4s.

V. **THE STUDY OF SOCIOLOGY.** By Herbert Spencer. Fifth Edition. 5s.

VI. **ON THE CONSERVATION OF ENERGY.** By Balfour Stewart, M.D., LL.D., F.R.S. With 14 Engravings. Third Edition. 5s.

VII. **ANIMAL LOCOMOTION**; or, Walking, Swimming, and Flying By J. B. Pettigrew, M.D., F.R.S. With 119 Illustrations. Second Edition. 5s.

VIII. **RESPONSIBILITY IN MENTAL DISEASE.** By Henry Maudsley, M.D. Second Edition. 5s.

IX. **THE NEW CHEMISTRY.** By Professor J. P. Cooke, of the Harvard University. With 31 Illustrations. Third Edition. 5s.

X. **THE SCIENCE OF LAW.** By Professor Sheldon Amos. Second Edition. 5s.

XI. **ANIMAL MECHANISM.** A Treatise on Terrestrial and Aerial Locomotion. By Professor E. J. Marey. With 117 Illustrations. Second Edition. 5s.

XII. **THE DOCTRINE OF DESCENT AND DARWINISM.** By Professor Oscar Schmidt (Strasburg University). With 26 Illustrations. Third Edition. 5s.

XIII. **THE HISTORY OF THE CONFLICT BETWEEN RELIGION AND SCIENCE.** By Professor J. W. Draper. Seventh Edition. 5s.

INTERNATIONAL SCIENTIFIC SERIES (The).—*Continued*.

XIV. **FUNGI;** their Nature, Influences, Uses, etc. By M. C. Cooke, M.A., LL.D. Edited by the Rev. M. J. Berkeley, M.A., F.L.S. With numerous Illustrations. Second Edition. 5s.

XV. **THE CHEMICAL EFFECTS OF LIGHT AND PHOTOGRAPHY.** By Dr. Hermann Vogel (Polytechnic Academy of Berlin). Translation thoroughly revised. With 100 Illustrations. Third Edition, 5s.

XVI. **THE LIFE AND GROWTH OF LANGUAGE.** By William Dwight Whitney, Professor of Sanskrit and Comparative Philology in Yale College, New Haven. Second Edition. 5s.

XVII. **MONEY AND THE MECHANISM OF EXCHANGE.** By Prof. W. Stanley Jevons. Second Edition. 5s.

XVIII. **THE NATURE OF LIGHT:** With a General Account of Physical Optics. By Dr. Eugene Lommel, Professor of Physics in the University of Erlangen. With 188 Illustrations and a table of Spectra in Chromolithography. Second Edition. 5s.

XIX. **ANIMAL PARASITES AND MESSMATES.** By Monsieur Van Beneden, Professor of the University of Louvain, Correspondent of the Institute of France. With 83 Illustrations. Second Edition. 5s.

XX. **FERMENTATION.** By Professor Schützenberger, Director of the Chemical Laboratory at the Sorbonne. 5s.

XXI. **THE FIVE SENSES OF MAN.** By Professor Bernstein, of the University of Halle. Profusely illustrated. 5s.

INTERNATIONAL SCIENTIFIC SERIES (The).

Forthcoming Volumes.

Prof. W. KINGDON CLIFFORD, M.A. The First Principles of the Exact Sciences explained to the Non-mathematical.

Prof. T. H. HUXLEY, LL.D., F.R.S. Bodily Motion and Consciousness.

Dr. W. B. CARPENTER, LL.D., F.R.S. The Physical Geography of the Sea.

Prof. WILLIAM ODLING, F.R.S. The Old Chemistry viewed from the New Standpoint.

W. LAUDER LINDSAY, M.D., F.R.S.E. Mind in the Lower Animals.

Sir JOHN LUBBOCK, Bart., F.R.S. On Ants and Bees.

Prof. W. T. THISELTON DYER, B.A., B.Sc. Form and Habit in Flowering Plants.

Mr. J. N. LOCKYER, F.R.S. Spectrum Analysis.

Prof. MICHAEL FOSTER, M.D. Protoplasm and the Cell Theory.

H. CHARLTON BASTIAN, M.D., F.R.S. The Brain as an Organ of Mind.

Prof. A. C. RAMSAY, LL.D., F.R.S. Earth Sculpture: Hills, Valleys, Mountains, Plains, Rivers, Lakes; how they were Produced, and how they have been Destroyed.

Prof. RUDOLPH VIRCHOW (Berlin Univ.) Morbid Physiological Action.

Prof. CLAUDE BERNARD. History of the Theories of Life.

Prof. H. SAINTE-CLAIRE DEVILLE. An Introduction to General Chemistry.

Prof. WURTZ. Atoms and the Atomic Theory.

Prof. DE QUATREFAGES. The Human Race.

Prof. LACAZE-DUTHIERS. Zoology since Cuvier.

Prof. BERTHELOT. Chemical Synthesis.

INTERNATIONAL SCIENTIFIC SERIES (The).—*Continued.*
(*Forthcoming Volumes.*)

Prof. J. ROSENTHAL. General Physiology of Muscles and Nerves.

Prof. JAMES D. DANA, M.A., LL.D. On Cephalization; or, Head-Characters in the Gradation and Progress of Life.

Prof. S. W. JOHNSON, M.A. On the Nutrition of Plants.

Prof. AUSTIN FLINT, Jr. M.D. The Nervous System, and its Relation to the Bodily Functions.

Prof. FERDINAND COHN (Breslau Univ.) Thallophytes (Algæ, Lichens, Fungi).

Prof. HERMANN (University of Zurich). Respiration.

Prof. LEUCKART (University of Leipsic). Outlines of Animal Organization.

Prof. LIEBREICH (University of Berlin). Outlines of Toxicology.

Prof. KUNDT (University of Strasburg). On Sound.

Prof. REES (University of Erlangen). On Parasitic Plants.

Prof. STEINTHAL (University of Berlin). Outlines of the Science of Language.

P. BERT (Professor of Physiology, Paris). Forms of Life and other Cosmical Conditions.

E. ALGLAVE (Professor of Constitutional and Administrative Law at Douai, and of Political Economy at Lille). The Primitive Elements of Political Constitutions.

P. LORAIN (Professor of Medicine, Paris). Modern Epidemics.

Mons. FREIDEL. The Functions of Organic Chemistry.

Mons. DEBRAY. Precious Metals.

Prof. CORFIELD, M.A., M.D. (Oxon.) Air in its relation to Health.

Prof. A. GIARD. General Embryology.

HUTTON (James).
    MISSIONARY LIFE IN THE SOUTHERN SEAS. With Illustrations. Crown 8vo. Cloth, price 7s. 6d.

IGNOTUS.
    CULMSHIRE FOLK. A Novel. New and Cheaper Edition. Crown 8vo. Cloth, price 6s.

INGELOW (Jean).
    THE LITTLE WONDER-HORN. A Second Series of "Stories Told to a Child." With Fifteen Illustrations. Square 24mo. Cloth, price 3s. 6d.

    OFF THE SKELLIGS. (Her First Romance.) 4 vols. Crown 8vo. Cloth, price 42s.

JACKSON (T. G.)
    MODERN GOTHIC ARCHITECTURE. Crown 8vo. Cloth, price 5s.

JACOB (Maj.-Gen. Sir G. Le Grand), K.C.S.I., C.B.
    WESTERN INDIA BEFORE AND DURING THE MUTINIES. Pictures drawn from life. Second Edition. Crown 8vo. Cloth, price 7s. 6d.

JENKINS (E.) and RAYMOND (J.), Esqs.
    A LEGAL HANDBOOK FOR ARCHITECTS, BUILDERS, AND BUILDING OWNERS. Second Edition Revised. Crown 8vo. Cloth, price 6s.

JENKINS (Rev. R. C.), M.A., Rector of Lyminge, and Honorary Canon of Canterbury.
    THE PRIVILEGE OF PETER, Legally and Historically Examined, and the Claims of the Roman Church compared with the Scriptures, the Councils, and the Testimony of the Popes themselves. Fcap. 8vo. Cloth, price 3s. 6d.

JENKINS (Edward), M.P.
    GLANCES AT INNER ENGLAND. A Lecture delivered in the United States and Canada. Crown 8vo. Cloth, price 5s.

    GINX'S BABY: His Birth and other Misfortunes. Thirty-fourth Edition. Crown 8vo. Cloth, price 2s.

    LITTLE HODGE. A Christmas Country Carol. Fourteenth Thousand. With Five Illustrations. Crown 8vo. Cloth, price 5s. A Cheap Edition in paper covers, price 1s.

    LORD BANTAM. Seventh Edition. Crown 8vo. Cloth, price 2s. 6d.

JEVONS (Prof. W. Stanley).
> MONEY AND THE MECHANISM OF EXCHANGE. Second Edition. Crown 8vo. Cloth, price 5s.
> Vol. XVII. of the International Scientific Series.

KAUFMANN (Rev. M.), B.A.
> SOCIALISM: Its Nature, its Dangers, and its Remedies considered. Crown 8vo. Cloth, price 7s. 6d.

KEATING (Mrs.)
> HONOR BLAKE: The Story of a Plain Woman. 2 vols. Crown 8vo. Cloth, price 21s.

KER (David).
> ON THE ROAD TO KHIVA. Illustrated with Photographs of the Country and its Inhabitants, and a copy of the Official Map in use during the Campaign, from the Survey of Captain Leusilin. Post 8vo. Cloth, price 12s.
> THE BOY SLAVE IN BOKHARA. A Tale of Central Asia. With Illustrations. Crown 8vo. Cloth, price 5s.
> THE WILD HORSEMAN OF THE PAMPAS. Illustrated. Crown 8vo. Cloth, price 5s.

KING (Alice).
> A CLUSTER OF LIVES. Crown 8vo. Cloth, price 7s. 6d.

KING (Mrs. Hamilton).
> THE DISCIPLES. A New Poem. Second Edition, with some Notes. Crown 8vo. Cloth, price 7s. 6d.
> ASPROMONTE, AND OTHER POEMS. Second Edition. Fcap. 8vo. Cloth, price 4s. 6d.

KINGSFORD (Rev. F. W.), M.A., Vicar of St. Thomas's, Stamford Hill; late Chaplain H. E. I. C. (Bengal Presidency).
> HARTHAM CONFERENCES; or, Discussions upon some of the Religious Topics of the Day. "Audi alteram partem." Crown 8vo. Cloth, price 3s. 6d.

KNIGHT (Annette F. C.)
> POEMS. Fcap. 8vo. Cloth, price 5s.

LACORDAIRE (Rev. Père).
> LIFE: Conferences delivered at Toulouse. A New and Cheaper Edition. Crown 8vo. Cloth, price 3s. 6d.

LADY OF LIPARI (The).
> A Poem in Three Cantos. Fcap. 8vo. Cloth, price 5s.

LAURIE (J. S.), of the Inner Temple, Barrister-at-Law; formerly H.M. Inspector of Schools, England; Assistant Royal Commissioner, Ireland; Special Commissioner, African Settlement; Director of Public Instruction, Ceylon.

EDUCATIONAL COURSE OF SECULAR SCHOOL BOOKS FOR INDIA.

The following Works are now ready:—

THE FIRST HINDUSTANI READER. Stiff linen wrapper, price 6d.

THE SECOND HINDUSTANI READER. Stiff linen wrapper, price 6d.

GEOGRAPHY OF INDIA; with Maps and Historical Appendix, tracing the growth of the British Empire in Hindustan. 128 pp. fcap. 8vo. Cloth, price 1s. 6d.

LAYMANN (Captain), Instructor of Tactics at the Military College, Neisse.

THE FRONTAL ATTACK OF INFANTRY. Translated by Colonel Edward Newdigate. Crown 8vo. Cloth, price 2s. 6d.

L. D. S.

LETTERS FROM CHINA AND JAPAN. 1 vol. With Illustrated Title-page. Crown 8vo. Cloth, price 7s. 6d.

LEANDER (Richard).

FANTASTIC STORIES. Translated from the German by Paulina B. Granville. With Eight full-page Illustrations by M. E. Fraser-Tytler. Crown 8vo. Cloth, price 5s.

LEATHES (Rev. Stanley), M.A.

THE GOSPEL ITS OWN WITNESS. Being the Hulsean Lectures for 1873. Crown 8vo. Cloth, price 5s.

LEE (Rev. Frederick George), D.C.L.

THE OTHER WORLD; or, Glimpses of the Supernatural. Being Facts, Records, and Traditions, relating to Dreams, Omens, Miraculous Occurrences, Apparitions, Wraiths, Warnings, Second-sight, Necromancy, Witchcraft, etc. 2 vols. A New Edition. Crown 8vo. Cloth, price 15s.

LEE (Holme).

HER TITLE OF HONOUR. A Book for Girls. New Edition. With a Frontispiece. Crown 8vo. Cloth, price 5s.

LENOIR (J).

FAYOUM; or, Artists in Egypt. A Tour with M. Gérome and others. With 13 Illustrations. A New and Cheaper Edition. Crown 8vo. Cloth, price 3s. 6d.

LISTADO (J. T.)
>   **CIVIL SERVICE.** A Novel. 2 vols. Crown 8vo. Cloth.

LOMMEL (Dr. Eugene), Professor of Physics in the University of Erlangen.
>   **THE NATURE OF LIGHT:** With a General Account of Physical Optics. Second Edition. With 188 Illustrations and a table of Spectra in Chromolithography. Crown 8vo. Cloth, price 5s.
>   Vol. XVIII. of the International Scientific Series.

LORIMER (Peter), D.D.
>   **JOHN KNOX AND THE CHURCH OF ENGLAND:** His work in her Pulpit and his influence upon her Liturgy, Articles, and Parties. Demy 8vo. Cloth, price 12s.

LOVER (Samuel), R.H.A.
>   **THE LIFE OF SAMUEL LOVER, R.H.A.;** Artistic, Literary, and Musical. With Selections from his Unpublished Papers and Correspondence. By Bayle Bernard. 2 vols. With a Portrait. Post 8vo. Cloth, price 21s.

LOWER (Mark Antony), M.A., F.S.A.
>   **WAYSIDE NOTES IN SCANDINAVIA.** Being Notes of Travel in the North of Europe. Crown 8vo. Cloth, price 9s.

LYONS (R. T.), Surgeon-Major, Bengal Army.
>   **A TREATISE ON RELAPSING FEVER.** Post 8vo. Cloth, price 7s. 6d.

MACAULAY (James), M.A., M.D., Edin.
>   **IRELAND.** A Tour of Observation, with Remarks on Irish Public Questions. A New and Cheaper Edition. Crown 8vo. Cloth, price 3s. 6d.

MAC CARTHY (Denis Florence).
>   **CALDERON'S DRAMAS.** Translated from the Spanish. Post 8vo. Cloth, gilt edges, price 10s.

MAC DONALD (George).
>   **GUTTA-PERCHA WILLIE, THE WORKING GENIUS.** With Nine Illustrations by Arthur Hughes. Second Edition. Crown 8vo. Cloth, price 3s. 6d.
>
>   **MALCOLM.** A Novel. 3 vols. Second Edition. Crown 8vo. Cloth.
>   **ST. GEORGE AND ST. MICHAEL.** 3 vols. Crown 8vo. Cloth.

MAC KENNA (Stephen J.)
> **PLUCKY FELLOWS.** A Book for Boys. With Six Illustrations. Second Edition. Crown 8vo. Cloth, price 3s. 6d.
>
> **AT SCHOOL WITH AN OLD DRAGOON.** With Six Illustrations. Crown 8vo. Cloth, price 5s.

MACLACHLAN (Archibald Neil Campbell), M.A.
> **WILLIAM AUGUSTUS, DUKE OF CUMBERLAND;** being a Sketch of his Military Life and Character, chiefly as exhibited in the General Orders of his Royal Highness, 1745—1747. With Illustrations. Post 8vo. Cloth, price 15s.

MAIR (R. S.), M.D., F.R.C.S.E., late Deputy Coroner of Madras.
> **THE MEDICAL GUIDE FOR ANGLO-INDIANS.** Being a Compendium of Advice to Europeans in India, relating to the Preservation and Regulation of Health. With a Supplement on the Management of Children in India. Crown 8vo. Limp cloth, price 3s. 6d.

MANNING (His Eminence Cardinal).
> **ESSAYS ON RELIGION AND LITERATURE.** By various Writers. Demy 8vo. Cloth, price 10s. 6d.
>
> CONTENTS:—The Philosophy of Christianity—Mystic Elements of Religion—Controversy with the Agnostics—A Reasoning Thought—Darwinism brought to Book—Mr. Mill on Liberty of the Press—Christianity in relation to Society—The Religious Condition of Germany—The Philosophy of Bacon—Catholic Laymen and Scholastic Philosophy.

MAREY (E. J.)
> **ANIMAL MECHANICS.** A Treatise on Terrestrial and Aerial Locomotion. With 117 Illustrations. Second Edition. Crown 8vo. Cloth, price 5s.
> Volume XI. of the International Scientific Series.

MARKEWITCH (B.)
> **THE NEGLECTED QUESTION.** Translated from the Russian, by the Princess Ourousoff, and dedicated by Express Permission to Her Imperial and Royal Highness Marie Alexandrovna, the Duchess of Edinburgh. 2 vols. Crown 8vo. Cloth, price 14s.

MARRIOTT (Maj.-Gen. W. F.), C.S.I.
> **A GRAMMAR OF POLITICAL ECONOMY.** Crown 8vo. Cloth, price 6s.

MARSHALL (Hamilton).
> **THE STORY OF SIR EDWARD'S WIFE.** A Novel. Crown 8vo. Cloth, price 10s. 6d.

MARZIALS (Theophile).
>THE GALLERY OF PIGEONS, and other Poems. Crown 8vo. Cloth, price 4s. 6d.

MASTERMAN (J.)
>HALF-A-DOZEN DAUGHTERS. With a Frontispiece. Crown 8vo. Cloth, price 3s. 6d.

MAUDSLEY (Dr. Henry).
>RESPONSIBILITY IN MENTAL DISEASE. Second Edition. Crown 8vo. Cloth, price 5s.
>Vol. VIII. of the International Scientific Series.

MAUGHAN (William Charles).
>THE ALPS OF ARABIA; or, Travels through Egypt, Sinai, Arabia, and the Holy Land. With Map. A New and Cheaper Edition. Demy 8vo. Cloth, price 5s.

MAURICE (C. Edmund).
>LIVES OF ENGLISH POPULAR LEADERS. No. 1.—STEPHEN LANGTON. Crown 8vo. Cloth, price 7s. 6d.
>No. 2.—TYLER, BALL, and OLDCASTLE. Crown 8vo. Price 7s. 6d.

MEDLEY (Lieut.-Col. J. G.), Royal Engineers.
>AN AUTUMN TOUR IN THE UNITED STATES AND CANADA. Crown 8vo. Cloth, price 5s.

MENZIES (Sutherland).
>MEMOIRS OF DISTINGUISHED WOMEN. Post 8vo. Cloth.

ANNE DE BOURBON.	MADAME DE MONTBAZON.
THE DUCHESS DE LONGUEVILLE.	THE DUCHESS OF PORTSMOUTH.
THE DUCHESS DE CHEVREUSE.	SARAH JENNINGS.
PRINCESS PALATINE.	SARAH, DUCHESS OF MARLBOROUGH.
MADEMOISELLE DE MONTPENSIER.	

MICKLETHWAITE (J. T.), F.S.A.
>'MODERN PARISH CHURCHES: Their Plan, Design, and Furniture. Crown 8vo. Cloth, price 7s. 6d.

MIRUS (Major-General von).
>CAVALRY FIELD DUTY. Translated by Major Frank S. Russell, 14th (King's) Hussars. Crown 8vo. Cloth limp, price 7s. 6d.

MOORE (Rev. Daniel), M.A.
>CHRIST AND HIS CHURCH. A Course of Lent Lectures, delivered in the Parish Church of Holy Trinity, Paddington. By the author of "The Age and the Gospel: Hulsean Lectures," etc. Crown 8vo. Cloth, price 3s. 6d.

MOORE (Rev. Thomas), Vicar of Christ Church, Chesham.
> SERMONETTES: on Synonymous Texts, taken from the Bible and Book of Common Prayer, for the Study, Family Reading, and Private Devotion. Small Crown 8vo. Cloth, price 4s. 6d.

MORELL (J. R.)
> EUCLID SIMPLIFIED IN METHOD AND LANGUAGE. Being a Manual of Geometry. Compiled from the most important French Works, approved by the University of Paris and the Minister of Public Instruction. Fcap. 8vo. Cloth, price 2s. 6d.

MORICE (Rev. F. D.), M.A., Fellow of Queen's College, Oxford.
> THE OLYMPIAN AND PYTHIAN ODES OF PINDAR. A New Translation in English Verse. Crown 8vo. Cloth, price 7s. 6d.

MORLEY (Susan).
> AILEEN FERRERS. A Novel. 2 vols. Crown 8vo. Cloth.
> THROSTLETHWAITE. A Novel. 3 vols. Crown 8vo. Cloth.

MORSE (Edward S.), Ph. D., late Professor of Comparative Anatomy and Zoology in Bowdoin College.
> FIRST BOOK OF ZOOLOGY. With numerous Illustrations. Crown 8vo. Cloth, price 5s.

MOSTYN (Sydney).
> PERPLEXITY. A Novel. 3 vols. Crown 8vo. Cloth.

MUSGRAVE (Anthony).
> STUDIES IN POLITICAL ECONOMY. Crown 8vo. Cloth, price 6s.

MY SISTER ROSALIND. By the Author of "Christina North," and "Under the Limes." A Novel. 2 vols. Cloth.

NAAKÈ (John T.), of the British Museum.
> SLAVONIC FAIRY TALES. From Russian, Servian, Polish, and Bohemian Sources. With Four Illustrations. Crown 8vo. Cloth, price 5s.

NEWMAN (John Henry), D.D.
> CHARACTERISTICS FROM THE WRITINGS OF DR. J. H. NEWMAN. Being Selections, Personal, Historical, Philosophical, and Religious, from his various Works. Arranged with the Author's personal approval. Second Edition. With Portrait. Crown 8vo. Cloth, price 6s.
> *⁎* A Portrait of the Rev. Dr. J. H. Newman, mounted for framing, can be had, price 2s. 6d.

NEWMAN (Mrs.)
>   TOO LATE. A Novel. 2 vols. Crown 8vo. Cloth.

NOBLE (James Ashcroft).
>   THE PELICAN PAPERS. Reminiscences and Remains of a Dweller in the Wilderness. Crown 8vo. Cloth, price 6s.

NORMAN PEOPLE (The).
>   THE NORMAN PEOPLE, and their Existing Descendants in the British Dominions and the United States of America. Demy 8vo. Cloth, price 21s.

NORRIS (Rev. A.)
>   THE INNER AND OUTER LIFE POEMS. Fcap. 8vo. Cloth, price 6s.

NOTREGE (John), A.M.
>   THE SPIRITUAL FUNCTION OF A PRESBYTER IN THE CHURCH OF ENGLAND. Crown 8vo. Cloth, red edges, price 3s. 6d.

ORIENTAL SPORTING MAGAZINE (The).
>   THE ORIENTAL SPORTING MAGAZINE. A Reprint of the first 5 Volumes, in 2 Volumes. Demy 8vo. Cloth, price 28s.

OUR INCREASING MILITARY DIFFICULTY, and one Way of Meeting it. Demy 8vo. Stitched, price 1s.

PAGE (H. A.)
>   NATHANIEL HAWTHORNE, A MEMOIR OF, with Stories now first published in this country. Large post 8vo. Cloth, price 7s. 6d.

PAGE (Capt. S. Flood).
>   DISCIPLINE AND DRILL. Four Lectures delivered to the London Scottish Rifle Volunteers. Cheaper Edition. Crown 8vo. Price 1s.

PALGRAVE (W. Gifford).
>   HERMANN AGHA. An Eastern Narrative. 2 vols. Crown 8vo. Cloth, extra gilt, price 18s.

PARKER (Joseph), D.D.
>   THE PARACLETE: An Essay on the Personality and Ministry of the Holy Ghost, with some reference to current discussions. Second Edition. Demy 8vo. Cloth, price 12s.

PARR (Harriett).
>   ECHOES OF A FAMOUS YEAR. Crown 8vo. Cloth, price 8s. 6d.

PAUL (C. Kegan).
> **GOETHE'S FAUST.** A New Translation in Rime. Crown 8vo. Cloth, price 6s.
>
> **WILLIAM GODWIN: HIS FRIENDS AND CONTEMPORARIES.** With Portraits and Facsimiles of the Handwriting of Godwin and his Wife. 2 vols. Demy 8vo. Cloth, price 28s.

PAYNE (John).
> **SONGS OF LIFE AND DEATH.** Crown 8vo. Cloth, price 5s.

PAYNE (Professor).
> **LECTURES ON EDUCATION.** Price 6d. each.
> I. Pestalozzi: the Influence of His Principles and Practice.
> II. Fröbel and the Kindergarten System. Second Edition.
> III. The Science and Art of Education.
> IV. The True Foundation of Science Teaching.

PELLETAN (Eugène).
> **THE DESERT PASTOR, JEAN JAROUSSEAU.** Translated from the French. By Colonel E. P. De L'Hoste. With a Frontispiece. New Edition. Fcap. 8vo. Cloth, price 3s. 6d.

PENRICE (Major J.), B.A.
> **A DICTIONARY AND GLOSSARY OF THE KO-RAN.** With copious Grammatical References and Explanations of the Text. 4to. Cloth, price 21s.

PERCEVAL (Rev. P.)
> **TAMIL PROVERBS, WITH THEIR ENGLISH TRANSLATION.** Containing upwards of Six Thousand Proverbs. Third Edition. Demy 8vo. Sewed, price 9s.

PERRIER (Amelia).
> **A WINTER IN MOROCCO.** With Four Illustrations. A New and Cheaper Edition. Crown 8vo. Cloth, price 3s. 6d.
>
> **A GOOD MATCH.** A Novel. 2 vols. Crown 8vo. Cloth.

PETTIGREW (J. B.), M.D., F.R.S.
> **ANIMAL LOCOMOTION**; or, Walking, Swimming, and Flying Second Edition. With 119 Illustrations. Crown 8vo. Cloth, price 5s.
> Volume VII. of the International Scientific Series.

PIGGOT (John), F.S.A, F.R.G.S.
> **PERSIA—ANCIENT AND MODERN.** Post 8vo. Cloth, price 10s. 6d.

POUSHKIN (Alexander Serguevitch).
> **RUSSIAN ROMANCE.** Translated from the Tales of Belkin, etc. By Mrs. J. Buchan Telfer (née Mouravieff). Crown 8vo. Cloth, price 7s. 6d.

POWER (Harriet).
> **OUR INVALIDS: HOW SHALL WE EMPLOY AND AMUSE THEM?** Fcap 8vo. Cloth, price 2s. 6d.

POWLETT (Lieut. Norton), Royal Artillery.
> **EASTERN LEGENDS AND STORIES IN ENGLISH VERSE.** Crown 8vo. Cloth, price 5s.

PRESBYTER.
> **UNFOLDINGS OF CHRISTIAN HOPE.** An Essay showing that the Doctrine contained in the Damnatory Clauses of the Creed commonly called Athanasian is unscriptural. Small crown 8vo. Cloth, price 4s. 6d.

PRICE (Prof. Bonamy).
> **CURRENCY AND BANKING.** Crown 8vo. Cloth, price 6s.

PROCTOR (Richard A.)
> **OUR PLACE AMONG INFINITIES.** A Series of Essays contrasting our little abode in space and time with the Infinities around us. To which are added Essays on "Astrology," and "The Jewish Sabbath." Second Edition. Crown 8vo. Cloth, price 6s.
>
> **THE EXPANSE OF HEAVEN.** A Series of Essays on the Wonders of the Firmament. With a Frontispiece. Second Edition. Crown 8vo. Cloth, price 6s.

RANKING (B. Montgomerie).
> **STREAMS FROM HIDDEN SOURCES.** Crown 8vo. Cloth, price 6s.

READY-MONEY MORTIBOY.
> **READY-MONEY MORTIBOY.** A Matter-of-Fact Story. With Frontispiece. Crown 8vo. Cloth, price 3s. 6d.

REANEY (Mrs. G. S.)
> **WAKING AND WORKING; OR, FROM GIRLHOOD TO WOMANHOOD.** With a Frontispiece. Crown 8vo. Cloth, price 5s.
>
> **SUNBEAM WILLIE, AND OTHER STORIES,** for Home Reading and Cottage Meetings. 3 Illustrations. Small square, uniform with "Lost Gip," etc. Price 1s. 6d.

REGINALD BRAMBLE.
> **REGINALD BRAMBLE.** A Cynic of the Nineteenth Century. An Autobiography. Crown 8vo. Cloth, price 10s. 6d.

REID (T. Wemyss).
   CABINET PORTRAITS. Biographical Sketches of Statesmen of the Day. Crown 8vo. Cloth, price 7s. 6d.

RHOADES (James).
   TIMOLEON. A Dramatic Poem. Fcap. 8vo. Cloth, price 5s.

RIBOT (Professor Th.)
   CONTEMPORARY ENGLISH PSYCHOLOGY. Second Edition. Revised and corrected translation from the latest French Edition. Large post 8vo. Cloth, price 9s.
   An analysis of the views and opinions of the following metaphysicians, as expressed in their writings:—James Mill, Alexander Bain, John Stuart Mill, George H. Lewes, Herbert Spencer, Samuel Bailey.
   HEREDITY: A Psychological Study on its Phenomena, its Laws, its Causes and its Consequences. Large crown 8vo. Cloth, price 9s.

ROBERTSON (The Late Rev. F. W.), M.A.
   THE LATE REV. F. W. ROBERTSON, M.A., LIFE AND LETTERS OF. Edited by the Rev. Stopford Brooke, M.A., Chaplain in Ordinary to the Queen.
   I. 2 vols., uniform with the Sermons. With Steel Portrait. Crown 8vo. Cloth, price 7s. 6d.
   II. Library Edition, in Demy 8vo. with Two Steel Portraits. Cloth, price 12s.
   III. A Popular Edition, in 1 vol. Crown 8vo. Cloth, price 6s.

   New and Cheaper Editions:—
   SERMONS.
      Vol. I. Small crown 8vo. Cloth, price 3s. 6d.
      Vol. II. Small crown 8vo. Cloth, price 3s. 6d.
      Vol. III. Small crown 8vo. Cloth, price 3s. 6d.
      Vol. IV. Small crown 8vo. Cloth, price 3s. 6d.
   EXPOSITORY LECTURES ON ST. PAUL'S EPISTLE TO THE CORINTHIANS. Small crown 8vo. Cloth, price 5s.
   AN ANALYSIS OF MR. TENNYSON'S "IN MEMORIAM." (Dedicated by Permission to the Poet-Laureate.) Fcap. 8vo. Cloth, price 2s.
   THE EDUCATION OF THE HUMAN RACE. Translated from the German of Gotthold Ephraim Lessing. Fcap. 8vo. Cloth, price 2s. 6d.
   The above Works can also be had bound in half-morocco.
   ** A Portrait of the late Rev. F. W. Robertson, mounted for framing, can be had, price 2s. 6d.
   LECTURES AND ADDRESSES, with other literary remains. A New Edition. Crown 8vo. Cloth, price 5s.

Ross (Mrs. Ellen), ("Nelsie Brook.")
> **DADDY'S PET.** A Sketch from Humble Life. Uniform with "Lost Gip." With Six Illustrations. Square crown 8vo. Cloth, price 1s.

Roxburghe Lothian.
> **DANTE AND BEATRICE FROM 1282 TO 1290.** A Romance. 2 vols. Post 8vo. Cloth, price 24s.

Russell (William Clark).
> **MEMOIRS OF MRS. LETITIA BOOTHBY.** Crown 8vo. Cloth, price 7s. 6d.

Russell (E. R.)
> **IRVING AS HAMLET.** Second Edition. Demy 8vo. Sewed, price 1s.

Sadler (S. W.), R.N., Author of "Marshall Vavasour."
> **THE AFRICAN CRUISER.** A Midshipman's Adventures on the West Coast. A Book for Boys. With Three Illustrations. Second Edition. Crown 8vo. Cloth, price 3s. 6d.

Samarow (Gregor).
> **FOR SCEPTRE AND CROWN.** A Romance of the Present Time. Translated by Fanny Wormald. 2 vols. Crown 8vo. Cloth, price 15s.

Saunders (Katherine).
> **THE HIGH MILLS.** A Novel. 3 vols. Crown 8vo. Cloth.
> **GIDEON'S ROCK**, and other Stories. Crown 8vo. Cloth, price 6s.
> **JOAN MERRYWEATHER**, and other Stories. Crown 8vo. Cloth, price 6s.
> **MARGARET AND ELIZABETH.** A Story of the Sea. Crown 8vo. Cloth, price 6s.

Saunders (John).
> **HIRELL.** With Frontispiece. Crown 8vo. Cloth, price 3s. 6d.
> **ABEL DRAKE'S WIFE.** With Frontispiece. Crown 8vo. Cloth, price 3s. 6d.

Schell (Major von).
> **THE OPERATIONS OF THE FIRST ARMY UNDER GEN. VON GOEBEN.** Translated by Col. C. H. von Wright. Four Maps. Demy 8vo. Cloth, price 9s.
> **THE OPERATIONS OF THE FIRST ARMY UNDER GEN. VON STEINMETZ.** Translated by Captain E. O. Hollist. Demy 8vo. Cloth, price 10s. 6d.

SCHERFF (Major W. von).
> **STUDIES IN THE NEW INFANTRY TACTICS.** Parts I. and II. Translated from the German by Colonel Lumley Graham. Demy 8vo. Cloth, price 7s. 6d.

SCHMIDT (Prof. Oscar), Strasburg University.
> **THE DOCTRINE OF DESCENT AND DARWINISM.** Third Edition. 26 Illustrations. Crown 8vo. Cloth, price 5s.
> Vol. XII. of the International Scientific Series.

SCHÜTZENBERGER (Prof. F.), Director of the Chemical Laboratory at the Sorbonne.
> **FERMENTATION.** With numerous Illustrations. Crown 8vo. Cloth, price 5s.
> Vol. XX. of the International Scientific Series.

SCOTT (Patrick).
> **THE DREAM AND THE DEED,** and other Poems. Fcap. 8vo. Cloth, price 5s.

SEEKING HIS FORTUNE, and other Stories.
> **SEEKING HIS FORTUNE,** and other Stories. With Four Illustrations. Crown 8vo. Cloth, price 3s. 6d.

SENIOR (Nassau William).
> **ALEXIS DE TOCQUEVILLE.** Correspondence and Conversations with Nassau W. Senior, from 1833 to 1859. Edited by M. C. M. Simpson. 2 vols. Large post 8vo. Cloth, price 21s.
> **JOURNALS KEPT IN FRANCE AND ITALY.** From 1848 to 1852. With a Sketch of the Revolution of 1848. Edited by his Daughter, M. C. M. Simpson. 2 vols. Post 8vo. Cloth, price 24s.

SEVEN AUTUMN LEAVES.
> **SEVEN AUTUMN LEAVES FROM FAIRYLAND.** Illustrated with 9 Etchings. Square crown 8vo. Cloth, price 3s. 6d.

SHADWELL (Major-General), C.B.
> **MOUNTAIN WARFARE.** Illustrated by the Campaign of 1799 in Switzerland. Being a Translation of the Swiss Narrative compiled from the Works of the Archduke Charles, Jomini, and others. Also of Notes by General H. Dufour on the Campaign of the Valtelline in 1635. With Appendix, Maps, and Introductory Remarks. Demy 8vo. Cloth, price 16s.

SHELDON (Philip).
> **WOMAN'S A RIDDLE;** or, Baby Warmstrey. A Novel. 3 vols. Crown 8vo. Cloth.

SHERMAN (Gen. W. T.)
> **MEMOIRS OF GEN. W. T. SHERMAN**, Commander of the Federal Forces in the American Civil War. By Himself. 2 vols. With Map. Demy 8vo. Cloth, price 24s. *Copyright English Edition.*

SHELLEY (Lady).
> **SHELLEY MEMORIALS FROM AUTHENTIC SOURCES.** With (now first printed) an Essay on Christianity by Percy Bysshe Shelley. With Portrait. Third Edition. Crown 8vo. Cloth, price 5s.

SHIPLEY (Rev. Orby), M.A.
> **STUDIES IN MODERN PROBLEMS.** By various Writers. 2 vols. Crown 8vo. Cloth, price 5s. each.

CONTENTS.—VOL. I.

- Sacramental Confession.
- Abolition of the Thirty-nine Articles. Part I.
- The Sanctity of Marriage.
- Creation and Modern Science.
- Retreats for Persons Living in the World.
- Catholic and Protestant.
- The Bishops on Confession in the Church of England.

CONTENTS.—VOL. II.

- Some Principles of Christian Ceremonial.
- A Layman's View of Confession of Sin to a Priest. Parts I. and II.
- Reservation of the Blessed Sacrament.
- Missions and Preaching Orders.
- Abolition of the Thirty-nine Articles. Part II.
- The First Liturgy of Edward VI. and our own office contrasted and compared.

SMEDLEY (M. B.)
> **BOARDING-OUT AND PAUPER SCHOOLS FOR GIRLS.** Crown 8vo. Cloth, price 3s. 6d.

SMITH (Edward), M.D., LL.B., F.R.S.
> **HEALTH AND DISEASE**, as influenced by the Daily, Seasonal, and other Cyclical Changes in the Human System. A New Edition. Post 8vo. Cloth, price 7s. 6d.
>
> **FOODS.** Profusely Illustrated. Fourth Edition. Crown 8vo. Cloth, price 5s.
> Volume III. of the International Scientific Series.
>
> **PRACTICAL DIETARY FOR FAMILIES, SCHOOLS, AND THE LABOURING CLASSES.** A New Edition. Post 8vo. Cloth, price 3s. 6d.
>
> **CONSUMPTION IN ITS EARLY AND REMEDIABLE STAGES.** A New Edition. Post 8vo. Cloth, price 7s. 6d.

SMITH (Hubert).
> **TENT LIFE WITH ENGLISH GIPSIES IN NORWAY.** With Five full-page Engravings and Thirty-one smaller Illustrations by Whymper and others, and Map of the Country showing Routes. Second Edition. Revised and Corrected. Post 8vo. Cloth, price 21s.

SONGS FOR MUSIC.
> **SONGS FOR MUSIC.** By Four Friends. Square crown 8vo. Cloth, price 5s.
>
> Containing Songs by Reginald A. Gatty, Stephen H. Gatty, Greville J. Chester, and Juliana H. Ewing.

SOME TIME IN IRELAND.
> **SOME TIME IN IRELAND.** A Recollection. Crown 8vo. Cloth, price 7s. 6d.

SONGS OF TWO WORLDS.
> **SONGS OF TWO WORLDS.** By a New Writer. First Series. Second Edition. Fcap. 8vo. Cloth, price 5s.
>
> **SONGS OF TWO WORLDS.** By a New Writer. Second Series. Second Edition. Fcap. 8vo. Cloth, price 5s.
>
> **SONGS OF TWO WORLDS.** By a New Writer. Third Series. Second Edition. Fcap. 8vo. Cloth, price 5s.

SPENCER (HERBERT).
> **THE STUDY OF SOCIOLOGY.** Fifth Edition. Crown 8vo. Cloth, price 5s.
>
> Volume V. of the International Scientific Series.

SPICER (Henry),
> **OTHO'S DEATH WAGER.** A Dark Page of History. Illustrated. In Five Acts. Fcap. 8vo. Cloth, price 5s.

STEVENSON (Rev. W. Fleming).
> **HYMNS FOR THE CHURCH AND HOME.** Selected and Edited by the Rev. W. Fleming Stevenson.
> The most complete Hymn Book published.
> The Hymn Book consists of Three Parts:—I. For Public Worship.—II. For Family and Private Worship.—III. For Children.
>
> *** *Published in various forms and prices, the latter ranging from 8d. to 6s. Lists and full particulars will be furnished on application to the Publishers.*

STEWART (Professor Balfour).
> **ON THE CONSERVATION OF ENERGY.** Third Edition. With Fourteen Engravings. Crown 8vo. Cloth, price 5s.
>
> Volume VI. of the International Scientific Series.

STONEHEWER (Agnes).
    MONACELLA: A Legend of North Wales. A Poem. Fcap. 8vo. Cloth, price 3s. 6d.

STRETTON (Hesba). Author of "Jessica's First Prayer."
    CASSY. Twenty-sixth Thousand. With Six Illustrations. Square crown 8vo. Cloth, price 1s. 6d.
    THE KING'S SERVANTS. Thirty-second Thousand. With Eight Illustrations. Square crown 8vo. Cloth, price 1s. 6d.
    LOST GIP. Forty-fifth Thousand. With Six Illustrations. Square crown 8vo. Cloth, price 1s. 6d.
    *** *Also a handsomely-bound Edition, with Twelve Illustrations, price 2s. 6d.*
    THE WONDERFUL LIFE. Ninth Thousand. Fcap. 8vo. Cloth, price 2s. 6d.
    FRIENDS TILL DEATH. With Frontispiece. Limp cloth, price 6d.
    TWO CHRISTMAS STORIES. With Frontispiece. Limp cloth, price 6d.
    MICHEL LORIO'S CROSS, AND LEFT ALONE. With Frontispiece. Limp cloth, price 6d.
    OLD TRANSOME. With Frontispiece. Limp cloth, price 6d.
    HESTER MORLEY'S PROMISE. 3 vols. Crown 8vo. Cloth.
    THE DOCTOR'S DILEMMA. 3 vols. Crown 8vo. Cloth.

SULLY (James).
    SENSATION AND INTUITION. Demy 8vo. Cloth, price 10s. 6d.

TAYLOR (Rev. J. W. Augustus), M.A.
    POEMS. Fcap. 8vo. Cloth, price 5s.

TAYLOR (Sir Henry).
    EDWIN THE FAIR AND ISAAC COMNENUS. Fcap. 8vo. Cloth, price 3s. 6d.
    A SICILIAN SUMMER AND OTHER POEMS. Fcap. 8vo. Cloth, price 3s. 6d.
    PHILIP VAN ARTEVELDE. A Dramatic Poem. Fcap. 8vo. Cloth, price 5s.

TAYLOR (Colonel Meadows), C.S.I., M.R.I.A.
    SEETA. A Novel. 3 vols. Crown 8vo. Cloth.
    RALPH DARNELL. 3 vols. Crown 8vo. Cloth.
    TIPPOO SULTAN. 3 vols. Crown 8vo. Cloth.
    THE CONFESSIONS OF A THUG. Crown 8vo. Cloth, price 6s.
    TARA: a Mahratta Tale. Crown 8vo. Cloth, price 6s.

TENNYSON (Alfred).
    QUEEN MARY. A Drama. New Edition. Crown 8vo. Cloth, price 6s.

TENNYSON'S (Alfred) Works. Cabinet Edition. Ten Volumes. Each with Portrait. Fcap. 8vo. Cloth, price 2s. 6d.
    CABINET EDITION. 10 vols. Complete in handsome Ornamental Case. Price 28s.

TENNYSON'S (Alfred) Works. Author's Edition. Complete in Five Volumes. Post 8vo. Cloth gilt, price 31s. 6d.; half-morocco, Roxburgh style, price 39s.
    EARLY POEMS, and ENGLISH IDYLLS.—VOL. I.
    LOCKSLEY HALL, LUCRETIUS, and other Poems.—VOL. II.
    THE IDYLLS OF THE KING (Complete).—VOL. III.
    THE PRINCESS, and MAUD.—VOL. IV.
    ENOCH ARDEN, and IN MEMORIAM.—VOL. V.

    TENNYSON'S IDYLLS OF THE KING, and other Poems. Illustrated by Julia Margaret Cameron. 1 vol. Folio. Half-bound morocco, cloth sides. Six Guineas.

TENNYSON'S (Alfred) Works. Original Editions.
    POEMS. Small 8vo. Cloth, price 6s.
    MAUD, and other Poems. Small 8vo. Cloth, price 3s. 6d.
    THE PRINCESS. Small 8vo. Cloth, price 3s. 6d.
    IDYLLS OF THE KING. Small 8vo. Cloth, price 5s.
    IDYLLS OF THE KING. Collected. Small 8vo. Cloth, price 6s.
    THE HOLY GRAIL, and other Poems. Small 8vo. Cloth, price 4s. 6d.
    GARETH AND LYNETTE. Small 8vo. Cloth, price 3s.
    ENOCH ARDEN, etc. Small 8vo. Cloth price 3s. 6d.
    SELECTIONS FROM THE ABOVE WORKS. Square 8vo. Cloth, price 3s. 6d. Cloth gilt, extra, price 4s.
    SONGS FROM THE ABOVE WORKS. Square 8vo. Cloth extra, price 3s. 6d.
    IN MEMORIAM. Small 8vo. Cloth, price 4s.
    LIBRARY EDITION. In 6 vols. Demy 8vo. Cloth, price 10s. 6d. each.
    POCKET VOLUME EDITION. 11 vols. In neat case, 31s. 6d.
    Ditto, ditto. Extra cloth gilt, in case, 35s.
    POEMS. Illustrated Edition. 4to. Cloth, price 25s.

THOMAS (Moy).
> A FIGHT FOR LIFE. With Frontispiece. Crown 8vo. Cloth, price 3s. 6d.

THOMSON (J. T.), F.R.G.S.
> HAKAYIT ABDULLA. The Autobiography of a Malay Munshi, between the years 1808 and 1843. Demy 8vo. Cloth, price 12s.

THOMPSON (A. C.)
> PRELUDES. A Volume of Poems. Illustrated by Elizabeth Thompson (Painter of "The Roll Call"). 8vo. Cloth, price 7s. 6d.

THOMPSON (Rev. A. S.), British Chaplain at St. Petersburg.
> HOME WORDS FOR WANDERERS. A Volume of Sermons. Crown 8vo. Cloth, price 6s.

THOUGHTS IN VERSE. Small crown 8vo. Cloth, price 1s. 6d.

THRING (Rev. Godfrey), B.A.
> HYMNS AND SACRED LYRICS. Fcap. 8vo. Cloth, price 5s.

TODD (Herbert), M.A.
> ARVAN; or, The Story of the Sword. A Poem. Crown 8vo. Cloth, price 7s. 6d.

TRAHERNE (Mrs. Arthur).
> THE ROMANTIC ANNALS OF A NAVAL FAMILY. A New Cheaper and Edition. Crown 8vo. Cloth, price 5s.

TRAVERS (Mar.)
> THE SPINSTERS OF BLATCHINGTON. A Novel. 2 vols. Crown 8vo. Cloth.

TREVANDRUM OBSERVATIONS.
> OBSERVATIONS OF MAGNETIC DECLINATION MADE AT TREVANDRUM AND AGUSTIA MALLEY in the Observatories of his Highness the Maharajah of Travancore, G.C.S.I., in the Years 1852 to 1860. Being Trevandrum Magnetical Observations, Volume I. Discussed and Edited by John Allan Brown, F.R.S., late Director of the Observatories. With an Appendix. Imp. 4to. Cloth, price £3 3s.
>
> **** *The Appendix, containing Reports on the Observatories and on the Public Museum, Public Park, and Gardens at Trevandrum, pp. xii.-116, may be had separately, price 21s.*

TURNER (Rev. Charles).
> SONNETS, LYRICS, AND TRANSLATIONS. Crown 8vo. Cloth, price 4s. 6d.

TYNDALL (J.), LL.D., F.R.S.
> THE FORMS OF WATER IN CLOUDS AND RIVERS, ICE AND GLACIERS. With Twenty-six Illustrations. Sixth Edition. Crown 8vo. Cloth, price 5s.
> Volume I. of the International Scientific Series.

UMBRA OXONIENSIS.
> RESULTS OF THE EXPOSTULATION OF THE RIGHT HONOURABLE W. E. GLADSTONE, in their Relation to the Unity of Roman Catholicism. Large fcap. 8vo. Cloth, price 5s.

UPTON (Roger D.), Captain late 9th Royal Lancers.
> NEWMARKET AND ARABIA. An Examination of the Descent of Racers and Coursers. With Pedigrees and Frontispiece. Post 8vo. Cloth, price 9s.

VAMBERY (Prof. Arminius), of the University of Pesth.
> BOKHARA: Its History and Conquest. Demy 8vo. Cloth, price 18s.

VAN BENEDEN (Monsieur), Professor of the University of Louvain, Correspondent of the Institute of France.
> ANIMAL PARASITES AND MESSMATES. With 83 Illustrations. Second Edition. Cloth, price 5s.
> Vol. XIX. of the International Scientific Series.

VANESSA. By the Author of "Thomasina," etc. A Novel. 2 vols. Second Edition. Crown 8vo. Cloth.

VAUGHAN (Rev. C. J.), D.D.
> WORDS OF HOPE FROM THE PULPIT OF THE TEMPLE CHURCH. Third Edition. Crown 8vo. Cloth, price 5s.
>
> THE SOLIDITY OF TRUE RELIGION, and other Sermons Preached in London during the Election and Mission Week, February, 1874. Crown 8vo. Cloth, price 3s. 6d.
>
> FORGET THINE OWN PEOPLE. An Appeal for Missions. Crown 8vo. Cloth, price 3s. 6d.
>
> THE YOUNG LIFE EQUIPPING ITSELF FOR GOD'S SERVICE. Being Four Sermons Preached before the University of Cambridge, in November, 1872. Fourth Edition. Crown 8vo. Cloth, price 3s. 6d.

VINCENT (Capt. C. E. H.), late Royal Welsh Fusiliers.
> ELEMENTARY MILITARY GEOGRAPHY, RECONNOITRING, AND SKETCHING. Compiled for Non-Commissioned Officers and Soldiers of all Arms. Square crown 8vo. Cloth, price 2s. 6d.
>
> RUSSIA'S ADVANCE EASTWARD. Based on the Official Reports of Lieutenant Hugo Stumm, German Military Attaché to the Khivan Expedition. With Map. Crown 8vo. Cloth, price 6s.

VIZCAYA; or, Life in the Land of the Carlists.
> VIZCAYA; or, Life in the Land of the Carlists at the Outbreak of the Insurrection, with some Account of the Iron Mines and other Characteristics of the Country. With a Map and Eight Illustrations. Crown 8vo. Cloth, price 9s.

VOGEL (Prof.), Polytechnic Academy of Berlin.
> THE CHEMICAL EFFECTS OF LIGHT AND PHOTOGRAPHY, in their application to Art, Science, and Industry. The translation thoroughly revised. With 100 Illustrations, including some beautiful Specimens of Photography. Third Edition. Crown 8vo. Cloth, price 5s.
> Volume XV. of the International Scientific Series.

VYNER (Lady Mary).
> EVERY DAY A PORTION. Adapted from the Bible and the Prayer Book, for the Private Devotions of those living in Widowhood. Collected and Edited by Lady Mary Vyner. Square crown 8vo. Cloth extra, price 5s.

WAITING FOR TIDINGS.
> WAITING FOR TIDINGS. By the Author of "White and Black." 3 vols. Crown 8vo. Cloth.

WARTENSLEBEN (Count Hermann von), Colonel in the Prussian General Staff.
> THE OPERATIONS OF THE SOUTH ARMY IN JANUARY AND FEBRUARY, 1871. Compiled from the Official War Documents of the Head-quarters of the Southern Army. Translated by Colonel C. H. von Wright. With Maps. Demy 8vo. Cloth, price 6s.
>
> THE OPERATIONS OF THE FIRST ARMY UNDER GEN. VON MANTEUFFEL. Translated by Colonel C. H. von Wright. Uniform with the above. Demy 8vo. Cloth, price 9s.

WEDMORE (Frederick).
> TWO GIRLS. 2 vols. Crown 8vo. Cloth.

WELLS (Captain John C.), R.N.
> SPITZBERGEN—THE GATEWAY TO THE POLYNIA; or, A Voyage to Spitzbergen. With numerous Illustrations by Whymper and others, and Map. New and Cheaper Edition. Demy 8vo. Cloth, price 6s.

WETMORE (W. S.).
> COMMERCIAL TELEGRAPHIC CODE. Post 4to. Boards, price 42s.

WHAT 'TIS TO LOVE. By the Author of "Flora Adair," "The Value of Fostertown." 3 vols. Crown 8vo. Cloth.

WHITNEY (William Dwight). Professor of Sanskrit and Comparative Philology in Yale College, New Haven.
> THE LIFE AND GROWTH OF LANGUAGE. Second Edition. Crown 8vo. Cloth, price 5s. *Copyright Edition.*
> Volume XVI. of the International Scientific Series.

WHITTLE (J. Lowry), A.M., Trin. Coll., Dublin.
> CATHOLICISM AND THE VATICAN. With a Narrative of the Old Catholic Congress at Munich. Second Edition. Crown 8vo. Cloth, price 4s. 6d.

WILBERFORCE (Henry W.)
> THE CHURCH AND THE EMPIRES. Historical Periods. Preceded by a Memoir of the Author by John Henry Newman, D.D., of the Oratory. With Portrait. Post 8vo. Cloth, price 10s. 6d.

WILKINSON (T. Lean).
> SHORT LECTURES ON THE LAND LAWS. Delivered before the Working Men's College. Crown 8vo. Limp cloth, price 2s.

WILLIAMS (Rev. Rowland), D.D.
> LIFE AND LETTERS OF ROWLAND WILLIAMS, D.D., with Selections from his Note-books. Edited by Mrs. Rowland Williams. With a Photographic Portrait. 2 vols. Large post 8vo. Cloth, price 24s.

WILLOUGHBY (The Hon. Mrs.)
> ON THE NORTH WIND—THISTLEDOWN. A Volume of Poems. Elegantly bound. Small crown 8vo. Cloth, price 7s. 6d.

WILSON (H. Schütz).
> STUDIES AND ROMANCES. Crown 8vo. Cloth, price 7s. 6d.

WINTERBOTHAM (Rev. R.), M.A., B.Sc.
> SERMONS AND EXPOSITIONS. Crown 8vo. Cloth, price 7s. 6d.

Wood (C. F.)
> A YACHTING CRUISE IN THE SOUTH SEAS. With Six Photographic Illustrations. Demy 8vo. Cloth, price 7s. 6d.

Wright (Rev. W.), of Stoke Bishop, Bristol.
> MAN AND ANIMALS: A Sermon. Crown 8vo. Stitched in wrapper, price 1s.
>
> WAITING FOR THE LIGHT, AND OTHER SERMONS. Crown 8vo. Cloth, price 6s.

Wyld (R. S.), F.R.S.E.
> THE PHYSICS AND PHILOSOPHY OF THE SENSES; or, The Mental and the Physical in their Mutual Relation. Illustrated by several Plates. Demy 8vo. Cloth, price 16s.

Yonge (C. D.), Regius Professor, Queen's College, Belfast.
> HISTORY OF THE ENGLISH REVOLUTION OF 1688. Crown 8vo. Cloth, price 6s.

Yorke (Stephen), Author of "Tales of the North Riding."
> CLEVEDEN. A Novel. 2 vols. Crown 8vo. Cloth.

Youmans (Eliza A.)
> AN ESSAY ON THE CULTURE OF THE OBSERVING POWERS OF CHILDREN, especially in connection with the Study of Botany. Edited, with Notes and a Supplement, by Joseph Payne, F.C.P., Author of "Lectures on the Science and Art of Education," etc. Crown 8vo. Cloth, price 2s. 6d.
>
> FIRST BOOK OF BOTANY. Designed to cultivate the Observing Powers of Children. With 300 Engravings. New and Enlarged Edition. Crown 8vo. Cloth, price 5s.

Youmans (Edward L.), M.D.
> A CLASS BOOK OF CHEMISTRY, on the Basis of the new System. With 200 Illustrations. Crown 8vo. Cloth, price 5s.

Zimmern (Helen).
> STORIES IN PRECIOUS STONES. With Six Illustrations. Third Edition. Crown 8vo. Cloth, price 5s.

Caxton Printing Works, Beccles.

www.ingramcontent.com/pod-product-compliance
Lightning Source LLC
Chambersburg PA
CBHW020229240426
43672CB00006B/462